ALONG DEEP LONELY ALLEYS

Baul-Fakir-Dervish of Bengal

ALONG DEEP LONELY ALLEYS

SUDHIR CHAKRAVARTI

Translated from the Bengali original
Gobheer Nirjon Pothey
by **UTPAL K. BANERJEE**

NIYOGI
BOOKS

First published in Bengali as
Gobheer Nirjon Pothey by Ananda Publishers.

Published by
NIYOGI BOOKS
D-78, Okhla Industrial Area, Phase-I
New Delhi-110 020, INDIA
Tel: 91-11-26816301, 49327000
Fax: 91-11-26810483, 26813830
email: niyogibooks@gmail.com
website: www.niyogibooksindia.com

Editor: Mohua Mitra
Cover Design: Debasish Deb

ISBN: 978-93-85285-69-1
Publication: 2017

Printed at: Niyogi Offset Pvt. Ltd., New Delhi, India

Dedicated to the memory
of my late parents

Contents

Walking lonely alleys for the mate in my soul

It is believed that the more mechanical civilisation advances, greater the incidence of artificiality in man. His face dons a mask—of civility, cordiality. Despite many efforts afterwards, the real face is no longer revealed, not even to himself. It is also said and believed that the rural folks are probably different. Though the artificial civilisation's glare does touch them a little, they are still simple at heart, full of life and hospitable to outsiders.

In this regard, my experience is different and a mixed one. I can vouch for at least eighty per cent of village inhabitants, that it would be difficult to define their thoughts. They may not wear masks, but they do cover themselves with an ineffable hardness. Beneath the apparent simplicity, that hardness is almost impenetrable. But if one can break open the hard exterior, the inside contains a really soft kernel: almost like a coconut-shell. Bitter exchanges spanning a few centuries, false assurances and shameless oppression have made the village folks suspicious of the urbanites. The hiatus between their aural-visual knowledge about the external world, and the theoretical information acquired from books by the urban people is so vast that they always retain a sense of pity for us. Their meek, sorrowful faces cover a huge feeling of fun which they exchange among themselves during leisure-time. Their fun and pity are expressed in such words as: "What would you see in this village besides dust during summer and mud during the rains?"

Or, "Sir, you seem to be carrying the tape-recording machine; what satisfaction would you derive from the rustic songs of ours?" Or, "We feel scared if you come this way once too often; who knows what you seek—votes or something else...." Between the lines are very cleverly concealed a quiet humour and an uproarious laughter!

Whoever has some practical experience in researching on folk culture would understand what I am really trying to convey. They have to necessarily overcome a barrier of resistance and suspicion. One easily gets a warm reception and hospitality for food and stay. Yet the sword of doubt remains forever raised. They are afraid—lest they lose something. "Do you know how much money Doctor Shasthi has made by copying the lyrics from Kuber Gosain of our village?" Someone at the *mazhar* of Lalan Fakir had told me, "Do you know, your poet Tagore had jotted down our Lalan Shah's songs in order to get Nobel Prize or some such thing? That has a valuation, I believe, of many hundreds of rupees..."

If these were the sayings and beliefs of the common man, better let me not mention what the extraordinary men held as their unspoken beliefs. But my job was even a more difficult one: dealing with Udasins[1] and Bauls[2]. The time-period spanned across the entire 1960s. The space covered Nadia-Bardhaman-Murshidabad in this Bengal and Meherpur-Kushtia in the other Bengal comprising countless villages. Among them lay hidden so many meta-religions: referred to as 'minor religious sects' by H.H. Wilson a hundred years ago and *upasak sampradaya*[3] by Akshaykumar Dutta. Their one-century-old narratives led me to enquire what the current status was of these worshipper communities or meta-religions; my initial wherewithal was a regular textbook-oriented

---

1 *Udasin*: stoic singer

2 *Baul*: mendicant singer of songs based on a folk philosophy called *deha-tatwa*

3 *Upasak sampradaya*: worshipper community

university degree and an indomitable eagerness to know. But, alas, I did not know the language, which is true, since I had to spend a clean five years to comprehend the folk religion's lingo. This was because their language was *sandha* (metaphorical, with different layers of inner meanings and abounding in earthly imagery). Let me illustrate with some of the preliminary stumbling blocks.

One

My query to a worshipper: "Are you a Baul?"
Response: "I've not set up a regular 'household' or followed its norms."
Query: "If you're a Fakir, do you have sons and daughters?"
Response: "Children? I've five thousand disciple-cubs (*shavak*) in my fold. They're my children. Don't you know the *fakiri danda* (the mendicant's stick) prohibits reproduction?"
Unanswered queries: "Are disciples not the *sevak*s (persons ready to serve) but a herd of *shavak* (animal cubs)? What exactly is a *fakiri danda*? Don't the lives of Bauls ever fall within the framework of a regular household?"

Two

My query to an Udasin: "What did you eat today?"
Response: "Call it *seva* – service to the soul – not 'eating'. Today's service comprised the *panchatatwa*..."
Query: "*Panchatatwa* (five philosophies)? You mean those professed by Chaitanya, Nityananda, Advaita...?"
Response: "No, not at all! *Panchatatwa* means a service of rice, lentil and three kinds of vegetables."

Three

I whispered my query to a senior Udasin at an *akhda*[4].

4 *Akhda*: religious assembly or settlement of non-conformist spiritual leaders or mendicant sects of Bauls and Fakirs

Query: "I heard in a song—

If vagina-phallus do unite
It's Yoga's best union in sight!

What does it mean? Is it alluding to copulation?"

The Udasin breaks into a hearty laugh and replies, "Copulation? It certainly is copulation! But, then, it has a different sense. Listen then:

Guru's words're phallus incarnate
Disciple's ears are in vaginal state!

Do you understand now?"

I realised that I had failed to understand earlier. There is ample scope for misunderstanding. The obstacle could come from another end. If one asks, "Are you from the Baul community?" The answer would be, "Yes, you could say that." Again if one asked the same Udasin—"Are you a Fakir?" The response would be—"Yes, I'm a Fakir too." Impatient at this word play, one could object—"You're saying yes to whatever I ask; tell me truly who you are!" Prompt would come the answer—"I'm a man. I worship mankind!"

What do all these words actually mean? What inferences do we arrive at?

In reality, the Udasins meditate on the basis of confidentiality. They reveal nothing outside their own community and deliberately talk in riddles to create confusion. To sum it up in a snatch: "Do not spill out the secrets of your meditation, nor scatter the details of your spiritual practice and attainment! Beware, guard yourself!" The core idea is:

Your meditation's matter—
Here'n'there, do not scatter!

Take care of you and yourself:
Both former and latter!

There is yet another kind of confusing stance. For instance, on another occasion, Imanali Shahji Fakir of Dha'para opened his notebook and urged—"Do write down, sir, and put all your matter together in 'harness'—the different 'ness' words, such as, darkness, dubiousness, wellness, formed-ness, formlessness, ovalness, emptiness, preparedness, callousness, completeness, nothingness...these are eleven open 'ness' attributes, while the remaining four 'ness' attributes are a secret."

I insisted on knowing—"What do all these mean?"

Shaking his head like a wise man, Shahji replied—"These are perfectly concealed doctrines of deep philosophy; you won't understand these intricacies."

Indeed, and more likely that Shahji himself did not know. He had probably procured them from somewhere and noted them down. Much like the pseudo intellectual urban scholars spouting "Truffeau" and "Goddard"...

Now I wondered how – when I first roamed from village to village looking for these sub-religions – I used to get bewildered listening to this obscure jargon. I was virtually stupefied in the musical soirees. Perhaps at the end of the carnival, the musical soiree would continue overnight. Hundreds of listeners would listen to those songs with gusto, with the singer pouring his heart into his music. And there I was – holding the highest insignia from the university – unable to discern any meaning whatsoever out of those songs!

These songs were known as 'wordy songs'. Someone would raise a doctrinaire point in the shape of a question at the beginning, and then another singer would provide an answer through another song. While the subject of the first song was referred to as *dainyata*, the second one was *prabarta*. All these

I learnt in a gradual process. Later, I noticed that if one could utilise these intimate lingoes appropriately, one could derive benefits hands down. For instance, once at a paan shop in our suburban town, a village-Baul was singing songs from popular records. I came out suddenly to say, "What's the use of those flippant songs, dear *sain* (venerable sir); let there be a *dainyata* song. These songs are filled with longing and a profound consciousness of human frailty."

The atmosphere, at once, changed dramatically. An amazing expression of respect for me appeared on the singer's face! It was as though the compassionate one had discovered the cognisant one! He commented forthwith, "How great, my respected sir! Then please listen to this: *My mind, travel to Shantipur first, proceed to Guptipara when alert...*"

I looked back proudly at the crowd gathered. It was, as if, to proclaim—do witness my vaunted knowledge, ye all! What was being stated in this song was that after the body and mind were at rest, the deeper secrets of the 'Guptipara' doctrines could be delved into, in peace. That was how I was initiated into the inner meanings of *amabasya* (dark phase of the new moon) as the menstrual phase; the bend in the river as the female vagina; the crocodile as human lust; the creepers as children; the moon-meditation as eating stool and drinking urine...and so on.

Aarjan Shanu Fakir of Got Palli had commented, "Are the secretions of one's body-matters to be disdained? Retaining the matter – namely, preserving and retaining semen – is our religion. To explain further, coital ejaculation of semen and impregnation resulting in the birth of a child are considered *apta-maran* (killing oneself). Impregnation is, therefore, taboo. But is ejaculation debarred? No, not for those whose lust is not dead; who continue to return to the 'gateway of birth' to impregnate. We call it 'the downfall in the vagina.' But then the feminine gender is not to be abhorred. Woman is the partner to our meditation: for *bindu-sadhan* (reaching the ultimate goal or the pinnacle of meditation) is attained through a *raser viyen*—'cooking' the sap of life to perfection. It is similar to boiling and evaporating milk on a low simmering heat at a confectionery, thickening and drying up the liquid slowly to a creamy condensed texture when it doesn't overboil! Likewise, lust is to be boiled repeatedly in order to conquer and pacify it. Our divine doctrine says:

The one who knows the secret of one's birth:
Knowing about all splits: is peerless on earth!
Semen, seed and sap combine
To create this body of mine—
Not knowing One who creates, conserves: I've no mirth!

We look for that real man, *Sain*, do you understand?"

After looking for folk religion and folk music in villages for years together, I came to realise that it was in part a conundrum, quite a bit of a ploy to fool the ignorant urbanites; but if one could strike the right person (knock on the right door), one could be rewarded with more than what one had expected. For this purpose, it is essential to learn their symbolic language, to develop the ability to distinguish between 'education' and 'conversion'. If one wished to ascertain someone's religious belief, one should not ask: "Are you a Baul?" Or "Are you a Fakir?" Rather, one should enquire: "Is yours the house of Sati-Ma or Deendayal?" Or, "Do you belong to the Patuli stream?" Immediately one would see a flash of clear recognition on the face of the Udasin. Once, by way of testing, a Baul asked me a cryptic question: "Did you do the job of digging the soil?"

I replied: "Yes, I did the job of the horse-shoe as well."

My last words worked like a miracle. The Baul then opened up to share quite a few things with me.

The secret *gharana* of folk religion carries a few distinctive meanings in its separate *bandishe*s (lyrics). If one does not evince their associated style and manner, the ustad (master) will not open up. It is difficult usually to gather *asli cheez* (the real crux), though it might turn out to be fairly simple at times.

Let me share an experience of mine, when I was attempting to fathom the original secrets of the Marfati (messenger) Fakirs.

On that occasion, I was privy to a doctrinaire discussion among two Fakirs late at night. It was after the days of *ambubachi* (three consecutive days in July when many Hindu widows keep a fast, traditionally) when the rains had ceased. Jahan Fakir and Shukur Ali were in a conversation, which I quietly heard. When daylight appeared, I discoursed with Jahan Fakir who belonged to Satgechhiya, Bardhaman (Burdwan in West Bengal), and was nearly illiterate, with no formal education and abjectly poor. His inner clothes and the loose cloak on top were all quite unclean. He refused to open up to me: with a world of excuses. Finally, to make him angry, I commented: "You all seem to be very fine. If you discard Shariat (scripture) or forget it, would you abide only by Marfati (messenger) then?"

He seemed visibly hurt at first; then apparently the light of truth suddenly dawned on him. Slowly, Jahan opened up. "Tell me, sir," he said. "Don't you read the First Book of alphabets first, and then the Second Book? But do you manage to forget the First Book by that time?"

This conversation seemed like a flash of lightning: coming from the mouth of an illiterate man. I was stupefied for a long time. Suddenly, I realised; Shariat was the 'means' while Marfat was the 'end'. Picking up courage, I said, "I realise you don't follow scriptures. But why don't you follow castes, what's the argument there?"

Very quietly, Jahan began to hum:

The Brahmin as quite a different caste,
Has Mother Nature made this steadfast?
Must you follow caste's tyranny, my brother?
Ballal Sen played the devil's trick
To create lineage and caste's prick—
Come, search the Vedanta and show me rather!

I liked his approach; my mind was fulfilled. Jahan seemed to be in a good mood and repeated almost to himself: "Man has made scriptures, and man, too, has created castes. Who has perpetuated Brahmins and Kayasthas among the Hindus, and Saiyads and Khondkars among the Muslims? Our Duddu has sung:

Ignorant man goes by own caste—
Which, his whole life, follow he must!
Dogs and jackals: they have all
Same lineage-caste, their wherewithal—
Separate caste is man's load: carried till the last!

That's why we looked for the true man. That man was neither in the Vedic rituals, nor in the Islamic *suras*, nor in *shalagram shilas*[5]—neither in ritual pestles nor in mosques. He who looks for man himself is the real Baul.

I interjected: "Then is the higher caste out? Are scriptures and the Quran null and void?"

: "Yes, please. To us, they hold no meaning. You stay with your caste and lineage, quoting scriptures, following the diktats of Maulavis and Brahmins. We don't follow castes. We believe that the poor man's god lives among the poor, amidst the common man. Listen to this song...

5 *Shalagram shila*: black stone representing Vishnu

Whom do you discard as the lowly men?
Perhaps Braja's Krishna in their den!
Calling them 'Sudra', 'Chanral', 'Bagdi' has had its day
And will now fall in total decay:
Their usage would die, as we say, this is our ken!"

Prophetic words of this song ring almost true today. The age of calling the supposedly 'lowly' classes by the names of 'Sudra', 'Chanral' and 'Bagdi' seems to be really over. But the protest inherent in these songs – the movement to resist – has also a tendency to create a new racism.

By a process of reductionism – discarding Vedas, Quran, Puranas, Brahmins, Maulavis, temples, mosques, ritual meditations, *et al* – by the end of 18th century, the Bengal of ours gave rise to a set of sub-religions whose list is both varied and fascinating. That list – as quoted in the book, *Vaishnava Bratadin Nirnaya* – comprises Baul, Nyara, Dervish, Sain, Aaul, Saddhvini Panthi, Sahajiya, Khushi-vishvashi, Radhashyami, Ramsadhaniya, Jagavandhu-Bhajaniya, Dadupanthi, Ruidasi, Senpanthi, Ramasnehi, Meerabai, Vitthalabhakta, Karta-bhaja, Spashtadayik or Roop Kaviraji, Ramvallabhi, Sahebdhani, Balarami, Hajrati, Gobarai, Pagalnathi, Tilakdasi, Darpanarayani, Bori, Atibordi, Radhaballabhi, Sakhibhavuki, Charandasi, Harishchandri, Sadhanpanthi, Chuharpanthi, Kurapanthi, Bairagi, Naga, Aakhra, Duyara, Kamdhenvi, Matukdhari, Sangjogi, Bar Smpradaya, Mahapurushiya Dharmasampradayi, Jagmohani, Haribola, Ratbhikhari, Bindudhari, Anantakuli, Satkuli, Jogi, Gurudasi Vaishnava, Khandita Vaishnava, Karan Vaishnava, Gop Vaishnava, Nihanga Vaishnava, Kalindi Vaishnava, Chamar Vaishnava, Haribyasi, Ramprasadi, Borgal, Naskari, Chaturbhuji, Pharari, Banshayi, Panchdhuni, Vaishnava Tapashvi, Aagari, Margi, Paltudasi, Aapapanthi, Satnami, Dariyadasi, Buniyaddasi, Ahmadpanthi, Beejmargi, Abadhuti, Bhingal, Manbhabvi,

Kishoribhajani, Kuligayen, Tahaliya or Nemo Vaishnava, Jonni, Sharbhalmi, Nareshpanthi, Dashamargi, Pangul, Beurdasi, Fakirdasi, Kumbhapatiya, Khoja, Gourbadi, Bame Kaupiney, Kapindra Parivar, Kaupinchhara, Churadhari, Kabirpanthi, Khaki and Mulukdasi.

It is a wonder that so many sub-religions coexisted in this land! Where did they vanish? Perhaps the reformist movements among Hindus and Muslims in the 19th century, the preaching of the Christian missionaries, rise of the Brahmo religion and the lifetime preachings of Sri Ramakrishna and Bijaykrishna created such a strong resistance that these sub-religions got shunted and finally receded to take refuge at the back of remote villages. On one hand the high religious ideologies of the times and on the other, the active oppressive policy of orthodox Muslims destroyed the Bauls and Fakirs to a degree. Sri Ramakrishna even maligned these secular religions directly to note: "There are two alternative ways of gaining entry to a house—either through the open main doors in front or through the lavatory at the back of the house; it is far better to enter by the front door, since an entry through the back door of the lavatory will surely soil the body." According to him, the process of spiritual attainment involving women and lucre was a dangerous one.

Bijaykrishna writes in the second volume of his diary of 1892:

> The Baul community follows many a disgusting practice, which cannot even be mentioned. Good people, of course, exist among the Bauls as well, especially like those practising Chandra Siddhi (the lunar realisation). If there are the four realisations: with semen, distress, poison and insanity: they deduce that all realisations have been accomplished. I protested, 'I won't be able to do that. I don't want to attain the kind of spiritual liberty that is achieved by consuming urine and stool.' Mahanta (the chief) got wild and said—'You've

> stayed for so long within our community and have come to know of our secrets; now you say that you won't follow the rest of the practice for the ultimate attainment! You've to adopt these practices as well.' I said: 'No, I won't.' Mahanta started abusing me violently and came forward to beat me; his disciples, too, started screaming: 'Beat him, beat him.' Then I remonstrated very strongly: 'How dare you beat me? Do you know who I'm? I'm a Goswami, belonging to the Advaita clan of Shantipur; and you're asking me to devour urine and stool?' They were shocked at the vehemence of my reprimand.

The check and resistance of the upper-caste Hindu ascetic practitioners considerably weakened the sub-religious sects. But several-times stronger was the struggle between the Fakirs and Dervishes and the orthodox Muslims. I wonder why these facts had been sidelined and avoided by those who had chronicled the social history of Bengal.

If proper accounts were taken, it would be seen that in the late 18th century, a very large number of lower-caste Hindus and poor Muslims gave up the larger Hindu and Muslim communities and joined the Baul and Fakiri religions in eastern and northern Bengal. It would also be noted that the deserters from Islam were very large in number. Lalan Shah and many ascetic religious leaders attracted several common men to their sub-religions through their honest living style, secular ideals and unitary thinking systems. This process led to a severe shock, socially and economically, to both ritualistic Vaishnava and orthodox Muslim communities. Naturally this gave rise to protests and reactions. Many Vaishnava booklets, like *Pashanda Dalan* (Chastisement of the Heretics), attacked Kartabhaja (the sect that flattered the leaders) and other sub-religions as 'heretics', 'perverted' and 'practitioners of prohibited paths' by misinterpreting their eulogistic theories and practices with the feminine form and certain other mystic practices. In the 19th century, Dasharathi Ray abused these communities in his *panchali* (ritualistic lyrics); the Jelepara satires of downtown Kolkata by wandering minstrels and professional comedians included many farcical acts and enactments of satirical songs taunting the Kartabhaja community.

The anti-scripture Bauls picked up their toughest fight against the Muslim followers of the Islamic law, in 19th-century Nadia, Jessore and northern Bengal. By emphasising the other behaviour-patterns of Bauls, such as, quadrilunar cycle realisation and certain abusive practices, the Islamic law-abiders emphatically opposed the singing tradition of the Baul. One sect of interpreters of Islamic religion intimated that music was inimical to their religion. They staged riots in the musical soirees of Bauls. Under instructions of the Alem community, physical repression began against the Bauls and quite often, their tufts of hair were forcibly severed.[6]

Out of fright, Bauls started hiding or discarding their exterior robes. The contemporary Wahabi, Faraizi and Aahl-e-Hadis reform movements harmed the Muslim Bauls a lot. The latter were forced to return to the ways of Islamic scripture. Many Muslim reformers of the time joined battle by issuing religious decrees against the Bauls. One can come across a commentary against Bauls and Fakirs in some of the contemporary writings, such as, those of Meer Mosharraf Hossain:

The knave guru, the false Peer,
The bangle-wearing bald Fakir:
They're the real devils, perfidious infidels...

6 The Bengali original book is titled *Banglaye Baul Birodhi Andolan: Prekkhito Lalan Shah*

The folk-poet Jonabali wrote thunderous verses:

Smash the head of the treacherous Fakir...

Baul Dhwangsha Fatwa (The Baul Destruction Decree), a book by Maulana Reyazuddin Ahmed from Rangpur was very popular among the orthodox Muslim community. He wrote in its second edition, published in 1825:

> In order to eradicate Bauls and Baldies from among Muslims, Bengal must constitute a committee in each district, each village, to congregate on each Friday, who would sharply and vigorously act, till even one Baul or baldy Muslim claims to remain extant. On the whole, it is the duty of Muslims to try, as best as possible, and rid completely the Muslim society of Bauls and Baldies.

Many such descriptions were available. The attack and false propaganda against Bauls and Fakirs spread beyond the boundaries of the 19th century into the 20th century. From the book, *Baul Dhwangsha Fatwa*, it is known that undivided Bengal contained some sixty to seventy lakh Bauls. Suffering from torture and oppression, their number has dwindled, rendering them cornered with their back to the wall. It is seen from written petitions that, under the leadership of Maulana Afchharuddin, a group of men chopped off the tufts of hair of all the Bauls – all followers of Lalan – assembled at the Chheunria Ashram hermitage in Kushtia.

It would, however, be wrong to surmise that all Muslims were against Bauls. In the 1927 Annual Conference of Faridpur Student Federation in 1927, Qazi Abdul Odud, an open-minded intellect, stated:

> One will get an idea of how Islam would succeed in a Bengali's life from this Marfat-follower, far more than from a Bengali Maulana; that is because, notwithstanding all the incompleteness, the Marfat-follower has within him some live faith, some pain of creation; his is a brand new birth within the tight wrap of strictures. Maulana, on the contrary, is only an imitator, a keeper of unsavoured texts—with a life devoid of relations and rhythms.
>
> As you know, our Alem community has used its full power against this Marfat-follower...It is important to speak up against the deployment of power by the Alems...to bring to their notice that they have not tried to use meditation against meditation; instead, they have sought to use the power of the stick to subjugate the relatively weak. In place of the meditation of the Marfat-follower, had our Alems tried to establish Bengal's unity with a wider, inclusive and more complete meditation, we wouldn't have got only the 'Baul Destruction' and 'Nasara Subjugation' decrees from them.

Spread over a century, such acts of chastisement and repression have made the community of Bauls-Dervish-Fakir weak and isolated, but unable to erase them as a whole. That was because the people from the lower castes could mingle easily in a secular fashion in the village society. A scrutiny would reveal that most of the sub-religions that sprung up in undivided Bengal were established either by a Muslim or together by a Hindu and a Muslim. Aaulchand, the founder of the Kartabhaja clan, was a Muslim and his main disciple Ramsharan Pal came from the cow-tending class. The founder of the Sahebdhani community was a Muslim Udasin and the chief of this cult Charan Pal, was a cowherd by caste.

In reality, the folk sub-religions of Bengal had at its foundation three streams: direct influence of the Muslim Bauls, Fakirs and

Dervishes; the antagonism among the lowest caste against the Brahminical domination; and the clarion call from the secular Vaishnava religion. This last stream needed a social explanation.

Sri Chaitanya appeared in our land almost in a timely role as a saviour. It was the 16th century when he evolved an open-armed, secular plan of Vaishnava religion: in order to resist the widespread conversion of Hindus by the Muslim rulers and to end the oppression on the lowest caste by the ritualistic, purist Brahmins. His way of religious practice was to preach the simplest creed: *Harernamaiva Kevalam* (*Hare Nam Kevalam* – chant Hari's name alone). A strong upsurge of popular wave added momentum to the Vaishnava religion.

But after the demise of Sri Chaitanya, divisiveness arose in Vaishnavism. The Goswamis of Vrindavan paid more attention to establish Chaitanya's theories by writing treatises in Sanskrit. There appeared hundreds of treatises and texts between the common Vaishnava devotees and their leader Sri Chaitanya. The helpless 'lower castes' drowned themselves in perversion and an unruly lifestyle. At that critical juncture came Nityananda's son Birchandra (or Birbhadra) as a leader and messenger. Birchandra re-converted to Vaishnavism the renegade perverted Buddhist Sahajiyas, the ignorant, copulation worshipping Tantric practitioners, and the illiterate distressed masses: hungry for salvation. This wave of Vaishnavisation began incorporating many secretive folk practices; breathing exercises and confidential meditative acts. New centres for meditation and spiritual practice appeared in the villages along with the Shripat. On the banks of the Ganga settled the Sahajiya Vaishnavas alongside Patuli, Katowa and Agradweep. People hailed Birchandra as an incarnation or avatar of Sri Chaitanya. They heralded their new leader with new words of felicitation:

Birchandra reappears as Gour's incarnation:
A blessed sight for those who missed Gour's vision!

In course of time, the folk-gurus brought the *Gita* hymn: *Yada Yada Hi Dharmasya*...(Whenever the faith is eclipsed...) and transformed it into such an axiom that a deep faith grew among the crushed, oppressed masses, leading them to firmly believe that Gouranga was an incarnation of Krishna and subsequently Birbhadra—Gouranga incarnate. Following this lead, we observe half amused, a curious development, exemplified in the initial declaration of the Kartabhajas—

Krishnachandra, Gourchandra, Aaulchandra /
are one in three, three in one!

It implied that Birchandra was removed and, instead, came Aaulchandra, giving rise to a new sub-religion for the believers in Vaishnavism. In no time, that sub-religion (that is, the Kartabhajas) was led by Dulalchandra Pal, whose mother (with the original name of Saraswati) was re-named Sati-ma. The latter had a clear resonance of 'Shachi Ma' (mother of Gouranga) in its sound. Alongside came the new chant:

The three have the same visage:
Sri Krishnachandra, Sri Gourchandra and Sri Dulalchandra—
Are three names of the same divine image!

How very well-planned was the ouster of Aaulchandra by Dulalchandra from the people's mind!

One hundred years ago, when Akshaykumar Dutta wrote the book, *Bharatbarshiya Upasak Sampradaya* (Indian Worshipping Communities), he gave an indication of the many sub-religions of Bengal and produced a general report. The problem was that Akshaykumar did not do any survey himself for his report. He collected material from all and sundry for his reportage. Some mistakes and partiality did creep in. In contrast, Bidyabhushan

Jogendranath Bhattacharjee did considerable fieldwork while writing his book, *Hindu Castes and Sects.* Akshaykumar wrote a very sketchy description of the Balarami community of Meherpur, whereas Bidyabhushan visited Meherpur and penned his narrative only after having met the widow of Balaram.

At the end of the 1960s, when I began enquiring about sub-religions, I preferred Bidyabhushan's methodology. The remaining part of this write-up is a truthful narration of what I could gather during my arduous walking tours—picking up vital information in its course. It covers the invincible folk forms of those sub-religions which could never be vanquished by civilisation, politics, science and scriptural dominance.

I had never heard of the word—*sahebdhani.* That there is a village Brittihuda in our vast land somewhere was also unknown to me. I read in someone's serial article in a suburban magazine that there was a famous folk composer, Kubir Sircar (Gosain), in Nadia in the last century. By looking at the published extracts from his songs, I felt Kubir's songs were worth collecting. After establishing contacts by correspondence, I descended one day at the Brittihuda village in the Chapra police station of Nadia. At Ramprasad Ghosh's house there, I was privy to see as many as 1,203 songs of Kubir—scripted by Ramprasad's grandfather, Ramlal Ghosh. They felt further encouraged to show me round the mausoleum-temple of Kubir, where lie the earthly remains of his wife Bhagabati and his spiritual-companion Krishnamohini as well. Peeping into the mausoleum-room of Kubir, I noticed an earthen lump, a decorated cot and bed, a flower-tray, a Fakiri mace, a twisted rod, a trident, a pair of wooden clogs and a low wooden seat.

"These are things that he used" said Gopaldas, the votary of the place, belonging to the fourth generation below Kubir.

I had never seen mausoleums of Vaishnava saints and got curious. I asked: "What's that earthen lump there?"

: "His head is placed there. As you know, our bodies are interred in a half-reclining position, with the dug-up earth providing support at the back and the legs stretched out."

I further came to know from the same notebook of Ramlal that Kubir was born on the full-moon day of Falgun 1194 (English calendar 1787) and died on the Tuesday night of 11 Ashadh 1286 (1879)—the sixth lunar day during the full-moon fortnight at the fourth measure of time. Then they showed me around the ancient home of Gurucharan Pal. Everything in display was seen but it still remained a mystery as to why the name of Kubir Gosain – a poet of 1,203 lyrics – was so unknown to the public.

On my return home, two things struck me like a streak of lightning within a few months. First, while reading *Sri Ramakrishna Kathamrita*, I suddenly discovered the famous song (by Tagore) quoted there:

Plunge in the sea of grace; drown, plunge:
Let my mind submerge!

(Doob doob doob roopsaagarey amaar mon!)

I discovered it was penned by Kubir. Secondly, while reading the book *Bharatbarshiya Upasak Sampradaya*, I was drawn to the mention of the Sahebdhani community and its creator Dukhiram Pal. His son: 'Charan Pal has become very famous in propounding the faith of this community...It has been some time that Charan Pal died...' (*Bharatbarshiya Upasak Sampradaya*).

After another couple of journeys on my own to Brittihuda village, I realised that there was Dogachhiya village on the west bank of the Jalangi and Brittihuda was on its east. Charan's father was from Dogachhiya. He was initiated by an ascetic and the

Sahebdhani sub-religion was founded. His son Charan Pal shifted home to Brittihuda across the river. The Sahebdhanis set up base here with their meditation centre. Among Charan's disciples, the principal one was Kuber (Kubir) Sircar, weaver in caste and poet-singer by profession. Kuber was initiated by Charan and made the head of the sect subsequently. He transformed himself to a Tantric composer. And following the local accent of Nadia, Kuber was pronounced as Kubir. One singer sang a Kubir song for me; I carefully jotted down the lyrics:

O, Shripat Huda's glory rises above Vrindavan's fame,
Where day and night you hear Deenabandhu's name.
Neelachal's interplay of blue—
More divine here and of a richer hue,
Hindus'n'Muslims have all seen the same.

Here Gosain Charanchand of mine
Holds sway as bright as moonshine—
Disciples, down a timeless stream they came.

My Charandas's name has sheer force,
To the woe-sorrow-sin stricken, gives recourse,
Spasm-cough-colic-screaming pain:
Tough diseases—peace and relief gain!

The last stanza is particularly noteworthy. It did seem that Charandas was reputed for knowledge and efficiency in medical sciences; it did not take long to understand that Hindus and Muslims were on an equal footing in the Sahebdhani sect. According to the census, the following statistics do emerge—Village name: Brittihuda. Pollice station: Chapra. District: Nadia. Location: 16 miles north-west from the town of Krishnanagar. Block no. 29. The livelihood of the residents is farming, trade and teaching. Total population: 3,450. Muslims: 525 households. Ghosh (cattle-tenderers): 60 households. Karmakars (carpenters): 8 households. Das (serving class): 40 households. Pramanik (barbers): 6 households. Garai (potters): 10 households. Weaver: 1 household.

In a village with a large Muslim majority, how a sub-religious sect, and that too a Vaishnava Sahajiya-centric one, survived with great success was a puzzle I was keen to solve. Dwijapada Pramanik, the headmaster of the village primary school, asked me to come on the full-moon day of Baishakh, when there would be a festival at Charan Pal's ancestral home.

I did visit the festival and witness how a large population from Brittihuda and the neighbouring villages participated together with great fervour and enthusiasm, regardless of their caste or creed. But it was also quite apparent that there was none from the upper castes. The ritual musical soirees stretched through the night, starting only after sudown. There was an occasion of listening to many *prabarta* songs by Kubir in response to *dainyata* songs of Lalan. I noticed that the Kubir songs were mostly sung by Muslim Fakirs, such as, Jaharali and Chhamed Ali. In between the songs, the audience roared: "*Jai Deendayal Jai Deenabandhu*".

I thought people were adulating Hari. Dwijapada broke my misapprehension. "Sahebdhanis worship Deendayal; their community is also known as the Deendayal cult. Sometimes they address Deendayal as Deenabandhu. This is their code language."

It meant that the 'Deenabandhu' in Kubir's lyrics that I heard the other day—

O, Shripat Huda's glory rises above Vrindavan's fame,
Where day and night you hear Deenabandhu's name...

...was the same Deendayal-Deenabandhu. Gradually I came to know that Hindus and Muslims were almost equal in numbers in the Deendayal cult. During the community feast, I noticed that the Hindus were serving the Muslims and vice versa. Actually, they do not wear saffron or other external robes, as this is a domestic sub-religion. Anyone could adopt the faith. Whoever we considered Hindu or Muslim in our naked eyes needed not be orthodox Hindu or scripture-following Muslim, but Sahebdhani. Jaharali sang all this while, traipsing around:

The head of this Vrajadham—
Is Sahebdhani's wealthy one!
Radha, too, is a Sahebdhani and a rich one!

What a wonder! They had created a Sahebdhani outside Vraja. It signified that they were a Naribhaja (female-worshipper) community. Meanwhile, Chhamed Ali had started the refrain:

All Creation is too large for my hold—
Allah happily resides in my throat,
And Krishna tucked safe within!

All these were purportedly Kubir's songs and seemed remarkably secular! I became determined to go to their roots.

From the broadside, the teacher Dwijapada was giving me a running commentary—"Charan Pal had three main disciples: Prahlad Gosain of Rukunpur, Ramchandra Gosain of Bamunpukur; and Kubir Gosain of this side. Out of them, songs were composed by Kubir alone. Oh, what lovely songs!"

I sought to know: "Are there no disciples of Kubir?"

: "How strange, haven't you heard Jadubindu's songs: I will arrange your listening right away. He was a poet of sublime emotions. Jadubindu Gosain was Kubir's principal disciple from Bardhaman's (Burdwan district in West Bengal) Panchlakhi village. That house still exists. Just look at Deben

Gosain there, Jadubindu's great grandson. O Deben, just come here."

Gosain came over with a shy smile and folded hands. Dressed in a white kurta, he was of lean structure and very fair complexion, with a curly mop of hair. I asked him: "Where's your Panchlakhi village?"

: "Sir, there's a road to Bardhaman from the Himayetpur crossing of Nabadweep. You will spot the Nadai bridge on that road, after you cross Nadanghat and before you reach Dhatrigram. Our Panchlakhi is alongside Nadai. Would you come once?

: "What shall I find there?"

: "There's the mausoleum of Jadubindu and his music notebook, with hundreds of songs."

Dwijapada intervened: "O Debendra, could you call Gopal's mother once? I would like him to listen to one of Jadubindu's songs."

Debendra was looking for his way in that crowd. What kind of name was Jadubindu? Was it some kind of vowel-harmony with Jadabendra?

: "Oh, no, no! It's Jadu and his meditation-partner Bindu that combine into Jadubindu. There's a song that you can listen to: '*At the Almighty's feet is this appeal from the sinner*'...where it occurs:

Jadu and Bindu, they're the two;
At Panchlakhi village, living they do.

Do you understand now the mystery of the Jadubindu names?"

By that time, Gopal's mother had appeared. She was a middle-aged, shy widow. "Tell me, sirs," she asked demurely, "What can I sing? Do I have my singing voice any more?"

Dwijapada replied, "Whatever you have, will do. Do begin." He explane to me, "Kubir's adopted son was Keshtadas; this woman is his widow. The old lady has a very sweet voice. She knew Jadubindu well and has a vast repository of his songs."

Gopal's mother began melodiously:

In whichever manner Gosain keeps me, I remain in that way—
What more can I say?
You eat and you feed,
You give, you give away indeed,
Your attitude is like the flying-shuttle of a loom to play!

Guru, wealth you give, woe you give,
Fault-praise, repute-offence: it's for you to bestow,
Yours is the clan, yours the glorious show,
You're Krishna, you're Kali, you're the heart's glow!

At times milk and honey, at times casein and sweet,
At times not even rice-broth of overnight treat,
At times arum-herb, sans salt, is all there to eat!

Says Bindu-Jadu, you're thief, you're sadhu,
You're Muslim, you're Hindu,
Hence Kubirchand is the name with which I pray!

Song after song followed in a continuous stream. Occasionally, the lyrics would be: "*My pasting mud all o'er wasn't enough*"; and at other times—"*Don't you, my mind, cross over the tortuous river's bend...*" Gopal's mother's eyes brimmed with tears as she sang on.

I left the concert avoiding people's eyes and attention in the enveloping darkness and headed for the interior of Charan Pal's ancestral home. Sharat Fakir, the then successor of Charan Pal, hurried down to me—"Please do come; I was aware of your arrival. Come inside right away, you'll see Deendayal's platform."

It was an open balcony, its walls decorated with lime. There was a near-dark compartment, outside which at least a hundred men and women were bowing down on earth: having vowed to offer sacrifices, provided their prayers were granted. There was a dim lamp hardly illumining the room. After the eyes got accustomed, I noticed a trident, a pair of tongs, a raised platform besides a few other things.

"Prostrate yourself," whispered Sharat Fakir in my ears. "Nobody outside our clan had seen Deendayal; you've got that chance."

I closed my eyes at the instant impulse and wondered how there was so much bounty for an undeserving conscious sinner! Sharat's eyes were pointed downwards, his clenched fist holding the Fakiri rod. His voice sounded like an oracle: "Come with me."

I followed him in the dim glow of the lantern to the vast roof of the commonly-owned mansion. It was a totally empty roof-terrace. The night was bathed in the bright moonshine of the full moon of Baishakh; Fakir gave me the sweet rice porridge as an offering after worship. It was dinner for Deendayal and tasted like nectar!

Resting his chest on the roof-cornice, Fakir looked away at the waters of the Jalangi bathed in moonshine. He muttered, "I've been awaiting someone like you for a long time. I've noticed you've been wandering around this village for over a few months. But you never came to me. You've been approaching people like Ramprasad and teacher Dwijapada. What do they have besides a few songs of Kubir? What can you make of those songs—could you follow their meanings? They are not like the folk music aired on the radio—you won't follow them unless you understand the essence of the Sahebdhani cult. I possess those theories, the notebooks of their chants. They are belongings of Charan Pal, all of which I'll give you."

I was totally unprepared for such a sudden gift on that Baishakh midnight, and was left speechless in bewilderment, for a while. All that I could ask later was: "What service could I be of, to you?"

: "It's not my work, but of Deendayal. This building is tumbling down; Deendayal's roof is nearly collapsing. The devoted disciples are all very poor. My mind tells me that you can be of use in creating publicity for Deendayal. Perhaps the government could take steps for re-constructing Deendayal's home."

: "But your sub-religious cult is confidential. Will too much publicity be good for it?"

: "I've given good thought to it. But I'm unable to carry on with the services and worships any longer. There are sacred feasts every Thursday; expenses for the daily worships; the grand events like the Rice Festival; the annual dole of hookahs and mats for the 'sitting' (sedentary) Fakirs; are these feasible any longer? So I was wondering...now that you've come and now that Deendayal has actually sent you, he would get his work done. Let's go, it is late night. I'll give you everything tomorrow afternoon."

I spent the rest of the night in great excitement. Lying on the exterior balcony of Dwijapada's house, I was virtually unable to get any sleep. I was also unable to share with anybody any information on what I was going to receive the next day.

It was morning at last. The day wore on. The gathered crowd gradually left for their homes with Deendayal's name on their reverent lips. I arrived at Sharat Fakir's home in the afternoon, as per our discussion. It seemed he was waiting for me and said: "Deendayal's food-offering rituals are just over. It's Thursday today, it's His day. It's the custom today to have food-offerings at all the platforms of Deendayal."

I could not but ask: "What did the word 'platform' signify? And what was meant by the term 'Platformed Fakir' that I had heard last night?"

Sharat Fakir proceeded to elaborate: "Deendayal's primary or base portal is here with us. But those among our cult, who are initiated, include some who have attained divine grace and are also allowed to establish his own portal or platform. These platforms have continued over a few generations. They are also entitled to initiate others and are named 'Platformed Fakirs'. We've a Baruni Fair on the 14th lunar day in the month of Chaitra at Agradweep where Charan Pal attained the power of uttering infallible words. Since his times, Deendayal's platform is established at Agradweep. I go there, as do thousands of devoted disciples. We conduct sessions of sacred vows, ritualistic prayers and there are festivities over three days. The platformed fakirs spread their platforms under individual trees and initiate devotees into holy chants. Do come over in the next month of Chaitra. You can stay with me under a tree for three nights and will get to see many things and learn a lot. Now come to the inner house. I'll give you a few things, but please don't tell anybody—as long as I live. Do I have your word?"

Conveying assent through silence, I followed him with excitement boiling in my heart. There was a large chest in the innermost chamber, which the Fakir opened with a big key, accompanied by a lot of screeching noise. He delved into it with his hands and fished out something wrapped in red cotton fabric. Respectfully touching his forehead with the bundle, he unwrapped the cloth to bring out some time-worn manuscripts and notebooks with yellow pages. They contained clear handwriting penned in lampblack ink. "They contain the secret information of our cult. And take this one—the real manuscript."

Trembling with excitement, I picked up a manuscript. There were secret hymns and meditation practices of the Sahebdhani cult penned in red ink from start to finish.

Fakir said: "These are the true hymns of the Sahebdhani cult and the secret nomenclature. One Muslim female ascetic taught these hymns to us. These are behavioural in nature, the whole of which was known to Charan Pal. His son was Tilak, whose son was Phatik, whose progeny was four: Rambhadra, Birbhadra, Pranbhadra and Manmohanbhadra. I am the eldest son of that Rambhadra. These manuscripts have transferred instructions over five generations before reaching my hands. Our practices are very secretive indeed, comprising the earth; the fluids and cranial meditation. I'll explain these to you. Kubir's songs analyse the theories of our cult. Its external meaning and inner essence are totally different."

I ran my eyes over those hymns written in a bizarre lingo and muttered them to myself:

Allahtalah Brahma Sain, all for your worth—
I drink the sap from this earth.
Chanting the 'Kling' mantra through you
I view crimson young shoots in yellow hue—
And drink the seminal fluid which I hath.
Every living moment my Guru I wish to see you—
Gosain Alek Sain, you're the sole witness in my view!
This age at which I eat four elements, I retain anew—
I beg you, O Deenanath, please, I beg you! (three times)

I realised that the four things talked about here, were human body fluids—faeces, urine, menstrual fluid and seminal fluid. Obviously, it had to be a top secret hymn.

The Fakir said: "The same philosophy has been expressed in Kubir's song in a different way. In the lessons of Charan Pal, he has said—

Women's mens and male semens are the same as seed,
And let passion stay away from this: as one in four indeed!
Do realise the creation theme—
As spirit in every body resides Allah Supreme!

Did you follow the phrase 'Shani Shukkul' here? Shani is blood, the female menstrual flow. 'Shukkul' implies male seminal fluid. Now listen to the true hymn of our cult:

'Kling Shling', in the name of Deendayal and Sahebdhani,
Guru's true! Four Eras are true! True are moon and sun!
Earth, Deenanath and Deendayal are all true!
True is Deenabandhu, else there's none!

Listen to another hymn:

'Kling' Sahebdhani Allahdhani Deendayal—the names ring true,
The four eras, lust, action, and the Lord: all are true for you!
Deendayal is Truth, Deenanath Truth, Deenabandhu spells Truth too –
Gosain is the compassionate Sain,
Other than you, none is mine!

There is another secret hymn, a coded and a difficult one:

Guru, you're truly an asset! Truth, you're stainless, I bet!
Earth, your name is Truth; lust is Truth;
Service towards all is Truth.
The Lord is Truth. Speech is Truth. Guru is Truth. Admit I do."

The Fakir stopped; but the seeds of many doubts raised their heads in my mind. Where had I actually landed up? What did all this mean? There were many words which I had never heard in my life. What should I do with them? As if to free myself from a strange bondage, I muttered: "I'm not able to follow any of this. What does 'action' mean? What is 'earth'? You mention Allah, and have also been addressing the 'Lord.' Who is 'Deendayal? What is 'Deendayal'?"

Sharat smiled pleasantly: "Do you think you would understand everything in a single day? These are actions and reactions gathered over a long time. At present, you should copy it all from the notebook. Do stay in this room today. Nobody would know. Copy down everything. I shall hand you all notes as well as the handbook of the talisman after that, and details of the Ayurvedic cures of diseases".

: "Won't you give me the notebook of Kubir's songs?"

: "Everyone seems to have the same demand. Can you tell me what is so special about Kubir's songs? Charan was the first to pen it all down; then followed Kubir. His songs simply deal with our hymns and beliefs, explain them. Do you think you would be able to reach the depth of those words and understand their deeper philosophies all by yourself? If you do, they would only be the immediate external meaning."

: "Is that so?"

: "Yes, of course. Well, listen to this song by Kubir. I can't sing, just listen to me reciting it:

It was first water-filled, above water earth was built,
Above earth were houses made by all—
Whoe'er is Allah, my brother, is Kala, Brahma-Vishnu, our father,
At Vishnu's feet did the Ganga fall!

Now please understand the sense. 'Khaki' is earth, a Persian word. At Vishnu's feet is earth, whence came the Ganga. Ganga implies earth. Water also implies earth. Earth also means water. The Hindu gets Ganga, when death comes. The Muslim gets earth, when dead. Both are the same. But when the Apocalypse strikes?

O brother, when Hindu dies, he gets the Ganga,
Muslim stays on earth here—
According to scriptures, this is clear.
When this earth alone will disappear,
Everything will be sans form, sheer.
The world'll go, Ganga'll meet Ganga water's sphere.
Do realise and witness: escape of earth's smear,
When the dead Muslim won't get burial: far or near!

The world'll be bare, home and hearth rare,
Do ponder on this judgment fair.
Water is part of nature; on water is earth's stature,
On this ground rests heaven-and-earth: this is the word mere!
To water-fire-earth, God gives birth,
Hindu-Muslim unaware, exist in the world with mirth!

Nature signifies divine power. 'Kule Alam' means God. So what does it all lead to? The Hindu's Ganga, the Muslim's earth: all amount to the same and nothing will remain forever. Only God and Nature will, along with water-fire-word. You Hindus and Muslims, discard your divisiveness and pray to the one and only Deendayal."

So the matter became clear. Continuing in the same breath I said: "The message of harmony lies embedded in your religious belief. 'Allahdhani' and 'Raidhani' combine to create your 'Sahebdhani'. It's a great wonder. I think this is because the first stoic who had initiated you belonged to the Kaderia Sufi community."

Fakir said: 'That may be possible. Do you know that we cover our heads with a veil when we visit the Deendayal cult?"

: "Oh, you put on veils, do you? There remains no doubt then."

Thus began my exchanges with Sharat Fakir. I used to go often to Brittihuda and spend my night there. There were midnight conversations. Once at the Agradweep fair, there was intense conversation lying next to each other on two mattresses under a mango tree. He wore white mill cloth and a white cotton wrap to cover his upper body. He would invariably hold his black Fakiri pole close to his chest, never misplacing it. Apparently it wielded divine power.

I was in deep slumber, cooled and soothed by the pleasant Chaitra breeze. Around twelve midnight, Sharat touched my body to call: "Wake up, wake up, you want to see my ritual practices, don't you?"

The whole fair was asleep. Thousands of people were in deep slumber, tired after the day-long festival of eating flattened rice. A pale sliver of a moon was pasted against the sky. In the thin darkness, I saw Gopal's mother and three other widows creating a rectangular cover around the Fakir with four dhotis. In their midst, the Fakir quietly sat eating rice. To see me baffled, Gopal's mother whispered, "We cooked the rice for Fakir at nine o'clock. He's eating at twelve midnight. His meal time is not for the public to see. Tomorrow for twelve long hours, he won't touch either rice or any other food. He will observe restraint and complete silence and remain seated all day. Again at twelve midnight he will eat some rice. This is his regular ritualistic practice at Agradweep. This has been going on for four ages."

After this, it was left to me to remain only an observer, because the Fakir was silent. In the morning after a bath in the Ganga, the Fakir sat on his platform in white robes, head covered with a white shawl, clasping the Fakiri pole to his chest with one hand. There was a vermilion-smeared huge trident planted in front, with a devotee sitting in scarlet robes. Men and women falling to the ground and shouting "Victory to Deendayal Gupta Babaji" gave offerings of salutation. Within a trice, a wave of devout disciples filled the space. A few hundred lay prostrate listlessly in wet clothes. The place instantly became muddy. I threw a glance at the Fakir to see that he was seated in a restrained posture. A brand new mat lay in front, where accumulated loose change and cash money; coins and currency notes gathered high. An accountant was keeping track of the money in a hardbound red notebook.

Later I came to know, by asking Gopal's mother, that the notebook was meant to keep track of the 'revenue' payable by the 'Platformed' Fakirs.

: "What revenue?" This was my question.

Gopal's mother replied, "Why, sir, their body and mind are pledged to the house of Deendayal; won't they have to pay a revenue?"

: "How much is that revenue?"

: "Can that be a fixed amount? One pays whatever one can: in cash, loose change, rice, pulses, peanuts, pigeon-pea, crops. That makes up the staple for the rice carnival. There will be a carnival on the other side, during the Baishakhi full moon. Then all the 'seated' Fakirs from here will go there. Each of them will be offered a mat and a hubble-bubble from the house of Deendayal."

I wondered how varied were the faiths, varied their customs and rituals. But how long would they last? Money was a scarce commodity among the guru clan. Their hymns and chants were rusting inside locked chests. The Pals had forgotten the Ayurvedic knowledge for want of practice. Sharat Fakir's children went to regular schools and colleges; they would never follow the clannish profession of Fakiri—begging for alms. At best, they would annually visit Agradweep in quest of some earnings.

The day wore on. On the mat before the Fakir was a collected heap of cash and currency notes, besides rice, lentil, potatoes and jackfruit. A few of the cult-followers began cooking in ten or fifteen earthen pots. Soon the spot beneath the tree became smokey. In the midst of this, Gopal's mother lovingly spread out a quilt, almost as large as a full grown man. She placed a pillow on the quilt and at the head of the quilt she built a tiny 'room' out of jute-stalks and covered it with a piece of red cloth. She then planted a saffron banner with a thin stick.

I was quite taken aback. Realising my consternation, Gopal's mother explained, "My boy, this is Kubir Gosain's platform. Charan Pal, when he was still alive, used to place the platform wherever the Fakir was seated and here sat Kubir Dadathakur. His family seems to be devoid of learning and education. My son Gopal is a dumb boy. Therefore, I spread out the platform for Babathakur. He comes regularly and sits at the guru's platform for a while. There, you can see Charan Pal making his presence felt through Sharat Fakir, now! His twelve-hour day is devoid of conversation, awakening of senses or attending to his bodily needs. Kubir Pal is sitting too, watching his Guru. Dears, please raise the chant 'Hari, Hari'. Glory be to Deendayal Gopta Babaji."

The entire crowd of the fair joined in unison. In this vast world of innate belief, I was the only 'Doubting Thomas': driven by self-flagellation, not willing to have faith in anyting without concrete proof. I was a total misfit. Presumably to get out of my self-doubt, I urged Gopal's mother to sing: "Do sing a Kubir song now."

: "Right you are, dear. Listen then to his best song. This song contains a bit of the real essence of our Deendayal cult. Glory be to Din Dayal Gopta Babaji. Listen:

Act now for man—
By dint of meditation, by force of devotion, catch man if you can!
Hari, Shashthi, Manasa, Makhal,
False are wooden portraits, earthen icons, Sakshi Gopal,
Why do you break your head at dead stone's van?

Between man and man, don't divide:
Do religious rituals with man alone,
Leave Vedas aside!
Knowing man true in theory,
Towards man, make your plan!

On pots and portraits, don't put mind –
Drink always love's nectar: of the priceless kind!
If you recognise Kubir's feet as Gosain's feet: in mind's pan!"

While roaming round, I happened to meet Deben Goswami, the great grandson of Jadubindu. An accusation came forth: "Oh why didn't you come to our Panchlakhi!" and the accompanying lamentation: "And what can you visit here? Besides our residence and the social hamlet of Jadubindu, what else is there? We don't get enough wherewithal to offer service and worship, nor do we get new disciples. The old ones are impoverished. We can't really manage any more."

: "Is there no other way of earning?"

: "I've little professional knowledge; seven dependents; they remain ill most of the time; run high fever. When I feel well, I visit Kalna Court and earn a little money by copying legal documents. Still do come one day. I've five notebooks on Jadubindu's songs. Sir, don't they sell any more? Do they have no value?"

Deben Gosain's eyes and face were crimson red. Was it because of the hot sun or a burning fever?

At night, when I mentioned the context of Deben Goswami, Sharat Fakir responded immediately: "That man is genuine, yet very miserable. He belongs to a grand family. Jadubindu had many disciples, but he couldn't retain them. If you couldn't preserve the heritage knowledge of Jadubindu's cult, it would all get ruined. He has five or six children, has no restraint and is caught in the spiral of births. Still do consider if you can do something for him. My problem is elsewhere. Perhaps I won't be able to retain Deendayal's legacy. Next disciple is not coming in the current era. As a saving grace, there are fifty hectares of land dedicated to divinity that would scrape through with the regular worship."

Fakir woke me up that night at nine o'clock, to tell me, "I would go into silence mode after another three hours, after my meal. Before that happens, let me show you the notes on the talisman of our clan. Try and see under the hurricane lantern's glow."

Indeed, there were some astonishing diagrams on the papers: various rectangles or words or letters or numbers. Some diagrams had cryptic messages like: 'Shafts don't hit in false knowledge; a hit assures cure' written below. Some say: 'Tarakbrahma talisman cures nightfall'. One has a message: 'The husband loves her'.

Another has: 'Menstruation is regenerated.' One piece has a betel-leaf shaped figure with the message: 'This paper is for capturing illusions'. Two talismans had even subjects like: 'Beginning of Love' and 'End of Love'. Besides, there were many hymns and instructions for several measurements.

Fakir pointed out: "These also belong to our cult. Once upon a time, they helped to cure many incurable diseases. They all came from dreams: to be worn by writing them on paper and wearing as talisman."

: "Do you distribute such talisman?"

: "No, I don't know the applications, never learnt them. Father died suddenly, had no time to initiate me into the subject."

: "Does that mean these, too, have no value: purely useless bundles of papers?"

The Fakir sighed deeply out of desperation. I wondered how much full of illusion the whole world was! On the other side, thousands of believing people were sleeping peacefully in the fair. The only one losing sleep was the architect of their guru's family, whose only concern was to save the crumbling residential site of Deendayal and recruit more disciples.

The night passed in one single round of sleep. When I woke up, the sun was up already. The ritual bath for Baruni was on in the Ganga. The fair was breaking up today. Sharat was sitting on the platform in silence. The Agradweep station was two miles away: straight after crossing the Ganga. On arrival at the station, I noticed that Deben Gosain was fast asleep on a cement bench; running a high fever. His whole body was burning. Smiling wanly, Gosain said: "I have been running such temperature since the wee hours of the night. I'll go straight to bed once I reach Panchlakhi, after boarding a train from Samudragarh. Let my Deendayal be put at rest now."

That I never developed intimate relations with the Sahebdhani cult was due to my own negligence. I really could not do much for them. Yet I did not break their faith. As long as Sharat Fakir was alive, I never wrote about, or told, anybody about the confidential matters of their cult. Perhaps, out of severe depression or deep worries, he suddenly passed away in a heart attack. I got the news and thought perhaps this chapter closed there.

But, suddenly after ten months, an agency from Delhi sent me a financial grant for collecting folk songs. I thought immediately of Deben Gosain and of the notebooks of Jadubindu preserved with him. After checking up from old diaries to trace the Pachlakhi address of Deben Gosain, I sent him a letter in reply postcard. I had learnt from experience that the village folks do not write letters often out of lethargy, hence the ploy of reply postcard. I mentioned about my arrival date and time, so that somebody should be at the bus-stop waiting for me. I also indicated the possibility of receiving rupees five hundred from me.

On the appointed day, I started off with a jute side bag. I had received a reply letter beforehand from Deben Gosain, in which he had written:

Respected Dada (Elder Bother),

I have received your letter and all the news. I owe you thanks that you have still remembered a wretched soul like me. Whatever, it is my great fortune that you are willing to come to my place at Panchlakhi. Do please come and stay with this poor man, do not hesitate.

Kindly note that a person will wait for you at the bus-stop.

Yours,
In distress,
Debenbabu

I boarded a bus on the Kalna-Chupi route from Hemaitpur of Nabadweep. It was around eleven o'clock in the month of Paush, in deep winter. I wondered if I would have access to the notebooks.

Perhaps I should not have written about money in advance. Of course, the money, if given, would at least help in the medical treatment of Gosain.

Conductor called: "It's Nadai Bridge, Dhoba...Won't you get down, sir?"

I got down; a 12-year-old kid quickly approached me: "Do come with me. You wish to go to our home, don't you?"

He resembled Deben Gosain: sharp eyes, aquiline nose and fair complexion, with a haggard touch of poverty. "Are you the eldest son? Why are you so thin?"

The boy did not reply, but continued to walk in front with rapid steps. He wore a pair of black underwears and a dirty vest, with a cloth wrapped around his head. The walkway was across fields of wheat and along a crop of potatoes. The boy did not speak much and barely replied to my questions. My queries did not cease nevertheless. "Does your father go to Kalna Court, dear?" The urchin nodded his head, "How many brothers and sisters are you?"' He indicated five with his fingers. "Is your elder sister married off?" He nodded in assent. After a continued stretch of ten minutes' walk, he declared, "That's our house" and raced off towards his home. It was an earthen room, with a roof of broken clay tiles and a small terrace. There were plants of the indigenous *sandhyamani* and marigold flowers. Meanwhile, the news of my arrival had reached home.

The lintel was tapering down. People's feet were visible underneath. I shouted. "Where's Debenbabu?" The boy rapidly came down with a water-faucet and a cloth-towel, "Please wash your feet." With sidelong glances, I could gather that it was a miserable, unplanned family. Two boys and two girls, all covered in dust, were observing me with surprised eyes. A lady – with lowered eyes and wearing a dirty saree, presumably Deben Gosain's wife – was laying a mat for me on the earthen balcony. But where was Debenbabu? Unable to suppress my curiosity, I asked, "Where has Debenbabu gone?"

The youngest boy, standing in front, muttered, "Dad is dead."

: "How's that? When? How did it happen? I just got his letter day before yesterday!"

The hapless woman broke down at my feet in uncontrolled wailing. Then she dried her eyes and said, "He passed away in the month of Kartik. He was suffering from TB for three years, but was unable to get himself treated. Please don't take offence. I got the letter written myself through my ritually-bonded brother." After a pause, she continued, "I didn't convey to you the news of his death, you wouldn't have come otherwise. Sir, we're very poor and helpless. Would we receive the money, please? Take with you all the notebooks."

Even now, when I open the notebooks of Kubir Gosain's songs, I recall the dilapidated home of Deendayal, the last gasp of breath of a rapidly-disappearing religious cult. When I read Jadubindu's lyrics, I see in my mind's eyes the pallid, fever-struck face of Deben Gosain and, at the same time, I hear a female voice, "I didn't pass on the news of his death, you couldn't have come otherwise." What a true statement it was!

It would be quite a different matter now. The time was sometime in the middle of the 19th century. The Brahmins were making oblations in the name of their forefathers. The venue was the Bhairav river in Meherpur in undivided Bengal. Taking handfuls of water from the river, as the Brahmins were meditating on their ancestors with deep veneration at heart, they suddenly noticed a lower-caste man making oblations standing in chest level water, not too far away. Observing closely, they could identify Balaram Haari from Malopara—the ghetto of the lower castes in the village. What an audacity! One of them burst forth in a sharp taunting voice: "What is it, Bala, have you and your people all begun to copy us and make oblations dedicated to your forefathers these days?"

Without the least hesitation, Balaram replied, "No, Sir, I'm irrigating my fields of spinach."

The surprised Brahmin said, "What are you saying? How will the water reach your fields from this river? Is it going via the sky?"

Balaram's undaunted response came pronto: "How are the waters of your oblation reaching your ancestors? Is it through the sky? Please understand, respected sirs, my water is reaching my field exactly the same way as your waters are reaching your forefathers."

This retort was followed by an instant dead silence in the air. The insulted Brahmins left, after casting poisonous glances at Balaram. What an audacity of the low-caste creatures! Filling his face with a taunting smile, Balaram Hari, too, proceeded towards home.

Who was this Balaram? Why did he protest so grudgingly? What was his cause of deep anger against the upper castes?

Meherpur was located in the Nadia district of Bengal in the 19th century. On the west of the small town lived the lower-caste people. In the Malo locality, Balaram was born in AD 1825, in the Malo enclave. His father was Govinda Haari, and mother Gaurmani. The Haaris those days earned their livelihood by tending pigs, selling vegetation-medicines, working as skilled fighters wielding bamboo poles and sticks, or being security guards for the rich. Balaram was the guard of Padmalochan Mullick, the famous rich man of Meherpur. Days were passing tranquilly, until one night all the jewellery of the Mullick household got stolen. The doubts converged on Balaram. Tied to a tree, he was beaten blue. Finally, as per the general consensus, he was chased out of the village. Bala became a stoic at the end. Fie, could the human mind be so low! Why was there so much hatred of the richupper caste for the low caste? Suddenly, a new man of protest was born in him. This helpless life, this injustice of the society, this fall from the faith moved him utterly.

After a few years, when Balaram returned to Meherpur, he was an entirely changed man. Wearing matted hair like a dispassionate spiritual soul, he showed no trace of the old Balaram. He founded his platform on the banks of Bhairav. The jewel thief had been caught meanwhile. And the repentant Mullick donated Balaram land and lucre where a temple came up. Over the days, waves of the low-caste people – long oppressed by the Brahmins – came to take refuge with Balaram, who gradually turned into their saviour. A new belief and faith were created. In common parlance, it was termed 'Bala Haari's credo'. Before long, around twenty thousand devotees and disciples gathered. Balaram's meditation-partner was a woman called Brahma Maloni.

The book *Bharatbarshiya Upasak Sampradaya*, by Akshaykumar Dutt – written more than 100 years ago – gives some information on the Haari community. There is more information in the book: *Hindu Castes and Sects*, by Pandit Jogendranath Bhattacharjee. He went to Meherpur and talked to Balaram's widow in 1892. Her first question to Jogendranath about his caste. Since Jogendranath was aware of their deep malice towards Brahmins and brahminical thoughts, he introduced himself simply as a human being. The lady then asked him to sit down and, despite being a Haari in caste, requested him to have some food. The surprised Jogendranath was, of course, not agreeable, but was nonetheless quite charmed by the illiterate lady's verbal felicity and leadership qualities. According to him, the Balarami community had no special symbol or costume for themselves. Most of them earned their livelihood by begging for alms. One more feature that he marked was that they did not mention the names of any particular god or goddess. The only significant aspect of this community noticed by him was animosity towards Brahmins. He expressed it in the following words:

> Bala Haari...was in his youth employed as watchman in the service of (the) local family of zeminders, and, being cruelly treated for alleged neglect of duty, he severed his connection with them. After wandering about for some years, he set himself up as a religious teacher, and attracted round him more than twenty thousand disciples. The most important feature of his cult was the hatred that he taught his followers to entertain against Brahmins. He was quite illiterate, but he had a power of inventing puns by which he could astonish his audience whenever he talked or debated.

Some samples of Balaram's oratorical powers and literary puzzles that Jogendranath had mentioned have been quoted. They were located in some old printed books:

- If there's no cook, who cooked the food? If nothing was cooked, what did you eat?
  The one who cooked ate it: that's this world's magical bit!
- Even when gone, he persists, even while staying, he's gone,
  Thus are you'n'me, dear, we're alive when dead, and dead, when we live on.
- He is what you are,
  What he is, is how you figure.
- The God of Death is a two-faced sack, hence his entrails are empty,
  He eats, eats, and eats in vain
  Do his insides those bits retain?
- If we open eyes, everything is there; if we close eyes, all is bare—
  Creation is in the day, not in the night; this is what is always right!

Balaram was, no doubt, a man of huge talents. But it is not true that he created a new religious belief based only on animosity against Brahmanism. In reality, the lower-caste people of this country became helpless for various reasons in the 18th century. There was no social security and certainty in their life. In consequence, they were frequently subjected to the oppression and dictates from the higher castes at any time. Balaram had to even desert his village. People like Ramsharan Pal of Kalyani, Lalan Shah of Kustia, Charan Pal of Hudo, Khushi Biswas of Bhaga village, Balaram Haari of Meherpur are the ones who tried to create a space of survival for the marginalised outside the frown of the upper caste.

It was not merely a protestation, but also a struggle for survival. It was no more living with a narrow analysis of the scriptures, but a free living within the catholicity of humanism. Therefore, they countered idol worship and the worship of evil spirits, avoided pilgrimages, resisted blind faith in Brahmins, deities and dependence on the scriptures and rituals by using the weapons of harmony, regardless of racial differences and employing simple religious practices based on the fresh wave of an enlightened mould of humanism. But the Kartabhaja Sahebdhanis accepted reincarnation. Balaram did not accept even that, nor did he accept the dual worship (of Radha-Krishna), since he was against Vaishnavism. This was the novelty of Bala Haari's credo.

But what did Balaram want to say through his religious faith? Defying reincarnation, he called himself 'Haariram'. He did not imply any separate community of Haaris, but linked the name to the ethic Bengali word '*haar*' (bone), meaning the Supreme Creator of *haar* or bones. The bone was part of the human body structure, around which the skin was the canopy. Inside lay the might—as blood. This was the human body, in which were bones, eyeballs, brain, intestines and bladders. All in all, there were eighteen constituent homes.

In the book, *Bharatbarshiya Upasak Sampradaya*, an interesting question-and-answer segment occurs as an interview of Balaram. It runs as follows:

Q. Where does Earth come from?

A. From decadence *(kshay)*.

Q. How did it originate from decadence?

A. There was nothing in the earliest times. I 'dissolved' my body to create this Earth. Hence its name is 'Kshiti' (Earth). 'Kshay', 'Kshiti' and 'Kshetra' (field) are all one and the same. I am Haari: the builder of the body structure and yet a married man. Like the thatcher who builds the thatch, I'm the builder of '*haar*' (the bones), hence my name is 'Haari'.

Howsoever strange the 'Haariram theory' seems, the mystery of the fundamental concept behind it is most fascinating.

ß

In 1971, when independent Bangladesh was born, I travelled immediately to Meherpur in quest of the Balarami doctrine. The land had been a part of Pakistan and so my curiosity was confined to manuscript pages. At last, I saw the Mullick mansion in Meherpur on the banks of the Bhairav and sat in front of the Balaram temple in Malopara. There were still a few people left from the community who worshipped and served Haariram daily. Their current leader ('Sarkar') began explaining to me: Listen, sir, our faith says:

Bone, marrow, semen, brain, intestine, bladder and heel,
In these eighteen dwellings reigns our Balaramchandra Haari, we feel."

I asked: "What is the theory behind this philosophy of eighteen?"

: "Well, please count, sir. The human body is made of a total of eighteen materials, such as, two nostrils, two ears and two eyes: which make six. And one mouth, one navel, one anus, one genital, which make it ten. Now listen to the four that father gives: bone, marrow, semen and brain. And the mother bestows another four: hair, skin, blood and flesh. These make the eighteen dwellings. And above all these is our Haariram."

: "Was Haariram an incarnation?"

: "He had stated that the Divya era prevailed before Satya, Treta, Dwapar and Kali eras. He was born during that period. That means he came before all other incarnations. There is the mention in our Sadananda's song:

In the Divya era Haariram had come,
In Meherpur is his home wholesome!"

I noticed that Bala Haari did not establish himself as an incarnation of either Ramachandra of Treta era or Balaram of the Dwapar era. He had put himself above them all. He had named himself 'Ramdeen'. What did Ramdeen mean?

Vrindavan sang on:

The letter 'Ra' means this earth,
Letter 'Ma' provides creatures their berth.
'Deen' is the letter that makes things bright—
Only if you remember his name just right!

I wanted to know whom the Balaramis worshipped. After all, they would be worshipping somebody. Somebody must be there warranting devotion; who was this entity?

Vrindavan replied: "We don't worship any idol or deity, any icon or portrait, any hillock or tree. We don't bow to anybody. We only pray to Ramdeen. It's He who is the creator. Hence Sadananda wrote:

Haariram's theory has secret meanings, outside Veda's purview—
Whoever has given up all faiths can catch its sense anew!
Knowing this theory, Shiva dwells in crematorium—
Knowing this theory, Sachi's Gora Nimai saint did become!"

The dialogue seemed unreal; bizarre were the beliefs. Soon the sun went down in the west behind the Balaram temple. A silhouette of the temple rose to my vision: surrounded by devoted men and women; with a vision of still conviction in their eyes and faces; a sense of proud charm. The Malopara temple was located at a derelict section of Meherpur. All around lay the wilderness of unkempt trees and creepers, and the broken remains of the homes of the deceased poor. Standing in their midst, Vrindavan cried out: "Those whom you call Brahma-Vishnu-Maheshwar are also creations of Haariram's hands."

: "How's that? How did it happen?"

: "Look, we believe that Haariram's yawn gave birth to Haimavati. And Haimavati went on to create Brahma-Vishnu-Maheshwar. Isn't that right?"

Night descended on the banks of the Vaibhav. I departed from the Haariram temple premises, after offering my quiet salutations. My mind was full of awe and respect. I asked Vrindavan: "I am keen to learn more on Haariram. Where else can I go?"

Vrindavan replied in dismay: "People have scattered after the Partition, sir. But you may get some information if you visit Nishchintapur under the Tehatta police station administrative zone of Nadia district. The wooden sandals of Haariram have been preserved at the Siddhapeeth of Beltala in that region. Radharani offers them daily oil and water. Go and tell her about me and convey that Bendaban (Vrindavan) from Meherpur has sent you. You will find Purna Halder and Bipradas Halder too, in Nishchintapur. Both of them are old now; however Bipra is still fairly fit. He knows many songs of Haariram, which you can hear him sing. Apart from them, there is our local 'Sarkar' Charu at Dha'para. Phani Dervish is there in Sahebnagar. Sir, please do visit them."

Before I take the readers to Nishchintapur, let them be acquainted with a few important contexts. What is the phenomenon of human worship? How did Nishchintapur get connected with Meherpur? What is the custom of worship of the Balaramis?

The Balaramis did not have much in common with the sundry alternative spiritual communities. They did not believe in the guru system, so there was no initiation into hymns or learning practices. Unlike the Sahajiya Vaishnavas, they did not have regular worshipping practices following certain sequential levels and hierarchical ranks like the 'founder-worshipper-achiever'. They did not have female companions for physical meditation practices, unlike the general practice of most other folk belief-systems. Hence there was little or no perversion; absence of the guru system meant no extortion from and exploitation of the devotees and disciples. The behavioural practice of their faith was very easy and simple. None belonged to the upper castes. Their participants were the lowest-caste Hindus, the marginalised and dispossessed men and some renegade Muslims. Those who changed over to the Balarami faith from the Islamic addressed Haariram as Hari-Allah. They did not have the tyranny of the superiors, higher castes or the guru. Hence there was no ritual platform, no taxation, no dependence on hymns and chants, no institutions, no seat of worship. There were only two places with seats of worship: one at Nishchintapur in western Bengal and the other at Meherpur in the east—now in Bangladesh. There were no ceremonial robes, no rosary, no string of beads, no games of trickery in this faith.

In reality, Balaramis were believers in worshipping humanism. According to them, the creation was Haariram's handiwork, not God's. One had to worship within the folds of one's household. They believed that as Haariram the master craftsman had created the human body with eighteen elements, it was He who ran that body. One of the songs said:

Haariram is the plumber working this machine.

Another song states:

Haariram created the human body—a unique contraption,
It's the power of blood that runs it, O my mind—
Without blood, the machine is not in motion!!

The original word '*bal*' signifies 'blood' in this context.

Even though Balaramis do not believe in reincarnation, they state – perhaps to covince people with a tilt towards Vaishnavism – '*Sachi's Gora left Nabadweep in tatters and tears*'; followed by the supplementary line—'*Kali era at Meherpur—you see the man after long years.*' Again, in order to bring credulity in Muslim minds, they sing:

To give credulence and direction to the absurd
Kind Allahtalah appears here as the human bard

But why this worship of the human frame and spirit? Why has there been an attempt to establish a human entity as the Almigty?

In reality, in the folk religious meditation practices of Bengal, there are two sides: *anuman* (surmise) and *bartaman* (premise). Radha-Krishna-Vrindaban-Kubja-Kamsa-Chandravali are all surmised in imagination, hence their worships are the worships of surmise. And the meditation of premise is concretely premised on the human body. In this body is located Vrindavan or paradise, where reside the elements of vanity-separation-despair-amour. After initiation from the guru and through formal ritual chanting along the path ordained by the guru, one can sustain a dual (man-woman), spiritually uplifting meditative process within the corporeal frame, receive divine perception and accept it as the proper path to salvation.

Again, the meditation of Balaramis is of another kind: outside *anuman and bartaman*. Explaining this, Phani Dervish of Sahebnagar had been candid with me: "We don't worship Radha-Krishna and Durga-Kali as deities," he admitted. "We say, *'Things we haven't seen with our own eye, / How can their worship and salutation we try?'*

"So we pray to Haariram; cry for him. At least, that man was born in the human form to salvage us, wasn't he, sir?"

But how did Meherpur get linked to Nishchintapur of Tehatta? In reality, when the district of Nadia had not been partitioned, Meherpur was a sub-divisional township within it. People from the neighbouring villages used to congregate at Meherpur for commercial transactions and litigation in courts. On some such errand, Tanu Mandal from Nishchintapur had been there once and met Balaram by sheer chance. Being attracted by the oratorical ability, divine power and sheer personality, Tanu adopted his discipleship. And from that instant Tanu started Balaram-worship at Nishchintapur; gradually, the lower-caste fishermen of that village became worshippers of Balaram. At Tanu's behest, Balaram must have come walking a few times from Meherpur to Nishchintapur. The people directly ordained by Balaram were Mahindar, Ramchandra Das, Jaladhar, Sadananda, Srimanta and Raju Fakir. Among women were ordained Natu, Daksha and Jago. Gradually in time, Bala Haari's doctrine spread out to Dharampur, Sahebnagar, Arshiganj, Natna, Dha'para, Haulia, Garibpur and Palashipara.

They used to meditate on their faith while keeping themselves almost out of sight, as they were the marginalised and the doomed poor. This apart, the Vaishnavas and Sahajiyas used to look down upon the Balaramis. The idea of worshipping Balaram could not be tolerated by them, since they were believers in divine incarnations. Kubir Goswami had stated in one of his songs: '*Like Balaram's disciples, if I may / Krishna's lore sounds bitter, I say!*' It was quite clear that the Sahebdhanis were not enamoured of the Balaramis.

That, of course, did not matter much to Balaram. His belief-system was well-established in his own lifetime. Everyone called him an 'orator', which meant that he had an extraordinary gift of the gab, enabling him to give in-depth analysis about all worldly matters and life in general. He used to hold three large festivals in a year by assembling all his disciples. These happened on Baruni—the eleventh day after full moon in Chaitra; on the last day of Jaishtha; and on the eleventh day after full moon in Kartik. Of them, Baruni's gathering was the grandest one, when the disciples used to play with red powder by placing Balaram on a swing. Balaram died in 1890 at the age of 65. The celebrations did not diminish in the least even after his death. But, due to the Partition of the land, the devotees of this community became somewhat dispersed. Still Nishchintapur remained their stronghold of sorts, where the regular celebration of ritual festivals and daily worship under the jasmine-tree continued without break. Of the five hundred households, at least four hundred were worshippers of Balaram.

I collected all this information from Phani Dervish of Sahebnagar in advance. That man was of a mellow temperament, but was most depressed by virtue of a large number of children. He would always repent: "O Creator, what's this you've done to me!"

It was Phani Dervish who pushed me to visit Nishchintapur.

Number 52 Mauja of Block Number one of Tehatta was formally called Nishchintapur. The name became Nishchinpur in common parlance. It was not a very secure place for the administration. Before I entered the village, someone from the block-office warned me: "Move around carefully; once upon the time the village was a terror: full of dacoits. Whoever they may be as Balramis or so on, 'safe bind, safe find'."

I, however, entered the village entirely unafraid. I was mentally figuring out that I was being sent by Meherpur's Vrindavan to accost their Radharani there, what should I be scared of?

Crossing long stretches of fields, the bus finally panted to a halt under a fig-tree, the engine catching its breath after the long haul. "Get down, it's Nishchinpur," announced the bus conductor.

A half-hour trudge down a dirt track led to the village. To begin with, I tracked Radharani down to the wood-apple tree. After the initial exchanges of acquaintance, she greeted me warmly and asked me to take a seat. The huge tree was quite a sight, with a large branch stooping down: almost to the point of breaking off. The branch was supported with brick-work. The wood-apple tree appeared quite ancient; it had been visited by Haariram several times, hence it was regarded highly sacred. There was a pair of old wooden sandals kept near the tree's trunk. Radharani came forward to enquire: "What are you watching, my boy? These are wooden sandals of Haariram's sacred feet. Observe them with devotion. These sandals have to be bathed with oil and water daily on the stroke of twelve. That's the order of 'Sarkar'."

: "Do you mean the local government by 'Sarkar'?"

: "No, my dear boy. Sarkar is our chief who resides in Dha'para. His name is Charupada."

: "Well, who performs the bathing?"

: "I do it. The onus of his service has now come upon me. I stay here day and night, all hours of the day; it's my good fortune."

: "What is served as food to Haariram?"

: Nothing boiled or cooked should be offered at his service; everything has to be fresh and raw. Soaked grains of pigeon-pea lentils, fruits and cane or date palm molasses are the usual fare. Steamed sweets – like sandesh or rasogolla – from roadside shops, won't do."

: "Is there any special hymn or chanting for his service?"

: "The food is kept under this wood-apple tree, with an offering of a couple of flowers. He accepts the service. And when I offer rice and water, the following words have to be uttered:

Haariramchandra, here I offer rice and water:
Do accept—
Theories of creed-caste-race,
the truths behind emotion and grace:
We learn from you a trace.
I contemplate you in mind and soul, I've no other desire—
Let me not a moment lose your sight, Haariramchandra, sire!

: "Where is the grand festival of Haariramchandra held?"

: "It's held right here, under this very wood-apple tree. The grand festival happens thrice: on the eleventh day from the full moon in Chaitra; the tenth day in Jaishtha; and the eleventh day from the full moon in the month of Kartik. The oath-taking, the mental offerings—everything takes place here; he resides here. But don't talk so much, dear, in this boiling afternoon of Jaishtha. Just walk up to that tubewell and come back refreshed, after washing your face. Let me offer you a share of his votive offering: the raw meal service.

Radharani served me a large pitcher of the molasses made from fresh cane-juice and cool water in a brass pot, with a lot of care. The humbleness of the home and the simplicity of the arrangement did not reflect in the taste, which was amply satisfying. The journey's tiredness disappeared in a trice, with a gracious pleasure descending over the body. I realised that the foundation of the Balarami's' faith lay deep in simple sincerity and unadorned objects. In the grandeur of large-scale worships of the devoted deities, we tend to forget that Haariram was not that kind of divinity warranting devotion. He had remained alive in every moment of the tired labourer and their daily remembrance.

The matter became clearer when I reached the earthen balcony of Bipradas from the wood-apple complex. Bipra was a fisherman, seemingly touching sixty: with a pair of long moustaches. As soon as he spotted me, he cried out: "Do please come right in. That you would come I was informed by the BDO, but no time was indicated. So, I was looking your way till the end of the day. Did you go, first, to the wood-apple tree-site? Victory to Haariramchandra! It's all a play of his wishes. May I hope that you'll accept the offer of our service this afternoon?"

As soon as I nodded in acceptance, he cried out again: "Victory to Haariramchandra! He gives right sense even to Brahmins. O my dear Kanchan, give this gentleman a towel and a waterpot. Serve him a little puffed rice and tea. Meanwhile, let me go to the river with my cast-net, to look for a fish, just in case."

I interjected: "Would fish be caught so late in the day?"

: "It's all up to the intention of the Creator; if he has sent you, he may send the fish as well," replied Bipra and proceeded with his net. The silvery flow of the rapidly-flowing river was clearly visible from the balcony itself. I could see very well Bipra getting down to the knee-deep water and, standing there, throwing his cast-net into the waters. Then, collecting the net back, he took one look and threw up his hand in the air. This meant he had met his end on a single try. He came up almost running. In his hand fidgeted a fresh-water carp of about 500-600 gram in weight.

I stood up on the balcony to greet him and exclaimed: "You seem to be a very expert fisherman, I can see!"

Bipra placed the fish on his balcony. Then he twirled his moustaches and said with a broad smile: "What is my skill in this at all? It's all his intention and your luck. Do sit down, Let me inform everybody." Bipra started humming:

Do tell me how does whisper the breeze,
The mind's like a lit-up creeper at ease!

Very soon, Bipradas's balcony filled up with a swelling crowd of Balaramis. There was not an inch of space left after a while. Our discussion continued over puffed rice and tea. The oldest disciple Purna Halder arrived and performing a full salutation, took his seat. Soon, a village Brahmin – a school teacher – came and introduced himself, inviting me to his home for lunch. Bipra remonstrated, "What are you saying? He's a Meherpur-returned person, a guest of Balaram himself. The Creator has sent a large fish for him. Besides, he is a self-realised man and does not distinguish among castes." Saying this, Bipra broke into a song:

At Haariram's feet, all castes unite—
O, their pure rite and true might: I saw at the sage's site!
In your water, the rice for all boils;
No separation in thirty-six castes recoils,
It is Haariram, none else who achieves this in the world's turmoils!

His was a very melodious voice, depicting also a mature sense of rhythm and tempo. In surprise, I had to comment: "How do you get to sing so easily, at every turn of phrase? Even your voice is so tunefully trained!"

Bipradas bit his tongue to correct me: "You're again making a mistake, sir! It all is the Creator's play. And, did you mention my songs? It's indeed worth a mention. All of you here might vouch—I certainly don't have a big stock of paddy at home, as I'm a poor man's son and a fisherman at that. But my humble home is a music stack." Laughing raucously, Bipra continued, "I'll sing Haariram's songs all through the night. The ribbon of your tape-recorder will get exhausted, but not the stock of my songs. What do you all say to that?"

Everyone agreed joyfully. Purna Halder egged him on, "Oh, and do tell them about your astounding memory".

Nodding vigorously and twisting his moustache, Bipra exclaimed: "Even that's the Creator's strange gift on me. I really don't forget anything. I haven't studied much, I've passed only the fourth standard; yet I know all the theories of Haariam and all the songs of Deenu Goshtha Sadananda by heart. But I don't know how long my memory'll stay, nor who'll sing these songs after I'm gone. These boys have more pomp than sincerity. Let me see whom the Creator commands me to teach. For the present, let these be captured by your machine. There will, at least, be an indication. In the afternoon, another customer of ours is supposed to come from Arshiganj. Let me see if he comes, perhaps that chap is lying in 'Bodhitan'; he can't keep his word.

: "What's 'Bodhitan'?" I could not resist asking.

Bipra clicked his fingers and said, "You'll get to know everything. These were confidential matters—outside the Vedas. Since the Creator has sent you and you've visited Meherpur, nothing'll remain unknown to you. For the present, please sit for a while. Have a bath and a serve of food. Meanwhile, let me take a quick dip and offer the raw meal service at the wood-apple tree.

Outside it was unbearably hot in the month of Jaishtha; on the balcony was the graceful gathering of the believing devotees. In my mind's canvas, the vision rolled on like a movie, of the mystic revelation of the Balaram temple at Meherpur—the innocence writ large on Vrindavan's face and the two eager eyes replete with hope and belief. I was left wondering how a disgruntled rebel had given these people a hymn of escapade, injected faith in their blood and put their feet back on the ground. What was this secret tide of change in village after village, trampling and crushing everything that traditional established Brahminical society stood for—blowing away the teachings of the Vedas, Vedanta and the Shastras? Yet, these were the poor, miserable lot, with heads held low in sorrow. Was there truly an inborn craving for dacoity in their blood? Did their ancestors selectively commit armed robbery at the homes of the Brahmins and higher castes? Was this in retaliation? Everything seemed so unreal to me.

I had observed in the Gazetteer that Nishchintapur was over 150 years old. Before that time, it was a wooded tract. Tortured by the upper castes, some low-caste people fled their homes and established a colony after partially clearing the forests. Subsequently Balaram had raised the bastion of belief and conviction needed for survival. The impassioned men, the early faithfuls – Tanu, Mahinder, Ramachandra, Jaladhar, Sadananda, Srimanta, Raju – did they leave their trace among this new generation? Their progeny was perhaps present here, among the new generation? Or were they in other lands?

The 90-year-old Purna Halder put in politely: "Everyone's information is not available. But then, Tanu has no successors, he never married. Deenu was in Aamjhupi of Bangladesh; his progeny is still there. Jaidev, grandson of Kunja, lives nearby in Bhabanipur. Dhananjay's clan is in Panchakoti. Raju Fakir's ashram is at the ghats of Palashipara. Sadananda's family is at Panchakoti. Mahinder, Srimanta, Daksha and Jago left for Meherpur in the company of Haariram. I don't know what happened to them after that. They were enlightened men; they must be with the Creator."

: "Well, aren't there parables or strange stories about the disciples of Haariram?"

: "All of them were unique persons; supernatural. They came in human form with Haariram only to enlighten us. But I heard that Srimanta of our Nishchintapur received a limb, while in the service of Haariram. He developed a tiny bit of a tail."

: "Then was he a reincarnation of Hanuman?"

: "How can I explain those secret doctrines? But then he was our first 'Sarkar' from whom originated our scriptures. All the learnings came from him."

: "Who was the Sarkar after him? How are Sarkars decided?"

: "After the old Sarkar dies, a new Sarkar is determined. We're not aware who succeeded Srimanta. But since the time I was born; I'd seen Goshtha of Sahebnagar. After he was no more, our Sarkar has been Charu Mandal of Dha'para."

: "A Sarkar's son can't become Sarkar, can he?"

: "There's nothing to prevent it. It can well be done, if the necessary qualities and merits are present. He must possess the ability to explain the doctrine of Haariram to all; must be acceptable to one and all. And he must be a worshipper of Nityan. Take, for example, Phani, the son of our previous Sarkar Goshtha. He was a well-qualified man, with mature knowledge and intelligence. But after Goshtha died, he couldn't be made the 'Sarkar'."

: "Why so?"

: "He had many children. Instead of transcending to Nityan from Ayotan, he was entrapped by Bodhitan."

: "I don't follow any of these terms: Ayotan, Nityan, Bodhitan..."

Purna turned solemn and said: "You should have all those matters explained by Bipradas. Now listen to a song and see if you can make sense of it." Purna began the refrain in a quivering voice:

Now remember him with devotion—
Or else there's no escape in motion.
Make Haariram's feet your principal notion.
O my mind, if at Bodhitan you remain—

You shall be caught in time's cyclic bane.
O mind, to Bodhitan do not tie down your motion—
Without Haariram's feet, there's no salvation!

Purna said: "What a game is this of the Creator! These lyrics are the composition of Goshthadas but his own son has been entrapped by Bodhitan."

In the middle of this, Bipradas came rushing in. Beckoning him near, Purna whispered something in his ears. Sprinting up, Bipra said: "Yes, certainly, everything'll be done. You will come to know everything. Those are matters of the late hours of the night: you've to listen to those doctrines under the wood-apple tree. I've brought the order of the Creator for the wood-apple premises. I'd also sing many songs. But as you know, first serve yourself and then serve the Lord—first comes the food, then come the prayers."

I asked: "Is this also the saying of the Creator?"

Tweaking his moustache, Bipra admitted: "No, these words are not from the Creator. This is from yours truly, his humble servant. Now, all of you go right home. Complete your bath and have some food. Sir is not escaping at this moment. Having come here, he has to stay three nights as per the custom."

When the day's scorching heat subsided, evening descended with an illusive charm. There was a strong cool breeze. And the moon hung in picture-perfect ethereal beauty against the sky. Bipradas and the singer from Arshinagar continued to sing, seated on the river-bank. Their songs were accompanied by the *ektara* – the single-string drone lute – and the *anandalahari*—a similar folk musical instrument. I didn't quite realise when the singing stopped or when the folks left. I was under the grip of overpowering sleep; my body was tired and there was the salubrious breeze. How could I be blamed?

It was into the late hours of the night when Bipradas called me up. Together, we proceeded towards the wood-apple premises.

The whole village was pitch dark, there was a dreadful silence all around. Lighting up a lamp, only Radharani was deep in meditation under the wood-apple tree. As soon as we both approached her, Bipra shouted:

Seed and machine together brought me in—
Hariramachandra is that blood and power.
Person, who knows this, over us, does tower,
I bow down a million times at his feet—
Whatever he says has Haariram's blood'n'power replete.

Afterwards, Bipra and Radharani offered flower and water on the wooden sandals under the wood-apple tree and chanted in duet:

We offer flower'n'water to Sri Haariramchandra's feet—
On the earth, we're now blessed complete.
Beauty'n'youth, mind'n'vision: we offer every bit.
I'm weak; you're the might for the weak. The all-knowing knows it all—
I praise your qualities. Do heed that I don't hear others' call.

Everything was quiet for a while. Gusty currents of wind rose. Bipradas's eyes were burning, Radharani was in deep meditation. Suddenly, Bipradas drummed on his cheeks to produce a beat and announced: "Right, victory to the judge Haariramchandra! Let's begin the doctrine of creation."

Keeping her eyes closed, Radharani said, "Haariram had the first right. From him were born Haimavati and Narada."

Bipra said: "And from this Haimavati were born Brahma, Vishnu and Shiva. Brahma had two offsprings—Ghamkanchani and Bhagavati. From Bhagavati came the demons Aghasur, Bakasur, Kamsasur and Lohasur."

Radharani said: "And Ghamkanchani had three children—Kalu, Murari, Basudev. This Kalu had offsprings like—Khagar,

Nagar, Neelambar and Manmatha. Murari's offspring are—Loknath, Jeevan, Aajir Methar and Bhushi Ghosh. Basudev's offspring are—Shanmriga, Gajakanya and Munibalak."

Bipradas played his cheek-music once again and announced: "Here ends the clan of Brahma. Now hear about Vishnu's clan from Radharani."

"Vishnu had a large family," said Radharani with closed eyes. "He had three children—Jho-kali, Muchhundari Kali and Musuk Kali. Jho-kali had no children. Muchhundari Kali's children were Hawa and Adam. This Adam's children were Habel and Kabel. Kabel led to the birth of Nikari, Jola and the Rajput race. On this side, from Havel were born Sekh, Saiyad, Moghal and Pathan."

Bipra continued: "Now come in closer to me. From Sekh was born four races—Jin Sekh, Pari Sekh, Haiduli Sekh and Dulduli Sekh. From Saiyad also came four races—Humani Saiyad, Ali Saiyad, Dumra Saiyad and Hurana Saiyad. From Moghal came four races—Lal (Red) Mughal, Neel (Blue) Mughal, Sunni Mughal and Shia Mughal. From Pathan also were born four races—Chhur, Chhurani, Ludhi, Lohani. That's all. Now is left the description of Musuk Kali's clan, Listen to it from Radharani's lips."

"Musukk Kali had three children—Parashar Muni, Namas Muni and Rishav Muni. This Parashar Muni had eleven children—such as the goat, tiger, snake, vulture, rat, mosquito, ***hajat***, horse, cat, camel and monkey. On this side, Namas Muni's children were twelve in number—Jarlal, Pharlal, Grahak, Naini, Shiuley, Nulo, Aaltapete, Mughalbere, Maldahi, Jhapani, Purkata and Chong."

Bipra continued to say: "Rishav Muni had four sons—Darashan, Narashan, Parashan and Padma. Now from Narashan came the barber, from Parashan the nurse and from Padma came the cobbler: Muchiram Das. Parashan's sons were numerous. Keep counting, sir: Dobey, Chobey, Tebey, Pathak, Pandey, Ubiddhi, Tewari, Mishir, Metel, Debel, Thakur, Bishan and Shukur. Are they not thirteen? Now let us end the creation doctrine."

Radharani said: "Only Shiva's clan is left out. Shiva's children are Kartik, Ganesh and Saraswati. Kartik's son is Arjun, while Ganesh's son is Bhuinmasur. And Saraswati is forever a virgin ascetic."

Making the deep, dark night tremble, Bipra announced in his resonant voice: "Here ends the creation doctrine. Right, say 'bravo' now, in the name of Lord Haariram."

Bipra and Radharani in their overwhelmed state—overcome with emotion and I, somewhat bewildered, shouted together thrice: "Bravo, bravo, bravo!"

There was no knowing how late the hours were. Everywhere was silence and stillness, only three strange humans were awake in this wide open world. All three of us had only single meals in order to listen to the creation doctrine. That was the custom. The one who enunciated and the one who listened to: both had to be deprived of food and sleep from 12 midnight. Everything was a little surprising somewhat. What were those messages that I heard all this while?

But I could not cherish my surprise for long. Bipradas said: "Now Radharani will spend the remainder of the night all alone. Come; let's go a little over to that side and talk. I would let you know about our worship of *tan*. That is the secret essence of Haariram."

As soon as we sat comfortably on the grassland opposite the wood-apple tree, Bipra began: "In our credo, there's no guru, no female companion for meditation. Haariram had left a statement that the most cherished meditation is that where 'the male has no female companion, the female has no male companion'. This is precisely what is termed as meditation on the path of 'Khastan'. But before you understand Khastan, you've to follow the pattern or layers of all other *tans*."

I had no more queries left, since Bipra was himself talking without a stop.

"Haariram's religion was not for the ascetic; but for the householder. Therefore, our primary meditation layer is Ayotan. That would mean, Haariram's chosen person would go to the gateway of birth, that is, have coitus with his wife only for the sake of reproduction. Hence there would not be futile coitus or daily coitus. In our faith, futile ejaculation was equivalent to homicide. Therefore, three and a half days after the woman's menstruation, that is, on the fourth day, the coitus should take place, desiring a healthy offspring. This is the custom under Ayotan. The blood's colour turns yellow after three days and a half. This 'three-and-a-half' is our realised doctrine." Bipra completed his sentence and began singing aloud:

O, from Vrindavan came the three and a half measure,
Let Ayotan keep to that treasure!

I asked: "Is this the essence of Ayotan?"

: "Yes, sir. But there are a few more things. Haariram had stated that the child born out of an early evening coitus becomes a thief. The coitus later in the evening but before midnight is sure to be a dacoit. So please understand that the most desirable union is after midnight. And the union in the early dawn hours gives birth to an angelic child."

Summarising the matter, Bipra asked: "Where does Ayotan's custom lead you then? Approaching the woman for coitus only for a child; that, too, at the crack of dawn: at three and a half. Coital union is taboo at other times. If the spouse is not menstruating, the union is futile; to sum up, lust is not Ayotan's custom."

I had never heard such an explanation of the theory of reproduction, so I grew curious. Gradually, Bipradas pointed out that 'Nityan' was the next step to Ayotan. The way to Nityan would be cleared after one got a child or two: by following the path of Ayotan, in all household chores and customs. One would then try to generate in the mind an indifference to home and family matters and a hatred for the female genital. Considering the female genital as a rotten hole, one had to discard it for ever. After creating a permanent breach with home and household and the rules and customs of this world, one would have to meditate on the liberated persona of Haariram—in solitary meadows, on the banks of rivers or under the wood-apple tree. Vrindavan of Meherpur and Radharani of Nishchintapur were on their way to Nityan.

But perhaps the most difficult way to meditate was of Khastan. Haariram alone was able to meditate in this manner; none else could do it. Khastan was the meditation for ultimate liberation. The world's light, wind, sky, trees, rivers, hills, and woods, meadows: they were all subject to their own domain. They were all free, not paying any tax to anybody for passing through their natural life cycle. Man had to pay the price for living through desire and the tormenting cyclic process of ejaculation and receival of the semen. The man who never ejaculated was the worshipper of Khastan. Only Haariram could achieve it; hence he was the creator of the worldly affairs.

Having followed up to this, I exclaimed: 'Perhaps now I've followed what Bodhitan is. Bodhitan is the forever bondage to lust and regrets for it. Isn't it so?'

"Exactly, Bodhitan is the condition of a conscious sinner. We all are that. Haariram had stated that the one who does coitus everyday and ejaculates has been entrapped by Bodhitan. All the disciples of Haariram seek freedom from this Bodhitan and wails. They shed tears for Nityan. Just look at me, for a change. Everyday I pray with my head down under the wood-apple tree and tell the Creator that I won't get Khastan in this life, but do advance me a little on the way to Nityan. Listen to this song of Goshthadas":

O mind, in Bodhitan, don't be locked, no—
Sans Haariram's feet, you've nowhere to go!

I see no other way, but for you to stay,
If ever again a human birth, Haariram's feet are your shelter so."

The plaintive melody of the song struck a deep quiet chord in the surroundings and rang true. My conscious mind was cleared of all uncertainty and pure truth shone bright like the glowing moon of pre-dawn. I could hear the hapless, head-hitting lamentation of all the world's lust-filled men: in the tune and sentiment of the song. I realised that it was not an artificial man-made theory of a folk belief. It contained within it the eternal sorrow of hapless tortured souls tied down with worldly fetters of physical desire.

Bipradas's wailing did not stop till long after the song ended. I closed up to him to rest my hand on his shoulder in sympathy. That giant of a man seemed to have shrivelled up so much in self-disgust. I held his hand and drew him towards the wood-apple tree, saying: "Be at peace; pray to Haariram. You're rather old now; what're you scared of?"

: "The animal inside my body is not yet dead, sir," Bipradas admitted reproachfully.

We both stood under the wood-apple tree, stepping into the shimmering glow of the setting moon. The lamp that was lit under the tree near Haariram's wooden sandals was not extinguished even by this strong wind. The light reflected in the face of Radharani who was deep in meditation. Looking at that, I wondered where the worshipper from Meherpur – the free soul with his unique mind rich with the ultimate realisation of truth—had gone. Where were his disciples: Tanu, Sadananda, Srimanta, Nutu, Jago and Daksha? The scripture that was created to establish himself, to save the tortured, downtrodden men had not been tainted in the least!

Deep faith in humankind

Perhaps every human being has an innate need to dive into the abyss of his own mind. Does everyone, then, wish to savour the deep loneliness residing within one's self? Is this why everybody complains about overcrowding, work-pressure: always trying to unwind the intricate and binding knots of duty to avoid the complexity of external crowds? Was this why people try to turn away from large gatherings and seek an endless solitude? But, many a time, I had witnessed just the opposite. Those who meditated and were worshippers of the body and soul – named 'Aaul-Baul-Dervish' in common parlance – had an eternal solitude embedded in themselves: through their deep, lonely practices. They cherished no fear of losing themselves in a crowd.

That was why they attended so many fairs and festivals perhaps, observed celebratory days and ritual observations all the year round. I had received numerous invitations to such fairs and festivals—"Come to the grand carnival on 14th Falgun, to my guru's institution, you'll derive great pleasure." In reality, the pleasure is mostly for the one who invites. These were not the weary, duty-bound social gatherings of big cities. There was somewhere a pleasure of receiving something from the call of the worshippers of body and soul. I asked many times about the kind of pleasure they derived, since there were also expenses galore.

: "Pleasure also lay beyond the reckoning of accounts: the sheer pleasure of meeting and watching people. We would be able to serve many people—and serve them better. That real entity would take shape and emerge out of all the castes and the creeds."

: "How would you recognise the real man?"

: "Oh, one can recognise, sir. Have you seen a flint? If you rub iron and stone, the real sparks emerge. Likewise, when man mingles with man, the real man is etched out. We've seen so much of this phenomenon. You won't get any of this if you gallivant in the Himalayas. Lalan had said: 'You get "man" if you hold "man" close/It has little to do with pilgrimage or ritual observations.' Hence I repeat: don't waste time by running after the Bauls and Fakirs. Mingle with people in the fairs."

I heard all of this from Royal Fakir, it was quite a few years ago. The name was 'Royal' Fakir and the man had some regal features in him. Tall and well-built, he explained easily to me: "Sir, the 'real' man moves around close to us, but it is difficult to spot him even after you have spent your whole life looking for him. The subtle space in between the two eyebrows is called the Arshinagar (the Town of Mirrors). There resides the *porshi* (the neighbour). This neighbour is the man of my heart—my soulmate. If you hold the mirror, you see the neighbour; if you hold the neighbour, you see the mirror. Does that make sense?"

: "I followed this much at least that you can't avoid man if you've to reach the Town of Mirrors."

: "Absolutely. Sir, you've realised the quintessence. Now, it's action and execution..."

: "What is that?"

: "That's the real thing," said Royal Fakir. "To know mentally; then to know in meditation and knowledge; and now to consolidate it corporeally, that's the point. For instance, you hear that wonderful fruits are hanging ripe on a tree. Only hearing is not enough. You've to look for it, hold an enquiry, climb up the tree and finally eat the fruit. But why on earth should one bother about such things? You may like to attend some of the grand fairs of ours,—well, you're coming with me. I'll explain everything. This is settled and confirmed. You'd first visit Ghoshpara at the time of Holi, that is, the fair of Sati-Ma. We shall start from my base the morning before Holi. Come prepared; you'd have to stay three nights. Well, that's final then."

I said: "Okay, it's final. But I should do a little research and reading-up in advance on that fair from books. It's, after all, a famous fair: dating back to some two hundred years. I'll check up some details on the fair."

: "Of course, you should check up the details. You're travellers on the way to knowledge, so you keep an eye on all external and physical matters. We're folks who work on emotions and understanding through the heart; we realise matters while travelling on our chosen path."

: "How long have you been going to the Ghoshpara fair?"

: "Oh it has been very long, my dear!" Royal Fakir stroked his white beard with his hands: "It's been since I gained consciousness after birth. That is, it goes back in time to my granddad-Gosain."

: "What does granddad-Gosain mean?"

: "Oh, you couldn't catch the meaning of that word, could you? As you know, what's my father's father to me? He's my granddad, isn't he? Likewise, my guru happens to be my Gosain. And the one who is my Gosain's guru, is my granddad-Gosain. Does that explain it?"

: "Yes, I do. Yet I don't follow how and why, those who have been following the path of asceticism create bonds of granddad-grandson, like a regular family!"

: "It's not only granddad-grandson, it's also the lineage of guru-father-disciple-child. The disciple addresses the guru's wife as 'mother-Gosain'. Disciples and devotees are treated not as people who serve the guru but his children. Everything is bonded well.

Our ways are the way of the sap, dear! Have you seen a palm-tree or a date-palm? All of them grow straight up, without looking back on earth. The religion of forsaking women and wealth is similar—it ceases to have any care for men and soil. Again, our Sati-Ma's religion is that of a householder: like a banyan tree. Prop roots are continuously sent down to grip the earth. The children and grand-children – the progeny – are always drawing sap from people and soil. Our journey is one of moving forward along with mother-Gosain; granddad-Gosain; et al."

: "Where did the faith of Sati-Ma or of the Kartabhaja begin?"

: "Why, it's from Aaulchand."

: "Who's Aaulchand?"

: "Aaulchand is the reincarnation of Gorachand. Gorachand had disappeared in the Gopinath temple of Srikshetra. Afterwards, he reappeared in the guise of Aaulchand in Ghoshpara. His rebirth at this point was designed to create the path of the Kartabhaja faith for the householders. He is the early master; from him originated this faith."

: "Then who is Sati-Ma?"

: "Well, then listen carefully in detail," said Royal, settling down gracefully. Aaulchand had twenty-two disciples. The chief among them was Ramsharan Pal; address Ghoshpara, Muratipur; caste Sadgop (milkman). His wife's name is Saraswati, from which comes Sati. Do you follow?"

I argued back: "How does it happen? How can Sati be derived from Saraswati?"

"It can happen, certainly happen," said Royal Fakir with a mysterious smile on his face. "You don't have a clue into the religion, hence this doubt. Well, let me explain. Saraswati begins with 'Sa' and ends with 'Ti'; so the two letters combine as 'Sati'. Do you follow now?"

I mumbled hesitatingly: "This sounds funny. Are there any more of such examples?"

: "Certainly. Take, for instance, the only child of Ramsharan and Sati-Ma—Ramdulal or Dulalchand. He took 'Lal' from Dulal and put 'Shashi' for Chand: to alter the name to Lalshashi. We refer to Lalshashi as 'Shriyut'. The book on music composed by him contains our songs of our faith. The name of that book is *Bhaaber Geet* (Sentimental Music), which we refer to as our book of law. Every Friday evening we sit together and sing from the book of law by Shriyut."

: "But why Friday, which is Jummaday for the Muslims. Then, was Aaulchand connected with Muslims or the Fakiri religion?"

Royal Fakir replied: "Well, my Gosain didn't divulge those deep secrets to me. But I can sing to you what Lalshashi's lyrics have said. Listen:

Since on Friday the creation was vent—
He ordained this: Wherever one is,
Should come and be present.
Whichever land the men reside, should together be heard—
For those twenty-four hours; then be dispersed.
This Friday at evening-hour, get blessed all—
Fulfilling each wish in mind: big or small!"

The famous writer Kamalkumar Mazumder was still alive when I had been discussing these matters with Royal Fakir. Everyone knows how deeply knowledgeable he was in folk studies and local cultures of this land. Before going to Ghoshpara the first time, I asked Kamalkumar: "Would you know anything about the Ghoshpara fair? I'm going there on the next full-moon day."

He was initially startled to hear this; then he screwed up his nose, saying: "That's an uncivilised place, sir; please don't go there. You might land in some trouble otherwise."

I was taken aback. We were chatting in a publisher's office. One researcher instantly pulled out *Sri Ramakrishna Kathamrita* from the racks and read a few extracts. It appeared that Sri Ramakrishna had expressed much distaste towards this faith of nature-worship. Again, he read the description of Babu culture from the book *Ramtanu Lahiri O Tatkaleen Bangasamaj*, by Shibnath Shastri. Apparently, the Babus "went visiting the fairs at Khardaha and Ghoshpara and the religious bathing festival at Mahesh, sailing by boats in troves with sex-workers, in order to get entertained."

It seemed that the hornet's nest had been hit. The researcher quoted, without stop, how much reprimand against the Kartabhajas was contained in the book *Bharatbarshiya Upasak Sampradaya*, by Akshaykumar Dutta. Right in 1896, Jogendranath Bhattacharjee had thoroughly castigated Ghoshpara in his book *Hindu Castes and Sects*. Even Mr Ward and Mr Wilson had not spared it. "Oh look, here it is, here it is," exclaimed the gentleman, opening the book by Benoy Ghosh and reading out an extract:

> This year during Doljatra, nearly 65 thousand people collected. Among the pilgrims, eighty-five percent people were women, sex-workers outnumbered housewives from elite families; among men, nearly everybody was illiterate.
>
> I saw nearly twenty patients lying prostrate under the pomegranate tree, in the hope of getting cured. Like folks from other religions, a little charlatanism was also freely practised by this sect. Disguising some known person as deaf and dumb, they were showing him healed after uttering words like: 'Let him speak'.
>
> I have heard from many that the amorous games of Sri Vrindavan's Krishna Lila are in vogue among the worshippers of this faith.

I sought to discover the exact period to which this description pertained to. I came to know that the newspaper *Sambad Prabhakar*, number 21, dated 23 Chaitra 1270 (1863), published this article which was dug out by Benoy Ghosh. I wondered how a rustic, folk faith could earn so much hatred and spurn from the learned folks of Kolkata. How did the customs of the Kartabhajas appear so drastically bad to one and all. True, the moralist Brahmo Akshaykumar or the orthodox Brahmin Jogendranath could be a little puritan to have acted against the Kartabhjas. But how was it about the open-minded, syncretist Sri Ramakrishna? How did he, too, misunderstand them? Was Kamal-babu intolerant about them, because he was pro-Ramakrishna?

The next day, while rummaging through the books at the Bangiya Sahitya Parishad, I came across a re-assuring fact in the fourth volume of the book *Amar Jibon* (My Life), by Nabinchandra Sen. In 1895, he had the administrative responsibility of supervising the Ghoshpara fair. With first-hand knowledge of that fair, Nabinchandra wrote:

> I felt that the Kartabhajas were nothing but an alternative approach by the Hindus for 'worship of the guru'. Their religion was a protest against the illusionism of the Vedanta. Ramsharan Pal – who was worth the worship of many by spreading a new religion in the midst of a land flooded with Vedas and Vedanta – could not have been an ordinary mortal. Truly speaking, what was wrong in worshipping such a person instead of worshipping imaginary idols? We often hear about 'harmony of scripture' these days. One can make out that this Ramsharan Pal realised it first. The thought that all religions and all customs are true—was only preached by Lord Shri Krishna, and no other religious preacher. Therefore, Ramsharan Pal, I bow to you respectfully. At long last, I have realised the essence of the Kartabhaja faith and have returned to my base with a heart full of devotion.

I met a professor friend at the library the next day, whose field was the 19th century Bengali society. On explaining my problem to him, he furnished me with a list of a number of books. Upon consulting them, it was revealed that, at the beginning of the 19th century, the Brahmos, Christians and Hindus of Kolkata were quite worried about the Kartabhajas. At first, certain views were widely circulated, like 'it was a faith of the lower rungs', 'they ate dirty and impure food', 'they used women to conduct Ras Lila in private', and so on. But, from among the Brahmins and the true Vaishnavas, many a person felt secretly attracted towards the Kartabhaja religion. To the lower-caste Hindus belonging to the Kolkata of the past, like the fishermen and peasants, oil-crushers, spice-sellers, businessmen, conch-sellers, weavers, et al., the Ghoshpara faith or 'true religion' came across as very simple and straightforward. They established 'portals of faith' in their respective areas. Groups of devotees came together for weekly Friday evening sessions. This was done in a clandestine manner to begin with and were continued later with open pride. From among the nine segregated upper-caste Hindu communities – the Varna Hindus – and in fact even from among the eminent personalities representing the wealthy and landed gentry, several expessed a great interest in the Kartabhajas. They were the likes of Maharaja Jainarayan Ghoshal of the Bhukailash estate. In the large tract on Krishna Lila that he wrote and published in the name of *Karuna Nidhan Vilas* in Banaras, he mentioned Ramsharan Pal as an incarnation.

The devotion of the Kartabhajas and the intensity of their belief brought a revolution in the mind of Shashipada Bandyopadhyay, a Brahmo activist. His biographer, Kuladaprasad Mullick, wrote:

> In the time of Shashi-babu, there were many portals of worship belonging to the Vaishnava community called Kartabhaja at Barahanagar. The garden of Nimchand Maitra at Banhooghli was one of them. Here, once a week, the lower-caste Hindus used to have a congregation and chanting of hymns and

> meditation in accordance with the special process followed by that community. Sri Shashipadababu used to visit them from time to time. He confesses that he felt particularly benefited from the sincerity of their meditation, by mingling in that group.

The worship of true faith by the Kartabhajas and their open-ended, inclusive syncretism put doubts even among the common man, as it was exemplified in the letter of a correspondent, published in *Sambad Prbhakar* of 18 Chaitra 1254 Bangabda (AD 1847). He wrote about the Ghoshpara fair, after witnessing it firsthand:

> The very large number of the followers of the Karta doctrine that was seen was not merely from the lower castes and folks devoid of ritual customs; people from the upper castes and the respected, educated and genteel society were also noticed...
> As Brahmins, lower castes and scheduled tribes ate and drank in that field together, irrespective of sect and caste consideration, which was an extraordinary sight –not seen and heard of elsewhere – it was a matter of great wonder that, as long as we stayed in that village, we did not find anybody unhappy. All of them passed time with cheerful countenance. Possibly the three days of Raas had a prevalence of happiness there.
> Dear Editor, many people express diverse opinions regarding Ghoshpara.We are low-witted persons, not daring to suddenly express public opinion on any subject. Until the secret doctrines of the Ghoshpara religion are known to us, we won't be able to resolve on them in any way. Although this religion is not according to scriptures and its external customs are not in accordance with traditionally accepted social customs and rituals, there is devout faith of many reposed in its theory and its stream of knowledge is enhancing instead of diminishing. We cannot, therefore, disagree to surmise that there may be some substance at its core.

In 1895, when Nabinchandra Sen went to the Ghoshpara fair, some gentlemen came to meet him one morning. 'Almost all of them were graduates well-educated and of good status. They were all Kartabhaja.' On perusal of all these descriptions, I was curious to know actually how many people joined the Kartabhaja school of faith at the threshold of the 18th-19th century, to persuade the orthodox Brahmins to stage the farce of Jelepara in retaliation, for reprimanding them, or, make Dashu Roy write his Kartabhaja Ballad at the behest of the pundits of Nabadweep: with the support of Pundits of Nabadweep. Their banter was too cruel and too indecent. Such as:

To Kartabhaja rites, let's all go.
If you seek to balance each side,
In anxiety, why override,
Losing both sides, eternally so!

Many here are having fun,
Worship preparations have begun,
They'll go to lonely places each Friday, or so!

Climb up trees, with flute and rest,
With hands, shall cover female breast,
Smiling, half lips shall make moist...
Then, with an immense happy glow!

It shall be Brajaleela I say,
Maidens enact the Brinda-Chandrabali play,
Or Lalita, or Sriradha if you may,
It'll be a great spectacle,
None'll stop, or put a shackle,
No action'll receive a blow!

Were only depraved practices and religious conflicts behind so much protestation and such ridicule? I did think the increasing popularity of the Kartabhajas and their organisational ability caused concern among the Hindus and Brahmos. But how many disciples did they have? And who organised them?

It was undoubtedly done by Dulalchand alias Lalshashi. He was an educated young man of the 19th century: adept in all four languages—Bengali, Sanskrit, English and Persian. When Ramsharan died in 1783, Dulalchand was only seven. His mother Saraswati Devi (later famed as 'Sati Ma') led the Kartabhajas for a while; then the leadership shifted to Dulal when he was barely sixteen. But Dulal passed away prematurely in 1833. Yet this short-lived man contributed towards the customary action and organisation of Kartabhajas for all times. Royal Fakir and his ilk sang his book of law *Bhaaber Geet* (Sentimental Songs) for over a century, to garner courage in their heart. Apparently Dulal verbally dictated those songs, while Ramcharan Chattopadhyay penned them down. Ramcharan was basically a Tantrik sage of Belur. Apart from him, the other intimate companions of Dulal were Bankachand, Kashinath Basu, Shambhunath Bhattacharjee, Ramananda Mazumder and Neelkantha Mazumder. There was a description of Dulal in the sixth volume of *Calcutta Review* in 1846. It is seen from there that Marshman and Kerry went to Dulal to have a debate on pantheism in 1802. Dulal's appearance was recorded thus: 'He was no less plump than Bacchus.' Was this man – in keeping with the mores of the 19th century – also overtly fond of sensual pleasures? Someone wrote:

> In order to make the Kartabhaja community a meeting place of all castes, Dulalchand took four brides from among Brahmins, Kshatriyas (warrior caste), Vaishyas (business caste) and Shudras (lower caste). He had five sons from his four wives.

The care and curiosity of the colonial officials for the Kartabhajas is worth our attention. M/s Kerry, Marshman and Duff used to keep a vigilant eye on Ghoshpara. In 1811, Mr W. Ward wrote the following description during the lifetime of Dulal:

> Doolatu, the son, pretends that he has now 400,000 disciples spread over Bengal.

Ward, however, brought down the figure to 20,000 in the second edition of his book in 1818.

When I was proceeding to Ghoshpara accompanying Royal Fakir's group, the latter was leading an amazing chorus:

> Victory to Sati-Mother, And to Karta-Mother—
> They curb trouble, danger, fear, disaster hither!
> Upon Mother's honour, fear and worry disappear,
> Doom's summons don't affect any further!

How this Sati-Ma gradually became Karta-Mother was also a mystery. This is because, while Mr Ward, and later Mr Horace Heman Wilson, mentioned the names of Ramsharan and Dulalchand several times in their writings in 1811 and 1828, they never mentioned Sati-Ma anywhere. Mr Ward, rather, talked about the myth of divine power and the ability to cure disease in the name of Aaulchand and Ramsharan. About Aaulchand, he wrote: "It is pretended he communicated his supernatural powers," and, about Ramsharan Pal: "He persuaded multitudes that he could cure leprosy and other diseases." The hint that Ramsharan made a huge amount of money and property by the trick of curing diseases was not kept a secret by Mr Ward. According to him, "By this means, from a state of deep poverty, he became rich and his son now lives in affluence."

The problem arises here: how did the stories and allegories about curing diseases spread in the name of Sati-Ma? There is a solution to the problem contained in the book called *Sahajtatwa Prakash* (Revelation of Easy Theories) by Monulal Mishra, a Kartabhaja devotee who wrote:

> After his (i.e., Ramsharan's) demise, Mahatma Dulalchand made proper efforts to spread the episodes about the supernatural powers of Sati-Ma, in establishing the school of faith of the Kartabhajas.

Royal Fakir was, of course, not aware of these allusions. He had only an explicit trust in his faith: without a single crack of doubt in the hard soil under his feet. He knew and believed that all ailments were cured once one rubbed the soil from under the wood-apple tree of Ghoshpara on one's body; followed by a bath in the lake of Himsagar; and finally, uttered the name of Sati-Ma with devotion. Holding on to my seat amongst thousands of devoted men in the mid-afternoon, I looked at the wood-apple tree: did the soil below truly cure all diseases? Did these thousands of men come here on the strength of that faith? Royal Fakir looked at my doubting gaze and smiled to say: "Sir, do have faith, there's freedom born of faith." Then he asked Dinuratan Dasi of his group: "Dinu, do tell sir about the greatness of Sati-Ma. He'll have peace of mind."

Dinuratan Dasi folded her palms upwards to bow to the invisible Sati-Ma and chanted in a balladic vein:

On Sati-Ma, whosoever keeps faith enough—
Gets rid of leprosy, asthama, pain and cough!
On earth, her grace makes miracles take shape—
The blind gets vision, hearing gets the deaf!
Placing faith in her, one gets wealth on earth—
She blesses infertile women, who to sons, give birth!
To Sati-Ma, those who willingly offer food –
Do escape from all perils, for good!

That the words of the lyric was much to everybody's liking in Royal Fakir's group, was clear from their vigorous nods of head. Royal Fakir said: "We've heard that Aaulchand Fakir was very satisfied by the devoted service of Ramsharan and Saraswati and at last, announced one day: 'It's time for my demise now.' Saraswati fell at his feet, wailing in disbelief. After much weeping and persuasion, it was finally compromised that Aaulchand would be re-born as a son to her. That child is our Lalshashi. He is the immaculate one. As Krishna is child of Yashoda in Gokul, as Ramchandra is child of Kaushalya in Ayodhya, as Gorachand is the child of Shachi-Ma in Nabadweep, so is our Dulalchand, son of Sati-Ma in Ghoshpara. This is, four-in-one, one-in-four. Do you follow?"

I realised that in the Kartabhaja school of faith, there was a talented order, behind which was Dulalchand's power of imagination and skillful intelligence. On one side was the doctrine of reincarnation, and on the other were the parables of cures from ailments. On the one hand it was the simple path to spiritual liberation—the easy worship mode; on the other were the sentimental songs. On one side were the flamboyant portals and institutions with their earnings, on the other was the offer of consolation to the widows and childless women. What was attractive to the educated men, being synergetic in nature, was tempting and full of illusions to the illiterate, because of the matriarchal hold of Sati-Ma. Dulalchand's personality and individual merits also played no mean role, as I was informed by Satyashiv Pal Devmahanta, one of the heads among Dulalchand's successors. A suave, educated man, Satyashiv startled me, while eulogising Dulal by informing: "Ramdulal Pal was nominated as a member of the Advisory Council to the Religious Congress of Chicago in 1893 (World's Parliament of Religions, 1893). I still have that letter: dated 17 April 1893. But Dulalchand had passed away much before, so the nomination was turned over to his grandson, Satyacharan Devmahanta."

"What is this phenomenon of Devmahanta?" I was inquisitive enough to ask.

Satyashiv Pal Devmahanta – majestic as a sal tree – was the fourth-generation successor to Dulalchand. He explained: "Devmahanta is a title. In our family, Ramdulal received this title from the king of Nadia."

: "What was the occasion for him to get the title?"

: "The fact of the matter is that there used to be a Chariot Festival in Ghoshpara on the full-moon day of Baishakh. It is held even now. Nadia's Maharaja ordained once that the festival must stop, since it was not according to scriptures for the month of Baishakh. Since he forced the chariot festival to stop, the devotees placed Dulalchand on the chariot and the latter started rolling on, without any traction. From that event onwards, Dulalcahnd became a Devmahanta."

In order to remove the fog screen of mythology, I quickly interrupted: "What's the area of Ghoshpara?"

: "The boundaries are with Kalyani sub-town on the south; Charbirpara on the north; Kalyani University on the east; and Charasbati on the west. Now the land aligned to the Thakurbari is 6.29 acres. Earlier, the Ghoshpara fair used to be held in 600 hectares of land, inclusive of mango and litchi orchards. There were around 3,500 trees. Under each tree would sit 'Sir'—a leader with his group. Then, during the last War, the British Government took away the land. After the War, the defence department of the government returned those 600 hectares for holding the fair. But, after Independence, the government of West Bengal protected only 30 acres for the fair. Out of it, there have been some illegal occupations; some colonies have also sprung up. There is a law-suit continuing at the Supreme Court."

After my first visit with Royal Fakir, I had been to Ghoshpara at least ten times. I only realised that the more the fair was getting crowded, the less was the space. But before going to that topic, let me finish with Royal Fakir. On the eve of Doljatra (Holi), Fakir took me out in the morning and showed me round the very large fair premises, acquainting me with everything. "This is Himsagar where the devotees and the diseased will bathe tomorrow." "Look under that pomegranate tree there; if one rubs its soil on the body and eats it, one will be relieved of every ailment." "Let's go to the east for a while; there's an assemblage of many Bauls, Fakirs and Dervishes there." Suddenly Royal Fakir exclaimed: "Why, here's the portal of Shivshekhar. Do come here, Sir, and sit for a while."

Shivshekhar turned out to be a curly-haired, well-built young man. He duly bowed his head in politeness. Royal said: "They have a very reputed 'Mahashay' ('Sir') family in Kumirdah village of Murshidabad district." After everybody had settled down, I asked: "Well, what's this phenomenon of the 'Mahashay'?"

Shivshekhar explained: "Our principal 'platform' or portal is here, at the main Ghoshpara base. The devoted and prosperous ones are accepted as direct disciples; they also have 'portals' in their homes and they intiate others. Those at home are called 'Sir' and, the ones initiated by them are known as 'Barati'."

: "How many generations have you been 'Mahashay'?"

: "It's running for six generations including mine. Before these six generations, our ancestors Nafar Biswas, Bhollagram's Mahabharat Ghosh and Hariharpara-Malopara's Tentul Sheikh were the three who reached this place while roaming around. They initiated disciples. The date was 28th Kartik. Since then, there's a large festival at our Kumirdah village every 28th Kartik. Do come this time and watch the enthusiasm around the festivities."

: "Could you name the six generations?"

: "Oh yes, please write them down. My name is Shivshekhar Mandal; my father was Jadulal Mandal; his father was Dukari; his father was Chand Singh; his father was Fateh Singh; and his father was Nafar Biswas."

I was mystified by the reply. From Biswas came Mandal, and in between was Singh. I asked a little diffidently: "Are you the Mahishya caste?"

: "We're Muslims."

Confusion was well-confounded. The name was Shivshekhar, the father Jadulal, and yet the religion Islam? I noticed that Royal Fakir was smiling silently. The feeling was akin to: "Sir, this is precisely why you've been brought here; to watch the fun. You'd be wonder-struck by watching the human activities."

Shivshekhar said: "Sir, we're born Muslims, but our rituals hold on to Sati-Ma's portal doors."

: "Don't you obsrve the rituals and customs of Islam?"

: "We have the Idgah at home; we observe the two Eids. However, we don't visit mosques. There's the portal at home: worshipped by six generations. Every Friday, there are prayers at Sati-Ma's sacred pot followed by the distribution of a mashed porridge, which comes with holy blessings."

: "Are there any regulations on food?"

: "Nothing very much, we just eat vegetarian food at home round the year."

Here was a vegetarian Muslim and the name was Shivshekhar! It was, of course, difficult to overcome the surprise of such a situation. One's superstitions and bias about casteism and racisim were so well-entrenched even in a highly-educated mind that the calculations did not quite tally. Looking at my bafflement, Royal Fakir smiled mysteriously and whispered into the ears of the singer of Shivshekhar's institution to sing a song. He immediately began, by strumming his single-stringed drone:

Caste is lost and all is lost
Indeed a strange situation—
With truth by Jove, none does agree:
A confused mass of consternation!

How surprising! Did Royal Fakir put me in the confounded group? By then, the unknown singer frowned and almost directly asked me in his song's third segment:

When you came to this earth,
What caste were you at birth?
While departing, which caste be—
None talks about it, of course!
Brahmin-sweeper-cobbler-tanner:
All're pure under the Master's banner,
Yet, none likes to see same scanner—
Death will not spare any source!

Was this a reprimand for me? Even before I could feel, the extreme logic of the rustic song hit me:

A secret meal with prostitute,
One's own caste, how does one refute?
Asks Fakir Lalan: what's caste absolute—
This blunder is beyond remorse!

Royal exclaimed: "Sir, there's nothing like a caste. All are the progeny of Kartababa. Hence says Lalshashi—'*There's no division between man and man; Why do you lament in each country's span?*'"

I continued to gaze at Shivshekhar, who had a shy smile on his face. I thought that it was a lesson well-learnt. Realising my predicament, he suddenly sprang up and pressing my two hands, entreated, "Sir, please don't mind. This is Sati-Ma's place, a portal of peace. Don't nurture any sorrow at heart. Royal, you have spite in your mind."

Royal responded: "There's no spite. With this sudden initial jerk, I enabled sir to stand on the right path. He won't err anymore; isn't that right, sir?"

Where was the right path, in which direction? What was the attraction than drew me, year after year, to Ghoshpara? Is Ghoshpara, the place itself, above dispute? The Kartabhaja sect that developed in the 18th century was initially the Sufi faith of Aaulchand. Mr Ward described Aaulchand as follows:

> About a hundred years ago, another man rose up, as the leader of a sect, whose cloth, or dress of many colours, which he wore as a voiragee, was so heavy that two or three people can now scarcely carry it.

The man, wearing such a monstrously heavy robe, established a sub-religion after the model of the Sufi sect, with which got blended the splendour of many talents over time. At the end, the 19th century Reformist movement, the uprising against idolatry, the anti-Vedas attitude and the syncretism blurring castes and creeds was all mixed up in this sect. An element of Islamic faith and some rituals of Christianity also entered its vitals. The personal god of the Sufis – whom they called 'Hak' or Truth – was the Truth that the Kartabhajas worshipped. I first thought that the word 'Kartabhaja' was perhaps created jocularly by somebody. But my initial surmise broke from one proud line sung from Dulalchand's *Bhaaber Geet*, where Dulal declared:

Realised and unrealised, men and women
I'll make you pray to the lord—
Before the lord's worshippers
I'll make you fools of own accord!

It goes without saying that this 'you' was directed to Brahmanism by Dulal. In order to curb Brahmanism, Dulal had proudly pronounced:

Worshippers of the Lord, this is a unique joy for you—
It's indeed worship of the self which is true!
The Vedic rituals they have no clue
It's the clever one's workshop, too!

But could the 'clever one' retrieve the final consequence? Evidently during the lifetime of Dulal, a sub-sect of Kartabhajas developed, under the name of 'Ramballavi'. In his book *Bharatbarshiya Upasak Sampradaya*, Akshaykumar Dutta mentioned the Ramballavis, to state that Srinath Mukhopadhyay, Krishnakinkar Gunasagar and Matialal-babu of Banshberia defied the leadership of the Pals of Ghoshpara and began the worship of 'Kali-Krishna-God-Khuda'. On getting this information, I followed the scent all the way to Banshberia. Ghoshpara and Banshberia were villages virtually facing each other across the Ganga. Upon my arrival at Banshberia, I found nothing of any consequence, with everything gone. There was no sign of either residence or progeny of Krishnakinkar or Srinath Mukhopadhyay. Upon hearing everything, an old man said: "I remember having heard of this sect in early childhood and that there was an institution of the Ramballavis right below the Banshberia Public Library on the banks of the Ganga; but I wonder if it still exists." When I went ahead – like a police search-dog – to sniff out the traces along the rough-hewn banks of the Ganga behind the public library, another old man rescued me. He informed that the real activities of the Ramballavis took place on the other bank, that is, in Panchghara village near Kanchrapara. On further detailed quest, I dug out a quotation from the *Sambad Prabhakar* of 1831 in the book *Sambadpatre Shekaler Katha* (The Narrative of Early Times in Newspapers) in the Banshberia library. One Jagatchandra Bandyopadhyay had penned a beautiful description of the gathering of Ramballavis at Panchghara village as follows:

> Some gentlemen got together at the residence of a member of a socially-depressed class at Panchghara village within our Kanchrapara neighbourhood; happily placing a brick-platform representing 'ultimate truth', with a wooden stool above and with garlands of flower on top; they arranged several food-items for feeding five thousand people from different castes sitting in the same row. One hundred Brahmins were invited from Triveni, Bansberia and Halisahar and each received the parting gift of a brass-plate and sweets. At that spot, Christians read the book of Bible; Muslims perused the Quran and the Brahmin scholars chanted hymns from the Gita.

On reading the above, does it not strike that a flavour of religious syncretism was latent in them? Would it not occur to one that there was less of Dulalchand's persona to it than the creation of his age? That their success shook the very foundation of the then contemporary Brahmo and Brahmin society of the Gangetic belt was beyond any doubt. Akshaykumar was so inimical that he even accused the Ramballavis of eating beef.

Standing in the midst of Ghoshpara, I often wondered how such a holy platform of syncretism among all religions became enmeshed in the glory of Sati-Ma. Was it due to the lack of proper leadership in the wake of the untimely death of Dulalchand? The latter died in 1833, after which Sati-Ma became the head of the community. She passed away in 1840, when Dulal's son Ishwarchandra sat on the Chief's platform. Ishwarchandra died in 1882 and then began the internecine fight for the platform.

That fight had not died yet.

In 1895, when Nabinchandra Sen went to Ghoshpara, Sati-Ma was no longer alive and Ramdula's son Ishwarchandra was also no more. Their two later successors had by then become two quarrelling chiefs to occupy two platforms. Witnessing them in the fair, Nabinchandra wrote:

> Now there were two members of Ramsharan Pal's progeny. Both were totally illiterate, yet both were the current chiefs... I had seen that the two foolish heads were occupying the two 'platforms' and thousands of pilgrims offering their devoted salutations to them and taking dust from their feet respectfully, after offering them money in obeisance.

Now, at the end of the 20th century, the same sight would be visible to one visiting the Ghoshpara fair. Inside and outside the Thakurbari, there would be thousands of devotees without any space for a foothold. Most of them were ignorant and illiterate villagers, who were farmers from Hooghly, Nadia, Murshidabad and Bardhaman districts. Three-fourth among them comprised women. Instead of two platforms, there were four at present, which would mean four chiefs. They were educated, yet certainly keen to offer dust from their feet and accept money for obeisance. Someone, resembling an accountant, was collecting 'tax' from the gentlemen and the task-holders, and entering the amounts in an accounts ledger. In front were arranged the photographs of the former chiefs, covered with coloured powder. My friend accosted an accountant with the question: "Are you collecting tax? Whose tax is it?"

I pulled him on one side and urged him to read a quotation in my notebook, taken from *Nadia Kahini* (The Annals of Nadia) by Kumudnath Mullick, which said:

> The Pal-babus had three kinds of earnings: (I) taxes, (ii) offerings and (iii) promised sacrifices. That is, according to them, the chief was the owner of everyone's body; since you are residing in them, you have to give taxes to the chief for them.

My friend – a short tempered man – grumbled with displeasure. One young man came forward and showed us a book—*Ghoshparar*

Kartabhaja Sampradaya (Kartabhaja Community of Ghoshpara), by Adwaitachandra Das. Having purchased the book for seven rupees in cash, my friend sat down and leafed through its pages. Suddenly, coming to the last paragraph, he drew my attention: "Oh dear, have you noticed this? Just read here." I read through the text:

> I offer this prayer at the lotus-feet of Sati-Ma entreating that the two partner-trustees should not be absorbed in trifling self-propagation, nor attracted by enmity and rapacity, but get together and be devoted to the amelioration of the Kartabhaja sect and its Thakurbari.

My friend exclaimed: "See, the protest, the resistance has begun."

Where was the protest? Year after year, the same scene was repeated at the Sati-Ma's fair. Thousands of illiterate, helpless, ailing people were squatting for obtaining divine favour. Under the wood-apple tree; they were throwing red-bordered clothes, conch shell-bangles, iron bangles or vermilion-packs used by married women, or tying pebbles as a symbol of an ardent plea to the tree. By rubbing the soil under the wood-apple tree to their bodies and even eating it, or by taking bath in a dirty, slushy pond, called Himsagar, or by drinking its turbid water, they were hoping that their ailments would be cured. The mute would speak, the lame walk, the barren woman would give birth to a child, the blind get vision. In a dysfunctional country, in villages engulfed by ignorance, the religious peddlers and middlemen were lurking around in secret, dragging these hapless creatures here under many pretexts. As a result, the long pathway from the Himsagar pond to the wood-apple tree was virtually a cesspool of slushy mud. Since the early morning, countless blind believers and superstitious men and women lay prostrate on the path in deep devotion, dragging themselves towards the holy destination, with eyes full of tears and faces glowing with deep faith; their clothes wet and unkempt. Many shy village-women – bereft of all shame and sense – lay on their faces, dragging themselves forward; in the hope and dream of curing a sick child, or a paralysed husband or to conceive a baby. Their young and nubile, bathed bodies hardly remained covered by their slippery wet clothes, drawing quick craven glances of the debauches and lumpens.

Where was the protest?

I stood on the banks of the Himsagar pond and watched the uninhibited fight for the 'holy' bath. The little pond had become defiled by mud and slush in consequence of the hustle and bustle of a few thousand people. Holding the mute boy by the tuft of his long hair, the religious middleman was bobbing him up and down in the waters and slapping him repeatedly on the cheek, ordering: "Do speak, say 'Sati-Ma', come on, speak up." The disabled mute boy received slap after slap, with nothing to put an end to his heart-rending misery! Where was any resistance against this torture? His unceasing flow of tears – breaking through his eyes – and the wailing of his cursed mother standing on the banks with tears streaming down—both mingled with the divine waters of Himsagar. Who was there to protest?

The fair authorities roared on the microphone: "Please remain restrained; do maintain the dignity of the ladies; nobody must touch their bodies."

"What does it mean?" My friend roared back. "What's all this I see and hear in this place? Is this my land? We declare to everybody that there's no religious extremism in West Bengal! Is that all wrong? Is there no remedy against this?"

Suddenly a youth shoved a 'little magazine' *Shabda* into our hands. "Read, please read and make your own observations," he said. Listening to his appeal, my friend responded: "You mean you get poetic inspiration even in such a place as this? Can't you stand up against these frauds?"

The youth replied earnestly: "This is the protest. Do read."

Settling down under a tree, the first passage that we both read from *Shabda* was a re-print from the *Utsamanush* magazine, titled 'Kalyanir Ghoshparaye Sati-Mayer Mela: Ja Dekhechhi, Ja Bujhechhi' ('What I've Seen and Realised at the Sati-Ma Fair at Ghoshpara, Kalyani'.) The writing began with an old report from an earlier year, in a boxed space:

> Even this year (1980), there was a large fair held at Ghoshpara from February 29....Carrying a baby girl, her aunt came from Dasnagar of Howrah to the Sati-Ma fair. Since the child got ill in the storm and rains, the aunt – listening to many people's advice – made the child take a bath in Himsagar (a severely-soiled pond in whose dirty water, thousands took bath in the pursuit of virtue) and made her lie down on Sati-Ma's platform under the wood-apple tree. Doctors were available at the fair, but there was far more faith in the divine power. In consequence, the child died. The aunt's deeply-anguished cries rent the fair's air. She kept sitting in the mud and slush, clutching on to the dead child.

There was an interruption in our reading. A gentleman approached us to ask: "Well, do you know where the stall of the Bandel Disabled Welfare Centre is?"

: "No, we don't. What's the matter? Is there such a stall in this fair?"

: "I heard on the mike. My boy is deaf-and-mute; do you see him over there?"

We noticed a little far ahead, a boy of about ten in the arms of his mother who stood with a pale expression. He was their only child. The boy stamped his feet and flailed his arms in uncontrollable rage and the frail mother was unable to control him. The gentleman said with a despairing gesture: "The boy is frightfully restless and unmanageable. We've been coming here for the last three years. We've made him eat the soil under the wood-apple tree and take a bath in Himsagar; but nothing happened. Could you suggest what should be done?"

: "Where do you live? What's your profession?"

: "Beleghata. I work in a factory."

: "Are you educated? Then why have you come here?"

The reply came in a despairing manner: "Well, everyone counselled me, so...His mother was entreating willingly. Someone said one had to come for three years successively. So we came; but what happened? Nothing actually. The one who escorted us extracted a lot of money from us. Damn it, everything is false. Now they're saying you didn't pray to Sati-Ma with enough devotion. Let it go, forget the rampant frauds. Let me consult the welfare centre."

We should also perhaps visit the disability welfare centre. We, too, needed some solid foundation below our feet. So we moved forward, following the hapless parents and their disabled son. Going ahead a little, we heard an announcement on the mike: "Come here, here's the disability welfare centre. Get your child examined in a scientific manner. Nothing could get cured by the water of Himsagar and the soil of the wood-apple tree."

We went forward and reached that reassuring centre, beckoning humanity. It was a small stall. On the benches inside were seated many helpless, unfortunate parents: with their children suffering from various disabilities: deaf-mute-imbecile-lame. A few bright young men were examining them with medical instruments and giving instructions. On a table was set a microscope to demonstrate how several bacteria thrived in the Himsagar waters.

"Haven't you been beaten up yet?" My question evoked laughter: like a flurry of pigeons flapping their wings and flying away. One youth said: "We are coming from Bandel over the last two years. There ought to be a protest against these superstitions, what do you say?"

I nodded in agreement, but could say nothing. I continued to wonder whether I would gain anything at all at the end of the deep, lonely alley. Yet I had been coming across so many houses of gods on the roadside. I didn't possess the necessary tenacity and depth of spirit to look for the 'man of my heart'? In the crowd, in the suppressed humanity, in the accumulated corpses of the abused value-systems, I did notice, from moment to moment, the manifestation of nascent life. When everything was done with, I had seen humanity – the free will of humanity – to get awakened. Was there gradual freedom then in this very way: after illumining the torch? I thought, even I did not meet the 'man of my heart', I would perhaps meet the 'man after my heart'. Take, for instance, these four youths from Bandel, or, the boy who shoved into our hands the *Shabda* magazine. Our crest-fallen human values stood up drawing support from their resistance. By picking up new inspiration, we braced up our heart and proceeded through the fair.

It was mid-noon and the scorching sun was up. In countless dens on all four sides, cooking was on in full swing. There were clouds of smoke and the musty smell of boiled rice. In the midst of all this, music continued. There were deep thuds of rhythmic beat music from afar. We slowly proceeded to stand in front of a den. A rural singer was singing a 'wordy' song using a play of words:

As man, you respect man,
As man, know man, if you can,
To recognise man, you should scan
Man—the precious jewel in the crown.

Looked at closely, the den resembled a vast tent. At least fifty to sixty people were spread out, either sitting or lying down, on mats or polythene-sheets. Cooking continued outside the tent. A kedgeree mix of rice and lentils was boiling in a vast cauldron. Inside the den there was a rectangular low wooden raised seat carrying the portrait of Sati-Ma. Water was offered in a copper-vessel. Flowers, leaves and coloured powder were spread all around. I explained to my friend: "This is what is called a platform or a portal. In the middle of this, that matted-haired man – wearing a white robe and fast asleep – was the 'master' and these were his task-holders. Do you follow?"

We asked a task-holder: "What's the name of your master and where does he live?"

: "Have you heard of Beldanga in Murshidabad? There is a small village called Byanyada in Beldanga. Our master's spread of mastership is there. His name is Trailakya Mahanta; you can see him sleeping there. Next to him is our Ma-Gosain, his wife. They are simple, guileless people."

I asked my friend: "Would you like to go in? On these people depends the whole year's running expenses of Sati-Ma. They are the master and his task-bearers, who pay the taxes and the salutation-offerings. This master recruits his new task-holders."

My friend replied: "I've realised that these very people form the cadre at the grass-roots level. And the master is the ladder. He might also be called Deputy Collector, couldn't he? But aren't they very seasoned men? What does your notebook say about them?"

As the master Mohanta was fast asleep; so, sitting in front of him, I took out the notebook from the side-bag and said: "There's a brief opinion about them in the book by Jogendranath Bhattacharjee in 1896. He writes:

> The agents of the Karta are required to pay over their collections to him, at a grand levy held by him at his family residence in the month of March.

"It implied this fair held during Dol yatra (Holi). Listen to the subsequent part:

> Each agent of the Karta is generally on very intimate terms with a childless and friendless widow in the village or group of villages entrusted to his charge, and through the instrumentality of this woman, he is able to hold secret meetings which are attended by all the female votaries within his jurisdiction and in which he plays the part of Krishna."

"Do you believe in all this?"

I said: "Perhaps in Jogendranath's time, all this happened. Who knows? I haven't noticed anything contradictory so far. In reality, everybody doesn't follow the affairs of Guruism. Besides, what are you observing here; are there only women? There are many male task-holders in this institution; could all of them be perverted? I've noticed many pure masters."

Trailakya Mohanta sat up in the middle of our conversation. He had matted hair tumbling down from his head, wore an unkempt beard and red powder along the parting of his hair: apparently a semi-literate, middle-aged rural man, devoted to his cause and service-minded. First of all, he made acquaintance with us and offered us sweets and water. Perhaps he was savvy to part of our conversation. Following its trait, he exclaimed: "The relationship between guru and disciple is like that between man and woman. That's why it's said:

For the blessings of your Guru condition yourself to the ways of Nature.
Give guru a husband's stature,
Then only, for work, you stay.

"These words mean that you have to forsake your ego and surrender everything at the Guru's feet. It's a difficult act."

Mohanta was speaking on incessantly and I was amazed to witness an intimate and selfless rendering of service. One woman disciple was first washing Mohanta's forehead by slapping water on it and then drying it up with a cloth's end with great care. Afterwards, she combed his hair, rubbed oil into it and tied a tuft. What a great feeling of sincerity and warmth of affection there was: as if she was his mother incarnate! Then she rubbed away the sweat on guru's face with cloth's end; fanned him gently with a hand-fan, sitting by his side; and virtually swallowed every word of his with the utmost keenness. I had not seen such a scenario much in my life. My educated brain was curious about rumours; seasoned in pornography and assessed news and events by reading about the court-cases and law-suits in the urban newspapers with a perverse bent of mind. Watching such an unsoiled relationship caused us some embarrassment and consternation somewhere; the calculations did not quite tally.

I came out with a sudden exclamation: "Our minds look at the ugly side in everything; could you explain why? Is this what could be called a vicious and impure spirit?"

Smiling an omnipotent smile Mohanta said: "Then listen to a song:

If vice were not there, would virtue gain respect?
Death's power would have been upset!
If there were no enemy or demon—
Lust'n'anger wouldn't be common;
The debris of fight'n'murder, you wouldn't get!
If everyone belonged to saints' sect—
Then criminal acts would've vanished, you bet"

Stopping his song midway, Mohanta looked at us for a while... perhaps to observe our reaction? I was not really aware. Then, with a sudden ornamental cascade of musical notes, he began singing:

Good and bad are two-in-one—
In action, they're separately done.

Unless separately placed,
Good and bad can't be run!
If new moon was not there,
Could full moon come into glare?

Such sequencing in the village lyrics, giving the status of morality, had always appealed to me. The song flowed on to explain the statement, as it were. Virtue and vice, lust and love, attraction and disassociation were all within the mind: they were only separated in the field of action. As soon as this was clarified, Mohanta indicated with his eyes to his female disciple, busy in service, who then started singing in the higher octave in a very sweet voice:

Guru's the trunk of the main tree:
In three worlds, prevalent and free—
Worms and insects, things moveable-immovable:
Otherwise, nothing there could be!

As long as this part was being sung, Guru Trailakyanath had his eyes closed. Suddenly, he opened his eyes: the latter were full of tears. He said: "You, sir, raised a very difficult question. This irrefutable song by Gaur Goswami came straight from the heart in response."

: "Irrefutable song?"

: "Yes, the lyrics of some of the songs can't be refuted. That would mean that the theory and the truth, inherent in the song, have been perennially proven. Written by a great master, it's not just an amalgam of concocted lines."

My friend's materialistic mind was also possibly affected a little. So he exclaimed: "Our mind was much depressed since morning, having looked at many staged falsehoods and deceptions. Your place has a certain calming effect. Well, can you explain to us the degree of truth behind the fables attached with Himsagar and the wood-apple tree?"

Mohanta gave a faint smile and replied: "If there was no truth, why did you come here in the scorching heat of midday? Would anybody summon a doctor without there being an ailment? However, the greatest force is the force of name-chanting. Hence said Lalshashi:

If you wish to seek more outcome
Than life's four noble pursuits—
Let your tongue have fun playing with
The juice of name-chanting's fruits!

"That would mean that the power of name-chanting is above the four goals of human life: virtue, wealth, love and final salvation. Yet only the chanting of name won't do, would it? There must be earnestness. Then there are different levels of ownership. According to our faith:

Female-hermaphrodite, male-eunuch—
To be Kartabahja, are qualified as such!

"Did you get the meaning?"

: "No, it all sounded a mystery."

: "There's no mystery at all. You have to discard the Vedic path. The Vedic path implies studies with complete abstinence; familyhood; withdrawal to the woods; and complete asceticism. None of these would lead to God: you have to be part of all this, with total indifference. It would be a female behaving as hermaphrodite or a male like a eunuch. When that status is achieved, you have to call Mother fervently. That's why the *Bhaaber Geet* (Songs of Sentiments) says":

If you're good for Mother, you get her affection—
If you truly call Mother, world's full of Mother's notion!

"This is why we perceive Sati-Ma in every space: in Himsagar, as much as under the wood-apple tree. She's everywhere but, according to the consequence of actions, some get to see her, some don't."

I noticed that Mohanta's discourse was getting more and more emotional. His task-holders were gradually inching near him, with fascination and surrender writ large in their eyes. It would be disastrous to let this status continue. In such situations, I usually dropped a brick: with a contrary statement. On this occasion, too, I got everybody startled by exclaiming: "Well, many people say that food is related to the body and physique, do you agree? Shivshekher of Kumirdaha village said he was a vegetarian. Are you a vegetarian as well, and don't take fish or meat?'

Mohanta's emotional languor ebbed away at this single question. The man was caught in the whirligig of words: he came out of it in one forceful jerk and said: "There's nothing like a vegetarian or a non-vegetarian; all are his creations. Of course, the food does act within the body. Its activity is to increase the body-heat. The meditative persons, therefore, seek to avoid the heat. It's not the three heats alone; the body-heat also hinders in the meditative practices. I don't choose between vegetarian and non-vegetarian food. I eat fish, but not meat."

: "Why? Is there any specific reason or, is it just a matter of taste?"

: "Does the worshipped do anything without a cause? He has to come to the right path: after a lot of realisation, much manipulation, many observations. Do you know why I take fish? Fish have no lust; their birth is not out of lust."

We, the two friends, picked up our ears. The common folks went about with some strange logic: some self-imagined, and some created by the guru. The statement, that the fish did not have lust and was not born of lust, had quite some novelty. So I asked: "Do fish have no lust? So, how are they born?"

Mohanta said: "The fish does not posses male or female organs. Hence, there is a common saying: the fish has no fishy organ. By rubbing body against body, they generate the seed of reproduction. That's what's called copulation. From that heat or copulation come the eggs. Hence, eating fish does not lead to lustful habits. What do you all say?"

Everyone nodded in appreciative gaze. One disciple said: "What can we say? We're the illiterate gangs from the remote villages. What all do we know? That's why we've accepted you as our guru. We say what you want us to say; we know what you want us to know. We can't move an inch without you."

Mohanta said: "The fish is the noblest of all living beings. It has the symptoms of meditators. Have you noticed that the fish has no eyelids, but only still eyes? It means that they are always meditating. That's why I always wail: 'Sati-Ma, why have you given me eyelids? Why haven't you given me eyes like the fish? Then I'd have continued to gaze at you!'"

I sat dumbfounded at the series of events. The server-woman wiped the guru's eyes with a cloth's end and fanned him vigorously with a hand-fan. Ma-Gosain exclaimed from inside: "The man has a lot of heat within."

After the weeping bout of the Mohanta came under some control, I asked

: "Does eating meat enhance lust?"

: "Not only lust, but all other desires get enhanced, such as, anger, jealousy, violence. Again, discretion is lost; one loses control over good and evil acts."

: "Is that so? Why?"

: "How can I explain to you, tell me? You're an educated man. Which meat would you prefer? Would it be mutton? Have you watched their method of copulation? Do they discriminate between mother, aunt and other female species? Don't you realise what man would come to, if he eats that meat?"

Goodness gracious, what strokes of words, what force of statements! I could not look at anybody in embarrassment. In order to avoid a decisive statement, I said: "I haven't tried to figure out such subtlety ever, hence my shaking you up. Do forgive me."

By then the man had become peaceful, quiet like still water. Smiling pleasantly, he asked: "What's wrong in seeking to know? But then, every knowledge doesn't have an answer, because everything has difference in names and difference in appearances. There are varieties in kinds and tastes, such as, between green coconuts and mature coconuts; between puffed rice and boiled rice; among flutes with names like *benu, murali, bongshi, banshi...*"

Interrupting the Mohanta's speech, I blurted out: "What are you saying? Aren't *benu, murali, bongshi, banshi*...one and the same? What's the difference?"

: "There's a lot of difference. *Benu* has five holes; *murali* three; *banshi* seven; and *bongshi* nine holes. Aren't they all different? They're different in appearances; and in their usage. Do you follow?"

I did, of course, follow. Though I was not the one who looked for slips and gaps, the words of the Mohanta somehow did not ring true and seemed to have a fleck of doubt. Was this all made-up or merely practised and skilled speaking? Did he create his disciples through the deftly woven web of words? He had talent, no doubt; and it was difficult to compete with the man. But having won the first round, Mohanta launched his second volley: "Had there been no holes, how old one come and go? Could you tell me how many holes are there in a human body?"

Ah well, finally I knew the answer to this. It was a common enough question! I answered in style, with an air of authority; "A human body has nine holes, as they're known as nine doors two eyes; two nostrils; two ears; and there're the mouth, the urinary channel and anus. Is that right?"

: "It's okay with men; for women, there's also the vagina, which is deemed the tenth gate."

Unable to answer such a simple question, I sat, head hung in glum silence. Then the Mohanta said: "When men meditate, each status gets a unique name. Take, for instance, these...*benu, murali, banshi* and *bongshi.* There are names attributed to the worshipper's states of meditation. Would you like to hear them?"

: "Certainly; I haven't heard such things."

: "How would you? These can't be heard at home. You have to come out; visit fairs and festivals; mingle with people. People're everything; there's nothing available beyond what humans possess."

In order to let him recall, I mentioned: "You were trying to say something about *benu, murali, bongshi, banshi...*"

: "Yes, I'll talk about them; that'd be the most important secret," Trailakya Mohanta brought his voice down to a bass, looked at me with a piercing graze and said: "When man's consciousness remains dormant, three holes play up; that's called the *murali* state. Three holes are the three qualities: virtuousness, spiritedness and ignorance; after which the self arises. That's called *benu*: with five holes. These are the mind, two nostrils and two eyes—these five. After this comes the *banshi* state when man becomes conscious. Then he plays with seven holes. Well, the total is seven. Man's fourth state is called *bangshi*, when there're nine holes. That is when the male and female organs are added to the seven of *banshi.* That's the final state of the meditator."

I was enchanted by Mohanta's sequence of statements. After a while, when the impact was reasonably diminished, I asked: "Is it your custom to practise cohabitation with your own consort or is it with another woman?"

: "What do you understand by consort and the other woman? Is it about one's own wife and the partner who is your companion facilitating your meditation process?"

: "Well, that's what's commonly understood."

: "It's all wrong. Our book of law states:

Chaste woman or concubine: none of them can perform—
Land gets different, but the easy land's the norm!

It implies neither own wife nor somebody else's. Own consort's meaning is entirely different. We hold that man and woman coexist within the same body—their cohabitation and union is perceived as the coitus within one's own domain. Anything, besides, is external coitus. The Kartabhaja sect practises this self-coital meditation. Now, tell me: can there be lust in this sect? Ours is an entirely different belief."

: "I've understood. But where do you place yourselves—among Aaul, Baul, Sain and Dervish?"

Mohanta replied: "That's a different path altogether. Esahuq, do you know about these?"

A middle-aged Muslim came crawling forward from the interiors; his name was Esahuq. It was noticed that he was not a Kartabhaja, but had come to the fair with Byanyada's group. Very respectful to Trailokya Mohanta, he came forward and said with humility: "I don't know aspects too well. But I had been once to Lalan's institution at Chhenur, where I heard a hymn which I wove in to my memory and can reproduce. Shall I?"

: "Yes please do."

Aauls have Fakir Allah,
Bauls Mohammed,
Dervish has Adam Safi:
This much's truly said.
Putting three sects together,
Ali made them the same—
And made them manifest
Under Sain-faith's name.

I remained quiet for a fairly long while and then asked Mohanta: "I couldn't follow anything. Am I getting entangled in a whirlpool, so to speak? I do want to know everything, but have I that ability? What do you say?"

Mohanta said: "Is there any limit to a man's ability? However, it need's the guru's benediction. Anyway, don't worry; I will take you to a place where there's a Fakir who regularly attends the fair of Sati-Ma. His name is Benowari Fakir. He is not a master from our sect, but does attend every time.'

: "If he's not a master, why does he attend?"

: "Well, this is a holy place where one obtains divine grace through austere practice. Therefore, many people come; there's much co-mingling; ideas are exchanged; one gets to know a few others. Let's go and see if we can locate him."

We could not find him despite going around on a long-drawn search. But someone said that the Fakir was ailing, so he did not come this time. "'What is his ailment," I asked. "I've heard that Fakirs never get ill?"

The man replied nonchalantly: "Sir, if there's body, it is sure to get shoddy."

I marvelled at the brilliance of such folk-sayings: "If there's body, it can get shoddy." I suddenly remembered what Royal Fakir had said. It was he who told me that visits to fairs and festivals allow to meet many people and gather much experience. It was he who held my hand, to take me round many fairs. The man was buried under earth at this moment, but his words were still alive. Whatever I had learnt through him about the Fakirs and masters from Ghoshpara would remain as a treasure in my mind for ever. On this day, as I went out from the Ghoshpara fair, I remembered all about Aaulchand, Ramsharan, Ramdulal and Sati-Ma. They liberated a community of depressed and humiliated people from the oppression of a religion: tainted by scriptures and casteism, and gave them the infinite potential of worshipping open-minded men. If their successors had put a tinge of greed, shoot of jealousy and cruelty of extortion into that sect, the grace of the original faith remained unsullied. There still remained intact their pure dictums and songs of sentiments. The intensity of belief and dedication of the Kartabhaja men – living in the inhabitation spreading from the villages up to Kolkata – were still so true. I had seen, with my own eyes, how so many masters and task-holders were drawn out of this sentiment from across even the Bangladesh borders, till this day.

After all the rituals were done with – stretching over the entire day – the fair fell into a stupor. The sheds of the different sects were lighting their evening lamps. The tired masses – after the continual, ritualistic prostrations on the ground in fulfilling their vows – lay fast asleep, at the end of the daylong inhuman labouring on the ground. The disabled boys and girls nestled close to the restless hearts of their parents. Only in certain gatherings, the refrain from the songs of sentiment continued to drone, weighed down by ignominy, self-doubt and profound regret.

Forgive our crimes, O lord!
Such judgmental lapses in every birth—on your earth
Shouldn't happen again: of its own accord!
Such futile blunders we can hardly afford!
In tens of millions, my mistakes abound—
Reduced to writing: their numbers can't be found!

It was not a deep lonely alley; the fair was teeming with the overwhelming presence of countless faces, thousands of people – holding on to tremulous hope and belief, with self-surrenders filled with the deepest of hopes – well on for two hundred years. The full moon seemed to be up tonight: in illumined salutation to the countless men and their combined devotion. Looking at those moonlit meadows and moving human streams, I, too, thought like Lalshashi:

The abode – on the road – like a tilting swing!

I figured out that Lalshashi did not transfer to his songs, the futile wailing accompanying the eternal and lifelong quest for the 'man of his heart' like the Bauls did. The 'man of his heart' was firmly lodged well within himself. So instead, he felt—what's the point in revealing the man of my heart to the world outside?

The famous newspapers of Kolkata ignored such news, but the suburban four-page press of limited standing often gave headlines to the torture of Bauls. I made and collected clippings of many such news-items. The news contents seemed mostly similar to each other. That is, in some village of Nadia (or Murshidabad), one (or one group of) Baul/s or Marfati Fakir/s had his/their tuft of hair and beard snipped out, the single-stringed drones broken to bits, and had been beaten up by orthodox fundamentalists. The news items ended there. The mind however, remained most anxious to know what happened later on. Did the outcast Bauls and Fakirs accept such oppression every time, or, did they build up a resistance? What did the administration do? Did the village politicians protest against the injustice? Nothing was known.

But, the news from my own sources invariably indicated that a Fakir, named Benowari, and his group, always jumped in favour of the Bauls at any such fracas and got involved in a *bahas* (religious debate) against the mullas, eventually winning almost everywhere. I had thought in terms of going to meet Benowari sometime or the other, but could not properly locate him. Did the man come out of nowhere like the 'Phantom' and plunge into the events? I had wondered often light-heartedly and laughed to myself. Finally, this time at the Sati-Ma fair, Trailakya Mohanta gave me the man's address. Benowari Fakir's permanent home was in the Mathpukur village near Dharampur at the Nadia-Murshidabad border. Some news about the man went round the air like the lightweight cotton seeds of the silk-cotton trees.

All Bauls and Fakirs of this region were apparently beholden to Benowari.

What did I care to depend on such hearsay? He was, after all, a man; and it would be enough to go and look him up. I recalled a song by Haariram:

Everybody speaks of the 'man'—
Who has done the search and scan?

Since I, at least, was never tired looking for Man, I packed some dry munchables and set out one fine day. Mathpukur was not at the back of the beyond, but the way from my home was a round-about one. But, still finally, I reached by mid-noon. I, had of course, dropped a post-card in advance, but the Fakir did not receive it, thanks to the efficiency of the postal department. It did not matter much. Along with the lean, tall-framed person lived a soft-natured man. They received me boisterously: "Do come; most welcome. How does it matter, if we didn't receive the letter? Your mind's letter has just arrived, with God's own seal. Well, that's good enough. Come up on to the balcony; sit down at this poor man's prayer hall. Yes, yes, we've heard about you, certainly. Now it's just a question of matching name to appearance! The latter does seem to be like a human all right! Ha ha ha! You would allow us to serve you a meal, wouldn't you? O ma'am Sahitan, do add some more rice for this gentleman."

I looked carefully at the courtyard to locate a young Muslim married woman – wearing a dark Begunfuli saree – lighting a fire in the earthen oven using twigs and dry coconut leaves. It was a huge community oven, which was usually kept on a slow fire with a metal cover on the embers. In the event of the sudden arrival of a guest, it would come in handy for cooking a quick meal. At that moment, the fair maiden Sahitan Bibi's body was dripping with sweat in the heat of the month of Jaishtha. Noticing her, I thought that Benowari Fakir had managed to acquire quite a youthful wife. Benowari brought a large mat of date-palm leaves from inside his home. Two hand-fans were arranged as well. After shouting out an order for a pot of tea and egg-omelettes to Sahitan Bibi, he seemed to have read my mind and expained: "It's not what you think. Sahitan Bibi is my salaried maid. You see, I'm alone and have advanced in age as well. She cooks my meals and sleeps on my balcony with her little child. Her husband has divorced her. Don't be surprised. There's always a divorced woman or two, in the homes of poor Muslims living in the countryside."

Although the statement was made quite indifferently, there was a tinge of anguish, a deep pain enveloping Benowari's voice. In order to cope with the situation, I exclaimed: "You live all alone. Why didn't you marry in proper time? Have you always been drunk on Fakiri?"

"Oh, no, no," said the man, laughing out open-heartedly and explaining; "I became a Fakir much later. Do you know what really happened? When a pumpkin or a bottle-gourd first ripens in the home-creeper, it's either offered in the service of the gods or kept to dry up for seeds. So, I was the eldest son to my parents, they didn't get me married, but preserved me for seeding. Ha, ha! I haven't been of any service to anybody, what do you say?"

The man seemed to be a very transparent one. I immediately fell in love with Benowari Fakir and said: "Seeds're the real things. It's only important to know where that seed is getting thrown: on soil or on stone. I do think your seeds would sprout up a whole forest. Isn't that right?"

"Absolutely right," said the Fakir while stroking his beard with his fingers. "Yes, I do have a handful of disciples; they will all come now. They're Jalil, Manullah, Abu Bakkar, Amaresh and Umid. Just look, Abu Bakkar is already here, as we're talking. Well, you're a lucky man; Bakkar's a good singer. You would be able to hear some good music today."

Wearing a white dhoti in the lungi style, draped in a white robe, and carrying a fully-covered two-stringed drone, the white figure of Abu Bakkar came up to the balcony and kneeled down in reverence before Benowari who sat with folded legs. Bakkar immersed his face in the lap of his guru, who sunk his fingers in his tuft of hair and placed a warm hand on his back. After the salutations were over, the disciple kissed the two big toes of his feet.

With the salutation process seeming a very novel one. I asked: "Is this what you call *sejda?*"

Benowari replied: "There's some controversy on *sejda* or salutation. Our Muslim superiors argue that it's taboo to offer *sejda* to anyone other than Allah. They question why Fakirs, as ordinary mortals, do *sejda* to other mortals. Our response is quite clear in this matter. We offer *sejda* because Khuda is in every mortal. This answer doesn't make them happy. We have severe confrontations on this issue from time to time. No, no, it's not bloody conflict; only *bahas*, that is, debate."

I said: "I'd heard in a song. The one who looks for Khuda in 'man' is the Baul."

Benowari said; "You'd be hearing plenty of songs the whole day today. Abu Bakkar has come. He's a pure songbird. Well, by the way, Bakkar, where has the bird flown, tell me?"

Bakkar replied: "The bird? It has flown away again. Let me check in which direction it has gone, I'd hold it by its limb and bring it back."

I exclaimed: "How's that? How can you, as a Fakir, tame a bird? Isn't it bondage?" Benowari kept laughing to himself and combing his fingers through his beard. Suddenly, the refrain of a song by Abu Bakkar came floating from the fringes of the house's backyards;

I've caught a bird right here!
The more it does flap its wing,

To tame it, peace I'll bring, –
I've planned to hold it back,
With a chain sheer;
I've caught, I've caught, caught a bird here!

Good heavens! Abu Bakkar was really holding a young maiden by her plait in his hands. A 13- or 14-year-old girl, draped in a green saree, shaking her head reluctantly and hitting Abu Bakkar with her fists. Her fair face had turned crimson in rage. Hanging her head low, she came and stood stubbornly facing the balcony. Bakkar complained: "She was hiding under the overhanging thatch and eating pickles. Just look here, she has rubbed pickle on my robe, scratched me and beaten me with her fists. Isn't there a remedy against all this? I demand justice."

"Justice my foot!" quipped the girl, sticking up her thumb and making a face.

Benowari said: "Justice has been done. If that youth comes to pick you up today, we won't permit you to go. That's all." The girl started to romp around the whole courtyard, by stamping her feet and allowing her anklets to tinkle. Benowari exclaimed: "I've never married, neither did Abu Bakkar. But just witness the illusion of this mundane world. Tell us, does Yakub love you that much?" The girl fled the scene.

I was taken quite aback by seeing the portrait of a charming home-life among the ascetic, family-forsaken Fakirs. By rescuing me from my mental state, the Fakir interjected: "She is the motherless daughter of my nephew; she's called Pakhi (bird). I tamed her here when she was barely five. She used to roam around like a free parakeet and peck on food-morsels and water. She used to even peck at us. Almost around the time when she had just about been tamed, the elder uncle of one of my disciples liked the 'bird' and got her married off to his son Yakub. Well, I thought, the illusion would soon be over.

Nothing doing! She escapes every day to come here. The 'bird' has remained a bird!"

Meanwhile, the tea and the omelettes were served. It was the 'bird who brought them out: as a very humble, peaceful maiden, looking like a coy creeper. Putting the dishes down, she ran away.

After the snacks were over, I asked: "You were talking about *sejda* then. What do the Islam scriptures say about it?"

: "Look, does anything happen with so many scriptures and evidences? We're the ones who got rid of scriptures; we're Fakirs. We state that *khad* means man or person:

The man, if you cannot snatch—
'Khuda' never you can catch!

"Abu, what does that song by your Arjan Shah Fakir say?"

'Khad' and 'Khuda' are one and the same—
Do worship, catching Khad's own name!

"It's the absolute truth. So if we obey 'Khad', we obey 'Khuda' as well. Isn't that so? Therefore, if we do *sejda* to Khuda, what's wrong in doing *sejda* to Khad?"

Do you know what the reality is? *Sejdas* are of two kinds. *Sejda-Abudiyat' or Ibadat;* and there is *'Sejda-e-Tahiya'* or *Tazim.* What's it, Abu Bakkar, could you explain it to sir? Why don't you give it a try? Let me also understand how much your ability has enhanced."

Abu Bakkar said: "Let me tell you what little I've understood from Murshid. Sir, please correct me if I'm wrong. Please listen, sirs. '*Sejda Abudiyat* or *Ibadat* is only meant for salutation to God, it has many attendant rules. And *Sejda-e Tahiya* or *Tazim* is a separate matter where '*tazim*' means showing respect. It means that one can do *sejda* to one and all. We Fakirs, therefore, do *sejda* to all individuals."

I replied: "When I was collecting Kubir Gosain's songs, I got the word *'sejda'* in one of his lyrics, but didn't quite follow the meaning. I'm able perhaps to understand it now."

: "Could you say what the song was?"

You all Momins and Muslims do regular pray,
God doesn't emerge, nor show himself, nay,
To whom do I offer sejda, *please say,*
Be thy own God in one's own mind, if you may!

Benowari exclaimed enthusiastically: "Well, this seems to be the genuine Marfati song—'God doesn't come in front, nor show his glimpse', how right! So to whom do I offer *sejda?* So, do *sejda* to God who resides in your own mind. Show respect to Khuda through all Khads in whom resides Khuda. How great! The mind becomes fine."

Meanwhile, Jaishtha was getting hotter. The smell of hot boiled rice was wafting across. Quietly a few more disciples of the Fakir had assembled on the balcony. We had not noticed them during our conversation and only saw them when Pakhi began reprimanding: "Won't you take a bath? And eat? Will it do by wasting time in idle conversation?"

Abu Bakkar said: "Let's get up, sirs, the babbler has started babbling behind. She won't stop before she gives us a peck or two." At once, he felt a tug at his tuft of hair by Pakhi. "My goodness," exclaimed Bakkar pleasantly and got up to have lunch, with us behind. Oil and towel were kept ready. We all took a plunge in the cold waters of the pond. On return to the balcony after bath, we found that the meals were arranged already: rice, lentil, fried vegetables, a curry of gourds and ripe mangoes. The four disciples sat in front. While eating, I suddenly noticed that all the four extended their right hands towards the guru, with noses stuck into the hands like ostriches. The guru offered four morsels of food – portions of his rice – from his plate to the four. They partook of the food with devotion and wiped their hands on their heads.

The customs of the Fakirs were obviously different from others and I was not sure what else I was going to observe during the rest of the day. After lunch, we lay down for a while on the date-palm mat. The conversation continued. On the other side of the kitchen, the large brood of young disciples were eating. Pakhi was prattling all along. I asked Benowari: "Do new entrants join the cult of Fakirs? Most minor cults are dwindling in contrast."

"Popular entry is always low in the way of Fakirs. It's even less nowadays. The way is undoubtedly a difficult one. More than the rites and activities, the accent is on comprehension, there is stress on respiration: on inhalation and exhalation. A mistake could cost one's well-being. It's hard to stand steadfast in its way, even harder to keep holding on. One of our songs say:

In Fakiri if you deceive,
You'll reach realm of hell,
For the cheat, that hell
Is the only place to dwell!

"Did you follow the song? Deception is taboo in Fakiri. It implies emptiness, cheating—utter falsehood. Lust, avarice, violence and jealousy have to be forsaken for ever."

: "Well, you haven't married. Are all Fakirs like that'?"

: "No, there're the householder Fakirs as well. But they aren't like householders under influence of lust. Preserving the sperm is their main activity. We call it the 'point' (*bindu*). This point or insect is the sperm, known as semen. We call it *nafs.* This *nafs* or lust is to be invariably kept under control."

: "In your Fakiri way of thought, is the role of physiology so very important?"

: "Marfat, as a word, has one such meaning. It's termed *elme tashrih,* that is, knowledge of the body. This is really anatomy'."

I perceived that in the illusion of mid-noon, I had entered the domain of some unknown kingdom which was terribly attractive. The one, lying down in front of me and effortlessly responding to my queries, was not a physical being, but a divine angel. A semi-literate rural person, he was a wizard in his scriptural knowledge and its running commentary. He was even stronger in his self-knowledge, as what could be called a powerful intellectual. Beside his domain of knowledge, I appeared to be a mere stone-picking Newton. Keeping that in mind, I sought information from the bottom of my ignorance and asked this knowledgeable angel: "Could you tell me something about the body?"

: "There's plenty to say. One part of the body is its physical entity. A major part is the heart. The main part is 'point'. As one crosses a passer-by while waking on the road, our Marfati way is also a meeting-point of many ideologies. The latter needs to be learnt and understood. The Fakirs don't proceed too far on the way of knowledge. Their way is that of the heart. Heart is the abode of God."

Benowari's dialogue had a deeper pull. That pull drew one deep within. It seemed the man had the answer to all my quests. But was that possible? Could it happen? My queries were, after all, not endless. The words drawn in pursuance of previous words, the questions illumined by earlier quizzes were all that I could seek from him. But, did I seem a fool by unilaterally raising non-stop questions before a wise man? Benowari's responses were steeped in fathomless knowledge, but did he regard my questions as mere childish prattle? I now asked with trepidation: "Fakir, sir, am I asking pointless questions? Perhaps I'm really bothering you."

"Not at all. In fact, I normally deal with illiterate farmers. Their knowledge extends at best to student scholarships. You've completely traversed the avenue of knowledge. I've also heard that you've kept company with many saints and sages. Your talk is a revelation of that. We understand where exactly the 'mirgel' fish swarms from the bubbles on the water."

: "I couldn't follow the meaning of your last words."

: "They're not difficult words. But you didn't follow because your ways are different. The fact of the matter is that 'mirgel' fish swarms in deep waters. As they breathe, bubbles of water surface above. These bubbles help fishermen identify the exact location of the mirgel fish and accordingly they cast their nets. Similarly, your words reveal your signs: where you are, how deep your position is."

I now gathered enough courage and went back to the topic left midway, to say: "You were explaining that the fundamental element of the Fakiri principle is to hold the 'point'. Well, what's the beginning of this 'point' or semen, and what's its destination?"

: "Listen then. Our Marfati ideology states that skin is over body; blood is within skin; flesh is within blood; fat is within flesh; bone is within fat; marrow is within bone; and within marrow is semen. Now you can understand how semen is the principal one among the fifteen elements of the body. In the semen resides the seed of life. You do understand that soul is the mainstay of life—the flower is within soul; bud nestles within the flower; consciousness is within the bud; mind is within consciousness; emotions and sensibilities are within the mind; the essence or flavour of life is within the emotions and sensibilities; love resides within this essence or flavour. And in that love lies the 'simple matter'. We're in quest of that 'simple matter' till the very end, hence love is our main support while we seek. Semen is at the core of all; therefore semen is to be saved. Loss of semen would cause disruptions on the way to 'simple matter'."

It was a well-argued web of logic: almost too facile to be accepted. Benowari had an extraordinary power of expression, and so was his praiseworthy memory. Perhaps from the holding of the 'point' came all this power, who knows? For the time being, while getting crestfallen by his sharp logic, I could only ask: "If semen is the main element, what is the origin of that semen? Is that element, too, man's congenital earning, like his blood-flesh-fat-marrow?"

: "If it's a birth-time acquisition, why doesn't 'point' come before youth?"

Admitting defeat, I said: "You please explain."

Benowari laughed and said: "Don't take me as a divine messenger or peer. For a long time, I've kept company with many gurus and Murshids, and followed the arguments of many Kamel Fakirs, before consolidating these thoughts in my mind. Whatever, the question now is: where does the 'point' come from, if it is not present from birth? A one-word reply to these question is: from the five natural elements. That is, food-crops and edibles are created under the influence of the five elements. From this is prepared the food for the the animal world. Man draws sap from that food. The 'point' is finally extracted and created from that sap of natural food and its peels. That's why it takes twelve to fourteen years for the 'point' to be created in the human body.

Whether we admit or not, this was an empowering factor for folk religion. These folks did not quote scriptures at every turn of phrase, but had a world of beliefs of their own. No Brahmin scholar or Maulana or Ulema had constructed that world, which was entirely created by themselves, with an organically sturdy frame. Lust and violation were equally confessed or accepted and condemned, respectively. In the theory of folk religion, there was more logic than emotion, because those who professed such faith had to constantly refurbish their ideology with logical arguments. Those who were converted to such faiths were also to be convinced with logical points. The village people did not get swayed by speeches as much as they were persuaded by logic. Their life was bound by the chain of logic. Sowing seeds led to harvest; rains contributed to large grains; fertilisers led to a large quantity of crops. On the contrary, poor seed would lead to bad harvest even if other factors remained stable and even excellent; even if everything else went fine, flood or drought would surely create havoc in a particular year. From that world of logic, I provoked Benowari: "In order to save the 'point', one has to have a good knowledge of breath-control. Everyone doesn't know this. Will men leading a normal family life not indulge in female-coitus in that case?"

"Why not," explained Benowari. "'Intercourse is meant for creating progeny. But lust for pleasure alone and for the fulfillment of one's own desire is a vice. We've a popular village proverb on this:

Do once a month, twelve a year—and less, if you can manage, dear!

"Do you follow?"

: "Yes, I do. Is that why you did not marry at all? What you had said in the morning about saving the seeds of the pumpkin and the bottle-gourd was presumably only a joke. What was it really then?"

: "It's my hatred for the vaginal opening for birth," the soft person suddenly turned steely. Straightening up, he said: "If one considers women as a whole community of mothers, can one lust for them? The route through which I am born belongs to my father. In that case, every woman carries my birth-mark. How can I lust for my mother? Am I an animal?"

My mind ached at his words. My whole body began trembling. The silence was so all-engulfing. It was so stifling. Benowari's face was tormented by remorse and hatred. Both his eyes had welled up with tears. He suddenly cried out in a solemn tone: "Abu Bakkar, let him listen to that song. Have you understood?"

Abu humbly nodded and sat down. He tuned his two-stringed drone, pulling it out of the cloth-sack. Then he closed his eyes, his voice rising to the fifth note in the upper octave, beginning his song in a high-pitched regretful and accusatory voice:

My mind, why did you leap
Into your father's bay—
In lust, your heart has become crazy and gay!

How much power did these lyrics possess—blowing in a sharp blast like a shaft into my ears and directly piercing the mind? How clear these words were and held how much resonance! It was not music, but a cry of lamentation of a lustful man. The more Abu Bakkar sang, the more he wept. Jalil, Manullah and all others had tears in their eyes. Abu Bakkar smoothly reached another half from the song's second half:

Why are you like this, my mind—
where you're born, there death you find!
You'll be taken through many alleys blind
Only in shackles, I'll say!

As lamps burning bright
Make insects flock to the light—
To die at last, as they might,
In the fateful ray!

By then Benowari had come back to his senses. Seeing that, I too recovered mental peace. The environment became less stifling. Exclamations like 'cheers', 'bravo' came from the Fakir in appreciation. To look at the matter, even Pakhi gathered courage enough to furtively glance from across the room's threshold. I thought again: how strong were the messages of such songs, making the heat in the mind melt down and cool the environs. Abu Bakkar had by then come to the composer's sign-off:

Siraj Shah Dervish says so—
In three worlds, high and low,
Why does Lalan go, to and fro,
Letting revelations stray?

Benowari came to sit next to me. Placing his hand on my knees, he said: "My mind has suddenly become very agile. That elusive 'simple matter' – the man of my heart – like the power in three worlds—resides in my mind. So why does one have to specially search for it in women? Why is there bondage? Why is there an illusion?"

Abu Bakkar stopped singing and kept looking at his guru with red eyes. "Let music continue": came the direction. He re-tuned his drone with a smile. Manullah used that opportunity to exclaim: "Bakkar, why don't you sing the song of the elephant to sir?" Pakhi clapped in support.

Bakkar began singing with a smile:

The elephant was in the fair on display—
Four blind men saw it and
Had their own things to say.

Was there a light breeze outside at the end of the day? In the room at least, there was a whiff of fresh air. Fakir's eyes were closed, with a faint smile on his face. Jalil whispered in my ears: "Baba's in a trance. His mental pain has ebbed away."

Abu Bakkar sang:

One said, 'To everybody, let me this to say,
I've seen the elephant on display—
Soft betel-nut trees there do erectly stay.

From top, thick above thin below,
The head like pumpkin sway.

Another said, 'Your words're untrue,
Let me tell now to you—
On four sides like trays, quilts hang, they do.'
The ignoramus gossip,
Everything appears false.
Yet another says, 'Listen with care,
Whatever you say, here and there,
Not a word is true—I dare.
Elephant is like concrete pillar,
Erect it does stay.'

Another says with a lot of noise,
'Very confusing is your voice,
I saw elephant like a sweet cane,
On the ground, it does poise.'

Gopal does fret, in regret,
How four blind men create a cacophony:
Confusing and gay!"

At the end of the song, Pakhi clapped happily Manullah said: "Pakhi has still a childish mind, so she derives gaiety even after listening to such a deeply meaningful song."

"Does this song have a deep meaning?" I blurted out, almost on a mistaken impulse.

Benowari said: "What does Allah look like? Does anybody know the appearance of God? Each one describes it according to his own guesswork, which is like the blind men looking at the elephant. The notion grows in accordance with the levels of meditation. At the end, there is no longer any concrete concept of God's appearance. One becomes assimilated in Him. That's the Sufi idea"

: "Will you explain a little about those levels?"

Fakir said: "Jalil, could you tell me about the system of Sufism? Let me see how sharp you are."

Jalil replied: "At first is the *belgaib yekin.* Then is *elmail yekin,* followed by *ainul yekin,* and then *huqqul yekin.* Oh, so sorry, sir, I can't recall the rest."

Manullah said: "You're very forgetful. Listen now. At the end is *hual yekin."*

Jalil bowed his head in shame. Benowari said: "According to Sufism, not to experience the self but to follow others is *belgaib yekin.* Then to believe in Allah through knowledge is *elmail yekin.* To believe through one's own sight is *ainul yekin.* There is another layer above these: to believe, knowing that it's the truth as *huqqul yekin.* And the last layer is *hual yekin.* It implies to get assimilated into Allah. Now you understand the value of the elephant song. Before Allah, we all are blind."

At this hour of dusk in late Jaishtha, I quietly offered *sejda* to the wise man, by silently stooping down in respect and humility. Comprehending my emotions with his inner grace, the man said: "Offer *sejda* to the *khad* within you."

Early next morning, I returned home. But, before long, I went back to Benowari Fakir at Mathpukur village. This was because I had in mind the context of oppression of the Baul-Fakir. I had not found out anything about it the other day. So, on reaching Mathpukur, I raised the matter immediately after taking tea and snacks. Who knows how disciples would congregate with the advancing day, there would be Fakiri songs and, in the melee of events, I would forget the main topic. So I directly came to the point: "Bauls-Fakirs apparently get tortured in Nadia-

Murshidabad. What kind of torture is that and why? Could you tell me who conducts it? "

: "Torture is first admonition; showing the fiery glare; then beating; breaking the drone and the drum. Finally, it's cutting the tuft of hair and shaving the beard and moustache. It's the last one which is most demeaning."

: "Why?"

: "Bauls have the ethos of preserving all their hair."

: "But who are those who carry out the tonsure? Are they common men?"

: "*Aalems* indulge in this activity. *Elem* means knowledge. I call those who do this as *be-aalem*, that is, ignorant. This activity has been on for a long time; perhaps a few hundred years. I've heard that during the times of Lalan Fakir or Panjushah Fakir, a *fatwa* was decreed on destroying Bauls in Jessore-Rangpur. Many people got beaten, some fled and the rest hid themselves. This was nothing new. I try to resist such oppression, and protest according to my capacity."

I looked at Benowari with a devout gaze. The civil society would never come to know about their contribution. In order to look for the man of their heart, they no doubt choose the deep lonely alleys; but from time to time, they felt compelled to stand beside the lamenting, tortured souls. That, too, was due to the urge of humanity. Long ago, Hemanga Biswas wrote in the *Ekshan* magazine, mentioning the diaries of Kangal Harinath, that once apparently the musclemen of Debendranath Tagore or Dwijendranath Tagore employed sticks to beat the subjects in Chheunria village of Kushtia district (now in Bangladesh).; on hearing that, Lalan Fakir led disciples from his Ashram to deploy stick-wielders of his own to reread that account, by the torturing musclemen. On reading that account, my regard for Lalan Fakir redoubled. Similar regard came to my mind, seeing Benowari Fakir. Folk religion did then bring quite a moral strength in man's mind: for staging protest and resistance. I suddenly realised that folk religion itself originated from protests. I also felt that my own religion did not give me any strength to protest, any weapon to resist.

I asked: "Do tell me why the incidents of oppression take place."

: "The main reason is fundamentalism. Most men are impatient, ignorant and illiterate. They fight about the scriptures, but haven't actually read them. The answer lies in the fact that most Bauls and Fakirs abandoned our Muslim faith, joined the sect and grew in numbers. That is frowned upon by Mullahs and Maulavis. It begins from there. There's more to it though."

: "Perhaps the real thing is the fight between the Islamic Law and its message, isn't it?"

: "It's very briefly so. The other thing is our indulgence in music. It's apparently anti-Islamic, prohibited. There was great fun on another occasion during a debate with the Chandipur Mullah on music. People came in large numbers from the surrounding ten or fifteen villages. I had Abu Bakkar accompanying me. I asked him: 'Bakkar, could you please sing for our Muslim brethren the song by Duddushah?'" He began to sing:

If it's a crime to sing—
Why is Quran Majid sung in a charged surrounding?
Raag, Ragini and tune
Are famed careers to commune,
There's such variation, why their conclusion's not a criminal thing?
In Arabic, Persian, or any other tongue—
Ghazal, Marsia are all sung,
When Nabiji goes to Madina, to welcome him the duff they bring.
Heaven's tunes are not a sin,
On earth, why are they unclean?
Says Duddu: 'Have you heard Fatwa against music ever ring?'

"Well, it was victory achieved in one song. The song's substance was that if music is not illegitimate in paradise, why should it be illegal on earth? It was an invincible song. And there was Bakkar's voice to go with it. Maulana' party fled. Thousands of people clamoured: let music continue the whole night. That was really quite an affair."

I said: "It's your habit to express things through songs. But one can't conquer everywhere through music. What do you do then?"

: "In most debates, arguments veer around explanation of Quran Sharif and Hadees. As for example, we're Marfati Fakirs; we believe that Allah has form, he can be seen. Maulanas don't admit this; they say Allah has no appearance. I then quote what Hazrat Mohammad Mustafa has said: –

During Qayamat, your saviour Lord will be seen—
Just as visible as this full moon has been!

"It implies that Allah will be as clearly seen as the moon of the full-moon night. What then? But there is a catch here."

: "Of what kind?"

: "What has been said here is that Allah will be as clearly visible as the full moon, but could everyone see that? No, to see Him, one has to adopt the Marfati path of ours. In an unknown path, one needs a road- guide. He's the Peer Murshid. One has to become a Bayet (disciple) to a knowledgeable Kamel Peer, only by signing a slave-bond to him and winning his heart."

For me it was virtually akin to entering a new world. As this world's subject was a grey one, so was its confusing language. But, at the end, the sense appeared clearly. Still there was a hitch. For instance, was the Murshid a mere road guide? Occasionally, he assumed an important role. Lalan Fakir, for example, said in one of his songs:

As Murshid is, so God is—
In mind, none should doubt on this!

What then? How about giving Murshid such a big recognition? There could be some confusion. Catholicity could not be universal. Instead of dragging Benowari Fakir in that argument, I pulled him to a social question, by asking: "Looking at this practice of Marfati meditation by you or Jalil or Manullah, isn't there dissent in the village society? Isn't there trouble, now that you don't ever go to the mosque?"

Benowari smiled and said: "You've hit the nail on its head. There's a conflict of mind from time to time. But then, we aren't persuading anybody to join our way. Besides, in our external behaviour, we tell everybody: 'say prayers', 'go to the mosque'. In fact, we follow our way by staying on one side of the village boundary; we don't put anybody into trouble and carry on with our music. People come in groups to listen to us."

: "But what about marriages? What about the social system?"

: "There's no difficulty. Many Muslims want to get their daughters married in our community. Do you know why?"

: "Why?"

: "There's no fear of divorce. Fakirs' children are peace-loving. Indeed, divorce is a religious torture. We hate the divorce system. We worship man. Then how can we insult man?"

:"And does the Muslim society accept your girls as brides?"

: "They adore it. Haven't you seen my Pakhi? She's hardly of marriageable age, isn't she? In spite of that, the elder uncle of one of my disciples forced me for her hands. Otherwise, he is an aristocratic Muslim, follows the Panchbena regularly."

: "What's this Panchbena?" I asked. "Even after living five or six hundred years within close proximity of Muslims, we know so little about them, have such scant knowledge. We didn't even wish to know. What's the reason behind this apathy?"

: "Your stance of screwing up your nose in contempt and our restrictive fundamentalism, are both responsible. Whatever, as you wanted to know, Panchbena, is according to scriptures, five obligatory rites for pure Muslims. These are also called Arkane Islam."

:"What are they?"

: "They're Kalma, Roza, Haj, Zakat and Namaz. Of course, there're some detailed specifications as well."

: "Such as?"

: "Such as, Namaz is fundamentally of two kinds: Jahera Namaz and Watune Namaz. The latter has no fixed timing for saying the prayers. That Namaz can continue all the time: in lying down or in dreams, everywhere. And Jahera Namaz is reading five times or Panchrokt. Their names and timings are all different. Would you like to listen?"

: "Please go on. I know nothing, having simply completed some futile formal education. I can tell you right now what the constitutional powers are of the American President; the news on Maradona's intimate details; or the quantity of India's loans from the World Bank. Otherwise..."

:"Well said," interjected the Fakir. "On what you wanted to know, the early dawn Namaz is called 'Fazar'. The Namaz at 12 noon-one o'clock is known as 'Johar'. The Namaz at three or four in the afternoon is 'Aasar'. The evening Namaz is termed 'Magreb'. And the night prayer is 'Ayesa'. Will you remember them, or, would you like to write them down. With that, write this also, in Lalan's words—

Panchrokt Namaz if reads one,
No invincibility has been won!"

: "Does it mean that you decry Namaz? Has it no value?"

: "I'm not saying that," Benowari explained for comprehension. "We want to say that the public display of

Namaz is of little consequence. The real Namaz is in the mind. Is religion achieved by sheer visits to mosque? More than that is the question: whose Namaz is this? Do we know Him? After committing injustice, sin and theft, can one read Namaz? Allah says: 'I am within you, how come you don't find me? *Afi aan phosekum aafala tofseroon.*'"

I tried to explain to Benowari: "I've understood that your religious meditation is somewhat like the *bartaman* (current reality) meditation of the Sahajiyas. They also say that *anuman* (tentative guess) is no religion. Krishna-Radha-Mathura-Vrindavan—have never been seen by me. Much more viable is man: hold on to him. Find within him Mathura-Vrindavan-Radha-Krishna. Your practices seem like that."

: 'Yes, there is a resemblance. But our principal difference from Shariat is that theirs is behavioural, while ours is based on realisation. Theirs is external faith, whereas ours is internal religion. You've seen Jalil, haven't you? He's a common illiterate farmer, working as a thatcher during leisure. When, twenty years back, he came to be initiated and guided by me, I asked him, 'Didn't the scriptural religion satisfy your mind?' He responded, 'Guru, the guesswork faith didn't fulfill my mind, I want to turn to man and meditate.' Then I initiated him."

: "Are the scriptures wrong then?"

: "Who said they're wrong? If Shariat wasn't there, would Marfat come? Do you know what Lalan Fakir once said in a debate? He said:

Shariat is my home's staircase,
Marfat is home,
Climbing the stairs
If I keep on straight,
How can I enter my home
Without my gait?

After I've done Shariat,
To Marfat I can roam!

What have you understood? Are we anti-Shariat?"

: "'No, I've understood. Marfat is not evading Shariat, it is a transcending religion. There is no Marfat without Shariat. But once Shariat is reached, one can't return to Marfat. Is my understanding correct?"

: "You've understood very clearly. Shariat and Marfat are like milk and butter. Both exist together in cohesion; but once butter is taken out, only butter-milk is left. What use is it then? That's why it's said:

For travellers along the Marfat path—
Books of scripture lie in the hearth.

"In that case what use are Haj, Roza, Zakat[7], Namaz? We've gone too far within. We can no more indulge in playing to the public. Therefore, we read the book of heart and look out for the man of our heart. If you find him, you need nothing else. There remains only Haqiqat, i.e., going along the way of Haq or Truth; and Tariqat, i.e., justice. Justice for what? It's for what I've done and what I'm doing. The one who is steeped in deep meditation is called Dervish."

There was silence for a while, for, Jalil had come to take us. Today we would have lunch at his place.

Jalil's home was the hut of a mere poor man. But there was nothing wanting in the sincerity of his service. Now he was making us seated, now fanning us with a hand-fan, or offering us palm-kernel and cold water, with molasses.

Benowari said: "It's because the poor have no external dazzle, that God remains stuck there. In the rich man's mansion, there is

7 *Zakat*: Process of sanctifying the spirit and the action of washing and cleansing it

a lot of glamour and style; so God slips out through the cracks. On this issue, there is a lot of debate between Aalems and us. Take, for instance, this Haj. Is Haj within the reach of the poor? That's why, one of our songs says:

If he's not visible here,
Anywhere else he would be rare—
For doing Haj, my mind, which Qaba do you go?
Not knowing the address of Haj,
What's the use of running to and fro?

"Do you know the real meaning of Haj? It's to draw the mind from outside and make it sit within. Jalil, why don't you tell sir the story of real Haj?"

Jalil narrated: "Once a true and God-fearing Muslim bachelor resolved to go to Mecca in the company of a few people of his village. The visit needed a lot of money, which could be collected thanks to God's mercy. Before departure, he decided to look up his bosom friend in the city, as it was not known if he could after doing the Haj. The only person on earth with whom he had any emotional bond was this friend. On reaching the friend's house, he found that he had passed away a few months back and his widow was financially under dire straits.

"The situation was like this that she had literally nothing to cook. But suddenly he got from the kitchen the whiff of cooking meat. He was surprised and wondered if his friend's wife had spun a yarn on her lack of funds, for, how could an indigent person cook meat? On enquiring, the friend's wife burst into tears and confessed that, after her children had fasted for three days, she had been to the abotaire and picked up the shank of a dead cow. While his friend's wife was cooking the shank of a dead cow collected from the abotaire, he was proceeding to Mecca for Haj by spending a lot of money! It was a shame, let Haj be shelved, thought this man! If he remained alive, he could perform many a Haj. Thinking thus, he gave away his entire money to them and returned to the village to tell the Haj-travellers that for some reason, he could not make the Haj. God willing, he would go next year.

"Here his fellow-villagers proceeded to Haj. On arrival, they seemed to spot that man everywhere and wondered what on earth was happening. Having said 'no' to them, did he travel with some other party? On return, they checked and confirmed that actually he had not gone. Then they accosted him to say: 'Brother, you performed the true Haj, not we'."

Benowari said: "This was the real meaning of Haj. If one did Khuda's work with sincerity, Haj would be accomplished. That one stood by the side of the poor, that one removed man's sorrow, was the indicator of the legitimate Haji. This confusion is there in our Zakat as well. Zakat implied gift. Yet most Muslims make a lot of pomp in Zakat. Well, because Allah has given you more, you're able to give. Then why is there such showing off? Give yourself away in his service."

I said: "I can see that there's no conflict fundamentally between orthodox instructions in Islam and your Marfati thoughts. The conflict is in explanation and practice, is that so?"

: "Exactly. But man is foremost in our eyes, for removing his mental debris. Take, for instance, our concept of Zakat. Zakat is of two kinds—Watuni and Jaheri. Watun means secret. One's favourite object has to be consecrated in Allah's way. Could you tell me what one's favourite object is?"

: "That can't be fixed, can it? Each one has it in one's own way. For instance, we Hindus have a custom that if you go to Kashi, Puri, Haridwar, Pushkar, etc., some object of one's temptation has to be given away to the Ganga or the sea. Someone throws away the mango, another throws the banana. The idea is that he won't eat that item for the rest of his life. I've also heard about funny matters on this count. For example, one person didn't like sour solutions of tamarind and hog-plum. He went to the Ganga of Kashi and consecrated to it both tamarind and hog-plum, exclaiming, 'Oh my god, I'm relieved now!'

"There's this one problem in our Hindu faith, there is little solemnity. We do have a habit to play with our religion. Indeed, these are not parts of observing the religion, but maintaining some rituals. If one pressurises somebody with a ritual by force, there's bound to be taunt and sarcasm about it. That's why in the interiors of all our homes, there's constant conflict. If the ladies say this ought to be done, we remonstrate that we won't do it. But perhaps I haven't properly replied to you. Do tell me truly what our favourite thing is."

: "Desire for our own happiness. This is what can be called self-gratification. Think it over; whatever we do has at its root self-gratification. If we pay a single coin to a beggar, there's self-gratification behind it. Avarice, possession, lust, luxury: they're all undoubtedly for self-gratification; even self-sacrifice is also a gratification. Discarding self-gratification is very hard. That's why it's said:

If self-gratification is there—
Inspiration will be truly rare!

Let me repeat again that to dispense with all forms of self-gratification is a mighty hard task. This is because some people feel happy by undergoing suffering. Even in renunciation, there can be self-gratification. That is one can see: how I've renounced everything! There's a very nice story about it, would you like to hear it?"

: "I've come here only to listen to everything!"

Making himself comfortable and relaxed, Benowari said: "Then listen. Jalil, you too hear this; I haven't told you before. Once,

Hazrat Mohammad had sat in meditation. After a long spell of meditation, Allah the Great bestowed him three things—poison, honey and attar ('itr' in Arabic). The poison was truly a deadly one. So he told his disciples: 'Have these what Allah the Great sent honey and attar for you. Drink honey to your fill and let attar make life around you aound life fragrant.' But he kept the poison for himself. That was just right; but even then there was a problem."

Jalil said: "What was the problem? He had kept the bad for himself and given away the good."

: "Even I didn't understand the matter earlier. During youth, when I had been to Mohammad Shah for initiation into the Sufi faith, the story came up once. At the end of the parable, Mohammad Shah said: 'Hazrat Mohammad no doubt kept the poison for himself; on that gesture, the disciple commented later that he took the sorrow and left for us the pleasure. Was that right to do? Even we seek to have sorrow. Hazrat deprived us of sorrow. Without sorrow, could we ever reach Allah the Great?' I was taken aback after listening to this explanation from Mohammad Shah. From then on, I realised what self-gratification was. To suffer oneself is also a great pleasure. What an unique arrangement this was, by Allah!"

I admitted: "It's a beautiful story; the definition of self-gratification was also a novel one. So it's clear that Watuni Zakat means to give away one's favourite thing. But what does Jaheri Zakat imply?"

: "Jaheri signifies according to us, the gift of only the one-fortieth part. You would notice during Jumma's Namaz that the devoted Muslims were giving alms to the poor, the miserable and the hapless ones: queuing outside the mosque. It's a job of great piety. But merely giving alms won't be enough. As a matter of fact, Jaheri Zakat has yet another meaning. According to us, Allah has given birth to us, after adding forty kinds of matter for our body to store. Take recourse to Murshid, to Murid, and give away, as

Zakat, the one-fortieth part of the special love of one's own along God's path."

I realised from Benowari Fakir's words that folk religion always followed a parallel path to the mainstream religious analysis. Outside the revelations from the scriptures and dictates of the priests, a marginal, yet powerful, world-view furnished the sap of soul to the roots of folk religion. It showed the right way with great precision, outside the vacuity of surmised dialogues. Not many people would be attracted to this path. But those few that congregated came only after logical verification, and did not vitiate thereafter. That Namaz was not real – *'By forgetting own self best / And merely looking to West'* – as per Duddu's dictates would never be explained to the majority of the people; *'Doing sejda, yet form not find / Is nothing but being stark blind'* would invite blows of the lathi on the head, if proclaimed in public.

The deep alleys of Benowaris over a few centuries, therefore had tried to mingle with the feelings of perceptive men and open-minded intelligence. It got blocked countless times and invited insult and body-blows. Tired, yet relentless, was that human sojourn. Truly, that path was a very lonely one; like this quiet afternoon at Mathpukur village. The whole village appeared to have fallen into a drowsy stupor. Only a dove or two cooed incessantly.

A full day passed in leisure and half-sleep; trails of thoughts leading to fragments of ruminations. In the adjacent room was Benowari who, after his rest, came and sat on my balcony. His face was serene and silent in meditation, with a pair of eyes and piercing gaze. It could be realised that the under-currents of his mind were busy in action. Apparently, the Sufi thought-system was intermingled with the deep interiors of the Fakiri principles. Jahan Fakir of Satgechhiya once had told me: "The main activity of the Sufis is to look for the principles or truth of Allah who creates, nurtures and destroys us." Was at this moment, Benowari immersed in that contemplation? Otherwise, why did he have such a far-away gaze?

I asked Jalil in a whisper: "Your guru doesn't seem to belong to this world. What's he meditating upon?"

Jalil told me in a very low voice: "Baba is observing Roza; this is the month of Ramjan."

I was startled. How come Roza was observed after so much of conversation and debate on Shariat? Besides, what kind of Roza was this? Just in the afternoon, he had a full plate of rice along with me. What then? My mind became full of doubts. After a while, he belched heavily with a crackling of fingers and looked at me questioningly. The mood was as if to enquire if I had any special question. Of course, I had a question, but was temporarily a bit rattled at the breathing excercises practised by the Kaderia Fakirs. Getting over it in a while, I asked: "Do you believe in Roza?"

Smiling pleasantly, Benowari said: "I am a believer in everything: Kalma, Roza, Haj, Zakat, Namaz; but my expression is different. Our activity goes on within. Allah's apartment is in the interior chamber of our heart. To go there is my Haj; my beliefs reposted there is my Kalma; my Wateni Namaz continues there; I've given my *nafs* the Zakat; and there's my Chhiyam of Roza."

: "Does Chhiyam mean fasting?"

: "It's austerity with fasting. Roza is keeping *nafs* in control. To fast during the day and gorge at night: that's the practice of a bat. Maintaining Roza outside and nurturing lust within is not real Roza. I fast for the whole day, but retain violence, jealousy and envy in the mind is spoiling the Roza of one's mind. By Roza, we mean self-regulation."

I kept looking at the man enjoying perpetual mental calm in amazement. It was as though his words were emanating from some complex source of wisdom of consciousness. It was as if the same distress of Allah was on the Fakir's face that expressed the message: "I'm within you, yet you don't seem to notice me." The person was sitting next to me, but appeared to have gone far away. What a wonder! Was this the same affectionate person looking after Pakhi? Was there such power inside the meditative contemplation? Perhaps this was called the realised condition. Jalil whispered in my ears in a deep voice: "Sir, his Shariat has been accomplished. Now he's on the asphalt road of Marfat, having climbed straight to fulfillment. Offer *sejda* to him."

I rose to my feet with respect and saluted him.

The sun was about to set. I bid farewell to the village of Mathpukur awash and glowing in crimson hues. I pleaded for the last time with Benowari Fakir: "I'm leaving for the present. I don't know when I'll be back again. Do speak out your last words. What have you received? What have you realised? Which final words of yours shall I fill up my mind with, while returning home?"'

Virtually like an angel, Benowari rose in great style and said: "That you can't know him is the ultimate knowledge. The ever sacred Allah hasn't kept open the road to reach him to his creation—mankind. Only one road is open— and that is the road never to know him."

After travelling for quite a distance and reaching almost the boundary of Mathpukur village, I looked back once towards Jalil's home. It was a cottage located beyond the paddy-fields stretching to the horizon. Against this backdrop was etched out a clear silhouette of two men.

Residents of a separate distinct world

Those Sahajiyas, who identify the body and the soul, have their main point as worship of the humankind. They often refer to their activity as 'catching man'. The question is: which man one should aspire to catch and who the real man of the soul is. They say mysteriously: what choice need be there among men, for, all men are the same. What can be got from one, you cannot apparently surmise ahead. A formal illustration of this was given by a Dervish, named Jehan. He had a colourful robe on, with a bizarre cap on his head. Around his throat were a piece of stone and a few necklaces of odd kinds. In his hands were *khelka, karoa* boat and a pair of tongs. He was sitting with eyes closed in meditation, in the Lalan Fakir graveyard at Chheunria in Kushtia. Evening fell. The graveyard, with its massive pillars and domes of the mausoleum, had the lacklustre rays of the setting sun illuminating the entire prayer-building with a faint glow. Just as the bright tones of a colourful bird died out in falling light, the Dervish's robe and the splendid glow of his necklaces lost their sheen to a pale silhouette. Slowly the winter evening descended wearing its dark shroud. At that moment, Jehan Dervish construed an original piece of thought, borne out of the amazing wealth of folk beliefs and philosophy. He asked: "Have you seen a spindle of thread? Likewise, everything has a spindle at its source; nothing is completely exhausted. With the pull, the next portion arrives. Man is quite similar to this. Whose tug pulls whom is a completely indeterminate factor."

It would be astonishing to think now that I got the proof of the Dervish's saying a few days later in the Moroldanga Poush Sankranti fair under Gaighata police station. Roaming there, I felt ravenously hungry. I chanced upon a large sweetmeat shop, which was frying hot Dhakai pancakes and honey-sweet wheel-shaped *jilipi*s (*jalebi*s).

It was a makeshift shop with an unsteady high-bench and wooden chairs. Water was served in tin-glasses and food on lotus-leaves. At my nose's level stood a cavernous clay oven, where the unique art of making fried, juicy circles of *amriti* and *jilipi* was virtually on display – with the 'craftsman' pressing a thick piece of cloth. He was a middle-aged, unshaven man, with white specks of stubble on his cheeks collected over the last five or six days. Watching the man's earnest devotion in creating concentric circles of his juicy *jilipi*s made me keen to talk to him. There it was, the spindle got pulled and was out! This was Manmatha Adhikari from the Ukhra enclave in the township of Haringhata. A baptised Vaishnavite, his family at home comprised a widowed sister with three siblings. "I haven't married, sir, I roam from fair to fair every year, barring the rainy season with this work. I keep observing people; time passes well. During the rains, I work around Harninghata as a hired cook. I manage with whatever work I get, catering food at weddings, the sacred thread ceremony, funerals and prayer meetings. There has been a recent addition of two more feasts: wedding anniversaries and birthday parties. With all these, I manage to survive."

This was what could be called, a pure 'perambulating trade'. One had to collect a basic capital, a few workers, some utensils, chairs and benches, bamboo and a tent-house. The rest of the job was only going round: from one fair to another. The schedule was fixed according to the lunar calendar. The owner was

Jogeshchandra Debnath, formerly of Barishal, wearing a cotton vest, aged around sixty, expelling worldly experience and cunning. On being asked, he quickly gave the list of fairs: "Take first, say, this Gaighata Paush Sankranti fair, which would run for one month. From here we go to Deorar fair or Yamuna fair in Swarupnagar police station during Maghi Purnima. From there it's on to Baruni fair in Thakurnagar on Chaitra Ekadashi. From there it is on to Jaleshwar fair in Gaighata on Chaitra Sankranti. Going like this, it would end at Banpur Matiari as the Ambubachi fair in the month of Ashadh. Leaving out the two months of rain, the season would start again in Ashwin."

Serving two concentric rings of freshly-fried hot *jilipi*s on the lotus leaf held in my hands, Manmatha Adhikari said: "Mercy be to Gouranga, I've seen some seventy-eighty fairs, by working with many owners in the last twenty years: what crowds of people, what happenings, how many businessmen, what scandals, how many storms, how much unnecessary fracas! But, all said and done, these were all very nice and happy events. Whatever you say, it is all Gouranga's game!"

In like manner, Manmatha Adhikari used the two phrases "mercy to Gouranga" and "game of Gouranga", as endless interjections to endear himself with me. In course of conversation, the spindle of contexts got unwinded.The man was easily capable of moving from one context to quite a contrary one. Utilising that opportunity, I opened up a question, long since concealed in mind: "With this business of leaving hearth and home for five-six months at a stretch, does everyone observe abstinence? There's the physical need of the body, isn't there?"

Biting his tongue, Manmatha said: "'Of course. In the game of Gouranga, all the confusion remains only with the body. Yes, in all fairs there's arrangement for that as well. Those special women are, of course, present. They put surma in their eyes, tinkle the anklets on their feet and walk past us to make their presence felt in good time. Whoever has the need, contacts them. These concealed arrangements are prevalent in all the fairs barring the Agradweep fair."

: "Why has that fair been suddenly excluded?"

: "'Mercy to Gouranga. That fair is the most sacred and pure of them all. Once you're there, you've to discard all evil thoughts and lust. That fair has a great air of piety. Would you like to know what kind of piety there is? Listen then. In the game of Gouranga, three hundred thousand people visit the Agradweep fair in three days; but you would notice no crow, no dog, no storm or rains ever raging there. There're deeper philosophies at work. Would you like to visit? Then I could give you all the clues and the directions. Sir, the Agradweep fair is the oldest of all."

I asked: "Mercy to Gouranga, who initiated the Agradweep fair?"

Manmatha waved his hands in the air, to say: "Oh, it's the play of Gouranga. Indeed, the Agradweep fair is the creation of Gouranga himself. It began with him."

I got startled: "Is that so? Did Gouranga himself found the Agradweep fair?"

Like a humble Vaishnavite, Manmatha replied: "'Yes, sir. In the game of Gouranga and as ordained by Him, I didn't have an education and remained an illiterate man. Yet, in my guru's portal Patuli, *Amiya Nimai Charit* is regularly read. There – and in the sacred words of my guru – I heard that Sri Gouranga himself had established the idol of Gopinath Jiu at the same site through his companion Gobinda Ghosh.The fair is held for three days around the Gopinath temple at Agradweep at the time of Baruni. It's called Aam-Baruni. I've been there many times with my shop."

: "When does Aam-Baruni occur?"

: "Sir, it's the Madhu-Krishna time, that is, the spring-time in Gouranga's game, that is, what's called the new-moon's eleventh day in the month of Chaitra, when the fair starts."

: "How do you reach there?"

: "You've to go by rail from Nabadweepdham station. The station before Katowa is Dainhat, and before that comes Agradweep. A couple of miles to the station's east is the Ganga. Gopinath's temple is across the Ganga. There is some arduous travel involved, in the game of Gouranga. He gets the devotee tested a little, no doubt. Nonetheless, do go once."

It was customary for me to collect some facts before the journey. The writing by Peterson in the Gazetteer from Bardhaman district appeared somewhat soulless:

> Agradweep is a famous place of pilgrimage and contains a temple of Gopinath, at which some ten thousand pilgrims gather every April.

A livelier description came from the verses of *Tirthamangal* by Bijayram. In the Bengali year 1,171 – that is, more than 200 years earlier – Bijayram had gone on pilgrimage with Jaynarayan Ghoshal, the king of Bhukailash. While returning from Tristhali, they alighted at Agradweep. They were delighted to see the Gopinath temple. Bijayram wrote:

We arrived at Agradweep then.
Gopinath icon's abode is there:
An excellent creation, looks very fair.

History recorded that three original temples of Agradweep were now on the Ganga's bed. The present construction was made by Krishnachandra, the king of Nadia district.

But why would the Nadia king Krishnachandra build a temple in Bardhaman without a good reason? From the spindle of this question came up another engrossing story. At the time of King

Raghuram, the father of King Krishnachandra, there was a huge riot at the Agradweep fair. A few people were killed, too. On receiving this news, the representative of Nawab Alibardi sent summons to the kings of Bardhaman and Nadia, and to the zamindar of Patuli. Each sent his respective representative. The angry Nawab began the talks with a basic query about the jurisdiction under which Agradweep fell. In sheer fright, Bardhaman and Patuli officials kept silent. Grabbing the opportunity, the shrewd Nadia representative said: "Agradweep was indeed under the king of Nadia. For various reasons, there has been a grievous mistake this time. Sir, there would never be such a riot again."

That was that, the crime was pardoned. Simultaneously, Gopinath of Agradweep came under the aegis of King Raghuram. Since then till today, Gopinath stayed in the palace of Krishnanagar at least six months a year. Was this apparently the administration of the then Nawabs?

A fairly old reference of Agradweep was available in the book *Jagannath Charitamrita* by the Oriya poet Dibakar Das. The book, written in the 17th century, stated in Oriya language:

To Agradweep Ghat if you go—
Sri Ghosh Gosain there you'll know.

This Sri Ghosh Gosain was Gobinda Ghosh; many people still called the fair as 'Ghosh Thakur's fair' after his name.

That such a distinguished person as Dulalchand, aka Lalshashi the famous leader of the Kartabhajas of Ghoshpara, had been to the Agradweep fair was proved by a mention in his song:

Once I went to see the
festival of Agradweep—
Many men-women they came to its den:
Their account you can't keep!

Rummaging through these annals, one could get a description of several established Sahajiyas. Even a more delicious narrative came from the writings of Kubir Gosain, the Sahebdhani songster:

Those shaven-headed men-women at Ghosh's bay
Stomach all the food-offerings twice a day;
Ramat-Nimat, the abstinent lads,
Aaul-Baul, the loin-cloth clads,
Ones with purist fads sacred beads, count away.
Stoic Dervish and Gosain
The smoking hermit Nitai:
Crazy always: on hemp to stay.

On the other side, the oval-portrait of philandering men and women of the Sahajiyas was also none the less attractive. One could see there—

On all sides, lover-women move around—
Calling anyone they see as: 'Come, soul-mate', a-whirling;
As per choice, if one's found,
Counting-garland's put on shoulder round,
Beckoning: 'hold, hold', as much as you can,
To your utmost wish, serve in amour's span!

Of course, I was unaware of the bad features about the Agradweep fair.

On the other hand, the visual love story of philandering love-obsessed Sahajiya men and women was also no less attractive. One could see there—

Love traders all, the women winded up and down—
'Come, my heart, my mate,' they shout to anyone they see in town,

As per choice, if one's found,
The rosary necklace put on shoulder round,
'Catch and hold on tight, if you can',
To your utmost wish, serve in amour's span!

Of course, I was unaware of the bad features about the Agradweep fair. I was intimated about this by a farsighted Fakir. He said: "Many kinds of people come to the fair with many intentions. All are not honest among them. Con-men, cheats, pimp, lascivious and evil men are, of course, there. There's, therefore, a saying about Agradweep fair in common parlance: *'The Agradweep fair / who pushes whom in the rear!'* That is, even obscene activities are on at that place. I, therefore, don't visit Agradweep any longer. The youth from the neighbouring villages come to the fair and indulge in obscene activities. The prestige of that fair has sunk."

I am not aware of any sociological study on Bengal's fairs. Had it been done, one could have obtained a picture of the society's evolution from the progressive change of the size, quality and characteristics of the fairs. For instance, it could be seen that the pen-picture that Dinendrakumar Roy drew eighty years ago in his book *Palli-Chitra* after witnessing the fair evolved around the bath-rituals at Murutia was substantially different from its present form. He wrote:

> The 'shops' of sex-workers were the principal feature of the fairs of this region. The more they come, the more is the income of the zamindars. Hence they enclose a portion of the fair for them. They are the scandal of the fair. I have heard that without granting their right to entry, the fair does not take off. Each sex-worker has opened a 'tonge', three to four cubits long, for their beauty business. There are a few hundred such 'tonge's on one side of the fair. Some three hundred sex-workers from different areas have arrived in the lure of

> earning money....Looking for their prospective targets, many are roaming around the site of the fair accompanied by loud tinkles of four pairs of their anklets and swaying many a thirsty heart of farmers, soldiers and cash-salesmen. In the crowded jungle of humanity, their delicate female forms appear as snakes and tigresses.

The sex-business patronised by zamindars no longer thrived in most fairs. There was no longer a cordoned space for the sex trade in the fairs. The *tonges* and hundreds of sex-workers milling about were now quite unimaginable. The reason for this is that the sex trade has become urban-centric and not too open. Yet in the olden days, people from villages with an agricultural economy were initiated into sex perhaps at the fairs. That was why there was still a respectful regard for the village fairs in the civil society. In the fairs of those days, quite a few girls got lost forever.

Let that be. But among the few elements that I did not know lay a major feature by which the name 'Gopinath' became 'Gupinath'. It was a matter of vowel mutation. I also did not know that the pronunciation of Agradweep would become 'Raggadweep' due to the rusticity of some regions. This I came to know when I was going for the first time to Agradweep from a stoic among the fellow-passengers in the train, who asked me: "Sir, are you also travelling to Raggadweep like us? Let's go. On other occasions, we had taken the river route; this time we're riding the 'ail'."

'Ail' meant 'rail'. It was an amazing alphabetic and phonetic arrangement of exchanges. 'Rail' became 'ail', while Agradweep was transmuted into 'Raggadweep'. Whatever, that was my first trip to see Gopinath of 'Raggadweep' by 'riding the '*ail*'. The station where the 'ail' stopped was named Agradweep, although the place was not called Agradweep. The place was Bahra. Agradweep was a village two-and-a- half miles away to the east of Bahra. The two villages were bifurcated by the Ganga. So the station was named after a village two-and-a-half miles away from the place! Perhaps this was the greatness of Agradweep.

It was in the middle of Chaitra, so the ground heated up by ten in the morning. Added to it was the vast strtetch of the dry sandy river bed. It was almost a mile-wide sand dune and proved to be quite an ordeal on the path of devotion, thanks to the mercy of Gouranga. But one did not feel the tiredness so much, as such a crowd of people travelled together and their continuous prattle livened up the journey. If one felt too thirsty, one could buy fresh palm juice. Or one would buy on the sand-stretch *bakhari*, which is a variety of an elongated green melon: juicy and cool. Someone went, carrying on the head a sweet pumpkin. In reply to the query: "Would you sell it?" she replied: "Not really, it's the first product of the plant. It would be offered to Gupinath." Out of the whole lot of pilgrims, three-fourth comprised women. From the dialect of most of the people, one could guess that they were from East Bengal. What was the matter? How come so many people from East Bengal were in Agradweep, in Gangetic West Bengal?

How did it happen?

From the spindle of this curiosity, another mystery got disentangled. Most of the lower-class men from East Bengal were devoted to Gouranga. At the time of Partition, many of them opted for the 'land of Gouranga', that's Nabadweep and its surroundings. Many had not noticed that the village fairs in West Bengal, which were associated with Krishna, were flourishing. It also went past notice that most of the other fairs were on their terminal state of survival. For, from village to village, there was these days such an efficient distribution system – thanks to tempos and matadors – that there was scarcely much to buy from fairs by the village folks. Fairs were now only for entertainment and by convention they followed narrow rituals and incidental ceremonies. But Agradweep's grandeur was something different.

It attracted hordes of people. The ferry service with ten boats on offer could not cope with the crowds crossing the river.

While travelling, it seemed as if everyone was in a great hurry to reach the destination; rushing and running along. "Shall we reach in time?" "Aren't we delayed already?" "What was the right time?"... When asked, "Why this mad rush?", someone replied: "The funeral will be over by eleven o'clock, hence such hurry."

: "Funeral? Whose funeral was it?"

: "You haven't been there earlier, have you? Funeral means Ghosh Thakur's funeral."

: "Does Ghosh Thakur mean Gobinda Ghosh? Who conducts his funeral?"

: "Who else, but our Gupinath himself. Today Gupinath will be suitably dressed in the traditional loin cloth *kachha* to conduct the funeral of Ghosh Thakur. Get moving, hurry up."

The breathless rush of this crowd was not something I could keep up with, nor perhaps did I want to. To my mind, such events at most created curiosity and fun. Could I, by any chance, remember that there would be Madhukrishna Ekadashi by the middle of April? Or, could there be a call of Aam-Baruni in my life? Yet, the rapidly-moving devotional crowd – rushing with me – remembered every such date separately and kept a count of them. This mad rush of theirs to witness the funeral ceremony of Ghosh Thakur and their dangerous leap to get on the ferry boat had a mental pull, of which – if properly counted and weighed – there was not even the tiniest fraction in the depth of my mind. Were they then the *'inhabitants of a separate, another clearly-drawn world'*, as described by the poet Jibanananda? They were undoubtedly separate. Because, in this huge solar world, their life of unassailable devotion and faith was entirely different from our kind of struggle for everyday existence It was clearly drawn, because their target was fixed, belief pure, behaviour determined and movement strictly along the path of devotion. They had no doubt or suspicion in their way. Two middle-aged widows were walking behind me, discussing various topics. One serious issue in their discussion was the selection of a proper guru. If there was a mistake in the choice of guru, there could apparently be an immediate disaster. One of them was telling the other: "I won't be able to keep company of a guru like Kalo's sister: by jumping around." Listening to that, it occurred to me that if jumping around was meant literally, it could imply the mental turmoil of Kalo's sister. That is, she was frequently changing her gurus, which was bad.

Replying to this the other lady said: "Is it easy to gain a guru? First of all, you've to gather respect by hearing about the holy man from the people. Then you are tempted to have the company of the holy man. From there on you have the pure company, leading to your perceiving the holy man as your guru. At the root of all this is the guru's message. I've finally acquired a guru. Well, dear, have you attained peace by having a guru?"

: "Yes, a lot of peace. Otherwise, why should I be running up to him so eagerly? I'm not all that tempted to see Gupinath. My guru has gone there; he has directed me; so I'm going. Do you know what my inner sorrow is? I haven't been able to perceive him as my own yet. But he has accepted me as his own."

Hearing all this, I could only be aware of their distinctly separate existence. I retraced a few of my steps and could not but ask: "Who is your guru? Where does he live?"

"Oh, my dear, have you overheard all that we were saying? What a shame! Let it be. Sir, our guru's name is Gagan Bairagya. Guru's aide is at Bamundanga. He has come here to arrange a festival. Do please come to our site; you'll get a lot of peace. Our guru is a simple man of utter peace. How would you recognise the cluster? Ask people the directions to the portal of Charan Pal. Here the Charan Pal portal is very well-known. My guru's portal is at its west under the pituli tree. O dear boy, do please come!"

Giving my consent, I advanced. I was feeling quite tired. It would have been nice to be able to sit down. But where could I sit on the hot sand-dune? Finally we reached the banks of the Ganga. We were to walk another quarter of a mile to reach the crossing ghat. At the moment, many people were bathing by the river. Chilly breeze was blowing. I found one Vaishnavi who had finished bathing and was painting ritual marks on her face, nose and forehead by holding up a small mirror. Beside her, her aged Vaishnava consort was smoking hemp. I sought this man out separately to talk to him. The man offered me a seat on the corner of his durrie. Ah, what peace!

Now began my urban series of inane questions. Which sect of the Vaishnavites did you belong to? Which was your system? Did it belong to Madhavacharya or Nimbarka or Ramanuja? Where was your guru-portal? The man had a smile of pity reserved for me behind his beard and moustache. He said: "Are all Vaishnavas the same? We're the Raat-tahaliyas (night-roamers). Did you understand?"

: "Night-roamers—what does it mean?"

: "It means our job involves roaming all night and singing God's name."

: "I haven't heard about it before. I've heard that there are two types of Vaishnavas: ceremonial Vaishnavas and Sahajiya Vaishnavas. Are there many more sects?"

: "Of course, there are. There are many not even known to me. And those known Vaishnavas would also be too many for you to digest. Listen. Outside the orbit of formal Vaishnavas and Sahajiya Vaishnavas, sects known to me, there are the Radhashyamis; Roopkaviraji; Radhaballavi; Haribola; Gurudasi Vaishnava; Khandita Vaishnava; Karan Vaishnava; Chamar Vaishnava; Kishoribhajani; Gaurbadi and our Raat-tahaliya."

: "Where do they all live? How do you recognise them?"

: "They're known by their symptoms. Their ritual activities are different; seed-chants are different; they've separate spaces assigned to them in fairs and festivals. Take, for instance, ourselves: our assigning the seed-chant and exchange of holy necklaces (marriage-vows) take place in Mohanpur Kenduli."

By then, the Vaishnavi had finished putting her ritual marks and even stamping the whole body with the 'Gaur' imprint. Those ritual marks stood out starkly on her dark skin. She threw a furtive erotic glance at me, which clearly bore the unmistakable marks of a permissive society outside our known social system. I sprang up and asked: "How long back did you exchange your holy necklaces and enter into bonded companionship?"

Revealing her thoroughly-blackened denture – resembling the black seeds of the custard-apple – the Vaishnavi said: "It was only recently in the month of Paush that we have exchanged the holy necklaces. Can't you make out by watching our fresh and nascent courtship? Do please sit down. Have a few sweet crunchy *batashas*[8] and water. Oh, you are drenched in sweat!"

It was difficult to reconcile to this nascent courtship between the middle aged man and the young woman. The girl must have put many a Vaishnava to perdition. I was, of course, cautious in my own interest. The Vaishnava holy man appeared most indifferent and stoic, puffing at his hemp. Any hint from the mundane world would at the moment be most worthless to him. By sincerely offering me sweet batasha and some Ganga-water on a brass-plate, the Vaishnavi settled down to plait her hair. She was also humming a song alongside. The scandalous words of the lyric (*'piriti'/piriti'* meaning 'love') took my breath away:

Friend, 'pi-ri-ti' has letters three—
Piriti's adoration is to be known: for its signs to see!

8 *Batasha*: sugar or jaggery candy

Love-shafts fly from eye to eye—
Then is born 'pi'!
Lips do touch: sip nectar much—
Then is born 'ri'!
From heart to heart emotions dart—
Then is born 'ti'!

At the end of the song, there was another fatal glance! Somehow surviving that shaft, I rose. The ghat was nearby. I had to cross the river.

On reaching the temple, it was discovered that the funeral ceremony was over. Someone said: "You've been too late, dear! The funeral is over for this occasion. You couldn't observe it. You don't have guru's strength. So what can you do? Today is the carnival of *chinre,* the flattened rice. Do sit at our portal and have some flattened rice and curd."

Next to the precincts of the Gopinath temple was Gobinda Ghosh's social chamber. It meant Gobinda Ghosh's tomb. On the morning of the funeral, Gopinath was apparently carried in there in his loin-cloth. In his hands were given sacramental rice and sacred grass. After a while, it slipped down, amidst a resounding clamour of the devotees, belonging mainly to the cowherd community. On all four sides of the fair complex, there were countless people.

Advancing from there, I walked up the stairs of the temple and looked inside. There was a most beautiful Krishna icon, made of touchstone: with a loin-cloth very smartly tucked up. There were plenty of Krishna temples all over India, but nobody had heard him performing his devotee's funeral ceremony wearing a loin-cloth in the traditional funeral style. The priest was resting by himself on one side of the temple. I badgered him with many questions. His reply came straight: "This is the height of God's affection for his devotee, and hasn't happened elsewhere in the world. The icon that you see was made by Vishwakarma with his own hands. Made of touchstone, the icon has its two eyes made from conch-shell."

I was not keen to hit the man from the believing world on a day like today. So I changed the subject and asked: "Have you been Gopinath's priest for generations?"

: "Not quite; from what I've heard, Nityananda Bhattacharjee was the first priest at the time of king Raghuram. From his hands the priesthood came to our clan. We belong to Bahra on the other side of the river. In our family, Gopinath's first priest was Madhusudan. His son was Trayonidhi, whose son was Trilochan. His son was Tarapada, who was Shyamapada's father. I'm his son. So how many generations are there: six? For these six generations, we're worshipping Gopinath."

: "Do you think your son too would become Gopinath's priest?"

: "Tell me, how can I say?" said the priest. "Even I'm not supposed to do this work. I was working in the Bengal Pottery. Did I ever think of settling down here in the temple in an empty field?"

: "How did you become the priest?"

: "It was my father who was the practising priest. Suddenly he took ill and sent me a telegram. I took leave and managed the daily prayers and temple services for a few days. But father didn't get too well. Then he said: 'Do take up the responsibility of the service. Everything said and done, Gupinath is like a son of the household.' I couldn't violate his wish, and stayed put. Four-five years have passed already."

: "How do you find it?"

: "At first I felt awfully bad. My mind was forever missing the life of Calcutta. This place's nothing more than an open ground. There are no residents in the neighbourhood. Only Gopinath and I were the sole inhabitants. Rarely did pilgrims or devotees appear.

Otherwise, I'm alone for the whole day, even during the night. I offer food-services; perform the routine session of worship; offer the afternoon and evening services. Besides, there's the child food-service to be taken care of. I go home perhaps once a month. I just manage to survive."

: "You don't feel so bad now, do you?"

: "Gupinath is there, isn't he? Now the heart has settled down. There's a kind of attraction, you could say; I don't get peace anywhere. I keep worrying about him, perhaps he's not being looked after well. I keep worrying when I'd return, and crave to see him for a while."

: "What's the reason, you think?"

: "What reason could there be? Everything is Gupinath's illusion. He's a powerful and dangerous being. This is a divine game in human guise. Sometimes I wake up in the night and find a delightful fragrance of flowers all around me. Yet, where are the flowers? At times in the dead of the night, I hear the sound of the latch opening in Gupinath's chamber, or it's being closed. It seems that he goes somewhere in the night, returning again towards the morning. I perceive it."

I kept looking at the priest, inhabitant of a separate and distinct world, and could not touch the bottom of my amazement. I could not possibly ask him why the omnipotent, omnipresent God would need opening any latch to go anywhere. Instead, I sought to know: "You were telling me about God's powers as a mortal, what was the incident?"

: "I see that you don't seem to know the event of Ghosh Thakur," said the priest with some compassion. "Listen then. Gobinda, Basudev and Madhav Ghosh were three sons of a Kayastha clan from the north-western plains of Gangetic Bengal. Their house was in a village called Kulai on the banks of the Ajay river near Katowa. They were companions of Sri Gouranga. It is written in the Adi Khanda of *Chaitanya Charitamrita*:

Govinda, Madhav, Basudev: three brothers dear
In their keertan dance, had Sri Chaitanya near.

So, once Chaitanya was travelling towards Ramkeli, together with Govinda Ghosh and other compatriots. Their custom was that they had lunch in whichever village they were crossing when it touched noon. In one of the villages after a mid-day meal, Mahaprabhu said: 'I could do with some mouth-freshener.' Immediately, Gobinda collected a piece of black myrobalan, gave him and kept a portion with himself. Next day, Mahaprabhu's entourage reached Agradweep. There, after the midday meal was over, Gobinda offered the remaining portion of the mouth-freshener. Prabhu was taken by surprise: 'How did you get it?' When he heard that this was the remnant from the previous day, he shook his head: 'No. Gobinda, you don't qualify for ascetism. You're still to get over your desire for hoarding. You should become a householder, get married and stay here.'

"What could he do, it was Prabhu's order. He stayed on. One day, Gobinda was taking a bath in the Ganga when he felt something floating by and touching his body. He first thought it was a piece of burnt wood from the cremation grounds. No, an inner voice told him that it was Brahmashila – a sacred stone– and that he should pick it up and bring it home. Prabhu had come back again. The sculptor carved out an icon with that stone. Mahaprabhu himself placed Gopinath in the thatched hut of Gobinda. This is the same Gopinath."

The priest stopped. I said: "But then you mentioned this icon was made by Vishwakarma?"

The irritated priest shot back: "Of course, it was Vishwakarma, in the garb of a man. Did you know that because they made the icon of Gopinath, the sculptors of Dainhat are so respected? Whatever that is, Gobinda was married then. He continued the worshipping service. Gradually a son was born. Meanwhile, his wife died suddenly. On the one hand was the rearing of the child; on the other, the worship of Gopinath. Gobinda could not manage both; things went haywire. Then at the age of five, the boy died. Gobinda went almost crazy in grief. He thought he could not become an ascetic and prayed to Gopinath: 'At your behest, I became a householder. You took away my wife; you snatched away my only son. Well, your prayer service shall be stopped. I shall not feed you. I won't eat myself; I shall kill myself. Let me see your justice.' Then the miracle happened."

: "Which miracle?"

: "Gopinath apppeared and said: 'Don't you have a vestige of mercy? If one son had died by a quirk of circumstances, would you starve to death the other son, too?' Gobinda sat up and exclaimed: 'Are you my son? Had my son been there, he would have done the funeral ceremonies. Will you do them?' 'Yes, I will, here's my word of honour.' Since then, the funeral ceremony of Ghosh-Thakur has been continuing. Every year, he dons the *kachha* – the special loin-cloth for three days – and performs the ceremony on the eleventh day."

: "Why for three days?" I wanted to know.

: "Vaishnava funerals are held for three days. But did you catch the real thing? Could you notice the actual grace of the benevolent God?"

: "What's it?"

: "If Gobinda Ghosh's own son were alive, he would have at most performed the ceremony for the few years he would be alive. But the merciful God here is performing the ceremony for 500 years. As long as the creation lasts, Gupinath will offer sacramental rice for the Ghosh-Thakur's funeral. Is it an easy matter? That's why this place has such a glory. So many people congregate! All kinds of holy men, ascetics, Bauls, Bairagis, Dervishes, liberated persons gather here. It's here that Charan Pal received his Deendayal. That's why on that north point is Charan Pal's 'portal' located every year. Do go and look it up."

I advanced to the north. Truly on the river-bank was Charan Pal's portal. A Fakir was sitting there, with a meditator in front, dressed in red robes. Innumerable men and women were offering curd, flattened rice, banana and puffed rice. For, it was the *chinre* carnival—the festival of flattened rice.

Although I knew all this, still I took the opportunity of asking somebody: "Do you know about the incident of Charan Pal coming here and receiving his Deendayal? Also, who is Deendayal?"

The man said: "Deendayal, friend of the poor, is the name of our worshipped lord, the Sahebdhanis. And Charan Pal was one of the earliest gurus in the clan of our gurus. His residence was in Dogachhiya in Nadia district. Once he was tending the cattle in the pasture.Then an ascetic came and asked for a drink of milk. There were only calves and bullocks among the cattle. There was just one sterile cow. So Charan asked: 'Where will I get milk?' The ascetic replied: 'The sterile cow will yield milk.' Miracle of miracles; Charan Pal mulched the cow and filled his pot with milk, but when he looked up he could not find the ascetic anywhere. The man was just there, where could he have gone all of a sudden? Looking for him, Charan Pal carried his milk-pot and ran helter-skelter, confusion writ large on his face. Where did the ascetic vanish? Crossing field after field, he reached Agradweep mid-evening and found him under a tree. After drinking the milk, the ascetic said: 'Go now; your wish will be fulfilled. You've received Deendayal. Today onwards, you'll be "Baksiddha". The next six generations after you shall also be Baksiddha.' Therefore sir, this is the episode."

: "What's Baksiddha?"

: "Sir, he's the one having the power of uttering infallible words. For instance, if the Baksiddha says, 'the lame shall walk; the dumb shall speak; the blind shall see; the infertile shall reproduce'—then it'll actually happen. He can show the sun rising in the west. By virtue of his words, he can feed rice to hundreds of thousands of people. Here, for example, is the order of Charan Pal, so there's never a storm at this fair, nor is there a single crow or any other bird on the trees, nor any dog or fox. All this is due to the powers of the Baksiddha meditator."

: "Are there other classes of such liberated souls?"

: "Yes, sir. Another one is called Sadhansiddha (realised by meditation). Kubir Gosain, disciple of our Charan Pal was Sadhansiddha. One of his songs narrates:

By meditation—realisation I've attained indeed—
My tears of devotion set love's trap in motion,
In touching those beauteous moon-lips I finally succeed.
With ample loving care, the jewelled treasure rare,
In my heart I store, prized.
Removing filth'n'dirt, I've been clean'n'smart,
Petty details I don't look at,
Pure path, I've followed and advised.

"Sir, this Agradweep is a most sacred place. Here was the play of Gupinath with Ghosh Thakur; here Charanchand became Baksiddha; here was Kubir's realisation through meditation."

Standing on that divine land, I gazed at the west-flowing Ganga. The evening was tinged with the dying hues of the setting sun. Painted in that fading dimness of colours stood the decaying palace of zaminder Hari Mallik. The glory of that mansion, too, was well on its way to set. I reiterated in my mind the lines from Dasharathi Roy:

On earth, Hari Mallik's clan is blessed—
As holiest of places, Agradweep is placed:
Where Gopinath is at play.

Suddenly darkness descended. At the sacred portals and sites, evening lamps were lit, along with lanterns and petromaxes.

There was noise everywhere, of countless people; sounds of single-stringed and double-stringed drones and drums; shouts of traders at the fair; and the loud drone of the wordy songs by Bauls and Fakirs. I played upon the thought that Agradweep now had throngs of people camping there—hundreds of thousands of the masses lietrally; by day after tomorrow they would all disappear after the ritual morning bath observing Aam-Baruni. There would remain only the emptiness of the vast grounds; the Ganga on the west; a few trees; the indifferent destitution of the crumbling ruins of the Malliks; and the 500-year-old legacy of the legendary icon of Gopinath.

I walked on, making one of the illuminated holy dens my target. The eleventh-day moon was not up yet. Before nightfall, I had to locate an appropriate site, otherwise, the night's meal and stay would pose a problem. I decided to take a peep into one of the clusters in front; I elbowed my way in, over the crowd's shoulder, to look inside. A combat of songs was in full swing inside. I plunged myself right in the middle of the gathering. Looking at my fairly 'civilised' appearance, someone said: "Do sit down, sir." Glancing at me through the corner of his eye, the singer continued:

On earth, Brahma is purest matter—
From this Brahma, everyone is born:
On other theories, don't bother to natter.

As the song was reaching its end, the singer – rival to this songster – slowly tied anklets round his feet. As soon as the song was over, everyone enquired: "Would you like to debate and curtail this song's premise?"

: "Of course, I will. Premises of such songs are child's play to me. At the mercy of Haariram, do I have only one song in my basket?" asked the man with pride.

Mercy of Haariram! But didn't that seem to be scripted in code language right away? I realised that there were certainly other followers of Haariram besides Bipradas of Nishchindipur (Nischintapur). "What's the name of the singer?" I asked. "Which village did he come from?" The singer responded to my questions: "Sir, my home is in Betai Jitpur. The name of this humble servant of Haariram is Ramdas Sircar."

Now holding the drone to his ears, Ramdas began the preamble with a resounding:

Balaramchandra Haari Gosain.
Bone too strong, a jewel of a brain,
Tarakbrahma Ramnarain.
Universe's owner, universe's lord,
Birth and death are of his accord.
Do please protect me.

Afterwards, Ramdas addressed the gathering with the following words: "Dear appreciative listeners and my mystic rival singer-friend. The essence of the song that I am going to present now contains the deep essence of our Haariram. In this gathering, the essence that was being presented so far had Brahma as the reality. And what we say is:

Oh, no, no, no, no, not that at all—
We heard: one Brahma, no second; He is over all—
Isn't that talking tall?
Haariram speaks of something else if you recall:

We hear Brahma's the Creator,
Vishnu is the Nurturer,
Shiva's the Destroyer,
Wherefore Brahma the 'Sole One', can you call?

Delving deeper into logic, when the song ended, everybody blurted out: 'Bravo! It's irrefutable argument.'"

Ramdas said: "The song's not irrefutable; it has its negation, too. But I won't sing that song in order to refute my own song. I only say that Haariram's theory is unassailable. So he said...—

Haariam's theory has a very deep essence—
Outside the Veda and Vedanta.
Nimai became ascetic knowing this substance,
And Shiva made the burning ghat his residence.

"Listeners, do say 'bravo' in Haariram's name."

Everyone roared: "Bravo! Bravo! Bravo!"

I did not generally miss such opportunities. As soon as Ramdas came out of the soiree for a smoke I took him to sit at an empty spot. Meanwhile the eleventh-day moon had appeared in the sky. I could clearly perceive the essence of Ramdas' personality in the moonlight. He had a sharp aquiline nose, a slim figure, hair parted in the middle and two beautiful eyes. Such people were usually touchy about their appearance. So I began a conversation from that angle: "You have a high nose, which is a good sign. You're not supposed to lie so low."

The heart warmed up to my words—as the proverb goes, the flattened rice was finally moistened with the right play of words! Flashing a shy smile, Ramdas said: "Sir, you've got the point well. Everyone says I've the symptoms of a meditator. Such a sharp Garuda nose is not for men on this Earth. Our Haariram had a principal disciple Tanu, he had such a nose. Have you listened to songs composed on Tanu?"

"No, I haven't," I replied. "I've been to Meherpur, to Nishchindipur. I've heard many songs from Bipradas."

Ramdas sang in a trice:

In Treta era, He was Hanu,
At Meheraj, He was Tanu,
Receiving the dust of his feet,
A devotee in all four eras it does make you.

Suddenly stopping his song midway, Ramdas paid obeisance by gazing at the sky. Then he began muttering to himself:

Haariram, Haariram.
He's full eternal Brahma, himself Shri Ram;
As Sita's lord, you made possible
Hanuman's creation—
So in your quality of showing mercy,
This worthless one, give salvation.
You're my mother-father. You're husband in notion—
At your feet is this submission!
Victory to Haariram, victory to Haariram,
Victory to Haariram!

I had mingled with so many communities of folk religion over time, but almost nobody had a completely Bengali chant. All of the latter was loaded with the Tantric practice sounds of Sanskrit origin *hring, kling, sling,* etc. Only Haariram's chant was a unique exception on all counts; it had been transformed into colloquial Bengali lingo very smoothly. In its pronunciation, the accent of faith was, therefore, worth hearing. Resting my thoughts on this, I asked Ramdas: "Why is there no Sanskrit in your chant?"

: "Couldn't you understand? Sanskrit is the language of the Vedic religion. And Haariram's doctrine lies outside the Vedas and Vedanta. This apart, there's the other argument."

: "Such as?"

: "We don't worship the future. All our meditation is for the present. Now, the Bengali language is the present dilemma. Here's where we're talking in that lingo, aren't we? And does anybody talk in Sanskrit? It's the language of surmise."

Splendid, it provided one more commentary on the doctrine of surmise and presence. I found Haariram's men quite meritorious and logical. One reason for this was that, for a long time, they had been moving on a path different from that of the Vaishnava and Bauls. They had to confront them at every step in theoretical combat, in order to allow Haariram's doctrines to edge in. For instance, in today's soiree for vocal music, Ramdas beautifully refuted their thesis of 'One Brahma, no second'. Of course, I did not tell the truth to Ramdas that 'Brahmo' and 'Brahma' were not the same. Folk singers did not have so much theoretical knowledge. Occasionally they got caught in the turn of the phrase or double entendre of the sentence. Whatever, it was my job now to extract information from Ramdas. So, I raised the point: "Ramdas, your faith does not have a guru."

Even before I finished, Ramdas said: "Yes, sir. We don't have gurus like Bauls and Vaishnavas. We've only one theory—that of as Haariram. Now again—

Million oceans: deep, sans shore,
One who knows can get afore,
The pen falls short of words less or more,
The path of pure raga gives form to the core.

"So, the doctrine of Haariram has to be known through raga. It has to be realised that I'm what he is. The difference is just that '*He's somewhat deep / I'm just a dip*'."

: "What does it mean?"

: "It means he has vast depth, while I'm like the seed of an apple: too small. But, then, I'm not to be neglected. Can one, who has learnt the glory of Haariram, be negligible either?"

I said: "What I wanted to ask you was these that while you've no guru, how you acquired so much knowledge?"

: "Sir, it's Haariram who's making me speak. But, yes, I've kept excellent company. Having been to Nishchindipur, did you meet Purnadas Halder?"

: "Yes, of course. He was quite aged then."

: "He's no more now. So, I had been to many places with Purnadas Halder, all over this region: Dha'para, Dhopat, Palshundo, Komthana, Hanspukur, Banne, Phulkalmi...Having travelled, I had heard many debates with Vaishnavas and Bauls. From there, I had acquired some self-knowledge. Now I can indulge in debates quite well. Would you like to hear about an incident?"

: 'Tell me."

: "Have you heard of Phani Dervish of Sahebnagar? It's about him. Near that Sahebnagar, there's a portal of the Vaishnava, where one evening Tarak Brahmo's name was being sung. I was then staying at Phani Uncle's home for a few days. Uncle said: 'Let's go and listen to the *naamgaan*—the music. Liberation lies in the name.' So we went and heard name-singing. Afterwards, the Vaishnavas sat down to eat from the earthen plates—the *malsha*. Of course, we couldn't eat from the Vaishnava *malshas*."

: "Why," I was in doubt. "What's wrong in post-worship offerings—the *prasad*?"

: "Oh, don't you about the stricture?" asked Ramdas with great self-satisfaction. "Then please listen with care:

We won't do other gods' praise or abuse.
Other gods' food offerings—, we won't use!

"That's final; it's a straightforward matter."

: "Then what happened?"

: "The more they insisted on our eating from the earthen pots, the more Phani uncle would refuse. The actual reason – namely, Haariram's taboo – he couldn't share with them, lest they felt hurt. We couldn't get away anyhow at the end. One of the Vaishnavas asked in a pinching voice: 'What's the objection? Do you hate us?' Unable to cope with it anymore, Uncle said: 'Dear sir, you seem to be bent upon making me say the very thing. The question is, we'll accept the service, but offer the service to whom?' The monk was stupefied by hearing his rejoinder. He said: "My goodness, your statement seems to have a lot of twists. Let me take you to our Mohanta.' He took us both to the Mohanta. Sir, do you understand who a Mohanta is?"

"Yes, I do," I replied. "He is the Vaishnava guru who heads that particular portal, isn't that so?"

Ramdas said: "But he's widely respected. He has a grand appearance: what could be called totally seasoned and well nourished. There was not a trace of householdership on him. The monk explained everything to him, as elaborately as he could. Hearing all that, he smiled and gazed at Uncle through his silver spectacles. Then he said jokingly: 'I can see that you've remained a little raw and is a greenhorn on the way to meditation. Here, both of us are sitting together, what's our difference? Both of us are men, devotees, meditators. What then?'

: "Then what was the reply that Phani Dervish gave?"

: "Oh, it was a most befitting reply. He said: 'You and I are no doubt sitting together, yet there's a lot of difference. Would you like to know what kind? You're sitting on a mat; there's a sack on top, is the third layer is that of a *kaantha*—the traditional cloth-tucked quilt a patched wrapper, then there's a bed-sheet. And here I am, born on earth, and sitting on bare earth itself. Isn't there a difference between you and me?'"

: "What happened after this?"

: "The Mohanta sat in silence for a while, venturing to answer a little later: "Whatever, why won't you accept the service? Don't you have someone to offer the service back to? Why, can't you offer it to the Supreme Spirit? Why isn't there any reply? So, you got defeated this time, did you?" Uncle tapped me and asked: "Ramdas, what could be the response to this, what do you think?"

Keeping Haariram in mind, I quickly replied: "Mohanta-ji, you've already offered this earthen plate of service to your Supreme Spirit. How can I possibly repeat the service and offer the same 'consumed' food to my Supreme Spirit?"

The Mohanta fell silent. Uncle quipped in: "Bravo, Ramdas! Congratulations to you! You've saved Haariram's name."

On the night of the eleventh moon, I was truly thrilled by listening to the account of such an extraordinary debating bout. It was quite true; the spindle from one narrative could unwind and lead on to such another narrative. The matter was quite a curious one, so I egged Ramdas on by asking: "Your wisdom seems to be riper than Phani Dervish's. Could you tell me what your main difference is from the Vaishnavas?"

Ramdas said: "It's their five doctrines; the counting of meditation-beads and the garland of basil seeds. We don't profess them. But where we've a conflict with the portal-based Vaishnavas is that they totally go against nature while we're householders."

I said: "What's wrong in not following Nature's way? Aren't there celibate faiths?"

: "Sir, could you evade Nature? Does the celibate Vaishnava not have a nightfall? Are the nightfalls at the sight of Nature, or, of men? Sir, you're making me angry to draw out my inner convictions. I will now become cautious."

I laughed and said: "Goodness, you've caught me there. So no more talking now; we'll get together at night. Now do sing a song; but not your Haariram's lyrics. They're far too loaded with cryptic theory. Sing some other song."

Ramdas said: "I'm singing such a song from which you'll easily get to know the real selves of the Vaishnavas. Listen—though the song doesn't belong to our cult, we still sing it—

Nadia's Gora—Chaitanya's name-sake—
From the Shaakta Bharati, the Shakti chant does take.
Later, from Ramananda's hand,
He seeks the Baul faith's band,
Worships Man and to the holy prime faith wake.
Chandidas, a Baul, did
Express pure human need,
Vaishnavas, this same theory their own make..
Deceitful ascetics, those
Steeped in the scriptures, verse and prose,
Yet not a letter of Truth on their path comes or goes

Rituals, clothes and garland sporting troupe
Faking prayers in their malsha *meals in a group,*
Day and night they spend in stupor, counting beads on rosaries fake.

Nadia's Gora – Chaitanya's namesake –
From the Shaakta Bharati, the Shakti chant does take.
Later, from Ramananda's hand,
He seeks the Baul faith's band,
Worships Man and to the holy prime faith wake.
Chandidas, a Baul, did
express pure human need,
Vaishnavas, this same theory their own make.
Deceitful ascetics, those
Steeped in the scriptures, verse and prose,
Yet not a letter of Truth on their path comes or goes

Rituals, clothes and garland-sporting troupe
Faking prayers in their malsha *meals in a group,*
Day and night they spend in stupor,
counting beads on rosaries fake.

I brought up the topic of the Haariram-Vaishnava conflict with Ramdas, much later after dinner. Then the whole fair had nearly shut down; it would be around eleven o'clock at night. Only in some over-enthusiastic clusters, music continued. Those were mostly hemp-smokers' gatherings. Their songs had neither head nor tail, as I had seen in my experience. Actually with the passage of night, all the clusters would host a large-scale rice-festival. Their arrangement was not a joke. Therefore, everybody was resting and sleeping as much as possible. I had no sleep. I could not sleep in a fair. So I depended on Ramdas as he sat down to count and chant Haariram's name. I asked him right away: "It's not to extract information from you; but I truly wanted to know why there's such animosity between Vaishnavas and yourselves. Is it jealousy? After all they're larger in number. You're only a handful, aren't you?"

Ramdas said with a most painful expression: "Sir, you're a learned man. Is the number ever the determining factor of truth or false? Perhaps, fundamentally Lord Haariram Chandra had clashed with the Vaishnavas of his time. Could there not be such opposition?"

"Yes, there could be," I replied after thinking. "Firstly, the Vaishnavas are dualist, they consider Shri Krishna as an absolute godhead and prefer to remain as devotees. And your faith is largely non-dualist. Haariram has called himself the Creator. Why would Vaishnavas accept this? They don't worship man, but are believers in reincarnation. They won't accept Haariram as a reincarnation."

"So why should we accept them?" Ramdas fumed as a rebel. "Does God reside in those ritual marks, garlands, sandal-paste signs and loin-clothes? I know all their affairs. Verbally they claim all races are the same, but actually their discrimination is no less there. Do you know that they've all kinds of divisions? There're Brahmin Vaishnavas, cobbler Vaishnavas, scheduled caste Vaishnavas, roaming ones, and many more divisions. Then what's the meaning of Gouranga's principal saying—'Everybody the same unto the lowest caste'? Then why don't the latter obey the Vaishnavas? Do you know the real reason? It's all the machinations of the conspiring Brahmins!"

Ramdas sang:

'Man' and 'man' on everyone's lips
O brother, who has searched or found him?
Trilochan calls in joyful glee, touching the high notes in his whim.

Stopping him, I said: "I've heard this song in Bipradas's voice. Where is the confusion here? Its theory is very simple."

Ramdas said with resentment: "Then listen to this part of the song:

Vrindaban hosts its Love Play—
The fortunate get to know and say.
For Radha-Krishna, it's a 'nay',

"*'And 'nay' for cow-maids: left alone'*: Could you follow?"

: "Is there something different to follow here?"

Smiling in self-indulgence, Ramdas replied: "The real essence is here. Vaishnavas perform keertan on Vrindavan Leela. They include the presence of Radha-Krishna and the cow-maids. But Krishna actually never participated in any Vrindavan Leela."

: "Oh, is that so?"

: "Yes, think it over. Brahma is the lord of creation, his place is in our head. Vishnu is the lord of nurture; he resides in the chest. Shiva is the lord of destruction; his place is in the genitals. Could you tell me what Vrindavan Leela is?"

: "Is it the union of male and female genitals?"

: "Absolutely. Then how does Krishna from the chest perform Vrindavan Leela? He does not. The taste or form of Vrindavan

Leela is only partially known too Maheshwar. But what does Krishna, Radha, or the milkmaids know of Vrindavan Leela? Here is the greatest mistake of the Vaishnavas. That mistake was pointed out by our Haariram Chandra. 'Who'll understand your glory in this world, Haariram?'

Just as the crescent moon stared at the fair-ground of Agradweep in silent wonder, I continued to gaze at Ramdas in total surprise. There have been so many elections, green revolution, Panchayat, nuclear terror, electronic technology, birth control, globalisation, stronghold of television: but did nothing dent their belief system? In the sleeping bodies of the countless people in the fair, were their minds also in deep slumber? In contrast to me, were they the inhabitants of such a clearly distinct and separate world? When this vast majority of people would wake up in the morning, their clear belief-system could destroy my stability. With that premonition, I fled the fair. I fled, and fled far.

A decade had been devoured between that flight and my recent trip to Agradweep last Chaitra. Of course, I came once and spent two nights with Sharat Fakir on this ground. But what did I observe this time? Along with Charan Pal's home, that huge kadamba tree and its surrounding forty square yards of area had slid to the depths of the Ganga.

A sudden sighting gave rise to doubts. How come, the very balcony where I had sat and where Ramdas explained the mystery of Vrindavan Leela had gone under the waters? Perhaps, in like manner, the Sahebdhani sect or the home of Bala Haari were also getting buried under the bottomless edifice of society. That would mean that it would become gradually difficult to unwind human spindles. Taking control of my disappointed mind, I begin searching for human links. At first, I stood at the portal of

Charan Pal, without its house. There was a temporary portal – with corrugated-tin wall and polythene canopy – where is seated the present Sahebdhani Fakir. This was the new Fakir who had acquired Sharat Fakir's place after the latter had passed away. He was seated with the Fakiri wand on his chest and a veil of white sheet on his head as per the custom. The new Fakir was seated on a new mat where a mass of loose change in coins of various denominations and ample currency notes collected—thrown in by the devotees. This was his earning for the whole year. Suddenly, from behind the corrugated walls appeared Sutosh Pal, an old acquaintance. He belonged to the clan of Charan Pal, but did not take up the Fakiri profession. Nor did he live in Brittihuda, the main cluster of Sahebdhanis. He lived in Natungram, where the worship of Deendayal also continues through generations.

Sutosh asked: "What's the matter? How come you're here after so many years? Is it to follow up on some new source of research?"

I replied: "Research on folk religion can be endless. I've come this time to observe how much Agradweep has changed in ten years. Immediately after my arrival I was indeed baffled to see the current situation. So much of the banks had been eroded away by the Ganga!"

: "This is the outcome of the release of water from the Farakka dam. I've heard of a greater extent of erosion along the opposite bank. Do come in; keep your bags in my tent. Let there be a meal service with us, here. Is it okay? Well, fine then..."

The tent was, of course, not ready yet. In a trice, four local men planted four bamboos and fixed a polythene sheet on top to make a cover. But what was there to sit on? Immediately, someone took some money from the gentleman and purchased a mat. Sitting on it, I sensed that Agradweep had quite a peripatetic 'bohemian' air about it. There was hardly – what is termed 'infrastructural facility' in economics – present here. Apart from some earthen vessels and dry branches for fuel, nothing was available. Everything was, therefore, to be carried along. It was quite a funny situation. For instance, having sat down in Sutosh Pal's tent on a mat, I blurted out: "I'm very thirsty, could I get some water?"

Someone immediately ran out with money. He returned after buying an earthen pot and a lid. Water was brought in it from the Ganga. My thirsty soul was saved by drinking the water. While I looked to and fro, suddenly the man in front, called Ramjan, offered a freshly-bought hand-fan. "I had bought it before the order came. You seem to be such a comfort-loving man," he said. I was ashamed. Sutosh said: "The rice-carnival is being held today. It's still sometime off. We should have something to eat now, what do you say?"

What could I say? Did I any longer belong to the age-group which could articulate such a need right away?

"O Mozammel, have you got anything with you?" shouted Sutosh Pal. "Give us something to eat.'"

: "Yes, sirs, I do have. I've brought some *murki* – freshly grilled sweetened puffed rice – from home and flattened rice husked on our own pedal. Do please have them, sirs."

"Deendayal has made a superb arrangement," I remarked.

I devoured the freshly made rice snacks, washed them down with large gulps of the Ganga water, which filled my stomach somewhat, and followed it up with a satisfied belch. Ramjan said: "Sirs, what you've taken has cast cement-lined moulds in your stomachs. It should hold good till two o'clock."

I smiled and kept watching their activities. They were four: Ramjan, Mozammel, Phoring and Badan. They all worked as shared labours in the paddy and jute fields at Natungram, belonging to Sutosh Pal. They did not have to gather here at all; yet why did they come? Mozammel whispered to me: "Sir, Babu has gone shopping, so let me tell you in confidence: we come here attracted by the Babu. If we didn't come, he won't be able to eat, sit or sleep. Hence is our coming. It's not for one generation; his father, his grandfather: someone or the other would come on every occasion. My father and uncles also came. That has been the rule."

: "Have you been accompanying him everywhere?"

Clamping his tongue in embarrassment, Phoring remarked: "Do you think visiting Raggadweep is the same as visiting all other? This is a place of knowledge and ultimate realisation; its glory and impact are quite different. Let me then share the truth, sir. We use this chance to take part in the rice-carnival of Deendayal. Indeed, there's no difference made here between Hindus and Muslims; everyone is equal in Raggadweep. You could go round all the portals. You'll see either a Hindu cooking or a Muslim cooking, and all eating the food together by sitting in a circle together."

: "It would appear that both of you are Muslims from your names. And are the other two Hindus?"

: "Sir, Phoring is a Hindu and Badan a Muslim. By the way, Phoring dear, what's your formal name?"

Phoring said with a pronounced swagger: "My name is Gobindachandra Mandal."

: "Goodness gracious, the name has such a lot of force!" remarked Badan. "The name 'Phoring' sounds much better. It matches your appearance perfectly!"

Phoring remonstrated: "Badna, your father's name is Madna. You're my water-spout for defecation!"

"Do stop mouthing obscenities here," Mozammel, as the seniormost in age, admonished: "Carry on with your work. Be fast with your hands. You don't have any sense of good or bad. You're badmouthing even in Raggadweep! Get on, dig the earth."

I continued to watch; they first dug the earth along a line, like a drain. Placing three new pots side by side, they checked whether the digging was in order. Ramjan explained: "Sir, this is called a *jol*. The pot shall be on top, the branches of the plants of pigeon-pea pulse will make the fire at the bottom for steaming and boiling.""

I asked: "How big could a *jol* be? I mean, what's the maximum number of pots it could hold?"

: "Say, around ten. You're going to spend the day here; you will get to see the digging of a *jol* a little later at the Charan Pal cluster: four in a sequence. A least, forty pots could be placed there. It's Deendayal's rice-carnival; everyone here would be able to get a portion of the sacred offering. The quality of cooking of this offering is also distinctively excellent. We won't be able to do it."

: "Why?"

: "You need a lot of physical power; devotion in mind; and the mercy of Deendayal."

: "Who would cook then?"

: "It's a system going on since Charan Pal's time. There's a village called Kamalbati near Debgram. The devotees from there have been cooking at the rice feast of Deendayal down the ages. There's lord Deedayal's mercy on them."

: "Of what kind?"

: "Sir, if I say, you won't believe! They lift and hold those large pots of hot boiling rice directly, without using any cloth, and bring them down from the oven with their bare hands."

: "Don't they get singed in the heat?"

: "It's a wonder, they don't feel the heat at all! Yet you would notice that when we cook here, the earthen vessels would become red hot!!"

I was amazed to hear this. I had come to Agradweep on earlier occasions, but never heard such yarns. I did not get to hear them, since I stayed in the noble company of Sharat Fakir. Unless one mingled with the sons of the soil, one did not get the true essence of the earth. Here were those four illiterate farmers prattling away in front of me; digging *jols* with dexterity; and digging quietly many other holes by obeying diligently the invisible regulations in silence. These were the poorest-of-the-poor devotees of Deendayal, whose participation made the real fair vibrant. I noticed that, after digging three pits, these were swapped with a mop of cow-dung neatly. I asked curiously: "Why do you have three pits?"

: "It's to keep rice in one, vegetables in another."

: "How's that? Will you keep them in pits? Won't they catch the mud and dirt?"

: "Nothing will happen. This is the hard and dusty soil of the western Gangetic plains, solid like stone. And as saving grace, there is the grace of Deendayal. You won't be able to make out anything when you eat!"

Badan swapped the three pits with a mop; Phoring sprinkled turmeric powder on them. Why was turmeric needed? That would remove the soil's deficiencies, according to Badan.

The dog-tired men finally sat down for a while. Their bodies were drenched as sweat streamed down; they wiped their bodies with a light cloth towel, twirling the same to fan themselves.

We both sat, facing the Ganga under a very old banyan tree. The fair had a lesser number of pilgrims on this side; it was somewhat empty. I told Sutosh Pal: "You're a highly educated person; what attracts you to come here every year?"

: "You could say this was our family responsibility. We are direct descendents of Charan Pal. It's our duty to be present in the rice-carnival and the feast, to ensure that the services are carried out efficiently and everybody gets served. Besides, it's my father's command. He used to come and, in his absence, I come. I derive a lot of mental peace. Also, Mozammel, Ramjan, et al., drive me here. As soon as it's the month of Chaitra, they start badgering: 'Babu, would you not go to Agradweep?'

: "Well, why are they so interested, tell me? After all, they're not meditators of Deendayal or his disciples."

: "This is a mystery difficult to unravel. There's something here, an attraction. The matter of religion is a very minor one. They come with a lot of trouble, and put in donkey's labour. They cook after digging *jols*; then go back after collecting everything. They still come, saying: 'Babu, without participating in the rice-carnival of Deendayal, there seems to be something missing.' Can this be explained with logic?"

I asked: "At home, you've Deendayal's platform; who worships there?"

: "Mostly, it's done by my elder brother. I also do on holidays when schools are closed. Then every Thursday, there's a special service-feeding of Deendayal. On that day, we offer him sweetmeats costing a rupee and a quarter. That's the custom. It is a rupee and a quarter: neither more nor less."

: "Well, if any disciple offers something personally on a particular day?"

: "Yes, then we consecrate his desired offering."

: "Generally, what do they offer?"

: "There's water, sweets or thickened milk pudding; or a simple mishmash of flattened rice, curd and sweets like the *sandesh*. Yes, I just remembered something special. Some people also offer mutton and thin fried paratha."

: "Mutton and paratha?" My hard-earned experience too, got a jolt. I had never heard of any folk-god being offered mutton and paratha! Then was there any Islamic belief working behind this notion? 'Saheb' of Sahebdhani had a clear Islamic association. No sooner had I put across the doubt to Sutosh, he replied: "The Muslim religion has quite a good impact on our sect. There're several Muslim disciples as well. In fact, the sect originated with joint cooperation between Hindus and Muslims."

I sought to know: "Have you noticed anything in your daily worship that resembles the Islamic religious practice?"

: "Listen then. In our prayer room, there is Deendayal's bedstead; it also has a mosquito-net. Everything connected with Deendayal is south-faced; yet we pray to him facing the west. Isn't this custom Islamic?"

: "Yes, quite so. Well, what're your daily rituals, in the worship room?"'

: "Daily, we've to give an oil-bath to Deendayal's hubble-bubble and stick. His daily service is rice, sweets, sweet betel-leaf and water. Then, one has to put tobacco and cinder in the hub of the hubble-bubble and offer it along, just as one does to a real person. Only, while firing up the tobacco-hub, blowing air into it is taboo."

In the middle of our discussion, Badan came in to say: "Babu, you've been called. Please go."

: "Whose call?"

: "Let's go. The *jols* that have been dug at the Charan Pal cluster that side will be ignited now. We've to go and stand there; this is the custom."

It was truly a sight to see. There were four *jol*s, one after the other, dug up in a line. There were forty vessels placed on them. Many progenies of the Pal clan, who were present at Agradweep, stood alongside. The cooks from Kamalbati offered salutations to Deendayal with folded hands and sought blessings. Betel-leaf, vermilion, oil and sweets were placed in their hands. Depositing these alongside the *jols*, they bowed down in obeisance to the *jol*s. One of them shouted:

Speak on love in Radha-Krishna's name,
Lord Nitai, Chaitanya, and Advaita: of fame;
Sriroop, Raghunath, Kaviraj Gosain,
Atalbihari, Karoadhari: saints all fine;
Honey-dripping words: in Deendayal's name.
Do utter 'Hari', 'Hari', and eternity claim!

Everybody, in chorus, said: *"Haribol"*.

In Baba Charan Pal's own name—
Say 'Hari', 'Hari' once again.

All of them shouted in chorus: *"Haribol"*.

Voila! Fire was lit in the four *jols*, starting the rice-carnival. Sutosh Pal explained: "All this ceremony is to prevent any hindrances; to obviate storms and rains, permitting everyone to partake of the rice-carnival services; to let cooking be smoothly done. Do you understand?"

I asked: "When is the rice-carnival due to take place, after all this cooking is done with?"

: "It would be fairly late. Before that, do have an early meal of fish-and-rice in my tent."

"Before that, let me go around a little," I said. "'That might reduce the slab of puffed and flattened rice!"

Going around, I noticed a portal under each individual tree. There was music being performed at some places. Elsewhere vegetables were being chopped and diced while the cooking progressed. At some places, surrounded on all sides with sheets, the *malsa bhog* or meals in earthen plates were being served in the pure Vaishnava tradition, with keertan being sung outside. Elsewhere, people were sound asleep. At one portal, a middle-aged widow was cooking broth in a vessel and stirring it with a piece of split-bamboo. I asked her: "Why do you use a bamboo-strip dear Aunt? Isn't there a ladle?" The venerable lady said, in a voice soaked in affectionate reprimand: "My dear boy, don't you know the customs of Agradweep? Ladles or spatulas are not permitted here. Only split-bamboos strips for cooking and banana leaves for serving food are allowed here."

What was cooking in the vessel was difficult to guess; something was boiling hard. Pressed by the boiling liquid, rice, pulses, brinjal, pumpkin, potato, raddish and gourd all surged upwards to the surface of the broth. It was indeed an unusual affair! I could not help asking the lady again: "What is cooking in there?"

: "Dear boy, you're a learned person. Couldn't you make out by observing? It's called *jagakhichudi*—a hotchpotch kedgeree."

So this was actually the proverbial *jagakhichudi* – the hotchpotch kedgeree – not just a figure of speech describing a 'situation' but a proper item of cooked food! I'd never seen it, only heard the term. I asked the lady: "Where do you belong?"'

: "Do you know Bholabhada? You've to get down there to go to Nangla Podmo. Our guru's portal is there. Guru's name is Rakhal Fakir. You see him sitting there."

The Fakir had curly hair and wore gold-framed spectacles on his eyes. He was clad in a dhoti and a 'terry-cotton' shirt. He took slow, relaxed puffs from a cigarette. Casting a glance at me, he continued his smoking. Coming out of the cluster, I stood at a point where cooking was being done for another group in a big vat. I stood there and observed a powerfully-built man—with a turban on head and clad in a deep blue vest, cooking a mixed kedgeree of lentil and rice. His whole mouth was red with betel-leaf juice. On being asked, he told me his name: 'Satish Bhugle'.

: "What kind of a surname is Bhugle?"

: "Sir, we're cowherds and milkmen by caste. Many people call us by worse names. Some say Bhemo Milkman; some call us Bhugle."

: "What do you do for a living? Follow the caste-allotted business?"

: "No, sir. I'm a cow-veterinary."

: "Do all castes and creeds come to Agradweep?"

: "Yes, all thirty-six castes and vendors from every business. See there at that cluster, those people are *jele* – fishermen – and *nikiri*."

: "Are the *jele* fishermen and *nikiris* different from each other?"

: "Yes, they are. Though both catch fish, *jele* fishermen are Hindus and *nikiris* Muslims."

There was no end to learning, I thought to myself. In these fairs, there was so much to see, so much to know! At the dawn of civilisation, people perhaps dug *jol*s to cook, dug such pits to keep food. In *Chandi Mangal* by Mukundaram, written in the sixteenth-century, where there was information about the low-born life of Kalketu and Phullara, we read: *'Look, there lies the overnight rice-water's pit.'* The poor folks dug pits in the raised front porches of their homes and ate rice and the overnight rice-water out of those. Perhaps one of its streams had remained extant in the Agradweep fair in a different form. This fair, according to mythology, was 500 years old; even in a strict historical sense, it would not be less than 300 years.

My thoughts were interrupted, when suddenly a lady – with a crown of leaves on her head and a garland of flowers around her neck – appeared in front of me, caressing my head, face and cheek with her hands, crooning: 'O my precious jewel, oh my star from the sky!' followed by a song in a sound melodious voice:

Flashy news comes over wire, and by wire,
This wire is not the wire that joins with Him everywhere!
If in the east you strike a passage, in the west comes the reply message,
Is that telegraphic wire – ask him by sending wire!

I was a little nervous about the event's abruptness. The lady disappeared as suddenly as she had come. But, while going, she swung her posterior in such an obscene manner that one did realise she was a crazy woman. Once that was clear, the embarrassment disappeared. The cow-vet Satish said: "She's Nachhrat (Nusrat) Bibi; her home is in Fazilnagar. She's mentally unstable."

: "How did you know?"

: "I'm a cow-vet, won't I know about people?"

The contrariness of his statement evoked my laughter. Was the job of a cow-vet to understand the ways of the cows, or, humans? Without being the least embarrassed, Satish said: "You're laughing, but it's true. You can't imagine how very far and near a cow-vet has to go. Wherever the mother-cow falls ill, I'm summoned. People're, therefore, well known to me. The cow-vet knows humanity, and the vulture knows the cow-vet. Between the vulture and the cow-vet, there's lifelong animosity."

It seemed to be a very strange statement. So admittedly surprised, I wanted to know: "I didn't quite understand why a vulture should peck you?"

: "Didn't you understand this? It's a very simple matter. Suppose, a dead cow is a vulture's diet. If the cow becomes well under the treatment of a cow-vet and is cured of its disease, the vulture's food goes missing. So it pecks the moment it sees a cow-vet and circles overhead for hours. Do you follow now?"

I realised that it was I, and not these folks, who was an inhabitant of a clearly distinct, separate world. Was it due to my mannerisms? Why did it happen this way? Why did I seek logic in everything? Why did I not derive joy out of everything? That was why I would never get the ethereal within the earthly. In order to escape the suffocating helplessness, I changed the topic and asked: "Satish, why did that Nachhrat Bibi lose her mind?"

: "Babu, that's a very sad story. Nachhrat used to love a Fakir, who was a hypocrite and harboured a venereal disease. Nachhrat went mad after getting infected by that disease."

I recalled that Ela fakir had apprised me on this aspect of Bauls and Fakirs long ago. There was little success, with most Bauls and Fakirs apparently turning out to be hypocrites or perverts. They succumbed to ejaculation with the slightest departure in their spiritual practice sessions with Nature. This was termed 'lock at the tenth gate'. Ela Fakir had let me hear two lines from a Marfati lyric by Buddhu Shah:

This room is locked with scriptures tight—
Won't open with false keys in a fight;
Buddhu has opened the door
With Guru-ji 'skey fitted right.

After singing the song, Ela had said: "If one is confined to the scriptural and formal systems, there could be liberation with the Marfati approach under the Guru's mercy. But if there were a lock on the tenth gate, it does not open any further. Apart from this, the other ejaculation is in erroneous breath-control."

"What kind of mistake was that?" I had wanted to know.

Ela had said: "Fakirs from the Kaderia sect have to learn a lot of respiration control, in the processes of inhalation and exhalation. That's called breath-control. Instead of learning from the really knowledgeable Murshid, wrong breath-control is bound to make one lose one's mind. Because the wind, instead of going to the right place, enters the head. Wind's pressure is a most serious matter."

I had confirmed Ela Fakir's statement later; this was absolutely correct like the Muslim jurisprudence. On one occasion, there was a festival in Jeevan Fakir's home at Palashipada on the first day of Baishakh. There was a soiree of Marfati songs at night. There was a confrontation between Sukuruddi, the young singer from Kulgachhi village and Yusuf Khan, the famous unparalleled singer from Murshidabad district. It was on intense fakiri doctrine. Yusuf sang at midnight:

Adding zero after one makes ten,
This is a statement: true and plain.
If two and eight get together,
Full ten, with 'nokta' they are then.
At ten places, 'nokta': the same,
The figure eight, it became;
Eight and ten: eighteen do claim—
Creates home in God's heaven.

At the end of the music, people became restless because Sukuruddi did not tie anklets on his feet. It meant that he would not rise and perform in the gathering again. This was because he was unable to present a sound rebuff to Yusuf's lyrics. He hung his head in shame. For a Marfati singer, the pain of this defeat went rather deep. Everbody came to know that his path of meditation did not yet stand on firm ground. Yet Sukuruddin's only consolation was that he was vanquished by the best. Still it was a defeat!

"Is there anybody in the gathering who would respond to this song?" someone cried out.

From the middle of the gathering, old Jeevan Fakir spoke up: "In this region, only Ejmali Shah could have responded; but do look at him and see his condition."

Fakir Abu Taher was sitting next to me. He pointed his finger with a pained expression. I noticed that, just outside the gathering – here the petromax light reached only dimly – a six-foot-tall man stood erect in the half darkness. He was fully bearded, with a cap on head, and with at least twenty medals dangling from his chest. Only his eyes had a vacant look. He was carrying a broken drone in his hand. It was a heart-rending scene!

Abu Taher remarked: "This is Ejmali Shah. We've never seen a more competent singer. His music created waves in the land:. Murshidabad-Rajshahi on this side, Kushtia-Jhinaidah on the other. Nobody could surpass him. Ejmali knew not only Lalan's songs, but also those of Panju Shah and Haur. You must be aware how difficult the doctrine of those songs was."

: "How did he get mentally deranged?"

: "He was a Marfati like us in Buddhu Shah's cult. Once, on a visit to Jessore, he fell under the clutches of one Kaderia Sufi. They practised some of the most difficult breath-control activities. Sitting here alone at midnight, Ejmali Shah used to practise these breath-control tactics and the associated loud shouts. Well, the wind went to his head. Definitely there was something wrong in the approach. He could not keep pace and became stark mad. Heis about our age and a good friend. He can't remember the songs any more. When any Fakiri gathering takes place, he only comes over with the medals dangling on his chest. We can't bear the scene."

My mind was filled with anguish, by listening to all this. Those medals were shining like a curse in the night. Could the lonely path to look for the man of my heart be deceitful to such an extent?

I returned to Sutosh Pal's tent with some apparent grief. Having seen Nachhrat Shah and having heard of Ejmali Shah, suddenly all the arrangements, entertainment and excitement of Agradweep dimmed in comparison and seemed pale and colourless. It did happen this way. In the brightest moment of success, the most melancholic event often came to mind. Still, wonder of wonders, when the mind became clouded by a person, often the cloud of sorrow was removed by another person. This was caused by Mozammel, Ramjan, Badan and Phoring. They were neither wealthy, nor literate. They called themselves 'ignorant people'. Yet they were shining with the lukewarm glow of life. As easily as they were singing songs on jewellery and rice-powder and dancing a little while ago, they had now finished cooking a three-course meal. As soon as I entered the tent, they began requesting me loudly to join them at lunch. Banana leaves to serve food and earthen tumblers for water had been laid out. There was hot rice, daal or lentil soup and fish in a light gravy cooked with green gourd. Food was piping hot; Sutosh began his meal. I had not yet got over the sultry heat and sat down for a little rest. Mozammel commented: "Is sir struck by a trance? It seems so from the signs. Don't have intoxicating habits. Otherwise, I'd have suggested giving him a bidi—an indigenous cheap cigarette made of tobacco leaves. At this time, a bidi helps in removing the ennui and clearing the head."

Ramjan remonstrated: "You propose recourse to bidi for every thing. Would the bidi accompany you to your grave?"

Mozammel said: "Sir, do you know what happened once? I just recalled this while talking about the grave. I was newly married then; and gone to my in-laws' place. There was a death in the family: of someone like a granduncle-in-law. We all had assembled at the burial ground. I blurted out suddenly: 'Give two packets of bidi with the dead body—what would he smoke there?' What a fiasco! I felt so ashamed, having said it and ran away from there."

Ramjan said: "Sir, when Mozammel is sad, do you know what he says? He says: 'Oh Mother Earth! Please open up and allow me in, with two bundles of slender cigarette.'"

I did not quite realise at which point Ramjan, et al., removed the cloud from my mind, spreading joy, cheer and banter. After lunch, I was feeling quite light in mind. I sat on a sack outside the tent, to watch the eating of Ramjan and others. On the question: "How is the food?" Phoring replied: "The rice is superfine. Such rice belongs to the babus, it does not suit the depressed ones like us." Ramjan said: "Sir, ours is the Musalmani food, with plenty of chillies. How was your food?" Badan said: "What do the Hindus understand of food and cooking? You better ask him this instead. Hindus eat unspiced vegetables in plain, insipid gravy and boiled vegetables—the core of the banana-tree trunk, arum-root and figs. Can one eat a proper meal without mutton? Can quality cooking be done without spice?" Phoring protested: "Still, you pine for the food of those Hindus! Sir, when my mother cooks something nice, she says: 'Dear, Oh leave a portion; Badan can have it with Phoring on return from the fields.' You, the wretched traitors!"

The day rolled on quickly enough. Sutosh was probably done with his forty winks. Coming out, he urged us to visit Charan Pal's site. All of us went together. All castes and creeds were present to accept the offerings of the rice-carnival, with rice, lentils and vegetables. With shouts and sounds from a few thousands of men and women and swirling dust raised by the sea of humanity milling about, the rice-festival took on a colourful hue instead of a pallid grey. I had often heard the following lines in one of Tagore's songs: *'Pother dhuloye ronge ronge aanchol rongeen...'* (The colours of wayside dust tinged the trails of clothes...) This was akin to witnessing the same in reality. Very large pits were filled with rice and vegetables. These were being served in earthen-plates by both Hindus as well as Muslims. Partaking of that sacred food, Ramjan danced, along with Phoring. We read the daily tidings of communal riots, heard of the artificial concepts of urban intolerance and resentment. Demands for Urdustan were raised by the divisive forces of imbecile ignorance and the Shiv Sena and Hindu fundamentalists flashed in retaliation. Why don't we ever get to read the news of the rice-festival of Deendayal?

Is it because we, the educated class created our own world with a clearly distinct pride? Would its vascillations and shift of ideology erode us away? I was having such random thoughts, when an aged widow came and held my two hands, speaking in a pleading voice: "O my dear boy, do express your recognition to me. I've been gazing at you for quite a while, wondering whether my child, my Gopal would recognise me. But alas, you didn't recognise me! Eventually, I came myself to hold both your hands. Would you know me now?"

I looked at her helplessly; but did not recognise her at all. Where had I seen her, at which fair, at which portal? It was so frustrating.

The old lady pleaded: "Don't be shy, Gopal my child. To err is human. Long ago – definitely ten years or so – we spoke to each other on our way to Raggadweep, while walking along that dry, sandy outcrop of the Ganga, do you recollect? We were walking together. I had my companion with me. Pity, she's no more. She was a good soul, a very virtuous lady. Have you recognised me now, my dear?"

Yes, I did now. I told her: "Yes ma'am, I've recognised you now. One statement of yours is still etched in my mind."

: "What's it, dear boy?"

: "You had said: 'I haven't been able to make my guru my own, though he has accepted me whole-heartedly.'"

: "Did I say that? O dear! You've still remembered it – that too coming from this illiterate woman – my precious? Is that some saying of a great man that you hold on to it? Then listen, dear. Those words are no longer true. Now, I've been able to accept guru as my own. Having left my home and hearth, I've taken refuge at my guru's feet at the guru portal. My guru is Sri Gagan Bairagya of Bamundanga. You must come right away to my guru's portal. My Gosain is there. Grandfather-Gosain has also come. Do let's go, Gopal."

Such an earnest entreaty holding both hands warmed the cockles of my heart. Who was this unrelated 'illiterate woman' who could drip so much love's grace so very intimately, I wondered! Did everybody gain something in Agradweep? Gobinda Gosain got Gupinath; Charan Pal got Deendayal; and I got this peerless symbol of affectionate humanism. I wished to hold the lady's hand with equal warmth and exclaim: "Take me to your community and unity. Snatching me away from my clear, separate, narrow, non-intimate world, connect me to your larger universe of faith and credulity." But I could not say it, though I suspected: the glow of my unspoken words was caught in the lady's eyes!

Avoiding all humanity, Gagan Bairagya's cluster was on one end in the west: in a low-lying land under a 'pituli' tree. Evening descended there, soaked in the essence of royal splendour. Incenses and many kinds of aromatic compounds made for a heady ambience. There was an evening's devotional soiree, with one singer extolling music and at least two hundred devotees listening in rapt attention. Aged Gagan Bairagya and his old matted-haired guru were seated side by side in the lotus posture, with eyes closed and a serene expression. He singer was singing the guru-doctrine:

Guru-asset is like sweet molasses, I see—
Without confecting in it, the mind sweetened can't be!
As molasses create and make,
So, for guru's service's sake—
The confectioner, who lies awake:
Is the blessed soul that be!
Service-maker's good confectioner,
Whoever does it gets the pleasure,
If you can't do, go below par,
On your foolish knee!

When the song was over, Grandfather Gosain told Gagan, his disciple: "Read *Shri Guru Tatva*". Gagan brought out a manuscript, bound by a red cover, and started reading: "Sri Gurudev is verily the expression of similarity and difference in the unthinkable entity of Sri Hari-Vaishnava." Grandfather Gosain gave the explanation: "That's why it's said that Guru-Krishna-Vaishnava is three-in-one, one-in-three. Then, what's said there, Gagan? Do read on."

Gagan read:

He is worshippable, considered as indivisible, par excellence—

'Sakshaddharitvena Samasta Shastrairuktah'.
Even then Sri Prabhu is God's daily prayable.

Grandfather Gosain said: "You're common folks, you won't understand such a lofty message from the scriptures. Let me simplify it for you, to say: Sri Guru is like a resort-base, while Shri Krishna is like subject-matter. So Sri Gurudev is a servant, despite being godhead; you're the servant of a servant."

All this seemed to me a rather intellectual affair. I crouched down to enter the gathering on the quiet. Some people respectfully made space for me. I realised that Grandfather-Gosain was the one-sided speaker. Who would compete with him? Only Gagan Fakir could compete with him, yet why should he proceed to refute his own guru amidst such an assembly of disciples and servers?

Grandfather-Gosain now said: "Do you know how a guru is? He's like a rudder of a boat. The boat has to reach the ghat, that is, near God. By itself, the boat can't move; it needs the rudder. If the rudder is steady, the boat reaches destination. Otherwise it would float away."

Gagan Bairagya told one of the singers: "What do your songs say, dear? How is a guru? Can there be meditation without guru?"

The singer sang in an empty voice, without accompaniment:

Those who say 'Hari' Hari'
And guru's name forget—
Like severing the tree's roots
And watering the top set!

"Hear, hear!" exclaimed Grandfather-Fakir, adding: "It's so very true. First is guru, then Hari. First is the way, then the temple. First is the meditation, then the reception."

Gagan Bairagya said again: "What else is said in the guru doctrine?" The singer sang on:

If the guru takes shape and is gracious,
He chants hymns in devotee's ears,
If guru you know my mind:
Krishna's vision you'll find—
With pleasure, you'll live in
Vaikuntha Bhavan, my dear.
If you err in guru as human—
Death'll punish, that's clear!

Grandfather Gosain added: "This last statement is important. Don't mistake guru as human being. He's very noble, very high. So it's said the sinner, who leaves guru and worships Govinda, is thrown into hell. Do say 'Hari' 'Hari' once, in the name of Sri Guru."

Everybody roared out Hari's name and the gathering was finally dissolved. Grandfather Gosain went to his own cluster. The venue was empty, but for the lady (whom I respectfully and to establish greater familiarity, called 'Aunt' by now) and I sitting on. In quite a contemplative mood, Gagan Bairagya came and sat down. We met each other. Aunt appeared gratified. Gagan asked: "How did you find our evening prayers for guru? Have you heard such prayers for gurus earlier?"

: "It's true," I confessed. "I had never heard it earlier. I haven't been to any other portal earlier where such prayer meetings for the guru were held."

: "Perhaps you've been more to Marfati Fakirs and the sect of Deendayal. Have you been able to catch the theory and process of ours?"

: "Theory and process can only be known after the practice-skills are observed. I haven't yet come across any practice of yours. Which sect is yours?"

: "Ours is the Patuli stream."

: "That signifies a Sahajiya practice. But your gathering for prayers to guru seemed very artificial, was it satisfying at all?'

: "That's an external practice, a ceremony for ordinary devotees performed in a superficial way. You won't be able to follow the core doctrine from it. I'll tell you the fundamentals later on. Would you stay for the night? Well, then I'll explain some of the things. Now, listen to these words from a confidential song:

Of that, he has no fear—
For him, who is, to guru, sincere and clear.
He can easily swim across;

Witty one gathers no moss;
The one who dips, he gathers jewel at the bend near!

"Could you make sense of this?"

I felt I could not comprehend much. Yet this much was clear that behind the shadowy mist of the song was the fire of a deeper life-style. The guru doctrine was perhaps not as simple as I thought it to be. Here, what could 'that' mean in the line—'Of that, he has no fear'? What did 'swim across' signify? What did 'bend' mean? What was the 'jewel'? I could make out very definitely that I was going into the depths of the doctrine; as if the clear but separate world's key lay here. A new thought arose in my mind.

Meanwhile, darkness deepened in all directions. According to calculations, the twelfth-day moon would rise a little later. Aunt had left for someplace. Suddenly, Gagan Bairagya came mysteriously to stand in front and, taking hold of my head and shaking it vigorously, hissed: "Forget everything. Whatever you've known is all wrong. Guru means the woman: the companion and partner in meditation."

In spite of being startled at his sudden behaviour, I shook my head vigorously in protest: "How could that be? We know that the husband is the highest guru. Is that wrong then? Then what is true?"

: "Truth is and lies in the feminine body. Carrying the signal near her, you've to swim. At her body' bend – that is, the tenth door – is concealed the highest jewel. Without getting drifted in a separate current, you've to plunge into the bottomless depth of the underworld. Then you'll get the jewelled treasure. At that bend comes the flood every month. That's called the deep, dark new moon: the woman's periodic menstrual cycle. In that flood at the river's bend comes floating the great fish: the unattached man. You've to catch him; you've to be steadfast in your union with him. That's what is striking gold or 'getting' the guru. Would bayou commit a mistake any longer?"

Gagan Bairagya's stern, hard face was still like a piece of stone. His two hands – like a pair of tongs – held my hand in a pincer-like grip, for eternity, or so it seemed from their power. I became restless, pleading: "Leave me alone. I don't want to know anything. I don't do meditation and worship. I don't know any ritual practice. I don't believe in this path."

Gagan's fiery red gaze was transfixed on my two eyes. Shaking me by my shoulders vigorously, the pain in his earnest voice showered down to that limitless dark: "Still you've to listen; you've to know. Am I not to share with anybody what I've realised in my mediation over all these days?" Suddenly, that apparently strong man broke down in tearful wailing and hid his face in my chest: "I haven't got a single man till this day: all are ignorant; all are superficial. I'm unable to continue talking according to their whims. Won't you listen to me?"

I agreed. But it was decided that I would first return where I had put up and bring my bags. After the evening meal, we would talk privately in the dead of night. I thought that the man was hugely relieved by getting my assurance. What an amazing experience it was! As though a repentant man felt somewhat consoled. I recalled from Tagore's play, *Visarjan* (Sacrifice), the dialogue:

Do you know what loneliness is?
I know. When I am brooding alone with a laden mind—
I seek to give, there's none to receive.

I was not aware that after acquiring some knowledge to the full, there could be such an unbearable anguish in keeping it accumulated in the mind. I realised clearly enough why Lalan, Panju Shah, Duddu Shah, Haure Gosain, Lalshashi, Kubir Gosain, et al., had endlessly written their songs. They had expressed their anguish in a like manner. Was this why the folk religions had such a profusion of songs? I understood where the pain hit Gagan Bairagya; he could not compose songs. Some ignorant and salvation-seeking men around him had an insatiable hunger for a holy refuge. They had to be fed with superficial practices and popular rituals. There were ignorant disciples devoid of meditation like the old aunt who stuck to Gagan Bairagya for receiving salvation. After all, this was not a Vedic religion, which catered for peace through scriptures and rituals. Folk religion was, at every step, religion for life's attachment. Is it possible to easily comprehend the people, for whom stool, urine, menstrual fluid and seminal fluid were not to be discarded? Their solitude was, therefore, of many kinds. First of all, it was meditation along the lonely, solitary path outside the path of popular religions' credo. Then, it was to live a hated marginalised existence, isolated from larger society. Even after that, there was the deep solitary resentment due to the inability to share one's realisation of Truth, even after an all-knowing status was achieved. Gagan Bairagya was unable to write. Lalan was most competent to write, but still he had to speak out:

Mental pain, with whom could I share?
I see none with such anguish and care!

Kubir said:

Fellow-sufferer, where is so—
Whom I could let my mind know?

What was this deep sense of anguish?

This agony was the meditator's agony. Indian saints and meditators in the Middle Ages or Sufi worshippers like Rumi realised truth from this agony. Side by side with such statement: 'After knowing Him, nothing remains to be known', we also see such a contrary statement: 'All learning begins after learning about Him'. Next to the pious saying: 'He has obstructed all means of knowing Him' is also the glowing statement: 'The ways to know Him are spread over all aspects of life'. Which statement was true out of these? Or perhaps all were true, valid at different levels of meditation.

I could easily comprehend that man's spindle never fell short. I was travelling, holding on to those endless spindles of people—in public and in solitude. Otherwise, what was my special job at this 500-year-old, festive Agradweep? Like the other handful of devoted pilgrims, I could have offered my annual obeisance to Gopinath inside his temple, and thereby ended the matter. Evincing full faith in the mythology of Ghosh-Thakur, I could have also witnessed the stone-icon of Gopinath and could believe that Gopinath actually wept at the time of offering sacramental rice during the funeral ceremony. Instead, Gopinath revealed to me man's weal and woe! Alongside the dancing ecstasy of Ramjan and Mozammel, there was the quiet presence of Ejmali Fakir's dumb quietude. Next to the perennially argumentative Ramdas floated the deeply repentant face of the lonely Gagan Bairagya.

In the intervening space of such thoughts, the formalities of going, coming, eating were all mechanically accomplished. The twelfth-moon shone brightly at midnight. Countless pilgrims lay around motionless, in sound sleep. Gagan and I crossed the bodies of the devotees, lying down after the satisfaction of feasting at the rice-carnival. At one point, having walked quite a distance, we reached the broken parapets of the Mallik residence and sat on a raised piece of land. Hearing human voices at some distance, we looked up to find two persons sitting facing each other, busy in a hot discussion. Before I could raise the question:

'who are they?' Gagan informed me that they were vintage Chistias who debated at midnight on Allah's true form.

Gagan Bairagya sat quietly for a while. The breeze from the Ganga was blowing rapidly, hitting at the mid-Chaitra night. Suddenly, like chanting a solemn hymn, Gagan recited:

In good or bad deeds, whoever engages mind—
Devotion to Krishna, he never does find.

"Why are you saying so," I asked. "Here, now at this hour of the night?"

Gagan replied, closing his eyes: "I'll now keep saying a few things. Please don't interrupt, let me say. I want to speak."

Nodding my head in approval, I sat down quietly.

Gagan continued to talk incessantly: "The biggest traps in life are knowledge and action. Here knowledge means the awareness about life and death. From that awareness comes the fear of death. What use is the knowledge that brings in the fear of death? Meditation gets hindered by that. Could you grasp the negative aspects of knowledge?"

I said: "This is a novel statement, at least for ourselves. By knowledge, we mean knowledge of scriptures. Knowledge is born from scriptures, hymns, and manuscripts and counselling. Then comes knowledge of materials and knowledge of Brahmo. Compared to Brahmo's knowledge, all other knowledge is mere trifling."

: "You've understood nothing. These are Vedic smokescreens. The real knowledge is self-knowledge. Before that knowledge, all other knowledge proves artificial. Without knowing self, could one know Brahmo? Have you heard this song?

I hear from everybody: 'I', 'I' and 'I'—
I can't get my 'I', howsoever I try!

This knowing yourself, finding yourself within yourself, is what's termed self-knowledge. Have you followed? Then, what did I mean when I said life's biggest traps are knowledge and action? One has to understand here that one has to leave the falsehood of knowledge through action and earn self-knowledge. Then the fear of birth and death would disappear."

I thought Gagan's ideas were very different. I waited to see what his ideas were on action.

Gagan pronounced—

An idea, concealed from Veda, is forbidden to say—
Vedic credo compels action: know, if you may!

"Do understand this matter now. The Vedic religion imposes only action on you; it does not allow you to remain free and healthy. From knowledge come the fears of birth and death. In order to rid us from that fear and avoid reincarnation, we perform action, chant hymns, worship the dolls, and carry out sacrificial fires. These are all futile actions. To take action with a purpose is a vice. Action is liberating; it should not be linked to selfishness. You keep getting involved with action."

I said: "It sounds very new. But why do we act in such a way? What's the way to escape from this?"

: "So finally I've brought you round", said Gagan. "Do you know why you act like this? It's because you treat your parents like guru. Can parents ever be gurus? They're tied by illusions, bound eight-fold. They are engulfed by lust. How can they be gurus?"

The words 'engulfed by lust' hit my ears like a thunderbolt from the blue! On this isolated river-bank in the middle of the night and sitting in the dilapidated Mallik-residence, I kept having a feeling that my consciousness would also now crumble. Perhaps to corner further my crushed entity, Gagan Bairagya exclaimed: "What do the parents do to us? Listen then—

Ensnared by lust, they had their intercourse,
In procreation, good or bad: they didn't judge the source.
They happily indulged in their moment of pleasure—
Enough to destroy them and myself at leisure."

"Stop please, stop at once," I bemoaned. "What're these you're talking about, from where?"

: "I won't. You Brahmins have kept us stifled for a very long time. Not any longer." Bairagya's face shone with revenge. "You're such believers in scriptures. "Are you the only ones capable of writing scriptures? Can't we, too? We've written this treatise—the Sahajiya manuscript. Listen quietly—

They happily indulged in their moment of pleasure—
Enough to destroy them and myself at leisure.
In between, when I keep floating around,
To rescue me, nobody's to be found.
Suffering confinement in womb for a while,
I landed on this earth, under their wile."

I covered my ears with two hands and shook my head in protest. By removing my hands forcibly from my ears, Gagan shouted, setting the wind trembling:

I was not keen at all to come out—
Under their joint will, this came about.

This scripture was intolerable, as it was impossible for me to accept it. I sprang up in a moment; should I sprint away? I didn't recognise all sides in the dark. The broken-down palace had its untrimmed concrete balcony jutting out high and low. Still I began walking fast, very fast. Gagan Bairagya ran even faster like an ascetic Kali-worshipper: with his open hair and unkempt beard flying in the wild wind. But he was unable to follow; in excitement, his foot slipped into a hole. He fell down straight on his stomach on the ground and could not rise. I deserted him to flee, as a man would discard his nightmare behind. Running breathlessly quite far at one go, I reached the river-bank and flopped down.

The night's cloak of darkness was gradually lifting. First, the birds woke up, then the people. Groups of people were moving, their shadows piercing the darkness. Today was the auspicious moment for the Baruni bath. The early dawn was the holiest time for that ceremony. I thought that I must leave the company of inhabitants of this distinct and separate world at once and reach the normal social system, where birth and death were accepted; where the beckoning of the body was considered normal; where the union of the parents was reckoned as pure, desiring an offspring; where life was lived in its own happy rhythm.

No, I could no longer stay here. Before anybody else, I would alone leave Agradweep. Very fast, I caught a ferry boat and crossed over to the other bank. The dawn was only half arrived. There was no end of pilgrims crossing but most were coming to this bank attracted by the Baruni bath. I was, therefore, alone to descend from the boat on the other bank. The lonely road meandered over the sandy outcrop up to the Bahra village. While I was walking on absent-mindedly, the first sunrays appeared. Fields full of crops and the sunlit sky attracted attention. Suddenly, did it seem that another person was walking some distance ahead? Yes, he was and, while walking, was from time to time pausing to look at the river. Because of his frequent pauses, I caught up with him. He was a most ordinary, dry kind of rustic person. I asked: "Didn't you take the Baruni bath?"

The man remonstrated: "Even you didn't."

I said: "I don't observe all this. I don't believe in it."

: "I used to believe, but don't any more. So, I'm fleeing my village for today. Everbody will take a bath in the Ganga today, only I won't. I can't stand this Ganga."

: "Why?"

On that wonderful dawn, the man pointed a finger towards one side of the Ganga and broke down weeping: "My fields and home stood there once upon a time. The demoness has swallowed everything."

I grasped the man's hand. This man belonged to me, not to another clear and separate world. He was entirely a man of my heart. I had been looking for him all this time. Finally, I got around him. I held him in the warmth of my two hands and realised that I had received my very own special treasure at this hour of the Baruni dawn—in my own deep lonely alley.

In my own home
I rest elsewhere

Like all other things, studies on folk culture, too, have some amount of adulteration. Perhaps, a well-turned-out professor or a smart alec journalist may suddenly be observed in the midst of a village fair. In a remote village, there may be a ceremonial or a regular function around the village deity going on. In days of yore, nobody ever went to these festivals. Over the last few decades, one part of the culture-lovers has somehow become interested in them. An astute culture-scholar once told me: "Sir, there are these days a total craze on two things: folk and foreign. You'll observe people having a lot of faith in anything foreign. Similarly, any folk element evokes a lot of appreciation. Bankura horse, Purulia Chhau-mask, Madhubani appliqué, Birbhum Baul music, Santhali dance are all much in vogue."

But that these folk elements, too, had so much adulteration was not known to me. For many years, having dealt with many kinds of Bauls, Fakirs, Sahajiya Vaishnavas, I did understand that there were plenty of low category, fake elements among them. Perhaps, there were many hopelessly hemp-addicted people or lascivious men or simple perverts among them. If asked anything, they would roll their eyes upwards and remark: "Is it easy to comprehend those deep matters?" They would also use some old shibboleths like—breath-control, five elements, Ida-pingala-sushumna, Triveni, sitting on a platform and enquiring on the esoteric, Guptachandrapur, Murshidabad, Guptipada, six mice, fifty-two shops in fifty-three lanes. My listening capacity was already abused with these words. The difficulty was that such clichés were so many in the Baul-Fakir lines that some brilliant words or sentences were confused or got lost. In an unnamed mausoleum in Bangladesh, I had heard a Baul song: *In own home, I belong elsewhere.* Listening to it, I was enthralled and felt a lightning over my body. Come to think of it, we looked for this thrill; though we seldom get it.

Many experiences were gathered, too. The simple folksongs, on first hearing, appeared too simple to bother about. Perhaps, after ten-fifteen years, or even after twenty years, the song's innards might suddenly open up. This was like a champak flower dried up in the leaves of a book. There was neither smell nor colour, still strangely captivating. Actually, just as the hidden treasures of fairy tales needed symbolic hymns, so quite a few Baul or Fakir songs had their meaning concealed in some wonderful, unrevealed words. To unravel those words, even ten to twenty years were not surprising. In these Fakirs' worlds, there was a prevalent relationship called 'Peer-Murshid', meaning guru and disciple. There was a long-standing dispute prevalent between Marfati Fakirs and Mullas. The orthodox mullas said that one had to approach Allah directly in order to reach him. Those gurus and murshids were the influence of Hinduism. Marfatis, on the other hand, opened Quran and pointed out that there was a hint at one place of accepting murshid.Why should I go into all that debate? What I had understood, in essence, was that many parts and words of Fakiri songs and Baul songs would have remained obscure to me, had some Fakir theoretician not explained them to me.

Let us take Imanali. On the very first day, the man astonished me and left me dumbfounded by saying: "Sir, the name has no power unless you've known its inner matter and essence of that matter. What's a word? Word gives only a sense. Behind that sense is the matter. Know the matter, only then the essence comes out by opening the skin of the word."

: "Such as?"

: "Such as, your writing the word 'fire' on a piece of paper. Will the paper burn? It won't, because the word 'fire' doesn't have the burning quality. Likewise, if you chant a name, would you get the named one? You won't, you've to understand his matter: where's he, how's he, where am I, what's the relation between him and me? That's why we Fakirs seek to hear everything in ears, comprehend them in heart and then see them with eyes: before acceptance."

After this, Imanali made another interesting statement. He said: "Sir, as you're running after songs now, won't you afterwards like to unravel its sense? You know what I say, do please run after the words. Then, look for the song. Words are the bait for the fish. The latter is the song. Eve before the words is the silence. Have you heard that song of Lalan? It said... *'When the silence will devour words...'"*

I got entirely immersed in a flow of bottomless consciousness. Let alone finding the bottom, I could not even make desperate strokes. Finding me gazing listlessly at Imanali, the latter observed: 'O dear, what are you looking at so intently?'

'Intent look' meant to plunge deep into the eyes, to blow out all consciousness. Did I have that strength any more? I only thought that I had savoured metaphysical poetry; tasted surrealism; but how come, a rural musician living 200 years ago penned a deeply-layered sentence like: 'When the silence will devour words'?

Imanali said with a smile: "Finally it's the silence that's the substance. There was silence in the creation's first day, and there'll remain silence on the last day. In between, we're creating noise over a few days—words. Even words won't stay. If you seize man, you'd get to know what man is."

The man as God, do catch—
Worshipping man, you'll get Nanda's son:
He's always there as your match!

I asked: "Where's he present?"

Imanali replied, "He's present within man. Everything's in man. That's why, it's said:

Guru's in human form,
Man has wish-fulfilling norm,
Man gets the treasure.
Again, man's the diver for another man—
O, you're man's guru,
Know only man, for good measure."

I was plunged in doubt. This sounded much like that song of Lalan: *'It talks, but doesn't appear before...'* or seemingly so. It was difficult to follow these statements of these Fakirs. When it seemed one was finally being able to follow, suddenly one was thrown into deep waters. I was trying to comprehend through my higher-education logic. Imanali was elucidating in the manner and language of his own sensibilities. The areas which I thought I was unable to follow, were mystic and extra-sensory. Even that was also an academic label: generating confidence after it was stuck.

In this sultriness of doubt and incomprehension, songs often lent a temporary relief. So I said: "I'd rather you sang a song."

The man – with a pronounced secular nature – began a song right away in simple melody:

Come, friend, let's go
Where Shyam sits, there—
I hear, the lord stays in a
Ha-Hey-Hu world's care.

I interrupted the song, asking: "What did you say? 'Ha-Hey-Hu' world? Do these expletives have any meaning?"

Without giving any reply, the song continued:

To recognise the unknown one,
To Shyamnagar, I had gone;
Sitting in the outer room, the Dark 'Kala' played his flute,
Hu-Hu-Hu-Hu sound was heard sweet absolute.
Shyam was the aim in this unknown land,
With Ha-Hey-Hu music strand.

Thereupon began my running behind words. Were 'Ha-Hey-Hu' then not onomatopoeic words? 'Hu-Hu' had been the mind soulfully pining away; 'Ha-Ha' was raucous laughter—had I applied such these words mistakenly done all these days?

Almost like the character Mrityunjay in Tagore's short story, *Guptadhan* ('Secret Treasure'), I wanted to strike my hands at the surrounding incomprehensible sultriness to speak out: "Monk, open the door." Imanali said: "Would you get the meaning of the words right at the beginning? Is it a dictionary that you open and at once the meaning stands out? Can you get all the words in the dictionary? Read the book of the heart."

I suddenly recollected a song across the ages,. In early childhood, I would often hear a beggar singing this near my home in Dignagar village:

With Hu-Hu, I've come around,
With Ha-ha, I'll go on rebound.

The child's mind had concocted a meaning of the song for the time being. That was, Hu-Hu was a kind of emptiness carried while coming to this world; while here was a similar wailing during departure, a sorrow for leaving behind everything.

But the inconsistency was finally caught now: there was a big chasm. But, for that matter, how could it be carried so far as to 'Ha-Hey-Hu' music strand'? What did the sounds mean?

In the college, I had taught academic philology: phonology, morphology, sematics; following Susan Langer's works. And how was it today?

My own news does not reach me at all...

Or,

No news comes prompt to hand—
Roam Delhi-Lahore and other land.

Then, was this the condition to be termed as: 'In my own home, I belong elsewhere?' Was I nurturing, in my Bengali body, another man who had read books from sundry other lands?

Sensing my trouble, Imanali said: "The road to words will open up. Do write down—'Ha' signifies Adam; 'Hey' means Allah; 'Hu' is Nabi. Have you got it?"

: "No."

: "Obviously, understanding the meaning is not everything. There're tea-leaves; there's sugar; there's milk. But all three need to be mixed to produce tea. But cold water won't do; you need hot water. Likewise, to understand Fakiri, a body is needed to begin with: a prepared body, a mature body."

: "How will a body be prepared?"

: "How's water heated up: in fire, isn't it? Body will be prepared in the fire of guru's advice. Catch a Murshid; don't let the scholar take over and dilly-dally on inane queries. Discard all deceptions, please."

Truly speaking, I used to avoid the Fakirs since then. First of all, I had not read the Islamic scriptures well; did not know Arabic and Persian words properly, let alone resolve the doubts inside the words. There're more confusions. Marfati Fakirs are against Shariat. Kalma (special Islamic prayers); Roza (annual fasting);

Haj (visit to Mecca); Zakat (donations) and Namaz (daily prayers) – all these they ignore – as self-drawn; practice-oriented. They're not merely materialistic; Lalan has called himself a 'material beggar'. From an excess of material doctrine, Bauls disregard the path of conjecture. They, in fact, don't accept any basis of imagination. This was expressed by Kangal Harinath – popularly known as'Shokher Baul' (a Baul by choice) – in this manner:

If, through imagination, the formless had shown form—
Then, leaving meditation'n'prayer,
Folks would use imagination as norm;
Many conjectures as norm.

From this material doctrine, they're believers in the body. They deny both earlier birth and re-birth. They accept that the body is nourished from the five elements. After life is over, the five elements get absorbed in the five elements again. Raising the weapon of logic, Lalan questioned:

Death reaches out to divinity per se
If all dead reach divinity
For both saint'n'sinner community—
Where is the need for prayers and chants
Over land and water, I ask if I may!
If the body is born from elements five
And blends with them, when not alive,
The divine parts, to divinity arrive—
Heaven or hell comes whose way?

All this logic, debates and counter arguments – for, as well as against – complicated matters. So I was not keen to enter those trying areas involving conundrums. But I did not discard them either. I was, so to say, waiting for my chance.

At that time, an enterprising young man, Akbar Ali Sheikh, came over from Berhampur. Prof. Shaktinath Jha had sent him to me, to extend an invitation for the third annual conference of the Baul Fakir Association in the coming January. The Association had Jha as President and Ali as Secretary; what was it all about?

First, Akbar Ali handed over a leaflet to me, whose gist was as follows:

Unlike Brahminism, Christianity or Islam, the Baul-Fakir doctrine did not belong to any sect or community. This was an approach to life's philosophy and life-activities. Men belonging to any religion could admit and practise this doctrine, while remaining steadfast in their own faith.

Those tenets of imagination or thought, which have no material basis and those which are not amenable to the five sensory organs, are rejected by the Bauls and Fakirs as conjectures. They do not take regard of the imaginary deities. The living man – as the highest expression of creation – is his subject of enquiry and respect.

The powerful stream of caste, creed and divisive credo of religions has mystified India today. We, the Bauls and Fakirs, oppose whatever divides men. Come; let us hold aloft our glorious message of humanism.

The words were indeed very nice. I started with a set of questions to Akbar Ali.

: "When and where did your association have its first conference?"

: "Our Association was established on 4 September 1983. The first conference was held in Swaruppur, Murshidabad, on 12 March 1984."

: "When was the second conference?"

: "It was in Hariharpara, Murshidabad, on 17 March 1985."

: "On this occasion?"

: "It would be in Goradanga village near Karimpur on the border of Nadia, on 25-26 January. Will you please come?"

: "I certainly have the intention of going, but before that, it would be necessary to know about the whole affair. Well, how did your Baul-Fakir Association come up?"

Akbar Ali quietly, yet clearly, replied: "The real reason was the need to be well-organised. You can say that we had to be united in response to the beatings and fisticuffs. Have you heard about how much torture is inflicted on the Bauls and Fakirs by the religious bigots?'

: "It would be wrong to say I've heard, but appropriate to say that I've read in the papers and magazines. Especially, this is perhaps more rampant on the Murshidabad side."

: 'Yes. The number of Bauls-Fakirs is high in that district; the number of mosques and Maulavis is also high there. So the incidents are more frequent on that side. Yet small incidents take place here and there, the news does not spread. But we get the news. We resist and complain to the administration."

: "Could you tell me about some current events of special torture?"

: "Yes, I can." Akbar Ali opened his diary and read out: "On 14 April 1984, a Fakir named Latif in Durlavpur of Naoda police station in Murshidabad district was killed by spear. On 13 July 1985, we were prevented from holding a meeting in Farazi Para in Jalangi police station and people were beaten up and thrown out. On 14 July, our Ruhul Amin in the Mirzapur neighbourhood of Baninathpur in Sargachhi was tortured; he was beaten up, had his hair and beard shaved and was driven out of his village. On 15 July, Abdur Rahim in Gopinathpur of Beldanga police station was tortured. Apart from these, stray incidents of abuse, warning, showing angry red eyes, etc., continue all the while. Even after these, if we're not organised..."

: "Yes, you've taken the right action," I said. "I'll of course come. I'll reach on 24th itself. I haven't, however, been to Goradanga village earlier. Can meetings and conferences be freely held there?"

: "There's no tension. It's a powerful base of the Fakirs. The village people're good folks."

On a late afternoon of the month of Magh, I reached the dust-ridden village of Dhulodoba in Goradanga. It was in Nadia district only in name; in dialect and accent, it was entirely of pure Murshidabad vintage. It was a small village with about a hundred and fifty familes, entirely of Muslim descent. Farming was the only means of livelihood. All this news could be gathered while walking along. Finally I reached the site of the conference. My palms responded to the warm handshakes of the organisers. Quite tired, I sat down under the canopy. There were sundry groups of Bauls-Fakirs gathered around. Smoking of hemp had begun in abundance. Shakti introduced me to Mazharul Khan—the head of this village and this area. Of medium build and wearing dhoti and shirt, he shyly showed his face and disappeared. Everyone was busy in one way or the other. By the time I got over my tiredness, puffed rice and tea were served. I started a conversation with Mazharul Fakir. He was a broad-minded, householder Fakir, from a moneyed farmer family. The responsibilities as well as the risk of the conference were mainly hitched on his broad shoulders. The attached large house also belonged to him. His sons, too, followed the Fakiri faith and sang Fakiri songs.

I asked: "You're holding the Fakir conference in this village. Will there be any resistance, or, any trouble?"

Laughing heartily, Mazharul said: "Who'll create trouble, and why so? There's no conflict with anybody. If you want the reality, out of one hundred and fifty Muslim households of this village, one hundred are followers of the Fakiri sect."

: "How did it happen?"

: "I've done it gradually. Could it be done easily? No, it took time."

: "Tell me a little, let me hear."

: "My age is now sixty. From childhood, I had been keen on Fakiri faith. From then onwards, I've moved with them. I had been fighting so frequently with my father at home; he had thrown me out. He was a pure Shariati Muslim, and we used to have debates. I, too, have read Islamic scriptures. I know Arabic, studied the Quran and understand the meaning of Hadis. On this side, no Alem Mullah could tackle me in debate. They no longer bother me."

I liked the self-confident man, I realised that, under Mazharul's personality, judgment and influence, the people of Goradanga village might not have become Fakirs, but are not intolerant about Fakirs, and are cooperative. Here under the banyan tree, now that cooking was in progress for hundreds of people, so many villagers have been lending their hands. Were those, who would listen – with heart and soul – to the Fakiri songs at night, Hindus or Muslims? Were they Shariati or Marfati? They were neither. They would be lovers of humanity then, mad after music. But the religious doctrines of pure Islam apparently consider music as irreligious and mischievous. Casting an aspersion, a moralist called Asad-ullah once wrote:

Which are those Peers who music instruments, play—
Use melodies to sing songs, give claps: happy'n'gay!

In reply, Abdur Rasid Chisti wrote in his book, *Gyan Sindhu* (Knowledge Ocean):

> The music which creates affection for Allah and his Messengers is termed religious music. But, according to the Fatwas of the Maulavis, if even this music is illegitimate, then why do Maulavis perform *bahaz* of realised seers at *majlish*es by singing

> Diwan and Masnavi lyrics from Maulana Rumi; Diwan Hafez; Diwan Shaman Tubrez; Diwan Lotk; Diwan Moinuddin Chisti; Diwan Zami, etc.? Does all the fault lie with Bengali music?

Really speaking, music was the language of Marfatis; the single-stringed drone was the symbol of their life. If that drone is snatched away and broken by someone, if singing was prohibited, then it was like interfering with the religious meditation of the Marfatis. Such injustice needed to be opposed.

Meanwhile, someone brought in Ruhul Amin. This was the same man about whom I had heard from Akbar Ali. In July last year, having shaven his beard and moustache, having destroyed his drone and having burnt his home, the religious bigots had thrown him out of his own village. In disgust and grief, he no longer maintained his beard. Deep resentment was visible in his eyes – as if someone had hugely betrayed him – and his speech equally solemn. Wearing a white dhoti and wrapping a white sheet around his body, Ruhul sat silently in front. I felt the prick of the dreadful bite of conscience.

I only held Ruhul's two hands in deep compassion. Ruhul looked up with painful eyes, perhaps searching for assurance in the vicinity of so many people.

In the meantime, there was a small gathering where – having tuned his two-stringed drone – an unknown Baul had started singing, which seemed to me very relevant for removing the sultriness of the moment:

Sain, in well-water, you've me, confined
In a dirty tank's bind.
There would be rains,
All my hope remains.
This condition of mine will disappear,
In how many days, shall I find?

In the well-water is stagnated the current of the flowing society. There are instances of religious fanaticism, killings, jealousy and malice on all sides.

The conference began after dusk fell. There were songs, more songs, speeches and promises to remain united. But, amidst everything, Ruhul's pain-stricken, resentful face kept floating in, like a super-imposed image. Still, I had the occasion to meet so many Dervishes and Bauls that night. The experience of dining was also of a very novel kind. Sitting on a crumbling jute-stick mat, it amounted to eating the mix of dal and rice, with mustard oil. It was then Magh midnight; even the backbone was shivering in the cold. Finishing the meal somehow, I just ran to the night-shelter. The bed was laid in the living room of a Muslim aristocrat. I asked the kind, civil host: "Is this your residence?" In a typically Fakiri style, he responded: "So the villagers say."

Outside, microphones were constantly belting out Fakiri music; it would continue the whole night. Next to me was Manullah, a half-crazy man, who chatted away. A resident of Madaripur and apparently a Fakir at one point of time, he lost his mental balance from a wrong dosage of hemp. He told me: "People call me mad. But I'm not mad. I'm just crazy; I can't tolerate the intolerable. I've composed a song on this torture on Ruhul Fakir. Do you know, I've studied up to the Matriculation class? My pseudonym is Nizami, under which I write."

I asked: "What does Niizami mean?"

: "The word Nizami means designer or decorator. But its latent meaning is 'garbage-destroyer'; sacred doer; reformer. Take, for instance, the sun. He is licking away all the debris, mud, uncleanliness."

Suddenly, he stood up on the bed and exclaimed dramatically, waving his hands: "When the human society gets completely submerged in a pit of waste and garbage, when the rusted, ruined boat is about to be sucked in by the tumultuous currents of the ocean, then you need the thunderous grip of a powerful boatswain; you need a Nizami. When the society and its people keep getting oppressed under a few human beasts like scholarly Mullahs, then only you need a Nizami."

Nizami sat down as suddenly as he had leapt up. Quite bewildered, I kept watching Nizami's shadow-play in the almost darkened room. Now he rose up, now he sat down and kept reciting:

O lord, the portrait that you've drawn of mine,
That portrait transforms with every birth on earth—
Therefore, I'm myself observing that portrait.

Whoever thinks hard becomes increasingly lonely;
The desire to live on arises, with Nature
as the centre; and the mind lives in hope, in a secret wait.

My way to freedom lies latent within thoughts,
The more I think, the more I'm silent—
What's the religion in the silent meditation of nature's beauty?

Through the medium of love, man can live
In honesty,
And a loveless life
Creates the death of good quality.

It was difficult to completely ignore Nizami's composition. Upon hearing, I could make out that it had a core quality. How did a half-crazy, half-Fakir write like this? Since the time we met and till this midnight, he was unceasingly smoking hemp. I realised his intoxication was the cause of his incessant talk. But all these were his instant oral compositions without any pre-planning. Indeed, the world of Fakirs was half layered with mystery. Spending the night with Nizami was an exceptional and extraordinary experience. For the rest of the night, whenever my sleep broke, I noticed Nizami was sitting up and clicking his fingers very loudly to exclaim: "Allah, Allah".

In the previous evening, he had precipitated another incident. A professor was lecturing on folk culture at the conference then. In his narrative, there was no stamp of experience about folk-life; on the contrary, there was a blatant exposition of bookish knowledge. He was constantly mouthing such terms and expressions as totem, magic belief, fertility worship, cult, sect and so on. Everybody was sitting through it and listening helplessly, maintaining civility. Suddenly from among the listeners, Nizami stood up clicking his fingers and said: "'Allah, Allah, give wisdom, give wisdom." The professor was bewildered and we were taken aback. But it worked. The professor desisted from disbursing further wisdom.

I had wondered at times that it would not be a bad idea to have a Nizami or two in everyday life. There was a dire necessity to sprinkle cold water on all kinds of hypocrisy and lecturing, pomposity and theorising. Whatever, I asked Nizami during the small hours of the night: "Don't you sleep the whole night?"

Nizami replied: "Only in the night I happen to talk to Him. Whatever the thought process, composition of lyrics, all these I do at night. He is seen at night; everybody remains asleep then. And tell me what sleep is. Nizami has written in his lyric...

I feel sleepy when there's no more logic.
For thinking with logic, to remain alive
Is the knowledge-power for proper life."

Clicking his fingers in appreciation of his own merit of composition, the self-indulgent Nizami said: "Ha, ha, ha, Allah Allah, Nizami has written rightly. You go to sleep, and bestow wisdom in the meeting tomorrow. Meanwhile, let me do some smoking. You must know that smoking is the royal habit. In smoking: king means royalty, ha ha Allah Allah."

It was, no doubt, a very interesting existence. A 30-35-year-old youth remained alive with intoxicants and verbal intoxication. He wrote lyrics of deep thoughts effortlessly. How did it happen? There was no inclination for food and sleep. I had heard that a Sufi meditator had two stages of worship: 'Fana' and 'Vaka'. To remain aligned with God, or the worshipped one, as a non-dual entity was Fana. And to exchange thoughts endlessly with the worshipped one in a standing dual relationship was Vaka. Which condition was Nizami's—Fana or Vaka?

It was perhaps none of the two: sheer morbidity or half-insanity. From that point of view, all Bauls and Fakirs were half-insane. Deserting one's own home and hearth for self-investigation in an outcast lifestyle from the physical point of view was no little craziness. *'Ba'* meant self, *'ul'* meant investigator; this was apparently the genesis of the word 'Baul'. Again, others said that 'Baul' had come from *batul* (neurotic). Who knows the reality? The meaning of the word 'Fakir' was comparatively quite clear: to leave everything to become a Fakir. By everything, most people thought of consumption, pleasure, wealth and treasure. But it was not so; everything meant leaving all kinds of sacraments: birth-death-rebirth-and the concepts of fear and social shame, even society. Nizami said when there is no longer the logic of thinking, man feels sleepy. At the moment, my logic for thinking was so strong that my sleep fled. Dawn was also creeping in slowly through the mist of the month of Magh. Nizami was murmuring, I asked: "What're you doing, Nizami?"'

With half-closed eyes, he said: "I'm saying my morning prayers."

I said: "Sorry, I had disturbed your prayers."

: "Not at all. Our prayers are undisclosed; it's going on within. The human voice doesn't reach there."

He completed his prayer by clicking together the tips of his thumb and second finger. Then he said with a hearty laugh: "You really can sleep well, as I see. You're sleeping so late, after sleeping all night!"

: "Where were the whole night-hours? I went to bed only at midnight."

: "Ha Ha, Allah Allah. Who knows when it's afternoon, and when the night-hours? Everything is the same to Nizami. I keep watching Allah's actions the whole day and grow mystified. One can't see anything at night. See Allah's judgement—then cattle and roses are equally dark. Only then *ruh*, that is, soul's light gets lit. Allah is to be remembered at night. Ha Ha. Allah is to be remembered at night."

: "Not to be remembered in the morning?"

: "In the morning, man has thought for his stomach, thought for his business. Haven't you heard songs in Khejmat's voice? Listen...

Like this worry for my stomach—
There's in life no other worry,
Rice on the low, lentil's on the low:
Wife's complaints forever show; and I am truly sorry.
In the morning, when I pray—
With worries heavy, I think in dismay,
How and what will I earn this day?
Post my prayers these thoughts I can't bury;
The fire of hunger makes my chant a wonder:
I count the beads stringed around my rosary.

: "Ha ha, Allah Allah!"

While listening to the song, I changed my clothes and said: "Well, now I'll go to the conference. Won't you go?"

: "I will; but now in my mind, a mega-conference is now going on. The speech for that conference, meaning a lyric, is what I'll have to write down at once, otherwise I'll forget. When at early dawn, daylight streamed in through the bay-window – it was Nizami's light – I composed a lyric. Would you like to listen?

In this universe, every sand-particle
Has a value for, each sand-particle
Glistens in the glow of light."

With the indulgence of the morning sun, I kept gazing at Nizami affectionately and continued my quest for his inaccessible mind. Nizami rose and recited dramatically:

Whatever I sought, I got,
You're the best.
Now take me to the last aeon—
Open the doorway.

I said: "Have you made me out as an angel?"

: "You're an angel, you're Gibrael, you're the messenger. You're Khad, you're Khuda. Within you, I've heard the resonance of Ha Hey Hu."

It was a strange language, a strange world; how much was I a denizen of a different world, of different language? Yet it was a wonder that this Nizami and I sat next to each other yesterday and shared a meal of rice-and-dal kedgeree with a drizzle of mustard oil. Were man's worlds of faith so different? "In my own home, I belong elsewhere." Or was it, "in another's home, I'm myself?"

In the morning session of the conference, I sat next to Mazharul Fakir. He introduced me to his son Manzoor. Yesterday I heard a beautiful *tattwagaan* in his voice. In between speeches passing of resolutions, I got quietly up: to go roaming towards the fields. In the green fields, full of crops, there was still a curtain of mist. Enchanted and alone, I kept looking around. A little distance ahead, date-palm juice was being boiled in a cauldron. A couple of drongos were leaping about on the ground in this early morning cold; two half-naked urchins were loitering about, on the lookout for fresh palm juice. Suddenly, a middle-aged villager appeared and stood in front, after saluting me. He was wearing a stitched loin-cloth and a vest. He said his name was Deldar Hussain Khan. I asked him: "Whoever I had met in this village had the title of Khan, what was the matter?" Smiling self-indulgently, he said: "You could call ours an aristocratic village; everybody is a Khan. They're *ashraf*, that is, *sharif*, civilised gentlemen."

: "Are they truly so?"

: "They must have been, once upon a time. The pride of the past still exists. But everybody is a farmer. Have you heard that saying? As they say:

His body stinks—he's Itr Ali;
That's a blind man—our Nazar Ali;
Not a single box he owns—our Dedar Bux!

"Our situation is somewhat like that! Whatever is the financial status, each of us is a Khayer Khan! But yes, Mazharul uncle is a true Khan. What powerful presence and courage! Amidst all the surrounding Shariatis, he has been upholding the flag of Marfati Fakirs."

: "Well, is there caste discrimination among Muslims?"

: "It's not there outside, but persists within. Look, this *duniya* – the world of Allah – is running on two things. Which are the two? They're the rich and the poor: Ashraf and Atraf."

: "Isn't there one more—Arjal?"

: "Don't count it among Muslims. Do you know who Arjals are? They are gypsies, jugglers, potters, cobblers and their ilk. They are of low class."

: "Who're the Ashrafs?"

: "Ashrafs are high class Muslims—Sheikhs, Saiyads, Mughals, Pathans. Among them, the Saiyads are the most blue-blooded of all. They also are of two clans: Fatemiya and Ulbi. They also have sub-clans—Hussaini, Hasni, Musabi, Rajvi, Qazimi, Takabi, Nakabi, and others. But would you like to hear all this?"

: "Why not? Those are living side by side in this Bengal for hundreds of years, yet are virtually unknown to us. Is this nice? From only this is born disbelief, sectarianism, violence. But how did you know all this?"

: "My father used to teach us orally. Then listen, among Sheikhs, the highest are the Qureshis, because Hazrat Mohammed was born in this clan. Other branches are—Siddiqi, Faruqi, Almani, Abbasi Khaledi, and some more which I don't recall. The main point is that Sheikhs and Saiyads came from Arabia. I've heard that the Turks from Central Asia were given the name Mughal. Afghans became Pathans. We're the descendents of these Pathans, that is, Khan."

I did not notice when Nizami had quietly come over. Before Deldar Khan could finish, Nizami said: "But you too are not aristocratic Khans; you're Atraf Khans."

: "Why?" I wanted to know.

: "Because the mixed class which was generated by the marriages between the foreign Muslims and the local ones was also considered aristocratic among the Atrafs. Their titles were Qazi, Choudhuri, Sheikh, Khan, Malik."

Deldar angrily asked: "And what are you?"

: "I'm neither Ashraf nor Atraf. I am Huq, Manaulla Huq. Huq means truth, Huqiqat. I'm not involved in the division of classes. Haven't you heard in Duddu's song?

In this land, Saiyads and Qazis
are seen to explain class—
As in Bengal, Brahmins do
explain to the mass.
Like Brahmins, they do the same,
Keep Qazi, Khondakar surname—
To appear aristocrat: they've this fuss.

Weaver, oil-man, sweeper, et al,
Are made low class, to be kept small,
Is this Islamic scripture at all?
With boasting: all to surpass?"

At long last, I could virtually step into a relaxed space. The protestation came from the Muslim society itself, didn't it? Lalan's disciple, Duddu had raised a sarcastic protest as a fitting reply to this class-division that was against Islam's scriptures. It was also clear that this reflected a social truth as well. Was then Ashraf-Atraf-Arjal modelled on the class-distinction of the Brahmins? Deldar's face was sombre, while Nizami appeared very happy. He accompanied me while returning from the conference. Talking incessantly, he said: "Everyone calls me crazy due to my hemp addiction. But let me tell you, our Bauls-Fakirs took birth from this point: in protest against the distinctions. The Vedic religion and Brahminism have wrought havoc."

I said: "Well, tell me: now that you call yourselves Marfati, what have you, as Nizami, done and achieved."

: "Do you know the scriptural explanation? Peer-Murshidi explanation is another one, which is set in 14-metre, such as—:

Shariat is the tree, its branch is the truth,
Tariqat are tree-leaves, Marfat is the fruit.

Marfat is not complete without Shariat,
Shariat's incomplete without Marfat.

"Shariat is the tree, but, tell me, what good is a fruitless tree? Huqiqat is the way, that is, the branch which would bear fruit. Tariqat comprises the systems of jurisprudence, and are the leaves whose shadows would protect the fruits. Fruit-bearing is the main aim; but the tree must be there. That part is Shariat. Our Murshid used to explain this in another way. He used to say:

Shariat is the group—
Tariqat is the road to lead the whole troupe.
Catch huq to go by that way,
That's Huqiqat, if you may,
Where shall you go? Marfat is through,
Marfat is secret doctrine, only for you.

"Would you listen to Nizami's own explanation? Marfat is the secret doctrine that you may not know by yourself. You've to know it through the guru; understand it through the body; meditate on it through respiration. This is what I call Marfat."

I quipped: "Your whole thesis is a huge mistake, which will be rectified through the beatings of the Mullahs one day, do you understand?"

"Ha ha, Allah Allah," said Nizami, by clicking his fingers and by beating himself twice with own fists. He added: "Only beat me, only beat me, Allah, barring the *la-makan*."

: "What's that? What's called *la-makan*?"

: "No messenger has given you that message, has he? Then listen to the scripture from the Nizami's mouth, which is a ballad of the madman. When Allah created man's body, he sent the spirit into it. But the spiritual substance emerged from the body, shaking violently. It said: 'Goodness gracious, it's burning there;

Satan's everywhere in the body.' Then Allah created *la-makan* two digits below the heart. Satan can't reach there anyway and the spirit resides there."

: "'And *nafs*?"

: "By *nafs*, we Fakirs mean the semen. It's difficult to control semen. Allah created the Prophet to control semen. But man is blind, so he doesn't foresee his own consequence. Man is deaf, so he doesn't listen to the prophet's advice. By controlling *nafs* well, one can reach Khuda; by being a slave to the semen, one falls prey to Saitan. Listen to Mansur's lyrics:

Khuda's in semen, Saitan's in semen,
We're slaves in semen's lap,
With shackles of illusion blocking our ken
We move around in the feminine trap."

: "For controlling semen, don't you pray for Allah's mercy?"

: "We pray for Allah's mercy all the time. Yet in the Marfati path, the main point is about self-control. Why should one drag Khuda for one's own carelessness? That's why it's said:

In own hands, birth'n'death stay—
Khuda controls birth'n'death: whoever does say?
Holding semen, life you save,
Otherwise, you get grave,
Ayurved decides what you crave: no scope's for play.
Letting semen waste and fall,
Lying on roads, like animals all,
Many folks die'n'stall but blame with Khuda, lay.

"Ha ha, Allah Allah, you've kept both the life-wand and the death-well in front. Ha ha, which one should Nizami pick up? Do you know what Allah is saying? '*Fazkuruni Waskurukum*', that is, 'I remember whoever remembers me'. Ha ha, Allah, even Nizami has a memory-lapse at times."

Meanwhile a lot of time passed, as though in a spell. At the intervals of the conference, meals were in progress, when everyone complained: "We didn't get to be with you and enjoy your company really well." What could I say? I was rudderless in a new world. Even if I knew the world of Sahajiya Bauls, the Fakirs' milieu was totally unknown. My only experience was the time I spent in the company of the Benowari Fakir, but how little that was! I was only looking with an open-eyed wonder at the people of an unfamiliar world.

Many unknown and unnamed Fakirs sat in front, while being served food. I had to know their functions and activities. It would not be the actions of the half-crazy Nizami. He was in a frenzy of sap—a *raskhyapa.* Manzoor came to say: "Abbaji is calling you." I went to Mazharul Khan's room. He said: "We hardly talked! Is any conversation possible at such fairs and festivities? Are you staying on today? We'll talk at night."

I replied: "No, I'm leaving this afternoon. Please don't nurse a sadness in your mind. I'll be back very soon. I've so much to know. Would you care to tell me?"

Holding both my hands and pressing them warmly with his hands, Mazharul retorted: "Now that you're going away today leaving a scar in my chest, this will have to be compensated by visiting again. You'll come, won't you? Fakirs are hard to be deceived by empty words and grand attire."

Could one leave by just resolving to leave? Were preparations not necessary? In my case, of course, there was some need of a mental preparedness. Before going to Mazharul Fakir, I took a little time to do some studies. I did want to know from him a lot of things, but on which topics? In order to decide that, I read the famous English book by Raffiuddin on Bengali Muslims. I sampled the background history of Farazi and Wahabi movements and their outcomes. Alongside, some descriptions could be noted about conflicts and encounters between purist Muslims and Marfati Fakirs. The clashes and struggles between the peer doctrine and Fakiri faith on one side and the orthodox Muslims were comparatively quite old.

In 1935, Enamul Huq had written directly in his book, *Bange Sufi Prabhaav* (Sufi Influence in Bengal):

> In the nineteenth century, there was an all-round arrangement for destroying Bauls. At that time, two well-known reformers arose among the Muslims.
> They were Maulana Kiramat Ali (died 1873) and Habaji Shari Atullah. Maulana Kiramt Ali's main fields of action was in North Bengal and Habaji Shari Atullah's home and field of activities were in East Bengal (Faridpur).

Here Baul implied Fakirs as well. The main targets of attack of the purists were Lalan Fakir and his professed ideology. The book, *Baul Dhwangsha Fatwa* (Baul Destruction Fatwa), by Maulana Rezauddin was the hardest hitting one in this respect. This apart, Mohammad Ali's *False Peer* and Mohammad Saiyad's *Marfat Nama* contained many critical and oblique references. In a book, concern was expressed about the Last Judgment (Qayamat) for Islam:

Imam Ghazzali writes in his book.
Qayamat willl have three signs in its nook.
When anti-scripture Dervish appears, at that time—Qayamat will soon appear and then fall in line.
According to documents, Alem won't do,
Read Quran and Hadis, you'll have to.
All Amirs and Sardars of this earth

Will be exposed: whatever their worth.
When these three bad signs'll be there,
True Muslims will be all rare.
That time has perhaps come now,
Anti-scripture Fakirs are many, anyhow.
Whichever exposed Sardars were there,
They became Murid in anti-scripture care.
On earth, howsoever Alems appear,
For false Dervish, they become peer.
Muslims are gone now, alas, alas,
Qayamat has clearly come to pass.

Someone discovered another evil sign for the pious Muslim society and wrote:

The youthful female class became Fakir en masse,
Left their husbands to be with the Peers.

In Rashid's lyrics published from erstwhile East Bengal, some hints could be gathered about the activities of the new Fakirs. Rashid said:

There're now pseudo-Fakirs many a one,
Non-Vedic, those pseudo-Fakirs, of Vedic rules they do make fun.
This is the difference main; but don't spread it beyond your ken ,
Men and women pray together, as companions then—With your sap, do travel up;, you must the bottom shun.

Meditating on five saps:
Be a success or you fail and lapse,
Holding poison in the body; carry it in a pot, don't leave gaps,
Your seeds you devour, so that birth and death remain none.

Here, allusions to adulterous meditative methods practised in copulation with females and hints at seminal fluid-drinking were clearly indicated. The body-yoga, practised by Fakirs, were also mentioned. Afterwards, Rashid said:

Your service-maid, for guru, if you laid,
Fear for other world would be all gone.

About the dominance of Fakiri faith at that time and other sects, there were some hints in another lyric by Rashid, such as:

Watching conditions in the Kali era, I plunge into worry and almost die;
How many men in how many ways do Fakiri to life apply.
Some say: Allah is air; Some say: Allah is fire;
Some say: Allah is water; Allah is held heavy and high.
Some treat the jewel of semen—
as Khuda and the Fakiri path try.
Some say: Sain floated formless in the egg's eye ,
The semen lent form to the egg and made it law, or nigh.
Some say: Fatema is Allah's mother—Hazarat Ali is then Allah's father;
the thought makes me cry.

Fakirs used to find counter songs in response to these songs in Lalan's compositions or Duddu's lyrics. They used to sing:

Kalma, Namaz, Roza, Zakat, Haj: to complete,
Observing them, you obtain Shariat's full treat.
I can make out sense,
These are not Shariat's essence.
Can more meanings be still there?
Sans Elem and sans Murid: the one—
To whom Shariat's bounds're unknown—
Only has the verbal flair!

This conflict was not today's, nor was it confined to a day.

It was nobody's case that this conflict was limited to West Bengal between Peer Fakir faith and Shariatism. Truly speaking, Bangladesh had this conflict and confrontation at its zenith. As an Islamist state, it had stronger demands of the Shariati law and the struggle for survival of the Marfatis was far more complex there. In February 1986, the writer Atiyar Rahman wrote in his booklet, *Aal Sadeed:* 'Bangladesh has no scope of freedom in socialism-Marxism-Washingtonism. As the largest Muslim country, Bangladesh has the progress of its land and nation rooted in the Shariati socialism.' M. A. Sobhan appealed for destruction of Lalan's burial in his book *Jalal-e-Faisala.*

In 1986, this Sobhan gave a speech in Kushtia on 'Peer Muridi Illegal', which came out in a printed form. He wrote there:

> We are Muslim inhabitants of a land or a region where the Peer-Muridi has spread like the aquatic wild plant over a long time... You know that I am a controversial man. I am continuing to apply fierce logic and debate against Peer-Muridi, Milad-qiam, Isle-sawar, Woras, etc., infidels today over a half-century... There is no Peer in Bangladesh against whom I have not waged a debate. We have eradicated ebullient Peers from Panti, Viala, Munsipur-Qutabpur, Kirtinagar and Benipur of Jessore. I have debated against almost one dozen Alems from among today's highest official Peers, that is, the powerful, cow-eating Atarpeers in Jugiya village in the suburb of Kushtia. Many of you have witnessed in what a pathetic condition they had landed, in this debate...Many of them had to flee, after their beards were clean shaven. I had confrontation with many... the Peer of Shambhuganj; Walullah Peer of Rajsahi; Peer of Bagura; Peer of Dahagram; and other Peers of Rangpur, Tangail, Faridpur, Dhaka, Tungi region and especially all the Peers of Pabna district...I have had my encounters with them.

In fact, all these conflicts, debates and encounters had less religious insanity and fanaticism behind them, and more of the rural mentality. In his book, *The Bengal Muslims, 1871-1906,* Rafiuddin Ahmed made a powerful comment: 'As a community, the Muslims were overwhelmingly rural in character and they contributed only a fraction of the urban population.'

Rafiuddin also pointed to another inequality, saying:

> Equally interesting and significant is the pattern of distribution of Hindus and Muslims in the various professions. Whenever the Muslims formed the bulk of the population, as in eastern Bengal, they belonged predominantly to the cultivation classes, while land-holding, professional and mercantile occupations were dominated by the high-caste Hindus.

Here remained a long history of deception and financial disparity. The majority of the Muslim class in rural life was perennially in the role of poor cultivator and the rites and festivities, economic progress and cultural high status were occupied by the upper-caste Hindu community. As a result, the Muslim society remained comparatively illiterate and rustic. Could one expect a widespread catholicity and indifference to a sub-sect of one's own religion? This apart, there was an inherent stream in the land. Those who were once Hindus were later the converted Muslims. Could they completely forget the Hindu rituals, festivals, sacraments and social customs? Witnessing the rural Muslims' observation of the Holi, Diwali, brother's felicitation, Bauni-tying, cow-worship, weekly celebration of Goddess Lakshmi, and other ritual ceremonies of Hinduism, Munsi Sameeruddin wrote in utter dejection:

The land's infidelity comes to one's mind—
Let me narrate it, for everyone to find.

Holi, Diwali and each such festive rite—
Performing 'Bauni'-tying, which is beyond Islam's sight.
'Bhaiphonta' for brother's health: being Muslim despite.
On Thursday the 'Lakshmi Day', money not to lend or borrow—
Such infidelity in land causes me huge sorrow.

Wahabi and Farazi movements were rooted in the purification of Islam, side by side with the eradication of grave-and-tomb-worship of Peers and Fakirs; and reduction in the Marfati practice of adulterous meditation and musical celebration. They did not accept the guru-disciple relationship. They also protested against the declaration of Fakirs that Allah could be seen. Fakirs were against *andaazi-sadhana*—where elements are left to the imagination during prayers. In an essay *(Baul Darshaney Bharatiya Bastubaader Upadaan* – 'Elements of Indian Materialism in Baul Philosophy' – in *Aneek*, Dec. 1985-Jan. 1986), Shaktinath Jha cited two beautiful quotations from a lyricist, named Aalep:

1. Without viewing Mohammad's form, worship how can be?
Only my ears've heard, but eyes didn't see.
2. Surmise and meditate: how can this be true?
Worship, after viewing the form, and attain the essence in you!

Sejda (salutation) was very important in Islam; Except Allah, *sejda* was prohibited for anybody else. In Namaz, *sejda* came as a significant sequence. Yet, Marfati Fakirs were reluctant to offer *sejda* to an invisible Allah. Their contention was reflected in Abed's lyrics:

Doing sejda without seeing is a case of wasted labour,
Sejda to a name, without his vision,
is doing the washerman's donkey a favour!

Contrarily, Fakirs did *sejda* to Guru-Murshids and to respected persons. In the person (Khad), they saw Khuda. As a matter of fact, the main protest of the Marfatis was against the external practices of Islam. Therefore, they were not attracted by Kalma, Namaz, Roja, Zakat, Haj: the five Shariati rituals. Here arose the sharpest misunderstandings. The confrontation which started with debates culminated in blood-letting conflicts or, like Ruhul, obligatory eviction from home.

Islam society was as cautious about the purdah of women as it was conscious about their willful habits and customs. The orthodox Muslim had never pardoned the non-Namazi women or female companions of Fakirs. The following description (quoted earlier):

Your service-maid, for guru, if you laid,
Fear for other world would be all gone

...captured the irritable victory-march of the Peers and Murshids of the rural society of that era, especially in the inner quarters – the sanctum sanctorium – of traditional homes.

In protest, the orthodox society ordained:

If there is a non-Namazi woman in anybody's home,
Divorce is appropriate, so says the holy tome.
After divorce, throw away the harlot to doom,
And hit upon her head with a hard broom.

Keeping in mind the history of these confrontations, hatred and conflict, I was getting ready for the context of a deeper discussion with Mazharul Fakir. Suddenly it occurred to me that, in spite of the manifold differences of the Sahajiya Vaishnava and Bauls from the Marfati Fakirs, there was one major similarity at one point. All three sects drank the 'two moons', i.e., stool and urine;

some believed in the 'four moons', i.e., stool, urine, menstrual fluid and seminal fluid, which they mixed to drink and rub on the body. This apparently detestable practice had taken many by surprise, who did not wish to go to the bottom of the process and understand the essence, by surprise. Drinking urine (*Shivambu* or Shiva's liquid), has recently shaken the civil society. There had been books about its physical benefit. Like drinking one's own urine, the system of drinking one's own semen in our country was also pretty old. The *Ganaswasthya* magazine, published from Bangladesh, carried an unusual analysis on *'Baulder Jauno Jiban o Janma Niyantran* (The Sex Life of Bauls and their Birth-control), in its April-May, 1984 issue, that caught my attention. Its special correspondent wrote:

> It is true that the human body has two animating antigens which are not part of the body's immunology system. These two are the tear's fluid – the tear drops – and the seminal fluid. If the fluid content of our tears or of the semen can somehow mingle with the blood, special antibodies can be created. Perhaps the seminal fluid-drinking male would generate antibodies in the body by his own semen, so that semen generation would be minimised. So, it is seen that the Bauls have very few children. Yet, it is to be noted that the female never drinks this seminal fluid.

Knowing such facts and analysing them, it would seem that there would be a different sociology prevalent around our folk life. The latter's rites and sacraments were very complex and secret. The secret moon-meditation had many symbolic names too. Some called it meditation of sap-eroticism; others termed it 'earth-work'. Generally speaking, 'sap' would mean 'urine'; 'eroticism' would refer to 'seminal fluid'; 'blood' would allude to 'menstrual fluid'; 'earth' would imply 'stool'. In music, they were called *adyachandra* (early moon); *saralchandra* (simple moon); *garalchandra* (poison moon); and *ruhinichandra* (blood moon)—to be concealed as pleasant names.

Before going to meet Mazharul Khan, I suddenly thought of Bimal Baul. At one end of our suburban town, Bimal lived in the cobblers' colony with his woman companion and meditated according to the Baul faith. He was a peace-loving friendly man, with long hair and beard, wearing saffron robes, with a bag strung around his shoulders, and carrying a *karoa*—the 'skull-cup' shaped out of a coconut shell in his bag. There was no consistency between Bimal's meditation and his livelihood. The day I went to Bimal's home after prior intimation, he brought a cake that he had baked at the bakery. Truly speaking, the offer of cake in a Baul ascetic's home was as unusual an experience, as was his open-ended nature. He did not hide anything from me.

Thinking about all this, I landed up in Bimal's ashram one day. His companion greeted me with tea and biscuits, and we talked generally about their meditation. Then Bimal and I sat under a *Tamal* tree (the egg tree) on the cemented balcony in the courtyard of the house. The evening gathered around us. Then I said: "I've never asked you; well, do you take the service of the four moons?"

Bimal did not hide almost anything from me; so, he brought out the black utensil from his shoulder-bag and said, showing it to me: "See this, I drink sap from this."

: "How many times in a day and night?"

: "As many times as I wish. The whole practice is so beneficial."

: "Benowari Fakir had told me that the urine secreted after the first round of instant sleep at night – induced by a full meal of rice – was entirely odourless; that urine was most beneficial for the body."

: "There're many opinions on this. But four moons are a very hard way of meditation. All these can be done if there's full control on the body. Otherwise, this can be harmful."

: "You're quite right. Benowari once told me; having done four moons, going out is prohibited. You can't expose the body to the sun. But once the four moons are assimilated, the skin becomes clearer and glowing. Well, Bimal, are you doing four moons, or, do you do it now?"

Bimal said: "I won't hide it from you. I can't take the earth; I find it repulsive. Other three moons are served and taken; there's a process for it, and there're doses. Don't ask me any further. Rather, listen to a song:

We've this process eternally on—
We defy the book of Quran, sans Nabi's instruction.
Following the laid-down rule, worshipping the sun-moon capsule,
Those meditating with the five saps, pierce the moon anon.
Simple moon, poison moon, ruhini moon to be born—
Mixing menses-fluid and semen: have drunk all, and I am done."

I said: "I don't want to embarrass you much. In what form do you drink the mix of the menstrual fluid and seminal fluid?"

: "We dissolve both matters in water and blend them with camphor and sugar: to make a drink like sorbet."

Man's habits and taste buds were, no doubt, great regulators. Year after year, I had been moving with them intimately, yet never could become one with them. Bimal and I were sitting side by side; still we had an indelible distance between us. Was it hatred? Who had classified food and non-food? Did the taste buds determine the boundaries between food and non-food?

I remembered Ela Fakir once telling me: "Our path is incredibly difficult. First, one to prepare the mind; then the body will respond. So we say: '*Shame hatred fear, the three have to be clear.*' Shame, hatred and fear are all in the mind. What we don't know has fear embedded. What doesn't tally in taste is to be hated. Shame is nothing but social shame."

It was so very true. Bimal, the breadmaker sitting beside me was, at this moment, residing in an immaculate space. He was a social being, but was above shame, guilt, hatred and fear. He was not hiding anything; not considering things worthy of hiding. He accorded respect and love to his unmarried companion of meditation. He did not fear the society; he had no hatred for it either. So he had nothing to lose. It was I who was contracting. Whose life's philosophy was right?

I was somehow unable to remain indifferent to the one whom I clearly did not know very well, and on whose tastes I felt contempt. He was, of course, quite indifferent to our way of high consumption life. He did not believe in the conventional social system, a healthy lifestyle, marital bonds and a regular family and the traditional rituals of worship; and was still self-dependent and happy. His companion was aged and not beautiful. The whole thing was a won. One's civilised and educated mind was clamouring to call Bimal a pervert. Was Mazharul Khan also of a perverted mind? How could that be? He was married, a family-man and was the father of his children. Who had said that Fakiri meant perversion? Did Baul mean the one defiled by lust?

My mind oscillated, hit by drafts of aimless thoughts. Eventually, I had to ask Bimal my long-suppressed question: "Well, tell me, I can understand your sap-meditation, the sap is contained within you body. But how do you obtain the menstrual fluid?"

Bimal made his voice very low: "This is a very confidential matter. Well, tell me, why live in the cobbler area?"

: "That has a straight reply. You lead an unsocial life-style. You don't have a married wife; you live with another companion. Will it be tolerated in traditional, aristocratic society and neighbourhoods?"

: "Yes, that's one reason. The real reason is that this is what you call the colony of people from the lowest rung. They are a totally mixed lot. There's not much of a social bondage. You can check and find out that most of them are not married man-and-wife. Perhaps there was an exchange of garlands in a Kali temple; there was affection and love. They live together; they have separations, too. But they give a lot of regard to Bauls and ascetics. They show great devotion, render service, call us home."

: "Why?"

: "They don't have Brahmin priests; no communication with high society. Yet they're quite scared of sin. You'll find all of them take initiation from the guru. Scared of the other world, they serve the guru very devotedly. There must be some guru or the other for each. Whatever the guru explains, they accept. But then, you know, all gurus don't have the same outlook; everyone is not a meditator either. Many are taken advantage of. In the name of service to the guru, there are rampant sexual transgressions."

I said: "How does that affect you? You don't profess to be a guru, do you?" Biting his tongue, Bimal said: "Goodness gracious, how I can be a guru? I haven't even completed my one-hundred-per cent education. Actually, we know some drugs and remedies: occult methods, incantation of enchantments and medicinal herbs. I give them during distress; they too give in return."

Suppressing my excitement, I said: "'What do you mean—'give' you? What I'm driving at is what's called menstrual fluid—do they give that to you?"

: "Yes, they do, even if I don't want to. They come home and give it in confidence. That's their religion."

: "What religion? Who told you?"

: "Please don't get so flustered. They treat it as their religion. Can you offer resistance? They've been taught that way."

: "Who taught them?"

: "Why, it's only the Bauls-Fakirs. Was that today? It has been going on for hundreds of years. Do you know how much they learn from Bauls about the body? Let me tell you something else. Please understand, when a virgin girl from these families begins to menstruate, then they donate it to us. Donate they must and we drink it. Such material is available after a lot of austere meditative practice and penance. Its drinking brings huge strength. Do you realise now why I live here?"

Truly speaking, I was in the throes of an inner turmoil, having understood quite far and deep. Man's ignorance was, no doubt, a blessing. Many mysteries of life were better left unravelled. From now onwards, the give-and-take under an unwritten agreement of the low-caste people would no longer remain closed to me. Looking at the labour-class of men and women, I would have the sharp sword of suspicion always raised: do they do it? Are they also implicated? An underlying current would flow beneath the politics, sociology, elections, state revolutions and atomic wars: the corporeal thinking on body, physical habit, sexuality, holding ejaculation and its regulation. As the night hid its darkness under broad daylight, the stream of saffron embedded in asceticism concealed the flower of desire.

On a morning of Chaitra, I reached Goradanga. Earlier, the whole landscape had been enveloped in the grey curtain of winter; now it was a brilliantly lit sunny experience. Grasshoppers were leaping and flying around in the erratic spring breeze. The villagers enquired about our destination. Whenever Mazharul's name was mentioned, all of them would say: "Go straight, it's a direct road."

Ultimately, the straight road, of course, took a turn and before my eyes loomed large Fakir's big mansion. Outside, there was a stack of green-pea pulse. On one end, threshing and beating of wheat in the machine was going on with a monotonous sound. Manzoor was supervising there. He came forward with a smile: "So you came finally. Do come, take your seat in the room. I'll call father."

Before father arrived, the little children of the house came in a cluster—looking at the strange creature from the town in amazement. Mustard was drying. Chick-pea plants were kept in a pile; weaning had not been done yet. The women of the house –wearing Begunphuli and bright green sarees – were busy with their daily household chores. It was an affluent household, with an expansive and a liberal mindset and related activities. There were three stacks of paddy, but no cow was visible. Where was the cow-shed? Manzoor came in to say: "Father is finishing his breakfast, please sit down for a while."

I asked: "Manzoor, why is there no cow in such a big household of yours?"

: "There were three or four. They've all been sold."

: "Why?"

: "Lack of labour; these days it's so hard to get farmers. A helping hand is not available for the house. You must know that keeping cows involves slogging like a cow. The women of the family can't manage everything any more. So...considering every aspect...I hope you're staying for the night? There is to be a musical soiree. We will inform everyone."

Meanwhile, Manzoor's maternal uncle, Khaibar, arrived. I heard his flute-playing last time. Actually, Mazharul Khan had set up a Fakir music group with the boys and the brother-in-law. The group performed in different villages. Mazharul composed lyrics and explained the contents of songs in the gatherings. They had sung a few times in the burial site of Lalan Shah in Bangladesh.

Mazharul entered the room, almost occupying the entire door-space. Six feet tall, he was proportionately broad, too, wearing white shirt and dhoti. In appearance, he did not look a Fakir at all. Actually, Fakiri was the name of a physical lifestyle; and mental excellence alongside. The outward attire, hair and beard were not compulsory in any sense. This apart, Mazharul was a full-time householder. Now, of course, his sons had grown up; they looked after every aspect, relieving their father and releasing him into his own circle.

After settling down, it took a little while to begin conversation. Meanwhile, flattened rice and milk arrived. Manzoor said: "Our village is so wretched that there isn't any sweetmeat shop. For sweets, one has to travel six kilometres and go to Nazirpur. We could not provide you proper hospitality; had we known before..."

Cutting him short, I said: "I was coming to meet human beings. Food is a minor matter. It's nothing but maintaining the body."

Interrupting me Mazharul said: "You didn't say it right. This world's called *duniya*, because two things're running this world. Could you tell me what they are?"

I recalled that regarding this, Nizami had mentioned—high-class, low-class; rich-poor. But it would not apply here; so I, quietly, looked up with questioning eyes.

Mazharul said: "*Duniya* is *du-niya*: those two are the tongue and the genitals. Every taste lies with these two objects; and tasting is living."

Truly speaking, I was startled at first: first, at the transparency of his materialistic thoughts and, second, at the style of his talk in the very presence of Manzoor. Manzoor, of course, did not look the least bit embarrassed or disturbed. That, too, was startling to my upper-class lifestyle and thoughts. Whatever, after recovering from the temporary shock, I said: "Could you please explain that matter of taste a little?"

: "Yes, that has to be understood. Look, Allah has created those two in our body for tasting purposes. But there's a funny thing in them: you can't enjoy the pleasures of taste using the two together, simultaneously."

: "Why?"

: "Think it over. When you eat pulao-mutton-sweets and derive the rare pleasure of the tongue, does man wish to engage in coitus then? Again, when one is having a sexual union, one would turn down the offer of pulao and mutton and look away. It's a strange rule: man goes by whatever is befitting for a particular time or moment. And also what you said about taking food simply for protecting the body—this is also in the context of Hinduism. Fasting, ceremonial vow, festivity and keeping the body within control are balderdash. Controlling the mind is following the path of true spiritualism. And protection of the body is the genuine faith. Our Fakiri sect says: five elements reside in fruits, roots, seeds and crops. From that food is born semen. Semen is life; its fall is death. Conserving semen is our credo."

It was very clear, very transparent thinking. Yet apparently to find a loophole, I said: "'Destruction of semen is a physical phenomenon. Is that unnatural?"

: "Why should it be unnatural? Vices and senses have also to be accommodated. Curbing the vices, abstinence, etc, are not viewpoints of the materialists. Didn't I have children?"

Over a cup of tea, Mazharul began again: "I'm now sixty. I got married when I was twenty. Between the ages of twenty and thirty, I reproduced my children, that's all. I've two wives; with three boys and one girl. The elder wife gave birth to the boys, while the younger one had the daughter. Well, I didn't beget any further.'"

: "You're talking as if giving birth is under your control."

: "It's certainly so in the materialist sect. Male is the soul, woman—the body. If the seed's pure and the body's fertile, there'll be an outcome. Again, there's no harm in ploughing without the seed. The Fakir knows how to retain the seed and how to control it. He has no fear of letting it fall. My sons, too, are into the Fakiri faith."

I did not want to surrender without a fight, so I asked: "Why did you marry twice? Is it because Islam is open to it?"

"Oh, no, not at all," said Mazharul with a laugh: "This was out of sheer necessity. My elder wife is very beautiful and also a very simple person. When the family grew, there were several children—she was a simpleton who could not manage everything very well. So I married again. The younger wife is a hardworking woman with a good head for accounts. It's she who has kept my family running and raised the boys. But she's not a pretty woman, mind you. Let this pass. Let's get back to what you want to know; you had several questions—please go ahead."

: "Would you tell me all I seek to know? And conceal nothing?"

: "Whatever I know I will say it all. Whatever is not known to me, I won't be able to say. You must know what Rasid said in his lyrics:

If a Jalem, as an Aalem poses,
Lannat's talk will put him into nooses."

: "What does it mean?"

: "Aalem means wise, Jalem means a dark ignorant fool. If, despite being ignorant, anyone poses as being wise, the noose of sin would go round his throat. So now you ask your questions."

I said: "You've faith in the present. What does it mean?"

: "Its meaning is conveyed perfectly and concisely in one of Lalan's songs:

One whom I didn't see with my eye—
Worshipping him: how do I comply?

The One who has no material form is treated by us beyond comprehension. We don't accept by surmise the One who can't be established by the senses. Hence, we first witness the appearance, then offer *sejda*. Again, because of this lack of form, we don't accept re-incarnation; there's no evidence. The form with which man is born it is lost after death; it does not return. Lalan has said so:

A name can be replaced by a name—
Where does one get the form same?"

: "Bauls also swear by the present. Tell me, where's your difference with them?"

: "Do you know where? Bauls adopt women as companions of meditation. That's not quite right."

: "Why?"

: "The one who's my companion or wife is the one who loves me intently. Is it correct to expose her in full public view? Her mind may become fickle. Instead of liking me, she may like somebody else. It's not correct to make the woman's mind restless. It's they who give us peace and happiness in the family and society; they're the ones who maintain an all-round balance. They're the ones who bear children. Their fickleness can tilt the whole world."

No sooner was I going to say that Mazharul's thoughts reflected the influence of the Muslim purdah system, than a poor villager entered home with his young son. The boy laughed out loud in his dreams at night, and often leapt up. Could the Fakir please give him a talisman?

Taking from me a piece of paper, Mazharul draw some illegible patterns on it and then folded it, bowed on it twice and packed it inside a talisman, before handing over to the man, saying: "Tie it on the left hand with a black thread." Keeping his faith in the Fakir, the poor Muslim went away with a gratified face. Returning suddenly, he asked: "Are there some food restrictions to be obeyed?"

: "Nothing at all, nothing. Only don't eat beef at home until the ailment cures."

As soon as the man was gone, I asked: 'How was this? What has beef got to do with talisman?'

Was this a Fakiri stunt?

Mazharul said with a smile: "You must know that the Imam from the mosque gives many directions; the Muslims obey them. Do you know what they say? Don't eat at the Fakirs' home. Listening to music is sinful; Fakiri songs are taboo. On the other hand, they like music. They're quite at a loss, and ask me: is Fakiri music pure or impure? They love to listen, but the Maulavis prohibit. Given a chance, I also take a slight revenge. I had said, for instance, that beef should not be eaten! Is a living creature a part of any religion? Everyone can eat everything."

: "Does God belong to any particular religion?"

: "Not at all. Haven't you heard that song?

Muslims think: Allah is in our team,
Could you think of such fools in your dream?
Allah is uncle to none—
How did you heed to such yarn?
Old age you did earn: unawares, it'd seem!"

: "Does it mean that Allah is mine, too?"

: "Yes, why not? Krishna is mine, too. Haven't you heard Kubir Gosain's song?

Allah is in the uvula in a happy state,
Krishna stays in the palate."

: "You consider Krishna as semen, don't you?"

: "Yes, his love-play of Raslila signifies the conjugal union of man and woman. In the woman's body is the Radha-point where Krishna unites with her."

: "Then what are kiss, embrace, erotic touch and so on?"

: "They're the twelve Gopals: companions of Krishna, like Shridam, Sudam, Basudam, etc. You must have heard their names."

: "Does Krishna then not reside in the feminine body?"

: "Yes, but his function is different there. Krishna is the nurturer there. As soon as the woman conceives, he takes his seat there: in the womb's flower. Drawing sap and blood from there, the embryo survives. Once the baby is born, it loses Krishna and wails, only screaming *'kahan kahan'*. This '*kahan*' means: "Where am I? And where is Krishna?"

ꕥ

A momentary silence descended on the quiet mid-afternoon of Goradanga, caught under the spell of the dove's incessant calls. Quite dazed, I wondered how this strange stream of thought flowed in a world which lay beyond our ken. Should we call them mistaken or just crazy? This had also to be kept in mind that life with such unearthly ideology had no conflict with the on-going rites of passage of life. The cycle of birth-death-marriage continued; the land was turning overproductive with high-quality fertilisers; the farmer was getting water-supply from deep tube-wells; modern machinery was weaning wheat on field after field. Amidst all this, the Fakir doctrine flowered; deep internal conflicts continued between the Shariati and the Marfati. Manzoors and Khaibars were increasingly adopting Fakiri and singing doctrinaire songs. The same Mazharul Khan played a leading role at lending a structure to the Baul-Fakir association. An ardent believer of the material world, the man was nonchalantly prescribing the esoteric talisman for conjectured diseases. The same man who refused to believe in the subjective surmise or imaginary thoughts built around a material object, admitted Krishna's presence in the body, without viewing with his own eyes. Was then Krishna not an esoteric icon, but just another name for the living stream of life?

The focus of thoughts was suddenly shaken, because it was getting close to the hour of the midday meal. On the same cot, where Mazharul and I were chatting, a wet light cotton towel was rinsed and laid out. Mazharul's plate of rice was served at one end, and mine, at the anther end. It was vegetarian food, with chilli and spice on the high side. No lady appeared from indoors, Manzoor supervised the meal and served us. At the end of the meal, I sought to know how the man came to the Fakiri line.

: "I was wise from my early childhood. This meant that, since the age of nine or ten, I had an ardent desire to know where exactly Allah resided. I used to visit mosques with my father, and studied Arabic and Persian, but was mentally dissatisfied. It was a faith based on surmises. At that point, there were many Aalem Fakir-residents around our village. I used to visit them under great secrecy. The secrecy was to stop father from beating me, in case he came to know. He was a pure Namazi Muslim: Shariat-governed, a wise man. Finally, there was a lot of chaos; I did not agree to obey and observe the Namaz, Roja, etc. You could say that my mind did not agree. Father beat me up hollow. The village folks, too, abused me and became enemies; I don't remember those things now."

: "Did the villagers eventually accept you?"

: "You could see now. Actually, I didn't go to beat anybody nor did I ask anyone to 'follow Fakiri'. I was following the path of mediation in my own way, I used to sing. If called by Mullahs-Maulavis, I joined their debates. Nobody could cope up with me in debate, nor can they even now in this area. There was a time, when for instance I didn't leave this room for a single day for ten long years at a stretch!"

: "Why?"

: "Fakiri meditation isn't easy, is it? Is it a show off to the gallery? There are many things like breath-control, body-yoga and others, which have to be learnt from the Murshid and installed in the body. Then only they come under control."

I asked: "Did everyone accept you thereafter?"

Giving a confident smile, Mazharul Khan said: "What could they do, but accept? At one time, I was socially ostracised in this village, I might say. And today I've brought everybody under the fold of the Fakiri faith. They've come on their own. Those who didn't come are not enemies. Well, I'm quite fine now."

I said: "You've been to Bangladesh. What's the situation of Fakiri faith there?"

: "It's excellent. And there are many great Fakirs there; there are many good singers as well. The doctrinaire songs of Jalal Rashid and others are most prevalent there. There are many Fakirs residing in Kushtia, Jessore, Faridpur and Rangpur. They're wise and conversant in Arabic studies."

: "I'll ask you a different kind of question now. I have with me an article published in Bangladesh: *Baulder Jaunajiban o Janmaniyantran* ('The Sex-life of Bauls and their Birth-control'). I've brought the article with me. There are one or two portions in it, which I want to get clarified from you, as to whether they have written the truth or not, because they sound very strange."

The Fakir asked curiously: "Could you read what's written?"

Taking out the article, I began reading aloud from one portion, Mazharul listening with great interest.

> According to them, the breast-milk of women was most beneficial to tuberculosis and other long-term ailments. Regular drinking of breast-milk could help in retaining youth and vigour easily and the lactating women also do not have children. I knew someone who made his youth and vigour long-lasting in this manner and was unparalleled in Baul music.
>
> Even though he died over the age of eighty, he never looked an old and doddering man with a decrepit body. Fundamentally, these are very secret activities in the Baul faith and are very little known outside the Baul society.

Mazharul became a little sombre after hearing the whole thing. Then he said: "Has all this been written down? These things are true. You would notice in the Baul groups, women of different ages. They are kept for many purposes. That breast-feeding women don't reproduce is quite true. Yes, please read what else is written, my mind is keen to know."

I continued to read again:

> Without a female companion, Baul faith is devoid of its core value. With the help of a wife or a specially selected companion, this faith completes its various necessary functions.
>
> The breath-control among Bauls stores the highest latent pleasure and peace of life. If one could control one's breath according to one's will, then it is possible to solve all problems and pain. The sex-life of Bauls has been structured and developed around this foundation of the breathing process.
>
> The male Baul treats the female as the base of his meditation. Along with his own conjugal satisfaction, he attempts to give the female partner also satisfaction: something not noticeable among the other ordinary village males. For this reason, the life of Bauls is a happier one, more inward-looking and introspective, and blessed with a higher level of satisfaction than the common households.
>
> Every Baul couple observes – regularly and with care – their monthly cycles in close detail. There is a strong religious logic in these observations, which is caught in a Lalan song. The song runs: *'Every tree blossoms, but every flower doesn't bear fruit.'* That is, there is no certainty that every monthly period will be flowed by an ovulation. The way to determine the presence ovulation is to taste the menstrual fluid. This taste has three categories: sweet like honey; saline; sour. If it is sweet like honey, the female is definitely fertile.
>
> Another important aspect of this monthly scrutiny of menstrual flow is to test its brightness or colour. If a drop of the fluid is put on a white paper or white cloth and placed in the sun, its true colour is reflected. Menstrual fluid's colour can be of four kinds: red, yellow, black and white. In the Baul language, these are red,

> '*jarad*', '*siya*' and white. These four colours have deep meanings. Here, too, red implies fertility.
>
> According to Bauls, there is no difference between the woman and the moon...it is to be noted here that, according to Bauls, males are not always fertile either. The male fertility considerably enhances during full moon.

Having heard everything, Mazharul *s*aid: "Everything that has been written is correct. And this is also true that all these are contained in the Baul songs. Haven't you heard: *'The moon has been touched by the moon'?* There's another song: *'The moon rises in the new moon'?* Have you heard it?"

: "I've heard, but didn't follow the meaning."

: "The time of menstrual flow of the woman is called new moon. At that time, the formless man comes to play as the large fish at the bend of the meandering stream. He has to be caught at that time, as it's the great confluence. You didn't understand anything, did you? Well, listen to a Lalan song:

Three days have three senses, let me have this say—
The witty meditator catches all in a single day.
After new moon, the first night
And before the second is bright:
Dervish Lalan says come there, he might
In his propitious way.

This means that, in between the first and second day of the woman's menstrual flow, the feminine body is the playground of the 'wise one'. If one can catch him, there is the pleasure accumulated over a million births waiting. But, however, if something contrary happens in ejaculation, then the meditator will be lost in the voracious lust of the erotic crocodile. The meditator will fail."

: "Well, it's clear now. But explain about the full moon, since you said earlier: '*The moon rises in the new moon*'."

: "Oh, when it's full moon in the sky, then men have a high tide; if, at that point, the woman companion too, has a new moon and menstruates, then that confluence of the two is the best ever hour fit for meditation. It happens very rarely."

I said: "Now I've realised that, for Bauls and Fakirs, the physical union is a hide-and-seek game. On one side is the fatal attraction of lust; next to the big fish resides the crocodile. If the fish is played around adroitly, the formless man of the soul will be caught in astute meditation; but if there's an error, it means a sure fall in the jaws of the crocodile. Have I followed right? Well, now tell me as we observe, there is a period of 'heat' in the animal world when the physical union takes place. Yet for man, the physical craving and lust persists through all three-hundred-sixty-five days, even at every hour. Isn't then human life the worst and vilest of all? Why did god give man so much servility to the body?"

: "Let me explain, first of all, what you call servility is really to be named dominance. The animal world has not received this dominance: they conjugate out of lust. To give birth remains their only aim. They don't derive pleasure; they don't have what you termed the 'hide-and-seek game'. Allah has given only man this pleasure, the physical ecstasy, the sensation of love; because He loves man most of all."

Now I gazed at Mazharul Khan with a deep look. I had received a new version of life from the folk religion. This life was like a strip of sand-dune between the two boisterous seas of lust and love: likely to be washed away, who knows, when.

In between the thoughts, the introspective householder self of the Fakir exclaimed: "Man has a voracious capacity for enjoyment, so Allah has arranged so many food-items for him. From food comes satiation and nourishment. From there is born semen. That semen is life, to catch which is man's highest skill. Again, those who're unsuccessful in it are lustful, and shall fall. Their life's like an animal. They're – like animals – dependent on others, the poor seeking alms. Like animals, they perish early. It's that group, which for fear of sin, observes fasts, goes on pilgrimage and keeps sacramental vows. They worship minor deities, wooden portraits and earthen moulds. That's why, the song says: 'Have human act.' Man's act is self-knowledge, to have dominance over body. Our path of faith holds a sign of it; only Murshid's guidance is to be sought."

I said indignantly: "Whatever you said so far is from the man's point of view. Does a woman have no role in the daily life and sex awareness?"

Mazharul said: "How can that be? Women have no desire."

: "What did you say? Women have no physical desire?"

Mazharul quipped back suavely: "You're married. Could you tell me honestly, doesn't the physical desire come from you first?"

I fell silent.

Mazharul said a little more pointedly: "Isn't the first physical attraction from the man towards his wife? Aren't the physical assets more on their side? Doesn't the male enjoy the female almost like a predator?"

Quite bewildered, I said almost helplessly: "Then how is a woman full of guiles? Doesn't her body respond?"

: "The male awakens desire in the female. Basically, they don't have desire. They're devoid of desire."

: "Then what does a woman seek from her man?"

: "It's, most of all, companionship and closeness. Every wife wants to serve her husband, wants to cook for him well. When you are back home from the world outside, you'll notice the woman wiping her husband's sweat, fanning him. Have you noticed any husband fanning his wife? Do ask all women, you'll find that they want their husbands to be always present in front, only to love them. The wives are mortally scared of the external world, lest their man does not return—if his body desires someone else. When a woman wants a child, one reason for it is the attraction to be a mother; but another reason is to retain a sign of the husband. Am I speaking the truth?"

Hearing that I would be leaving before the evening, everyone felt sorry. Manzoor brought in roti made of rice powder and *payesh*—milk thickened and sweetened with date-palm molasses. While eating, I asked: "There's no cow at home, you had to buy milk for this dessert, didn't you?"

Manzoor shyly lowered his head.

: "How much did it cost?"

: "Rupees seven per litre."

: "Seven rupees per litre in an out-of-the-way village? We get good milk cheaper in the cities. Well, Manzoor, vendors take away all the mangoes raw, don't they?"

: "Yes, there's no way we can retain mangoes on the tree; they are all stolen."

: "Whatever fish is caught, also goes away to the city markets, doesn't it?"

: "Yes, there're direct bus services; besides, they fetch good prices from the city market. Villagers can't, of course, buy at that rate."

: "How about kerosene oil?"

: "We get a little through the rationing, the rest has to be purchased in the black market."

Mazharul Khan came back again and sat down. He said: "Such a flying visit is not sufficient. I thought you'd stay at least for the night; I would have Manzoor and Khaibar sing for you. Leave it at that. When you've promised to come back again, this poor Fakir shall remain waiting for that moment. You came, so we had some academic discourse. Where are people here, otherwise, for discussion? So were you satisfied with the responses for what you sought to know? We haven't studied in schools and can't talk coherently. Man, of course, has boundless queries. What is it, you seem to have become silent!"

"No, I've not fallen silent," I replied. "There's no end to questions as well. But I am the one who has been asking you a continuous stream of questions since morning; I'm only making you talk."

"Oh, that doesn't really matter", said Mazharul. "I'm not wise enough to keep things hidden either. Whatever little I know, I'm always prepared to talk about, subject to the suitability of the other party. Tell me, which are the other questions you might still have? Your time of departure is drawing near."

I had in mind the subject of a virgin girl contributing her first drop of menstrual fluid, as mentioned by Bimal Baul. Come to think of it, it was perhaps the most secret element and private context of folk religion. But Bimal could only give the information, unable to analyse it. It was not possible for him to do so either. I was tempted to put it across to a theoretical scholar like Mazharul. No sooner had I raised the question – with due respect and after thinking it over well in mind – Mazharul's face lit up in a strange glow. He uttered in a very low voice:

Slaked is a million births' thirst—
Drinking a drop of water first!

Saying this, he heaved a deep sigh.

"What happened?" I asked. "Did I hurt you unawares? Then let us drop that subject."

: "No, nothing of the kind. It has struck a blow at a very delicate point of my mind. No no, you've nothing to do with it. Whatever that is, as you were saying – about the first menstrual flow of a virgin – weren't you? It's a very sacred thing; it comes to the service of the Baul-Fakir as a great stroke of luck."

Taken by surprise, I blurted out: "Is it true? Is the statement not elusive then?"

: "Elusive? Yes, it's elusive in a manner of thinking. It's like rainfall without a cloud. Would you like to listen to this Lalan song?

Without cloud there is rainfall—
The pure witty knows its sense, all.
There's no morn or afternoon,
There's no time: late or soon,
Big or small.
Between clouds, creation begins,
King Indra's order knows
Always on call.
The sapless, with sap glow,
Everyone cannot know,
God's skill can't stall.
O, its one drop's touch
The creature gains as much:
Immortality's hall.

"Did you understand anything?"

: "Yes, I did; something still remained unclear. Is the rainfall without cloud that's talked about, the first menstruation of the virgin? That's why, it's sung: *'There's no morn or afternoon, / There's no time: late or soon'*—is that so?"

: "Yes, you've followed it well. Even this you might have understood: *'Between clouds, creation begins'*?"

: "Now I've understood. Just check up if I've followed properly. It has been said that, under Indra's orders, cloud gives rainfall, and only then does the cosmic creation continue. Likewise, under Sain's creativity, the sap gathers, from which life's creation is sparked off. The start of a woman's menstrual cycle implies that her reproductive ability has been set in motion. Isn't that so?"

As I analysed in this manner, I was thrilled within. Was it not a wonder that, simply relying on my bookish knowledge, I was able to easily follow the most difficult mystery of folk religion? It was clear how much a guru one needed as a guide in this faith. I had heard earlier that there was a word *barjakh* in the Baul doctrine, which meant a place in between heaven and earth. The souls resided there awaiting the Last Judgment. The Marfatis called their guru *barjakh* since guru was the connecting bridge between man and God. There was, since this morning, a powerful warmth of life in my mind, which had at its root Mazharul's company and symbolic presence. I had read these songs in *Lalan Geetika* earlier, but did not understand a wee bit. Mazharul was, no doubt, a great *barjakh*.

With a confident tone, like a *barjakh*, Mazharul said: "We believe that the taste of a drop of that sacred menstrual fluid lends immortality to man. That's why, Bauls-Fakirs have always retained adolescent girls in their groups and kept a vigilant eye on them. The ability to drink the first drop at the start of their menstrual flow lends enormous power to the body and mind. So we say: '*Slaked is a million births' thirst / Drinking a drop of water first!*'

Mazharul suddenly became absent-minded. His deep sigh this time was not so clear. I realised that he did not get that rare, sacred drop in his life despite all his efforts. Did the gathering darkness of the impending evening made his face sombre? Or was it some other pain?

The bus-stop was at one end of Goradanga village, where I was standing alone. Suddenly a villager advanced and introduced himself as Ramjan Khan. He practised homoeopathy from a rented room near the bus-stop. As could be seen from his appearance, he was a self-satisfied man. After preliminary civilities, I asked: "How are you keeping in this village?" "We're very well" said Ramjan. "We live together in great happiness. There isn't much scarcity. There is no political turmoil. People are peace-loving."

: "But we hear that people in villages live in great penury; there is much poverty, much suffering."

: "How's that? When we go to cities, we feel so sorry for you. You live in such congested localities, being lumped together. The roads and lanes are horribly dirty. Nobody cares for anybody else. If someone goes hungry, none'll keep track of him. There're beatings, murders, injuries, snatchings, strikes, power failures. Truly, we discuss about you from time to time. You must be surviving with such difficulty!"

By this time, Manzoor had appeared with his bicycle; he was on his way to the next village and stopped over, after spotting me. Ramjan said: "You know, Manzoor, I was telling him all this while how bad the city is. One wonders what joy they derive from living there! Do you recall, Manzoor, the time when Altaf's old grandmother was suffering from the winter's intense cold last Paush, and how we all subscribed to buy her a quilt? Please understand nobody in our village fasts for want of food; on hearing about it, we arrange to supply him food from one house or the other. And how is it in your cities?"

Quite surprised, I stared at Ramjan for a while. Was the man argumentative or quarrelsome? Was he a simple man or a very cunning one? Indeed, there was no sign of devilry on his face, but quite a smug, contented look.

I said: "So I gather life is fine here and you're keeping quite well. It's indeed nice to know. Yet, in an affluent household like Manzoor's, there's no chance of keeping a cow; one has to buy milk at seven rupees a litre. There's no mango. Fish is not available. Kerosene is quite dear. There's no helping hand available at home. There's no physician, no library. Newspapers don't reach you. One has to go to far-away Nazirpur to buy sweets. Well, brother Ramjan, by village, we understand plentitude, waste and expense. Could you tell me, is man's living philosophy to constrict and dwindle, or is it about expanding vision in all directions? Indeed, as you've accepted that you would never drink milk; never eat fish; never enjoy a mango or get sweets; read books, read newspapers—is this life? Is that what's living well means? We've not accepted any of these factors. Are you really living well, as you claim?"

Manzoor Khan and Ramjan Khan looked at each other for a while. Then Manzoor replied: "That's true, Uncle Ramjan, we're not truly well; but we don't seem to realise it."

The bus appeared before the conversation was over. While boarding it, I looked back for the last time at Goradanga village and at the bewildered faces of Ramjan and Manzoor. The speeding bus quickly severed the tenuous link with one village: among a hundred thousand electricity-less, kerosene-less, silent villages of Bengal.

Folks cannot fathom 'Gouranga'

How much was the knowledge derived from the pages of books different from that culled from the work-a-day, run-of-the-mill life? Quite a while ago, we studied semantics in the philology class. The meaning of words, as we know now, could apparently be quite different at other times. The reason was that while the 'high'-class people perhaps created a word, the supposedly 'lower'-class people changed the meaning of it altogether, by their continuous oral usage. A nice example was the childhood rhyme:

The camel goes with head held high,
The spider hangs from the wall: well nigh.

The Sanskrit word used for then spider was Urnanava. While studying semantics, we came to know that it was not Urnanava, but Urnabava—originating from the Sanskrit root word *bav*, meaning the one who wove the thread. But whatever the root, the common man believed that the spider secreted a sap from its navel in order to create the web. Therefore, Urnabava became Urnanava: dealing with navel. Such behaviour-pattern of the illiterate folks – who could not even correctly spell or pronounce the word 'pronunciation' – was exposed by our professor tauntingly, who quoted some more ludicrous and illogical examples of word distortion by these people. We were not aware then that those who distorted the pronunciation, or changed the meaning of the word also had sarcastic comments in store about the scholars.

A few miles away from Katowa lived Prankrishna Gosain: a Sahajiya Vaishnava. He asked me with a smile: "What does 'Krishna' mean?"

Who could stop an itching scholar, like me, who had studied Vaishnava treatises? I said boastingly: *"Krishnastu Bhagavana Swayam."*

: "How did you know?"

: "It's written in the Vaishnava treatises. *Ujjwala Nilamani..."*

Interrupting me, Gosain said: "'Stop, please stop; it's all by surmise. We go by the present. Now listen, Krishna doesn't mean God; Krishna means man: the one who can cultivate. Krishna signifies the man who is well versed in the matters of the earth, the field—also a seer of sorts. Someone who understands the land, is able to cultivate accordingly and sow seeds. Seed also means Krishna, that is, the semen. Have you understood?"

Under the depths of bottomless waters, I asked: "Then who's Radha?"

: "Radha? Radha's the field."

Startled, I said: "Does then Chaitanya mean something beside what we normally understand? Do the names like Advaita, Nityananda, etc, also carry different meanings?"

Smiling gently, Prankrishna hummed:

Radha-Krishna story that you sing in the song—
If you think they're of Vrindavan, then you're wrong!

I said: "How's that? Did you compose those lyrics on the spur of the moment?"

Gosain laughed loudly and said: "What, has the mirror cracked?"

: "The mirror?"

: "Yes, there was this big mirror which used to reflect the sun. Now you see, the hand suddenly dropped the mirror and it broke into smithereens. What would happen now? You wouldn't be able to see one whole sun! As many suns as the pieces, isn't that so?"

Prankrishna slowly rose and went over to the Ashram-site. An ascetic wearing a white robe, he had white matted hair. Suddenly he turned around and returned, with his gleaming eyes scanning my bewildered face, to retort: "How much would you know by reading scriptures? Are all scriptures sacrosanct? Kabiraj Gosain penned *Sri Chaitanya Charitamrita.* Do you know what some people say about it? They say:

The book, Chaitanya Charitamrita, is—
Quite bitter in taste to some, not a bliss!

"Then what? No book is irrefutable. Only irrefutable is the doctrine on the Supreme. What can I tell you? You're *a-Chaitanya* ('unconscious'). Become *sa-Chaitanya* ('conscious')."

That was the beginning, at least two decades or more, ago. When my effort to become *sa-Chaitanya* (conscious) started, the trumpet for celebrating 500 years of Chaitanya had nowhere been blown. In other words, my pathway to receive Chaitanya was very lonely. But one more point should be noted. It was easy to be transformed from *a-Chaitanya* to *sa-Chaitanya*, as suggested by Master Gosain, but it was far more difficult to mould an opinion, set for once, into a totally new one. The idea, already formulated in my mind on Vaishnavism and Chaitanyaism, were not at all easy to change. It was like having finished learning a song in a wrong tune and then re-learning it in the correct tune, which was far more difficult. I faced hindrance at every step. How could a person, who had carefully studied books like *An Early History of Vaishnava Faith and Movement* by Sushil Dey, Shashibhushan Dasgupta's *Sri*

Radhar Kromovikaas: Darshane o Sahitye (Gradual Evolution of Sri Radha: in Philosophy and Literature), Bimanbehari Mazumder's *Sri Chaitanya Chariter Upadan* (Elements of Sri Chaitanya Charit) or *Sri Chaitanya Charitamriter Bhumika* (An Introduction to Sri Chaitanya Charitamrita) by Radhagobinda Nath, forget his old academic studies? Simultaneously or later, I had read the English books by Kennedy and Deemak. Out of necessity, I had consulted *Sri Gouriya Vaishnava Avidhaan* (Sri Gouriya Vaishnava Dictionary) by Haridas Das, *Sahajiya Sahitya* (Sahajiya Literature) by Manindramohan Basu, or leafed through the seminal works like *Haribhakti Vilas and Sri Chaitanya Charitamrita.* Are these all external approaches? Nonetheless, I gradually realised that there were two clear ways to comprehend Chaitanya. One was to wade through the scholarly tomes; the other was to get formally initiated into the Vaishnava faith, to go through the path of practice. I was familiar with the first path; the second one was complicated for me; because I had no sincere devotion in my heart, hence the futility of formal initiation. But, out of sheer nowhere, a third way opened up: via the Sahajiya way. Almost like the Third Eye, this way opened up such a vista that I had never thought of knowing.

Sonadanga was the station following Bethuadahari. In a dark and dingy room of the railway yard of Sonadanga lived Ela Fakir. He was blind, but his mind was illuminated. He told me on the first day: "If you wish to know about Gora, go carefully through Lalan's lyrics."

I exclaimed: "How's that? How will I understand a Vaishnava through the eyes of a Fakir?"

His blind eyes lighting up in a flash of smile, Ela said: "He's the original Fakir: our Gora Fakir. Shaving his head, draping a cotton cover and carrying a beggar's bowl, Gouranga is the original Gora Fakir. Lalan says:

Listening to an unknown man's word—
To shave head, Gourchand came forward.

What did you follow? The unknown man is Aalekh. Getting his news, Gouranga adopted asceticism. So read Lalan first; but before that, visit the pilgrimage centres. Have you seen Nabadweep, Shantipur, Bagnapara, Kalna, Katowa, Kenduli, Fulia, Agradweep, Srikhanda, Khardah, Guptipara, Jeerat, Mangaldihi, Gopiballavpur?"

I said: "I had seen some, not others; but what shall I get from pilgrimage? Indeed, Lalan had said: 'Those pilgrimage vows are futile actions'; then what?"

Ela said: "Do you know for whom the pilgrimage vows are not required? It's for those who have acquired self-knowledge. For you, the outside knowledge hasn't been known yet. Leave those confusions; first go round the pilgrimages and then come back."

So I went round many holy places over a period of time and witnessed the food offerings, prayer services and worships, and five doctrines of the Vaishnavas. After a thorough understanding, I went back to Ela Fakir again.

Fakir said: "Did you get to understand everything? Did you notice the outward show of rituals? Did you see how in the temples they put Gouranga to bed for the night and wake him up next morning? Did you observe the worship of the wooden images and portraits? Did you see them putting the *raskali*—the sacramental marks? Did you see them wearing the *dor-kaupeen*—their saintly loin-cloths? How did you find it all?"

: "It was all quite nice. They were all very devoted, reading books, performing keertan."

: "Which keertan is genuine?"

: "Why, the Naamkeertan! With Hari's name comes liberation in Kalyug—the mythical Kali era."

"Is that so?" Ela Fakir smiled dubiously: "Will mere uttering of the name 'Hari' bring salvation? Then listen to what Lalan has said:

What would mere words do, if you ignored the path indeed!—
If words could produce your crop, why sow the seed?"

I remarked: "What does that have to do with Hari's name? Do you know the power of name?"'

Without replying to me, Ela sang the second stanza of the song, followed by an elaborate *taan*—a melodious composition of rising and cascading notes:

Mentioning molasses, is mouth sweet?
Is darkness gone, if day you don't meet?
So, only Hari's name you treat –
To Hari, it doesn't lead.

: "What did you follow?"

: "I understood that singing only Hari's name won't do; one has to understand its essence."

: "'No, only essence won't do. You've to know his location, that is, where does he reside in the body; what his activities are."

I said: "What's the way to understand them?"

: "It's here that you need a guru. Without a guru, it is impossible to catch the true essence of Gaur and understand him. This is why Lalan says...

Sans a guru, Gaur to worship—
It is into hell you dip."

I felt that there should be another side to understand Gouranga and the Gouriya Vaishnava religion: contrary to one I had known so long. Ela Fakir was trying to attract me to that side very skillfully. First, he explained to me that idol worship was futile; then he showed how trivial the core of Hari's name was. Yet, was the ceremonial meditation in Gouriya ideology wrong?

Could there not be parallel ways of meditation? On another day, when I raised the point with Ela, he laughed it out outright, saying: "Can truth be of two kinds? The outcomes, of course, can be different."

"Of what kind?" I asked him.

: "Outcome would depend upon the recipient, know it for certain." If you sow good seeds into stone, will you get good crop? Similarly, if you stored curd in a copper container, it would turn into poison. There's a song that says:

Lion's milk doesn't stay in an earthen pot—

What then? Do you understand now the difference in outcome by way of recipients?"

: "It's understood. But can't one worship Chaitanya in one of the two ways? If ceremonial Vaishnavas use pure rituals for wooden icons or chant names, what's wrong with it?"

: "Wrong? Listen to Lalan's words:

The breast that gives milk to the bonny child—
Oozes blood if leeches suck it in the wild."

Startled, I said: "What powerful force of logic! But here it's not according to the recipient, but according to the entitled. Milk is as much true, as is blood. But the outcome is according to the entitlement. Well, but how come, your understanding of Chaitanya is correct, and theirs is incorrect? How are you so much beyond doubt about it?"

: "We've understood because we've reached out and latched on to the human soul. That's why we don't need scanty loincloth, sandalwood paste markings, garlands, celibacy, Vrindavan, Mathura or anything else. Rather, we say:

Accept as true this man-based play—
Discard your loincloth; the 'Hari'chant don't you say!"

:"I understand. But why object to celibacy? In every religion, sacrifice, ascetism and celibacy are highly appreciated and applauded."

: "Who applauds? Only you become celibates on the one hand and give bravos; not us. Can life move without Nature? Where did you come from? Have you descended from heaven, or, been born in your mother's lap? Who is that mother? Isn't she your father's Nature? We believe that 'the sign of manhood resides in nature's bosom.' Besides, how far will you go discarding nature and donning loincloth? Will you listen to some core fact? Mahaprabhu himself experienced the companionship of nature. Through Lakshmipriya and Vishnupriya. Advaita had two natures. Nityananda's was the same case. You've studied quite a lot; could you tell me how many were celibates before and after Chaitanya?"

After some counting, I replied: "That's true. Srinivas Acharya had two wives and Shyamananda had even three. Roop, Sanatan and Srijeeb were celibates." Catching my words, Ela said: "Now, you've caught it right. Leaving nature out was a canard they've perpetuated. Mahaprabhu never said it. Do you know, his associate Ramananda Roy used to meditate with the service of two temple dancers? Did Chaitanya forsake him, or, stop the topmost secret dialogues with him? Whatever, you, dear, consult your books and check whether what I've said is correct or not."

What I got from the books and manuscripts could, of course, never be conveyed to Ela Fakir; for, by then he was under the grave. But what I culled out was no less engrossing. First, my attention was attracted by a most unusual statement by Ahmad Sharif, a noted scholar of Bangladesh, in the Dhaka Bangla Akademi journal's issue of Magh-Chaitra, 1370. Sharif wrote: 'Rumours have it that

Chaitanyadev himself had a secret meditation process. This meditation was based on adulterous coitus.'

More explosive information than this was available in an article of Bangiya Sahitya Parishad journal of year 91, issue1. Prof. Ramakanta Chakrabarty had given there an introduction to a biography of Chaitanya by Nrisingha. Nrisingha had written his manuscript, *Sri Chaitanya Mahabhagavatam,* in Sanskrit. Gopinath Adhya, of Banchharam Akrur Lane of Calcutta, had donated the manuscript to the Parishad. Retrieving the manuscript from the dark and dingy vault of Parishad, Ramakanta wrote his introduction. Written in the year 1665, the book appeared quite nascent and immature. But, at the same time, Ramakanta Chakrabarty's remark seemed correct, namely: 'As an unusual commentary on Gouranga Leela – a localised and mixed version created perhaps in the middle of the 17th century and limited to an ignoramus community of Vaishnavas – (it) was quite valuable.'

Now it was observed that the manuscript, *Sri Chaitanya Mahabhagavatam,* by Nrisingha stated, in page 51K, the following most unusual factoid: 'Gouranga, expert in *kamashastra,* used to adopt the *kaya-vyuha* process to indulge in conjugal union with countless women companions.'

It must be admitted that this was dreadful news and perhaps somewhat matched Ahmad Sharif's comment. So, more enquiries were warranted: but in the academic world, not down the emotional pathway.

Someone intimated, in passing, that Sri Nandan Ghosh of Bernia village had a collection of pen-scripted manuscripts. Ghosh was dark skinned and of robust frame with an equally matching thunderous voice. He was informed in advance. As soon as I got down from the bus, he welcomed me vociferously, making my arrival public news.

Soon Ghosh took me to his hut. He said: "We are Sahajiyas. You must know that Sahajiya Vaishnavas have several streams, such as the Nityananda stream, Patuli stream, Roop Kaviraji stream, and the Beerbhadra stream. Ours is the Patuli stream—with initiation and learning at Patuli village. Our Gosain's name is Satyadev Mohanta, who expired last Shravan. Yes, you've heard right, I've many penned manuscripts. But what do you wish to know? The moon meditation or the begging doctrine, the corporeal chronicle or the Radha doctrine?"

How would I know all that? I asked him if he had anything leading to Sri Chaitanya's adulterous path of meditation for salvation. Smiling pleasantly, he opened the wooden chest, brought out a longish manuscript bound in red cotton cloth and touched his forehead with it. Giving it to me, he said: "This is *Adya Kaumudi* by Mukunda Das. Do read it and copy down notes. You're here the whole day, aren't you? The meal service will be late. Till then, handle the manuscript. Information on Mahaprabhu's adulterous meditation is contained here." Reading on for quite a while, my eyes were suddenly arrested by a hymn in *Adya Kaumudi*. It said:

Becoming ascetic, Prabhu took a concubine—
Sarbabhauma's daughter Shati turned out just fine.
Maid Shati was Mahaprabhu's companion, other—
For steady coitus: as a common man would, rather.

Reading all this, I was plunged into greater depths of doubt. Who was Shati who was understood to be Sarbabhauma's daughter? Was this topic of Basudev Sarbabhauma, something which I had missed and not read elsewhere earlier? When I informed Ghosh about it, he said: "People from the Gouriya faiths won't naturally divulge it, for it's contrary to the asceticism theory."

I thought his statement had logic. But why should Chaitanya behave like the 'common man' and practise *atalsadhan*—a life of steady coitus? Answering this question, Ghosh said with some conviction: "Then you don't seem to know the truth. Do you know why he appeared on earth? And about his three desires?"

"Won't I know this?" I said fluently. "Whatever, let me put it across in simple Bengali: first, to know what the essence and charm of Sri Radha's love-play was; second—how sweet the grace of Krishna's love – experienced by Radha – was, and third—to perceive the extent of pleasure that Radha derived by perceiving Krishna. In order to fulfill these three desires, Gouranga took birth in Nabadweep, in the womb of Shachisindhu."

Ghosh asked: "Where did you get this fact? Who told you?"

: "Why, it's in the scriptures—written by Swarup Damodar."

: "Bunkum. Who obeys those scriptures, written by that sect of Brahmins-Vaishnavas? They're all rubbish, all beside the point. Will you listen to the real reason—why Mahaprabhu came to Nabadweep? Then listen carefully."

First rose the humming notes of the tune, followed by the lyrics:

In Vrindavan resided Rasaraj our King—
Their game of desire he followed not, a sound push was what he got—
To reach his 'Nadey'[9] and start living.

This was one of the wonders: there were only songs and songs. All the logic of folk religion was strung in songs. But what was the game of sap that Krishna did not fathom in Braja, for which he had to come to play in Nabadweep? I had to interrupt, to remark: "What nonsense are you singing? What did Nanda's son lack in Braja?"

: "Don't you know? He didn't have a simple nature, so he couldn't carry out Sahaj meditation. How could God have a Sahaj

9 *Nadey*: A colloquial usage and a popular local reference to the district of Nadia—in association with Nemai Chandra, later Sri Chaitanya or Sri Gouranga. This is where Chaitanyadev took birth.

nature? How was it possible? He was not born out of the lustful desire of his parents—blending seed and menstrual fluid? So he was, by nature, devoid of lust and desire. Without lust, there's no excitement of love. Sahaj meditation is not possible without love; so he had to be born in Nadia. This birth was from the seed and the menstrual cycle—associated with a lustful function of body. He took to asceticism to surpass that lust. Adopting Shati as his soulmate and companion for *parakiyasadhan*, he performed his meditation with the assistance of the 'other woman'—to achieve *sahajananda*. Listen to the three desires now, in a song:

One, oh, I'd wear my loincloth around my waist;
Two, I'll carry the begging bowl at my best;
Three, the man of my heart in my mind, I'll rest.

Do you understand now, the last desire is the cardinal one—*'Man of my heart, in my mind I'll rest.'*

I understood that I was gradually moving from '*a*-Chaitanya' to '*sa*-Chaitanya'. Returning home, I began exploring more books and manuscripts, looking for the fair maiden Shati. These were not Vaishnava scriptures, but simple Sahajiya lyrics or collections of Fakiri songs. Leafing through some, I stumbled upon the context of Shati. How very romantic—it was not merely confined to the Patuli stream, but also pervaded Marfati music. I found there:

For Gobinda Chand, Shati was the concubine—
To woo which moon, Gora for Shati made a bee-line?
Holding Shati's crimson feet—
Performed the Sahajiya treat.

But immediately thereafter, the folk composer highlighted a self-contradiction: to raise an embarrassing question. He sought to know:

All three worlds for her beg—
Gora's unbalanced for her to peg.
Then forsaking women's dreg:
Why does Gora whine?

It was truly a burning question. All living beings of heaven, earth and the netherworlds were hankering after coital pleasure; Gouranga himself was unbalanced for that woman's companionship; how did the same man counsel forsaking feminine company? Was there some adulteration in this matter? I recalled Ela Fakir's surmise—perhaps Mahaprabhu did not instruct the forsaking of nature. Ela believed this was the vicious plotting of the six Goswamis of Vrindavan. But my mind was keen to know another matter. Human reproduction was an outcome of the blending of seed and the periodic menstrual cycle and hence man had a penchant for erotic desire within the spirit—this statement had an unambiguous and clear perspective of life and a healthy admission for sex.

Really speaking, our birth had a certain process. It might sound obscene to our highly-educated urban ears but did not feel bad at all, when Jeevan Gosain told me quite casually at the Agradweep fair—"Birth is a providential phenomenon. The man or cultivator – well versed in the earth and the field – sows his seeds by dropping it into a woman's womb at the right moment. It's similar to adding a portion of curd to warm milk for it to curdle and set. The supreme seed keeps floating in the world of the mother's womb: indefinite, shelterless. Suddenly the soul appears. The floating seed, tossed by currents, suddenly becomes elongated from its round shape. Now from this oblong shape suddenly appear two moulds—becoming, well, the body and two legs. Another splurge of wave shapes the two hands and a head. Then come intelligence and growth."

Talking so far, Jeveen Gosain caught up with a question-and-answer song between guru and disciple. This was a wonderful composition by Deen Sharat! The disciple says:

This upside down country Guru, where is this land?
Feet-up, head-down: the folks there walk and stand!
There each river and each stream
Has an upward flow, it would seem,
Sky'n'wind, below water lie—
Human life there is fairly grand!
All the people who live there,
Don't eat with their mouth, their nose breathes no air,
Stool'n'urine they don't pass—
Yet they eat, and live a life simple and bland!

This was clearly a song of corporeal doctrine, describing the human embryo's incubation period in the womb. Stopping the song midway, Jeevan Gosain had a short break and then began another cryptic song—replying to the first lyric on the guru's behalf:

My mind, from that land you took a final bow—
Having lived feet-up head-down there, and how!
As seed, you were in your father's head,
Out of lust, into womb went ahead,
Seed and mens' fluid together led
To the round shape now!
Earth, water, energy, fire and space
In five months, five elements apace,
In seventh month, your guru did
The sacred hymn allow.
Sun 'n' moon didn't reach your den—
Under water, in dark, you lived months ten,
Umbilical cord in mother's navel-lotus

Fed like a suckling cow!
Deen Sharat says: meditation's fruit
From a prison to this land, brought you as offshoot,
Forgetting that illusion's in cahoots—
What's for salvation now?

There was no lack of clarity in this song of Jeevan Gosain; there it was only a chronicle of human birth. At the end, there was a moral, as was common in all epical mythology. Thinking of the moral, another aspect arose. The core point of the moral was that after travelling through many vaginas, one was blessed with the human birth after much effort and meditative practice. But, having been born in this garb, one forgets one's promise! Being born as a human, one was here to focus and serve fellow humans. Under guru's instructions, instead, how did you get caught in the web of lust? Moving on to the next thought—there was still a way; spot and catch the guru of this mortal life and learn Sahaj meditation. Remember Chaitanya too. Having been born as a human being, he, too, had to take Shati to complete his Sahaj meditation; only then did he receive his salvation.

Here that song of Lalan's would be relevant, where it has been said:

Would Gour come again?—
What's done for human-worship, he did already with great pain.

Another song could be culled as prelude to this song, which too belonged to Lalan. It would be seen there that there was a sequence for Gouranga's birth from Braja up to Nadia:

Leaving Braja, to Nadia he came,
In earlier birth, it was laid the same;
Now leaving Nadia, where's he game?
Tell me: where's his path lain?

Indeed, there was no authentic, practical information about Chaitanya's death. No biography of Chaitanya narrated the event of his death. Some wrote, he was assimilated in the Jagannath icon; some wrote that he let himself drift into the deep sea in a moment of emotional fervour. Only Jayananda wrote that he died of the injury that he sustained while dancing in Puri. Here the folk religion suggested a simple solution. Their logical sequence went somewhat like this—why did Chaitanya appear? It was to explain to the illusion-ridden human beings the power of Sahaj meditation and to realise its depth himself. Only that much knowledge was not gleaned in the play of life in Braja; it had remained incomplete. Yet, after achieving that completeness in Sahaj meditation, where did Chaitanya disappear? One answer was as follows:

Some say: doing his own worship
To his own land, he did go,
Lalan feels—which tryst to keep
With which land, does one know?

Chaitanya went to his own land, his deserving abode. He had come to promote popular education. He departed by keeping an idealistic model before the people; after having completed his task, having eradicated differences among caste and creed, and having brought a new devotional surge among people. Now what would happen to us? How should we receive him and understand him? Would we get him only by surmise?

I got the answer in the Baul-Fakir Association's conference in the Goradanga village. Those were the days of biting winter in the month of Paush. It was a gathering of all the Bauls and Fakirs from the neighbourhood of Nadia and Murshidabad. The smell of marijuana was renting the air. The cold was hardly tackled by a thick blanket. Sanatan Das – the 70-year-old ascetic – had started singing: with less music than self-surrender. His was part singing and part explanation. He was both a singer and a narrator: with sudden delving into dance. What a dance it was, with what an earnestness! He sang away:

It's all accounted for in human land.
Three craftsmen of dexterity have created every city,
All threaded as one—the three attributes' strand.
Virtue and vice—while they add strength and girth—
Creatures enter a chamber of illusion along the earthly path;
Like a lotus, its petals inwards out in all its worth.

: "I'm describing mother's womb, dear! Three craftsmen are Brahma. Vishnu and Maheshwar; and three attributes are: purity, spiritedness and ignorance. The lotus with its petals inside out is the flower of the mother's womb. All life begins there, dear! Now listen:

Now the creator starts making the soul,
After knowing outcome of its action as a whole:
First month for flesh'n'blood to cover the seed;
Second month for navel'n'bone indeed—
Third month with three qualities brain to breed;
Fourth or eyes ears, lips, skin and hair...

"Is man made in one day? Is he an animal that he would only survive his years anyhow? Man has to perform all the rituals and actions; he has to understand everything. He needs consciousness, knowledge of good and bad, consideration of truth and falsehood. Hence his process of construction is a slow one.

Fifth has hands 'n' feet;
Five essences get added to make the soul complete;
That day the being's form 'n' size are on treat.
At six months are placed the six passions in each seat.

"Five essences mean five elements. All the world's flowers, fruits, crops are made of five elements. The embryo draws five elements from the stream of blood in the placental flower of the womb. In six months, the being gets a form, size, as well as the six passions come to inhabit, namely—sexual lust, anger, greed, infatuation, vanity and envy.

In the seventh month, seven metals each—
Comes there with own power to reach.
In the eighth, eight solutions come for consumption.
In nine months, nine doors are seen—
In ten months, the ten senses are no more in the womb, where they had been.

"Nine doors imply two eyes, two ears, two nostrils, the cavity of the mouth, the anus and the sex organs. When ten months are over, five knowledge senses and five activity senses come alive. Then the foetus squirms within the womb, saying: "Liberate me from this dark; save me from this painful womb; this is full of blood and slippery too."

The Creator then asks: "Would you remember what to do once you're born?" "Yes, I'll remember. I'll meditate on and serve mankind. Nonchalantly, I'll perform the service." But in reality it happens the other way round. Therefore—

Gosain Kala calls—Gopal, come on to hear;
Wind-master, eyes have come out so dear—
Now the creature lies crying on the earth, devoid of essence clear!

"At the time of birth, the head indeed comes first; it has eyes. Those eyes view the earth first and illusion hits hard on those eyes. He cries out and in the process, the essence gets lost.

'Where, where, where': he wails to say,
The being has no clear bonding—
With where he appears and has to stay!

"He only cries: 'Where, where? Oh where's He, and where am I? Where was I, and where have I come? Where did my Creator disappear?' Then the mother puts him to her breast. Holding it with two hands, the baby sucks. The baby's lust is born; his vow is washed away. My dear brothers, this is life." The narrator Sanatan Das stopped.

My goodness, this was unalloyed Freudian thought-process! But what had this to do with Chaitanya? At the end of the music, Sanatan Das was pulling at his hemp in the room above. Without being scared, I went right in and asked: "What was the link of the Gouranga doctrine with the song you sang?"

With a universal gaze, Sanatan said: "Everything is linked with Gouranga or the Chaitanya doctrine. Take, for instance, our two gurus—initiation guru and teaching guru. Now, initiation guru is like Krishna, and teaching guru is like Radha. Then the initiation guru and teaching guru are getting linked in the disciple's body. Then disciple is Chaitanya. Would you like to listen to more of this?"

It was quite a new statement, without doubt. Being inspired, I said: "Would you tell me more? Please do. I haven't heard these statements before."

: "Yes, you are misled. We've to understand our doctrine with this body. Then listen to the Chaitanya doctrine. Where was Chaitanya born and with whose seed? His father was Jagannath Mishra. Who is Jagannath? He is the lord of the world, that is, where the animate being and God have blended. His birth was from that blended seed. The combination of seed and the Radha entity is Chaitanya. In order to understand the Chaitanya doctrine, therefore, you need nature. Is there a religion possible without nature? Nature is necessary for the *anandaswarup rasa*—the sap in the form of joyous pleasure. For getting unparalleled consciousness, too, you need nature. Now did you follow everything?"

: "Can the whole thing be followed? I've followed some, the rest is unclear. It's not very simple."

: "Then hereby I lock my mouth," said Sanatan Das. "You can't now make me open up to say anything more. But yes, hemp has induced trance as well as high philosophy and emotion. Rather, let me sing a song, you might get an answer to your queries:

In Roop's doors, Sri Roop does reign –
She can open Roop's locks,
If she does deign.
If one gets into Sri Roop,
The lock opens: to get out of the loop.

"What did you follow, dear?"

I replied: "Sri Roop is the feminine body; is that correct?"

Sanatan came forward to ruffle my hair with his fingers. Then, smiling with his brightly glowing eyes, he said: "So you've completed comprehending Nityananda! Do make some progress. You're bound to get Chaitanya and Advaita."

I had goosebumps all over my body.

I said: "I seem to comprehend quite a bit; but everything is not clear yet. Tell me what I should do. Where should I go?"

: "Where exactly have you been?"

: "To all the Vaishnava places of pilgrimage, namely, Nabadweep, Shantipur, Khardah, Bagnapara, Agradweep, Katowa, Adi Saptagram..."

: "These are all Shri Pat. But you've not been to too many Sahaja clusters. Do visit Nasratpur once; and Patuli."

Having attended and performed the rituals at the Baruni bath in Agradweep I got down at Patuli on my return journey. It was a beautiful village on one hand. On the other side, the market township had come up with new houses, shops and cold storages. I had no business on that side! Rather, there were many hutments towards the Ganga, sprawled out with their earthen courtyards, housing the Sahajiyas over the last 200 - 300 years. They performed a secret physical esoteric activity. The name of that particular meditative process and its related faith was called the Patuli stream. Their external attire was a cheap white loose robe of coarse Markin cloth, their loincloth—the Janata dhoti; they all wore their hair long—collected and tied in a raised knot. They wore garlands of tulsi wood around their necks and held dry coconut-shell bowls in their hands. Many followed the two-moon meditation, and some observed the four-moon one. The pure, celibate, gentle Vaishnava community heartily hated these Sahajiyas, calling them heretical perverts. "Fie," they blurted out in disgust upon hearing the Sahajiya name. "They take Gouranga's name, despite eating all the waste."

I knew some of these facts; so had not much difficulty at the Patuli portal of Sadabrata Adhikary. In passing rather, I raised another topic, saying: "Well, what is the significance of your head-tuft as well as the robe and tulsi-garland that you wear? Are they playing off to the gallery or something else?"

: "You have asked an excellent, pertinent question, which nobody else has asked till date. Then listen as to why this dress. You must have seen a field of spinach crop? A most ordinary thing; however, it still needs to be fenced off for protection. Otherwise, the goats would munch on them. The meditator's robe is his fence:

the protective talisman. Everything said and done, we're only human. The mind does get diverted into evil thoughts, evil deeds. Whenever that happens, we keep our hand on the garland, the tuft of hair, the robe. We tell ourselves: aren't you a monk, wearing an ascetic's costume? Well, the self-control returns, escaping from a dire fall. Did you get it?"

I realised that the man had the analysing ability in him, that is, he was wise. Perhaps I could get from him some inkling into the Gour doctrine. But as per the rules of the game, I could not raise the topic all at once. It had to be done in a roundabout way. So I said: "It's well said. But everybody can't express with such clarity. Is this expression coming from within you?"

: "No, expression doesn't come from a mere clear perception. The words have to be mulled over. Have you seen some great meditator? Their inside is filled with clear wisdom. But you can't make that out at first sight. They are silent, at peace with themselves, without any outward expression. And those who're narrators have to sharpen their exteriors, irrespective of what is there inside. Take, for instance, this hurricane lantern. Perhaps there's light inside, but can you get illumination unless you keep the glass-surface clean? For the meditator, therefore, both inside and outside have to be kept clean."

: "Would that mean mind and body?"

: "Yes, only then the desire, action and wisdom would remain under control. They're three-in-one: indivisible."

I felt I could raise my query now. So I blurted out: "Well, what's your doctrine, in a nutshell so to speak?"

: "In a nutshell, it's a core hymn, which is secret. But to elaborate a little:

Earlier, you were Radha in my heart—
Now I'm Radha: as your integral part.

"Did you follow?"

: "Yes, I did. In Braja, Radha was in Krishna's heart. In the Nabadweep stage of their game, Radha had Krishna within her. Therefore, it's 'Krishna-in, Radha-out'. That's why Chaitanya is 'Gouranga', clear-skinned."

Sadabrata said: "You're almost there. But Gour's fair complexion has another interpretation. One of the songs contains that doctrine—O Haridasi, please give me my *sarinda*; let me sing a Mahat lyric."

Finally Haridasi could be spotted. She was an ascetic in a white blouse and white cotton sari. On her nose and forehead there were the red-earth paste ritual marks. She was a strikingly dark-skinned woman. She lowered the musical instrument on the earthen balcony and very devotionally took her seat on one side. While the drone was being tuned and in the process produced a few tinkling notes of music, I took the opportunity to ask: "Aren't we to listen to Haridasi's singing?"

Giving a sweet smile, Haridasi nodded her head. Many people had told me that the songs of the Vaishnavis hailing from the western-Gangetic plains of Bengal were worth listening to, on all accounts. I had, of course, heard many Vaishnavis sing them at the portal of Meera Mohanta at Agradweep; but then they were on fair grounds, where music of deep essence was rare. Meanwhile, the *sarinda* had been tuned and Sadabrata had begun singing on an upper octave:

Gour, please do appear again.
In the ritual fire's crackling noise
Ears are rent in piercing voice,
If it's purely of your choice—
Jump into the funeral: to be lain.

I had never heard such a song before. Gour, do appear again: where would he appear, and, in which form? Is the fire of lust implied by 'the ritual fire's noise' and 'jump into the funeral'? Apparently then, the meditator was inviting Gour to merge with his own body. What an unusual song! The rest of the song was:

If you're burnt in that fire –
You'll be carrier of the pyre;
Action will be blessed then,
With golden hue: fair and plain
Gour, please do appear again.

Stopping the song, Sadabrata said: "Did you get the meaning of Gora's appearance? The colour of lust is black, deep black. Plunging into that lust to purify the latter, love is born. Love is of a golden hue. Gouranga is love personified. Hence his colour is golden too.'"

What was surprising was that all folk faiths were trying – through their songs –to convince me that Gouranga was not any person, nor an incarnation, but was consciousness at a meta-level. He would not be available in an idol or through chants. He would be accessible in a mix of meditation, in a process of purification. The matter began to attract me. I said: "Isn't there any simple and easy song of yours pertaining to Gouranga?"

: "What's easy—to listen to, or to understand? What I sang is also a very easy song, provided you follow. Well, now listen to a simple song. Come Haridasi, hum the tune."

Closing his eyes, Sadabrata used an upper-octave note on the *sarinda* and Haridasi caught on:

Oh guru, I use my gaze and see Gour in everything...
Chand Gour is my rosary,
The Gour-talisman, on my neck I sling,
Putting my Gour-jewellery on,
I slowly do my stepping.
Gour's collyrium on my eyes,

Gour's bracelet, Champak-bud,
Gour's on hair—the chandrahaar[10]*, my moon-garland,*
Gour's my mark, nose-ring.
Gour's my saree, conch-shell,
The cord to bunch my hair, my ladle-bell,
Gour's the bangles on my two hands,
My breasts' cover and its drawstring.

At the end of the song, I noticed Haridasi's eyes were full of tears. In the world of belief, I was a questing atheist: highly a misfit. I asked: "Are the lyrics describing Gour the lover?"

"It may be," said Sadabrata most nonchalantly: 'Those are of your concern. And our concern is only one—when shall we attain Gour."

The difference between the inquisitive and the devotee was that between knowledge and faith. Indeed, I wanted to understand: layer by layer, sequentially, by classification. They realised in stages from perpetuator, meditator and the initiated. Their knowing was vertical, mine was horizontal. I wanted to catch Chaitanya through the web of social truths, while they sought to assimilate Chaitanya within the orbit of personal perception. Yet, nothing was acceptable to them, that is, to folk religion, without the logic of the myth. That was why they liked to remain within the confines of themselves. There arose no conflict with the upper class. Therefore, we had a sense of fun in our curiosity about them. They, too, derived fun out of our Vedas, Puranas and consciousness of class and caste, but had no curiosity. I had heard two hymns about Chaitanya many times. One of them was:

Satya, Treta, Dwapar, Kali: four eras were wrought
Within them, a Divine era Gora[11] *himself brought.*

---

10 *Chandrahaar*: A necklace with moon shaped motifs

11 *Gora*: A shortened endearing reference to Gouranga or Sri Chaitanya

Here was a straightforward cancellation of our Puranic Era classification and reincarnation theory. In the catholic thinking of the lower class, the words 'Divine Era' were a new creation. Here the Divine Era was a time-period of idealist dream, which was not patronised by the Brahmins, nor governed by the royalty, nor sheared by caste and class. If Gouranga had brought up any ideal of creating a healthy society, it was a free society: glowing in humanity, warm in physical faith and earthy in lust and desire. Placed in this stance, the folk religion had another say:

On this earth, Gora has brought a new law—
In the justice of that law, Ved-Puran did thaw.

This nascent law, brought by Gora, was then the brave hymn for the under-privileged. Empowered by this law, they put humanity at a higher pedestal than the scriptures. Opposed to the worship of holy pots and portraits, they ascribed Krishna-Radha myth in males and females. The picture of the Sahajiya religion was clear even to foreigners like M.T. Kennedy. The latter wrote in clear-cut language: 'The worshipper is to think of himself as Krishna and to realise within himself the passion of Krishna for Radha, who is represented by the female companion of his worship. Through sexual passion, salvation is to be found. The Radha-Krishna stories are held as the justification of their practices which are secret and held at night.'

Now, this Radha-Krishna story, the Barai Buri-Chandrabali-Aihan myth, Gouranga-Vishnupriya-Shachi-mother trilogy had, behind all or them, a clear-cut logical sequence which at least I had not read in any study. There was another expression of folk religion – in poetic songs, musical tournaments, serial story-telling and narratives – where the Puranas were so much interpreted and re-interpreted, orally and among various singers that they needed an analysis that had not been penned down. Had this been done, we would have got the likes of Damodar Dharmananda Koshambi in Bengal.

From such thoughts, I told Sadabrata in the afternoon, after the lunch-service: "I've some sundry questions: would you like to reply?" Once Sadabrata agreed I asked: "Well, what does your belief say? What was the guilt of Vishnupriya? Why was she forsaken by Mahaprabhu?"

Smiling like an omniscient man, Sadabrata said: "The one who was Sita in Treta era, was Vishnupriya in Kali. Do you recall the elusive deer episode? Without heeding Lakshman's prohibition, Sita crossed over the line to give alms to Ravana and the latter abducted her at once. The violation of the prohibition then induced Mahaprabhu to forsake Vishnupriya. Have you been thinking about Shachi-mother?"

: "Yes, certainly. Why did Chaitanya make her weep, without fulfilling his mother's debt?"

: "Shachi-mother was Kaikeyee in Treta era. Suffering the pain of her son's separation, mother Kaushalya cursed Kaikeyee to suffer likewise, the pain of a son's separation in the Kali era. Hence was the appearance of Nimai, the ascetic."

: "Are there similar explanations about the villains Jagai-Madhai?"

: "Yes, in every age, the worship of God has been practised to look upon Him as an enemy. The ones who were Jagai-Madhai in the Kali era were initially the heaven's gatekeepers, Jay and Vijay. Under Brahma's curse, they were born in human form and inimical to divinity. Before this happened they were the Ravan-Kumbhakarna duo in Treta era and the Shishupal-Dantabakra duo in the Dwapar era.

How wonderful! I had to appreciate. Then I asked my last question: "Well, Chaitanya was initiated by Keshavbharati: what was its significance? Why should God be initiated?"

: "It happened to establish the Guru theory. Even such an event is not new. As was sage Sanak in the Satya era; sage Vishwamitra in the Treta era; sage Garga in the Dwapar era, so was Keshavbharati in the Kali era."

That Sadabrata was getting caught in his own web, he could not comprehend. Otherwise, it was very clearly understood that those who accepted the Divine era to be outside the ambit of Satya, Treta, Dwapar and Kali, should not refer to the latter four eras in support of their myth. Here the self-portrait of the somewhat simplistic thinking process of the lower strata of society was palpable. On one hand, they were making their new, contrary myth in protest against the privileged class's Purana and other myths; on the other hand, they were seeking support of their own myth – hewn out of their own logic – from the Purana of the 'upper' class! It was protestation and cooperation: at one and the same time!

That day Sadabrata saw me off up to Patuli station. The afternoon's Bandel-Katowa local's whereabouts were as inscrutable as the Chaitanya doctrine. Nobody knew when it would arrive. I was seated on the cement bench on the station premises. Kathmallika flowers silently fell on the head from above. There was a gusty breeze blowing. Some passengers gathered in twos and fives....Suddenly a group of Bauls materialised as if from nowhere—probably from some fair or festival nearby. All of them smoked some hemp to begin with. I quietly moved up to sit in their midst. Then, I dragged myself to the Baul group, i.e., the group-leader, to sit right in his front. I asked him: "I wish to know about some doctrinaire points; would you please tell me?"

With eyes crimson red from the hemp, the Baul Gosain drawled: "You want to know doctrines, have you completed your self-learning of doctrines?"

I realised it was the routine formula; I would be tested. I replied: "Do ask."

: "Who are you? Where have you come from?"

: "I'm a human, I was in my father's head: as a seed."

: "Well-done. Where did father's seed come from?"

: "From grains, corn, fruits and roots. They had five elements as their base."

: "Well, very well said. So what are five elements?"

I knew that it would hurt the questioner's ego, if all questions were tackled promptly. So I pretended to be a bit foolish and said with a troubled expression: "Earth, water, energy, wind and space: these are all I know. I don't know what their essence is, though."

Ignorance worked on such occasions. It happened exactly that way. Sieving his hand through in his beard, Baul Gosain said: "Space means Chaitanya; wind is Nitai; energy is Advaita; earth is Gadadhar; and water is Sribas."

: "Then how is the body made of five elements?"

: "You are right. Your learning phase is over. Well, I will ask you one more question. If you answer this correctly, you'll get the response on the doctrinaire question. Now do you agree to that? Well, tell me how Hanuman's face was burnt? Don't you tell me that Lanka's fire singed his tail and that same fire blackened his face! –That is simply rubbish! Go on, tell me now."

My goodness! Finally I was to manufacture myth and that too, after taking into account the lower-class logic! Were myths born from such predicaments as mine? However, I had a brainwave. I was aware of the sensitive feelings of the village folks and keeping that in mind, I said: "Hanuman was asked by Ramchandra to show his signet-ring to Sita at the Ashok grove and reassure her with the following words: 'My mother, you needn't be afraid. Preparations are being made for war in order to rescue you.' But, having said all that, Hanuman added on his own some superfluous words: 'My mother, if you want to see Ramchandra, climb on to my shoulder, I'll take you across the seas in one leap.' O ignorant Hanuman, how could you aspire to rescue Sita! This audacity of his was the first fault. And the much bigger fault was that Hanuman wanted Sita to climb on to his shoulder. It meant that he had the desire to touch her body. He was an animal, after all. For these two faults, his face got burnt."

"Bravo!" exclaimed the Baul Gosain. I was immensely relieved.

The Baul Gosain appeared to be quite pleased. "Listen to a song," he said. "Let me see whether you can catch the essence of this theory or not. Listen and ponder:

When you sleep, he's awake,
Your Guru: he's the one,
He's within your body,
Pure love for him is done!"

This was a difficult one, I thought to myself; was this the Chaitanya theory? When I slumber, my consciousness remains awake. But the next portion followed quickly:

Creatures move to and fro,
Only with that force, they go,
All their weal and woe—
Only in this pot are won!

Did men move and talk by virtue of their consciousness? Or, was the soul's statement being made here? But, was everything the harbinger of pleasure and sorrow? Now came the subsequent part:

If you do his worship,
All the knowledge you can keep;
From earth's troubles, you can leap:
Out and away: for ever gone!

No, this was certainly not talking about the soul or consciousness in this song. Meditation by soul or consciousness was a mystic matter. Why should the materialist Baul sing that song? What was this meditation about, which could leap out of birth and death? Now came the last bit:

When he goes away,
He'd make you a corpse of clay,
Sale'n'purchase, finish you may
In world's fair of great fun!

Wonderful! I knew I followed. I said: "You talked about breathing, didn't you? Breathing was then the guru! He led, and then I moved. Without him, I was only a corpse! And by controlling that breathing, one had the feeling of death while one was alive! There remained no sensation of the real body and mind. Have I followed correctly?"

: "Well followed. Do follow a little more. From the flow of breath emanates the movement of the seed. From breathing control comes protection of the seed. The seed is Chaitanya, the seed is Krishna. Another name of the seed is the jewel."

I felt suddenly the blast of a gusty wind. Was the song *'To know him, subjugate guru'* finally clear to me? Did guru mean breath? It meant Krishna, that was, Chaitanya. Totally beside myself in my joy and excitement, I said: "Have I understood the Chaitanya doctrine?"

: "You haven't followed all, but have now made some progress and found a bearing on this path," noted the Baul. "While still fresh and hot on this, listen to another song:

Which Krishna's the world's lord?
That Krishna is Nature,
Not Krishna as Mathura's God!"

Stopping the song, he asked: "What did you understand? What's the meaning of 'Nature'?"

I said: "Nature signifies the seed."

: "Right, right. Now listen—

In living creatures the seed resides,
Permeates the universe on all sides
Krishna is thy name.
Whoever's the male, is Radha's alone; and he guides!"

What was the third theory? If Krishna was the seed, then the male body which possessed it was Radha! Could 'Krishna-in Radha-out' have this explanation as well? Holding both the hands of Baul Gosain, I pleaded: "Please talk, talk a little more. Sing the remaining part of the song."

Suddenly there was a great commotion all around. People were running helter skelter; the Bandel-Katowa local train had appeared two hours late. Standing up and looking at my tearful eyes, the Baul said: "You've to wait a little. But you'll get to know him."

A strict path to know Chaitanya was contained in history, scriptures, and biographies. There was yet another path: secret and isolated. The second path once took me quite far, again, in a reverse flow, got set aside, after pushing me into deep mystery. I could, therefore, not resolve through which path I should fathom Chaitanya. Should I consider him as a historical iconic man, religious leader and a social visionary, or, as a beacon of light in a deep, lonely alley? Another question arose from this dichotomy of approach. While the upper-class Vaishnava society reckoned him as a leader, considered him as a reincarnation for worship and even made idols and charted out the methods of worshipping him, the lower-class folks obeyed him in a formless manner, through secret rituals. Was there reflected, in this approach, an unclear social thought-portrait: carrying an indignant protest? Was it from any deep sorrow – for rejection of rights – that they concealed Chaitanya from a person to an idea?

These leads should be explored from the contemporary times of Chaitanya and the history of the Vaishnava community of the post-Chaitanya period. In reality, there was a kind of decadence in the Bengali society since the time of Chaitanya: decadence in Brahminism and the Vedic culture. It implied the decadence of race, religion, scriptures and feudal society as a whole. On one side was the social leadership of the Brahmins and the upper class; on the other side was the Muslim royalty; in between arose Chaitanya's dream to herald a Vaishnava society. The confrontation was unequal, yet the ideals were humanitarian. Everyone was equal, only Hari's name would earn salvation; Vaishnava would have to be most tolerant and the humblest of the humble. Chaitanya, indeed, had these three core messages in his religious movement.

The idea was excellent, and wonderful as a thought, but mighty difficult to bring into practice. Alongside his new ideology was his profound devotion, indomitable courage and splendid physical grace: non pareil. Attracted by his formidable persona, so many men ran to him with devotion, or passionate love, or for self-protection or even protest; they came to be by his side, to be under his .protection. Here it was to be noted that because Chaitanya was a Brahmin, his messages were adaptable, acceptable to all, and respected by everyone. Had he belonged to a lower class, could his resentment against religious divisiveness, chant-imagery and scriptural practice be tolerated by all and sundry? Here remained two vital gaps in the Chaitanya movement. He moved into natural leadership – without having to earn it – precisely because he was a Brahmin. Again, it was in the peep-hole of Brahminism that the seed of future fall of Vaishnava society had remained sown. Within one hundred years from his death, the Brahmin-Vaishnava faction removed the marginal and communal Vaishnavas from the mainstream. Vrindavan loomed larger than Nabadweep. Those who were side-tracked did love Chaitanya and so, not able to make a dent and get space in the high-class Vaishnavism—created a different path of Vaishnavism. Returning from here, the seed of evolution of the minor faiths around Chaitanya had to be looked for. From this defeat and rejection emanated their meditation of secrecy. Comprehending while not comprehending Chaitanya as a person, they perhaps began thinking of Chaitanya as a metaphor from this point.

History recorded one more thing. The amount of resistance that Chaitanya got from the Muslim royal power during the first phase of his religious movement, was a hundred times less than the obstruction he got from the contemporary Brahmin society and the Hindu social leaders during his time. Smarta Raghunandan made out several regulations on Brahminism and his batchmate Krishnananda Agambagish – to whom the Kali idol and Kali worship were sacred – were canons of Shaktism's idolatry. It was not the end yet. Why ultimately Chaitanya had to leave Nabadweep and why he could not return to the Gangetic Bengal in the last eighteen years of his life, had no easy answer. One explanation, was, of course, skillfully documented in the lyrics of the folk musicians. It was stated there:

At Mahaprabhu's victory time,
All the land's rogue Brahmins did
Call him a 'madcap' sublime!
Gosain's human incarnation
Was a holy-bodied notion.
Seeing it as sinful commotion,
Named it 'epilepic' fit of crime!

So, first taunt was to call him 'mad' and then to name him an 'epileptic patient'. Yet, when Mahaprabhu's victory march could still not be forestalled, then what did the scheming Brahmins do?

When they saw nothing untrue,
Vaishnava: a caste they did brew;
Brahmins wrote, in black and blue,
Scripture's notes: to fall in rhyme.

This was the perennial ploy of the Bengali Brahminical society. It was salutary to recall that, much before Chaitanya's birth, many Brahmins and high-caste people took shelter in the remote and far-flung places – far away from the developed townships – to evade torture from the Turkish invasion. The local non-Aryan society's superstitious folks sought to worship their ancestral gods and goddesses, such as, Chaandi, Manasa, Dharma and some others. Their deities had no anthropomorphic forms and they searched out shapes of stone-pebbles, trees or even wild animals and snakes. Their parables of violent actions and vengeful stories moulded their oral tradition of feminine narratives of sacramental vows. The newly-arrived civil society – the Brahmins and other high-class people – soon mingled these with Hindu Puranas, using imagination and skills, to frame Mangal verses or Mangalkavya. That was how the orally-transmitted rural sacramental ritualistic ballads got the high pedestal of sophisticated literature.

The itinerant narrators roamed from village to village with these Mangal lyrics. This also opened up a means of livelihood, because the gatherings stretched from one Tuesday to the next. This is how, shoulder to shoulder with the non-Aryan society, the Brahmins and Vaidyas – both flaunting sacred threat – received due respect and recognition. The scheduled castes were also pleased because their stories got accepted. They could hold their heads high. Thus, the snake-goddess Manasa became Shiva's daughter; aboriginal Chaandi became Chandi—the symbol of Durga; unheard-of stories of the untouchable class got acceptance of the aristocratic class. Brahminisation was complete.

The same thing happened for Sri Chaitanya as well. When the Brahmins witnessed the endemic impact of the widespread acceptability of the Vaishnava faith and when the mercantile class and the working-caste people began respecting him, – then the Brahmin society began writing scriptural annotations and analytical biographies. If a count was taken of how many Vaishnava scriptural books and lyrics had been composed, ninety-five per cent of it would have been written by Brahmins. But, of course, they were no logger Hindu Brahmins, but 'Brahmin-Vaishnavas', that is, Brahmins converted to be Vaishnavas by chanting hymns and secret mantras at their initiation. 'Vaishnavasmriti-sastra' scriptures gave clear-cut instructions that a Brahmin had to be initiated by a Brahmin-Vaishnava in order to become a Vaishnava. A lower-caste Vaishnava was not entitled to initiate a Brahmin into Vaishnavism through hymnal vows. Narahari, Narottam and Shyamanada did not obey this dictum; they were, of course, rare exceptions. It was a historical truth that the mainstream Vaishnavism of Bengal and Vrindavan was Brahminism-oriented. Chaitanya himself was a Brahmin. His two main associates, Advaita and Nityananda, were Brahmins. Out of the six Goswamis of Vrindavan, Roop-Sanatan, Jeeb, Raghunath and Gopalbhatta were five Brahmins. In the post-Chaitanya period, leading Vaishnavas like Janhavi Devi, Ramachandra and Veerbhadra were Brahmins. In the Vaishnava faith of Bengal in the seventeenth-eighteenth centuries, the Bengali theoreticians, Srinibas Acharya, Bishwanath Chakarabarti, Narahari Chakrabarti and Radhamohan Thakur were Brahmins.

A colleague professor-friend said: "Vaishnava movement is really a history of fragmentation. However much Chaitanya wanted to eradicate racial and caste distinctions, nobody – other than Nityananda, Narottam and Shyamananda –could ignore the influence and prestige of Brahminism. Bimanbehari Mazumder has informed that, out of 490 direct disciples of

Sri Chaitanya, 239 were Brahmins; 37 Vaidyas; 29 Kayasthas; 2 Muslims; 16 women and 117 lowest classes. One more aspect was to be considered, namely, that in Chaitanya's time as well as later among Gouriya Vaishnavas, there was no central organisation. In Vrindavan and Nabadweep, that is, in Brajamandala and Gaurmandala, there was no coordination. In consequence, everyone proceeded to act of their own accord. There was no definitive plan or direction of the Gouriya Vaishnavas to eradicate racial discrimination."

I asked: "What's your opinion about Nityananda?"

: "Nityananda was a lover of life, with a catholic temperament. He was fond of decorative attires; and loved commotion and pandemonium. He had a Tantric background and was full of the sap of life, without any consciousness of caste and creed. Chaitanya had asked Nityananda and Advaita from Puri to propagate Vaishnava religion widely in Gangetic Bengal; he had asked Roop-Sanatan to go to Vrindavan to compose scriptural commentaries. There was no coordination between the two. The consequence was pretty bad. However, we were talking about Nityananda who had a grand personality. If you read *Prem Vilas,* you'd notice that he was more inclined to the path of wisdom than the path of devotion, in his old age. As a result, he increasingly took up more the task of propagation and Vaishnava initiation. He literally shook the whole country. It was Nityananda (alternatively, Veerbhadra) who converted 1200 bald male and 1300 bald women – the perverted Shakti worshipers of Buddhism – into Vaishnavism. His spirited and proud declaration was:

Nityananda himself – if you take the name –
Each lower caste into Vaishnava: I convert the same.
I make no distinction in caste or creed,
Make them dance in keertan *with love-devotion's seed!*

This egalitarian, broad-minded message of Nityananda was not likely to be palatable to the higher class and especially the upper ranks of Vaishnavas. His own disciple Vrindavan Das gave ample hint in *Chaitanya Bhagavata* as follows:

Watching Nityananda under Mahaprabhu dilation—
Some are happy, some disbelieve the notion.

And there were even some among the Vaishnavas who were so inimical to him that they believed in, *'Hearing Nityananda's name, get up and get away!'*

I said: "That's why, after Nityananda passed away, his wife Janhavi Devi and son Beerbhadra went to Vrindavan later on to contact the Goswamis there and take instructions. It meant that Nityananda's popular movement fell again in the hands of the higher class."

My professor friend brought out from his almirah the book *Chaitanyottar Jugey Gouriya Vaishnava* (Gouriya Vaishnava in the Post-Chaitanya Era') by Nanigopal Goswami and read aloud:

> As long as Sri Chaitanya was alive, there was no lack of order in the Vaishnava society. But after his passing away, the fire of communal hatred got ignited in order to retain the self-interest of the leaders and, sooner than later, there arose internal groupism within a few years, leading to several, mutually-quarrelling sub-branches: the group of Gaurnagar theory; the Advaita community; the Gadadhar community; and the anti-Nityananda community...Whoever could become a leader, became so whichever way. When the Gouriya Vaishnava society was disorderly in this manner, there arose worse confusion with the establishment of 'guru-ism'.

I commented: "The responsibility of initiation and learning remained with this guru, so Gour-worship without guru became impossible. Guru came up between Gour and his devotee. In those days, the book *Haribhakti Vilas* about Vaishnava practices magnified clearly the self-interest of the Brahmins. Brahmin here meant the 'Brahmin-Vaishnava.' *Haribhakti Vilas* accepted the caste-base of the society and the Brahmin's apex role there. This treatise went against the lowest class, giving prohibitory orders against any of their donations, even suggesting atonement procedures if an untouchable was sighted. It issued a fatwa that the Brahmin guru was the best of all and it was only a Brahmin who could initiate any caste. It was, of course, said that the lowest class could also initiate in their own caste and even at lower level, but never a Brahmin."

My friend said: "That was why the lower caste people went over to the Sahajiya line. In the lower caste, Haribhakti Vilas was not in vogue in the lower class, being written in Sanskrit and, in turn, Brahmins were indifferent to them. Their mention was riveted on the Mohantas. Taking this opportunity, many semi-literate, illiterate and even perverted people pretended to be the gurus of the lowest class. They interpreted adulterous relations, adolescent worship and the secret rituals and practices of Chaitanya-sadhana. Who had gone to inspect them at that time? Here listen to what Ramakanta Chakrabarti has said. I'm reading from *Society and Change*, first volume, fourth issue:

> Non-Brahmana Vaisnava gurus sought new (field) in tribal areas when they freely preached their own versions of the legends of Radha-Krishna and Chaitanya. Most of these versions were deeply (mixed) with sex and fundamentally different from the orthodox Vaisnava concepts, which had been couched in Sanskrit and which were, therefore, incomprehensible to the common people.

Hearing this commentary, I recalled the statements of Mazharul Khan of Goradanga village. He had asked me once to read the final volume of *Chaitanya Bhagavata,* where it was apparently written that Nityananda was the principal one, not Chaitanya. I searched out the instance in the book where Mahaprabhu tells Raghav Pandit, the Brahmin scholar from Panihati village:

Raghav, let me tell you my own secret—
Other than Nityananda, a second I didn't get;
Whatever Nityananda gets me to do—
I follow the same, let me tell you.
All my actions're at Nityananda-gate—
Candidly this I'm telling you, mate!

Later on, when I went again to Mazharul Fakir, he asked me if I had found the right place in *Chaitanya Bhagavata.* As soon as I nodded my head, Fakir asked: "Could you tell me what the meaning of 'Nityananda-gate' is. You can't, can you? It signifies the female vagina. Gouranga has indirectly stated that you've to go to the Nityananda-gate in order to understand the fundamentals of Chaitanya doctrine."

Had there been a thunderbolt in the room, I would not have been more shocked. Mazharul probably gave the ultimate example of how the sudden novelty of explanation could turn a pure treatise upside down. But this was not his own innovation by any means; the matter had passed on by word of mouth in utmost secrecy among the Baul-Fakirs, no doubt, over a few centuries. The Vaishnava community abounded in many fascinating instances as to how a treatise could be explained involving the concept of binaries at several layers. This side had not been properly studied till today. But something that needed to be especially noted was how far the concept of 'Nityananda-gate' – as explained by Mazharul Fakir and his preceding folk gurus – had reached: the sheer extent it had spread to. Hearing this, many would be vexed; many orthodox Vaishnavas would be quite hurt; but folk beliefs could not be toppled so easily. The folk gurus, ascetics and monks had said many such things, which ran parallel to the approved mainstream, were still propagating such thoughts and would continue to do so in the years to come.

Actually, complications had emanated 400 years ago. After the times of Chaitanya-Nityananda-Advaita-Gadadhar-Sribas, Bengal's Vaishnavism became self-centred and went into a divisiveness and contraction, from which Srijeev Goswami's initiated and tutored team of Narottam-Srinibas-Shymananda and, later on, Krishnadas Kaviraj, Bishwanath Chakrabarti, Narahari and Radhamohan – who were all from Vrindavan – made valiant efforts; still Vaishnavism could not be saved from the inevitable decadence and break-up. At the end of the seventeenth century, Narottam made the last effort to unite all Vaishnavas of Bengal by calling a mega-conference at Kheturi. But could the spontaneous popular power of Vaishnavas stop the rigidity, purification and leadership of Brahminism of *Haribhakti Vilas*? Did the mega-conference not ignore the marginalised and insulted lot? By naming them as 'racial Vaishnavas', were they not pushed into the hands of the perverted and uneducated gurus? And, taking that as advantage, did the Sahajiyas and Baul-Fakirs not gradually pull many among the lower-class folks gradually into the attractive and lively stream of nature-meditation along the path of rasa? In like manner, a historically acclaimed person like Sri Chaitanya became a layered symbol of secret worship? Nityananda became a deep symbol of body-centric sexual meditation. Krishna and Radha were ascribed a symbolism focusing on the physical union of the male and the female! On the other side, the puritan Vaishnavas were busy in establishing the faith of Krishna-Radha and Gouranga through temples and mutts: as wooden or stone icons.They laid down instructions for worship and wrote out scriptures and lyrical narratives. Giving everything a divine and unnatural interpretation they wanted to sit firm on their pedestals, against the flow of life...*'People failed to follow Chaitanya's sense'* was indeed a tragic utterance.

It should, of course, be stated at this juncture that it was not at all easy to establish Gouranga as an incarnation in Gangetic Bengal itself and recognise him as Supreme Power. This was because the Vaishnavas of Vrindavan never admitted the existence of an independent Chaitanya doctrine outside the Krishna ideology. They used to consider Chaitanya as 'means' and Krishna as 'end'. On the other side, the Gouriya Vaishnava community was keen to establish Gour supremacy. But, here in Bengal itself, a group of Vaishnavas founded Gour-Nitai icons in the temple, while another group established Gour-Gadadhar icons. After the Kheturi mega-festival, Narottam stated the dual icon of Gour-Vishnupriya—something challenged by the Vrindavan Gosains. Ramchandra Gosain, the adopted son of Janhavi Devi, wife of Nityananda, created a sacred portal at Baghnapara, where there was admittedly quite some expression of Sahajiya Vaishnava thoughts. There was resistance from the country's royalty in establishing Chaitanya as a supreme deity. In the eighteenth century, the Sri Gour idol in Nabadweep had to be kept under the earth's cover for six months in fear of the wrath of local royalty - Maharaja Krishnachandra - also the recognised head of the Brahmin society.[12] Kartikeya Chandra, the dewan of the Nadia royalty, clearly noted in 1875:

> The majority of the Brahmin community was constituted of Shakti worshippers and had very few Vaishnavas; among the lower class, most were Vaishnavas and some Shakti

12 See *Sri Sri Gauriya-Vaishnava-Jeevan* (Part II): Sri Haridas Das; p. 84

> worshippers. The kings were Shakti worshippers, but inimical to the Vaishnava faith.[13]

This record towards the end of the nineteenth century showed that most from the 'lower' rungs of the caste structure were of the Vaishnava faith. The mainstream Brahmins were inclined towards the Shakti doctrine. The remaining lot of grovelling Brahmins – landless and decadent landlords and other royalty, having lost their sheen and gloss under the stringent laws of the Permanent Settlement – were naturally keen to be Shakti worshippers under the powerful deity Kali, rather than show humble devotion to Krishna; they were also naturally more inclined to the five principal vices. However, by the end of the seventeenth century, the royalty, mercantile class and zamindars tried to start afresh and arouse the Vaishnava faith de novo. That history is worth noting here.

In the mega-conference on Vaishnavism at Kheturi, in the seventeenth century, there were a few proposals adopted, out of which one was to propagate Vaishnavism on a wide basis. The work on promoting and propagating the religion on a wide basis stated from two centres: Vishnupur and Kheturi. The Vishnupur king Veer Hambir and the Kheturi king Santosh Dutta got directly connected with this movement. Kings of Mayurbhanj, Panchkot and Paikpara, too, gradually came forward. Thanks to the efforts of Rasikananda, disciple of Shyamananda, in the Jharkhand-Odisha region, many of the royalty and nobility of Odisha came forward as well. In the Gangetic West Bengal, there came a wave of Vaishnavism. Vaishnavi centres sprang up at Baranagar, Ariyadaha, Panihati, Sukhchar, Khardaha, Kanchanpalli and Kumarhatta on this side of the Ganga and at Mahesh, Aakna, Bishkhali, Jeerat, Guptipara and Adisaptagram on the other

13 *Khitish-Vamsavali-Charita*. Manjusha edition 1986; p. 19

side of the Ganga. Besides Kulingram in Bardhaman (Burdwan) district, places like Kalna, Purbasthali, Patuli, Katowa, Dainhat, Agradweeep, Kulai, Shrikhanda, Dakshinkhanda; Mainadal and Mangaldihi in Birbhum district and many places in Murshidabad and Maldaha districts created a Vaishnava environment. Several Vaishnava Smriti books, biographies of Mohantas, collections of lyrics and poems, research and listing of different Vaishnava streams and books on the days of maintaining sacramental vows were written. Twenty-four hour meditation, worship and keertan were scheduled according to the rules of *Haribhakti Vilas.* Vaishnava gurus and acharyas gave up their clan-surnames and adopted the surname of Goswami. Vaishnavas of both householder and ascetic classes were respected in the society.

Meanwhile, the signs of social evolution were indicated in two ways. In the eighteenth century, on one side was the rise of the Shakti cult and Shakti music. On the other side was a wide-spread Sahajiya connection among the lower class. Sahajiya stream was not new in this country. There were different currents of faith, according to the Buddhist Mahayana sect and the Tantrik meditative practices involving women as physical conduits, already prevalent in folklife. Vaishnava Sahajiyas adopted a lot of these ideologies and practices. The Sufi and Marfati influences brought in a fair impact from the Islam religion. In the villages came up organisations like the Satya Sangha, Kartabhaja, Sahebdhani, Khushi-Biswasi and other minor folk sects, which combined the Hindus and Muslims across villages. Perhaps on the very model of Chaitanya, conversion-centric minor sects originated. The strangest element was that the Sahajiya Vaishnava branches began using the names of famous Vaishnava gurus as their creators or authors of their treatises. Names of such noted gurus as Nityananda-Beerbhadra-Narottam-Krishna Das Kaviraj-Roop-Kaviraj began being inducted into their mainstreams. Was it the way of bringing legitimacy of some kind in their non-scriptural nature worship? Was it a process of keeping alive a spirit of some cooperation within the depths of protestation?

Sukanta Mazumder was an ascetic once upon a time in Gouriya Vaishnava society, but was now back as a householder. He had lived in mutts and temples for at least fifteen years, studied scriptures, adopted the saffron attire but finally being disappointed due to various reasons, had given up that path. Yet the habits had become internalised and remained ingrained in blood. The Vaishnava humility and modest nature were assimilated within Sukanta. I used to go to him from time to time to clear my doubts. Once in passing, I asked him: "Please tell me something about the genesis and promotion of Sahajiya-ism in Bengal. Was their spread due to a reaction against the orthodox Vaishnavas?" Making such initial overtures as "What little do I know?" and "How little have been my studies?"' Sukanta said: "To speak the truth, Sahajiyas got established even before Mahaprabhu. You'll get many hints in Chandidas's lyrics. In Gangetic Bengal, there's a folk-tale prevalent on Krishna-Dhamali, that talks about Krishna, Radha, Ayan Ghosh and Barai Buri. It's a tale of illegitimate love. You must know that there's no mention of Radha anywhere in *Bhagavata.* Jaydev created Radha from the folk origin. In that story of Krishna-Radha, Baru Chandidas wove desire, anxiety, deceit and separation: to make it popular. Sahajiyas used to like very much this story and songs. Then, the Buddhist Sahajiya and Tantrik practices seeped into them as a gradual process. All these were very secretive."

: "But were the Sahajiyas a religious community then, as they're now?"

: "I don't think so. This was a secretive practice, confined among the society's extreme marginalised classes. But after Mahaprabhu, those who came out as Sahajiyas seemed very organised and conscious. Truly speaking, the orthodoxy of the

Gouriya Vaishnavas and the Sanskritism of Vrindavan could not be tolerated by many in the lowest class. They were looking for protests. The Sahajiya Vaishnavas woke up from Gournagar Sadhana by Narahari Sircar of Srikhanda; Manjari Sadhana of Nabadweep and alternate explanations and expressions of adulterous meditation. Keeping in front Sri Chaitanya's path of secret meditation, countless manuscripts, called *Body Chronicles,* were penned. Could you ascribe them all to be compositions of the lower class? Could you insist that the higher class did not aid the Sahajiyas from inside? Later on, of course, the purist Gouriya Vaishnavas established themselves only in Nabadweep, Shantipur, Khardah, Srikhanda and such other places, while Sahajiyas spread out in many villages and many clusters. Perversion also crept in among them. Then began several Vaishnava sub-communities."

: "Could you tell me exactly when these sub-communities began?"

: "Only towards the end of the eighteenth century. In order to explain it, I've to tell you the story of Vaishnava Totaram Babaji. Would you like to listen to that?"

: "Of course, I would. You're the most apt person to tell such things", I said.

With a modest look, Sukanta accepted self-adulation. Then, pondering over it a while, he said: "Born in the eighteenth century, Radhamohan Thakur was the scion of the clan of Srinibas Acharya. He died in 1781. You could call Radhamohan the last Vaishnava intellectual of Bengal. Once in Vrindavan, a debate was held among two Vaishnavas, the moral choice between *swakiya* and *parakiyabaad*[14]—

---

14 *Swakiya and parakiyabaad*: The concepts have roots in ancient India and have been parallely in vogue among many breakaway sects and faiths of Hinduisim in later eras. The former refers to a relationship within the confines of marriage and family with a companion who is socially and legally accepted while the latter refers to the practice of and philosophy behind keeping a companion or soulmate (*sadhansangini*) outside the ambit of marriage and family, purely for practising certain secret meditative rituals or sadhanas using different concepts of physical union.

one's own versus an adulterous romantic relationship: which path was the correct one? In the judgment of the Jaipur royal court, one's own relationship won. The opposite party was unhappy and demanded the opinion of the Gouriya scholars. The king of Jaipur then sent Krishnadev Bhattacharjya, his courtier and pro-own relationship school, to Bengal. The debate took place in the court of Nawab Murshidkuli Khan of Bengal. Being vanquished by Radhamohan in the debate, Krishnadev wrote out a letter of defeat. Well, since then the doctrine of adulterous relationship reigned in Bengal. Let me say something here. According to the Gouriya Vaishnava faith, the adulterous relationship is a pure, lustless concept. But Sahajiyas did not accept this concept. By adulterous relationship, they understood and explained it around a female companion outside marriage kept solely for meditation and salvation through physical union. Gradually, the 'worship' of adolescent girls and maintaining physical relationship with someone else's wife came to be recommended for this sect."

I asked: "Did they not compose 14-metre verses to support this adulterous relationship?"

Sukanta replied: "Of course. As you know, just as Gouriya Vaishnavas quote Sanskrit hymns from Vrindavan at every step, so do the Sahajiyas cite 14-metre verses. Would you like to hear a 14-metre verse supporting adulterous relationship?

Own coitus has no passion, it's always there—
Adultery has pain and sorrow: an event rare!

"Now listen to the argument. Why is an adulterous companion needed to comprehend Gouranga? What's wrong with one's own relationship? The reply is: Shri Krishna himself had his own companions like Satyabhama-Rukmini-Kubja, yet why did he have to take refuge in Radha's love? The analysis said: in one's marital relationship, there is no hindrance and no embargo from the society. Therefore, it lacks challenge and passion. In an adulterous companionship, there's the romance of pain and suffering. From anxiety to the physical union, there is an involvement of self-flagellation and the courage to forsake the clan. It requires the strength to ignore the brow-beating of society. Love's real depth blooms here."

: "But why did you raise the context of Totaram Babaji?"

: "Indeed, all the minor Vaishnava communities grew out of adulterous relationships. They discovered that the theory of Purush-Prakriti (union of Man and Nature) worked quite well with the Krishna-Radha ideology. Krishna was their 'subject' of meditation, while Radha was the 'object'. The 'attribution' meditation went ahead regardless. Totaram Babaji registered his impatience about this practice. The information about first thirteen minor communities came from him. Totaram was a scholar from the Dravida country during the reign of king Krishnachandra. He came to Nabadweep to study Nyaya; he went to Vrindavan from there and finally returned to Nabadweep to become a portal-based Babaji. But, pained by the Sahajiya Vaishnavas and other minor communities' practice, he declared:

Aaul Baul Kartabhaja Nayda Dervish Sain
Sahajiya Sakhibhavuki Smarta Jaat-Gosain
Atibari Churadhari Gour-nagari:
Tota says—with these thirteen, no favours I curry.

It was to be noticed that, out of the thirteen minor communities, against whom opposition had been mentioned here, Aaul, Baul, Nyara, Sain and Dervishes were not Vaishnavas at all. But Totaram had expressed his intolerance against Jaat-Gosain and Gour-nagari, which left a big evidence about the Vaishnava divisiveness. This intolerance as well as divisiveness made the Vaishnavas even more divided. Another 14-metre verse contained that proof. This said:

There were thirteen minor sects in the entire early time—
It's now three-times-thirteen: difficult to keep faith prime!

In like manner, fifty-two minor communities had already been born. Now the question was: which 'prime faith' was being talked about here as 'difficult to keep'?"

I remarked: "Why, the pure and conventionally ceremonial Vaishnava religion is being discussed here. But yes, the point raised by you is a legitimate one. But did the catholic, casteless, creedless Vaishnavism that Mahaprabhu dreamt about and Nityananda wanted to preach, remain at the end as the welfare-seeking faith for the entire population, inclusive of the lowest class? Did it not become stultified in the Sanskrit scriptural messages and explications by gurus and Mohantas? In that ivory tower of high-class Vaishnavas, how could common, salvation-seeking folks take refuge? Sahajiya Vaishnavas, caste-Vaishnavas and many divided Vaishnavas would only increase in number! On the other hand, those who followed the social Smriti doctrines became the high class Vaishnavas of the present days—for dealing with the spiritual canons of Vaishnava religion. The Smartas whom Totaram considered ineligible were now the most respectable Vaishnavas. Watch the strange fun of history! Just at this moment, who are theVaishnavas? Number one, those are celibate Gosains at mutts and portals; number two—are the caste-Gosains ignored by them and the hated Sahajiya Vaishnavas; number three are the householder Vaishnava gentlemen who are initiated by hymns, chant Hari's name and yet follow the Smarta tradition prevalent in the Hindu society. They need Brahmin priests during ceremonies surrounding birth, marriage and death. They're in the majority. What, Sukanta, am I right?"

"It's quite correct," Sukanta agreed and said: "Nobody then followed Chaitanya properly. But what the body-centric Sahajiyas refer to in their meditation, as chronicles and treatises, are also pretty strange. They've written those chronicles and treatises themselves, but put them under the authorships of Roop Kaviraj, Krisnhadas Kaviraj, Beerbhadra, Nityananda, and even Narottam. They also claim that Roop Kaviraj was the disciple of Srinibas Acharya, based in Birbhum. The thrown-out, dissident man was apparently their earliest guru. They sing as follows:

He who has devotion in Sri Roop's feet—
Man's action he does duly treat.
At Sri Roop's feet, lowered:
Gets Sri Roop's salvation reward—
The God of scriptures—can beat a retreat!

I said: "Indeed, Sri Roop is used here in two senses. Sri Roop is Roop Kaviraj and Sri Roop is woman. Isn't that right? But you must be aware of the Gouranga doctrine which is prevalent secretly at the folk level? From what I've followed, Radha has a male body, in whose jewelled centre is Krishna. This is Gouranga in a single body. To comprehend that Gouranga, one needs the Nityananda-gate."

Sukanta said: "You almost talked as though it was a formula! No, no, it's not that easy. There's a little gap in between your knowledge. There's some more complexity in Krishna-Radha which I, too, don't know. That's as peer practice. And I've heard that only some people from the Dervish faith know it. I haven't met the right persons from the Dervish faith. You should be on the look-out."

I thought: where do I look for it? Will the significance of Gouranga remain unknown to me?

A festival during the Ambubachi rituals was held every year at the grave of Aahad. On one such occasion, I came to know Khejmat Fakir of Badlangi quite closely. Fakir told me: "You've been around the villages of Chapra police station, but we've not seen you in our Badlangi village. Come once this time, on the occasion of full moon in the month of Kartik, when we've the anniversary celebrations of my Gosain. There'll be a big carnival. There'll be a big musical soiree too, where many an Aalem, Dervish and Fakir will come from across the border. You can listen to their music—comprising highly esoteric songs. Would you please come?"

I had nodded my head with the usual nonchalance, as was our wont on such occasions and completely forgotten about it later. In our urban calendars, where was the mention of the full moon of Kartik month? But Khejmat did not forget. He had duly sent a post-card, seven days before the carnival, written in red ink. What was a further wonder, the incomplete address simply read: 'Sudhir Chakrabarty, Professor, Krishnanagar'. Still the postal department managed to deliver me the letter. Can one not go after this?

On my way there in a bus, I was, of course, quietly wondering how someone, whose name was Khejmat Fakir, could have a guru named Paramananda Gosain? I was quite confused. The carnival was indeed on the death anniversary of this guru. On arrival, I raised this point as the very first topic. Respectfully they let me sit on a uniquely-crafted cotton-quilt with exquisitely embroidered motifs of the elephant, horse, lotus, the conch-shell; on one corner was embroidered the name 'Maidani Bibi Badlangi'. As soon as I praised the work, Maidani Bibi herself came over with a shy face and sat in front with a hand-fan. Khejmat instructed: "Give devotion to sir." Maidani bent over to perform the salutation.

Even this was no small wonder! I had never received salutation in a Fakir's home earlier. In fact, they do not do salutations. And instead of calling it salutation, 'giving devotion' was a feature I had not heard of, barring the low-caste folks who came from Faridpur. Looking at my surprised eyes, Khejmat said: "What, aren't you surprised? Our Gosain was a scheduled caste from Erakandi of Faridpur. All this is learnt from him. I am a Fakir by birth, not by action. As Liaqat Fakir's son, I am called Khejmat Fakir by the people. Of course, I've gone the way of Fakirs for quite a while. Ten years back, I suddenly had the fortune of gaining an exalted guru in the Matua fair at Betai-Jitpur. My Gosain's portal is at Kulgachhi. My initiation and grooming have all been done there; we are Sahajiyas by faith, following the Nityananda stream."

Slowly the afternoon faded. There was a slight cold wind. The villagers were coming by twos and threes. Khejmat was very busy with his hospitality. Bauls and ascetics had come. One or two songs were sung: mostly from the learners; I understood they were under training. The Bangladeshi group was about to arrive. I was roaming to and fro. On one side of the courtyard, kedgeree was being cooked in a huge vessel. Noticing me there, Khejmat said: "Sir, you must be feeling lonely. Do come this way. A singer has come from Nasratpur, who knows songs by Jadubindu. His voice is not top class but is expressive. He knows the theories. You can listen to his songs."

The Nasratpur singer was called Mohan Khyapa. He made me sit with due modesty. Khejmat said: "Sir, please allow me to go. Probably news of the Bangladesh team's arrival has come." I told Mohan Khyapa: "Would you sing Jadubindu's song on the Gouranga doctrine? You'll have to explain the theory though."

"How deep would I know of theories, tell me! The one who can explain will provide words to my mouth to explain things, of course. Before that, let me sing a lyric by Kubir Gosain, guru of Jadubindu." Tuning the two-stringed drone – the *dotara* – he began his song:

O kind guru, I haven't anyone but you!
While I eat, sleep, comeor go—
Sing your qualities, I do.
You're Brahma, You're Vishnu, You're Jesus, you're Krishna,
At life's end, I should fathom your own hue!

Quite startled, I stopped him midway in his song. What did Mohan Khyapa say? What a wonder, how things mingled and where? "You said: you're Brahma, you're Vishnu, and you're Krishna: all that is fine. But, how is it that you bring in Jesus? Is it about religious reconciliation?" Listening to my analysis, Mohan said: "'No, sir, my Gosain has given another theory for this song."

: "What's it?"

: "He says, and that's correct, that other than the 'point' or semen, whatever you call him – Brahma, Vishnu, or Krishna – He's the only one. That's why, another song says:

'Gour Gour Gour': you always say—
That Gour's within you, all the way!

"Do these words not mean the same thing?"

Dispelling the mist of Kartik, the full-moon night was awakening. There seemed to be another moon rising—to illumine my consciousness. The mist was clearing. I was chanting a hymn to myself, which I had read in the scriptures: *Ekashchaitanya-chandrah Parama Karunaya Sarvamavishchakar*...I have so often recited this hymn tonelessly in front of the students. Was today that discovery going to be fulfilled? Meanwhile, the Bangladeshi group had arrived. Mohan was singing Jadubindu's lyrics:

Good company, those who keep—
Of Ganga-Gouranga, they've a peep,
At times, sacred Suradhuni enhances its current's leap!

The music continued. Only I ventured out, breaking through the Kartik mist, into the meadows where there were several heaps of stacked paddy. I explored within myself and finally found the essence of the song. I realised clearly that the 'Ganga-Gouranga' together meant the movement of the seed down the way of the Ida-Pingala-Sushumna channel.The increase of the current meant excitement. Having the mobile Krishna within oneself, savouring sex by controlling the movement of the seed: was this the essence of Gour doctrine? This could neither be present in the scriptures nor in poetry; nor could this be explained through writing. Was that the reason why this doctrine could be transmitted through guru and disciple in the folk perspective? The transmission remained oral, yet it was not to be uttered everywhere; the practices were all action-oriented, yet they were secretive and quiet.

However, I did not realise then how much I had still to comprehend. The night was spent almost in a trance. The meal-service with rice, followed by endless songs, the moonlit night—all passed as if without my conscious knowledge. I was sitting on Maidani Bibi's cotton-quilt by spreading it on the balcony. The music had ceased. Everything was quiet. People were sleeping anywhere and everywhere. From far away came the repetitive sound of a husking machine. Waking up in the early hours of dawn, the women and girls were already sieving the paddy. The Bangladesh group had taken refuge in a balcony not too far from mine. Everyone was tired after the long journey by road and was in deep slumber. Only one old Fakir chanted on his beads, murmuring to himself. He was of a distinguished lineage, wearing a gorgeous robe. He was a Fakir of the Barkheda region of Kushtia.

I had only one thought in mind after looking at the Barkheda Fakir. He seemed to have conquered hunger, thirst, tiredness—everything. I had heard that till now there were many powerful Fakirs in places like Kushtia, Jessore, Rajshahi and contiguous areas in Bangladesh. By powerful, I meant the power of self-control, exercises in breath-regulation and conquest of physical pain and sorrow. Having started three days back from Kushtia, this group had arrived mainly by walking all the way: a minimum of sixty to seventy miles. Yet, since the time they arrived here, this man had been sitting ramrod-straight. Till midnight, he was present in the gathering of vocal music. Now, everyone of the group was in deep sleep, yet the Fakir was sitting alone, chanting deep within himself. Apparently they performed the chanting and related acts in their breathing exercises and said Namaz through breathing as well. That Namaz was *watul* or concealed. The breath exercises began with the Aisa Namaz of the previous night, culminating in early dawn as Fazar Namaz.

I had no sleep, no Namaz either. As a solitary questioning soul, my only companion was a song of Tagore:

With a free wandering soul, I roam apace,
Looking at everyone's face...

It was true; I had spent half my life looking at faces. Whatever these apparently ignorant and illiterate people had shared with and taught me, had I received even a fraction of that knowledge from the so-called civil, educated society? Just this evening, would I have ever found from my bag of knowledge and wisdom, what Mohan Khyapa, a singer from the common run, had shown me as a way to illumination? I was seated on the embroidered cotton-quilt stitched by Maidani Bibi. Could I – with my scanty understanding – ever match up to the imprint of sincere service and the salutary ode to beauty that were woven in it? The Barkheda Fakir sat, his eyes quiet and at peace;; it was a wonder what wealth he had drawn and accomplishments he had achieved already for his soul from life! Did I have even the slightest share of that peace and certainty in my wealth, achievements and easy flow of daily living? I thought of such things; I pondered on my newly-acquired insight into the Chaitanya doctrine. That Baul Gosain in Patuli station had told me: "You'll need a little more time; but you'll get to know him by and by." How much more time? The thread of thoughts suddenly broke at the shriek of a night-bird. Was the night drawing to an end? The slight nip in the air in the wee hours sent a cold wintry shiver down the body. The eyes burnt slightly. With an almost weightless, blank mind, I savoured in the unique human environs, an overwhelming sense of awe. A faraway earthy scent rose from the crops.

I was lost in my thoughts. The sudden sound of quiet movement broke my reverie. I noticed that the Fakir had risen very quietly from the balcony and was on his way to the tank for a wash. And almost immediately, as if on cue, Mohan Khyapa appeared from nowehere and whispered to me in breathless excitement: "I've got news. That Aalal Fakir is a most knowledgeable Murshid; he is over a hundred years old. I've been waiting in hiding since the wee hours for daybreak. Sir, let's go to the tank and catch him. This is the perfect hour. Those people of Barkheda have told me that before the Fazar Namaz and immediately after the morning cleansing rituals, whatever you'd ask the Fakir, you'd get a response. For the rest of the day he'll remain silent. Come, let's go. Don't you want to gain the knowledge of any deep theory?"

To learn a deep theory? Certainly, I knew very little of the Chaitanya doctrine itself. Sukanta had said that Dervishes knew it well. Had the chance come at long last? Like one driven by a dream, I went and stood quietly under a bakul tree. Now it was only a matter of wait. The moist eathy fragrance told me of the presence of wild flowers. A hazy darkness clung on. One, two, three, four... progressed the moments. Some seer had said: "This is the hour of God's awakening". There he was—Aalal Fakir climbed up directly towards us. There was a distinct wet swish; was the end of his robe dripping water? His eyes held a faraway look—preoccupied and lost in a different world. Mohan Khyapa and I sprang up, right in front of him, almost like assassins. Initially a little startled, he then collected himself and looked up with pardoning eyes, peaceful and bright. "Tell me, dears," he said. "What do you wish to know?" I conveyed my desire—eagerly nurtured over many days. He smiled a little. Then raising his hand, he said: "Do you know, dears, the jewel point in the head is indeed Krishna. He travels up and down the spinal chord, following the wind in the body system, right to the mouth of the penis. His game of love is at the Nityananda gate. First, Krishna travels from the site of the jewel downwards to the mouth of the vagina. Then the meditator – using the power of the breathing exercises – forces the downstream flow to turn back and move up. When He travels downwards, He is the *dhara*—the 'flow'. Turning round from the mouth, when He goes upstream, He is 'Radha'. This pattern of flow and ebb continues, transforming *dhara* to Radha and Radha to *dhara*, the flow. This flow and ebb – mobility and freeze – is called Gour. Did you follow? The flow is white in colour, Radha is yellow. It takes many years to place Gour within the body, dear. Only if Nityananda helps, you'll get Gour. Get hold of Gourchand. You'll earn peace."

The sound of moving feet intimated the exit of the Fakir. I was left standing in the depths of silence; like a tree. Daybreak arrived gradually and stood facing me—a colourful, pure and fresh-as-air clear dawn.

On the reverse bend of deep lonely alleys

Those who seek the real soulmate – the man of the heart – must necessarily discover that deep lonely alley to begin with. But when I was lost in the quest of the people – who were in turn searching for the person of their heart – my path used to be crowded by countless folks. At every step, they confronted me. They had enormous curiosity and that was all personal. "Where are you coming from?", "Whose home do you want to visit?" "Why should we tell you all that you wish to know? What do we gain in return?" "Does anybody of this village know you? How then can we trust you?", "Do you know, two years back, an official from the government came to count how many husking machines were there in the village. After counting he left, immediately after which there was the tough robbery[15]."

What was a 'tough robbery'? On the first day, I could not digest the strange adjective. Later on, I found that the word 'tough' was locally used to mean 'wonderful' or 'ferocious' in the Bagri area of Murshidabad. Ishanali of Beldanga once described the ravaging floods by saying: "Sir, on our side this time, there have been difficult floods." While having the festival kedgeree at the home of

15 *Tough robbery*: the word 'tough' translated from the word *kathin* in the original Bengali book. *Kathin* is the ethnic word that is used in these parts of Murshidabad in West Bengal to signify 'wonderful' or 'ferocious'

Shibshekhar in Kumirdah, someone exclaimed, for my ears: "It's a tough kedgeree, isn't it?"

But let it be. For the moment, let me come away from the 'tough'. The earlier discussion was on the suspicious nature of the rural folks. They had so many questions, so much of disbelief harboured in them, and yet those questions would elicit the most indifferent replies.

On a particular occasion, we had taken the village road to Satgechhiya. On both sides stood the ridges of earth circling the farmland; in between lay the narrow foot trail. The crops smelt fresh, mixed with the fresh earthiness of cow-dung. Sickle in hand, the farmer had stopped to look at us. Under a solitary strange tree in the middle of the fields, sugarcane juice had been placed on the boil. As the question came up in my wife's mind, she asked: "What tree is that?" On being asked, the person who was boiling the sap laughed and replied casually, throwing a question in the air: "That tree? Hello, folks, do you know what tree it is?" Then laughing raucously to himself, he replied, "It's then a 'who-knows' tree, or, a 'don't-know' tree!" Then came his piercing, naked question: "Well, where are you coming from? What's your destination? With you, is the one your wedded wife, or, a female companion?"

Pacifying my indignant wife with a quick wink, I managed to get the address of an off-the-beaten-track quiet cluster of Bauls. I did not take long to understand the indirect hint of a female companion. I recalled the warning from Ela Fakir: "Sir, you've come down this path; be very careful. There are all kinds of people here. All of them pose as Baul-Bairagis and ascetics. Are they all truly so? You listen carefully now, and do remember! Bairagis are of five kinds—Chyatasti, Pyatasti, Malatepa, Oshudhbecha, and Ayalakhyapa. Do you follow?"

How could I possibly follow? I was a sophisticated man from the urban culture. On top of it, I was adept at dispensing academic knowledge at the university. Luckily the blind Ela Fakir could not see my helpless face. Smiling to himself, Ela had said: "Listen, I'll explain to you. Among the Baul-Fakirs, most of them are 'Pyatasti', that is, they have taken to the order simply to fill their stomachs. They don't pray, but are the greedy ones; they are only good at feasting. And 'Malatepa' means those who are empty from within; they're only counting their rosary beads with their eyes closed. Beware! Do you know what the Oshudhbecha are? They know some basic medicinal plants and roots, and some dietary practices; they sell that information without any deeper knowledge of meditation or worship. And Ayalakhyapa means the addicts of hemp. More than prayers and meditation, they're attracted to the hemp-smoking. They all sit with their eyes up, faces down, and a permanent happy smile hanging on their lips. Avoid them as much as you can."

"And Chyatasti?" I had kept track of the fact that Ela had missed the first name he had uttered.

Ela remonstrated angrily: "You uttered the obscene term finally? That term is bad, very bad. Listen; let me explain, that name implies those who only enjoy women in the name of faith and meditation. Dear, keep clear of them."

: "How would I identify? One can't recognise them at first sight!"

: "You'll understand. They would be known by their ways. The Almighty would help you identify. That bad name that you uttered—they would be seen at the clusters which teem with women; the unattached female companions. Strangely enough you'll notice that they all look rather simple and innocent."

That term 'female companion' came up again a second time, after the episode with Ela Fakir, in Satgechhiya village. There was nothing more of note that day. The next Sunday, I went again, alone this time. The man boiling the sap gave the directions on this occasion: "After you cross two fields, you'll notice a tamarind tree; that gives you the direction. Well, you walk a quarter mile on the right to reach the river. The Baul-cluster lies across the river on the other bank."

Following the complex directions, I reached the precincts of the portal. The squeaky clean courtyard was full of children – of different age groups – outnumbering the pigeons strutting about. It was a quiet summer afternoon; a hot wind rose from the dry sandy river bed on the south and blew across the expanse of the Baul cluster in strong gusts. Wandering about for a while, I climbed on to a corner balcony and peeped through the window to look inside the room. Lo and behold, what a scene it was! I saw a middle-aged man with two women perched on his two knees. The man wore his hair long, which descended in silky curls with a neat parting in the middle. He wore a white vest and a white dhoti, with a bidi, quite obviously stuffed with hemp, stuck in his lips. The two buxom ladies in service were engaged in a mock fight over who would light the bidi while the man – evidently overripe in maturity and much-exposed to the ways of the world – calmly sat with his eyes closed and a gratified smile hanging from the corner of his lips. By Jove, it was a scene straight out of the Kalighat-pata paintings. Inevitably, I remembered the word 'obscene' mentioned by Ela Fakir. And I recalled the cautionary words: "Careful, remain careful yourself."

Could I bear to stay on the balcony any longer? I rushed out into the garden. There was another wonder waiting there. In mid-Jaishtha,[16] there were many mango-trees laden with mangoes—fully ripe, luscious and succulent to the core. The yellow mangoes swung among the green leaves was and made a pretty picture and a novel sight indeed, especially in rural Bengal. This was because vendors arrived in the spring months of Falgun and Chaitra –

16 *Jaishtha*: the second and hottest month of summer on the Hindu calendar

when the blossoms appeared and ripened – to strip the trees of all the raw green mangoes and ferry them across to the commercial hubs. And here was a garden at the ascetic's cluster where nobody had stolen the ripe mangoes!

Noticing my gaze turned upwards, a service-woman came forward. She said: "Are you surprised by the sight of ripe mangoes? Behind this is our guru's pure grace. Would you like to listen to that episode? About five years back, one vendor came to this cluster's garden to steal mangoes. But the man didn't know of our guru-thakur's grace. As soon as he touched the mangoes, his hand got stuck. He sat there flailing his arms all night like a night-blind bird, its wings flapping wildly."

: "I've followed and know the rest. Let me tell you the remaining part of the story. The wild flapping continued for the entire night, yet the hand wouldn't get dislodged! Your guru-thakur knew about it all by virtue of his meditational power. In the morning he called everybody and rescued the thief by the power of his chant. The thief got hold of the guru's feet and pleaded: 'I didn't know of your power, Babathakur. Otherwise, would I have ventured to commit this dirty crime? Please save me, Sir.' Since then nobody touches the fruits and produces of this garden. Am I right?"

"Perfectly right," the surprised service-woman came forward with respect and gazed at me for long. Then she said: "Which guru-thakur are you, sir? How did you know it all?"

I replied: "I had heard the same story in five other clusters, that's how. Do you know something? This thief was a 'pretend' one and your guru-thakur is actually a shrewd conman!"

Very quickly I got out of there and came to sit down at the tea-shop attached to the cluster and collected the guru-thakur's memorable profile. His original home was in the village linked to the cluster and, by caste, he was a cowherd. His father was a simple farmer. After the school leaving merit examination, he joined a Sahajiya site at Patuli. Since then he had been with the *sahajananda* sect. His father tried to pull him back home with a quick marriage. Nobody knew why the bride committed suicide by hanging. By then, he had established his own portal here. India was a secular country, where meditation and prayers had no hindrance in faith or deed. Thereafter, his faith found home in the portal and lust in his deed. The narrative history behind such a dignified and remarkable man, such as this, was like holy nectar, manna form heaven. Dusk fell while I listened to the stories. The service-women lit the evening lamps. Wearing his wooden clogs, the 'venerable' guru made a round of the courtyard in his wooden clogs. He threw a glance at me as though I was a fallen sinner and he, an exalted mini-'Sainbaba'.

But I could not help wondering where this fairly large number of service-women came from. Though I had not thought about it earlier, I had the answer coming quick enough. In this wretched land, there was no end to widowhood and therefore no lack of service-women. In the villages, was there any shortage of poor, dependent, childless widows? In order to escape the lascivious brothers-in-law, they took refuge in the gurus and rushed to their portals. Had anybody cared to chronicle the social history of who or what attracted them; how they were seduced and flushed out of their homes and who gifted them the venereal diseases? All at once, I recalled a scene at the Madan Gopal fair of Rukunpur. On that occasion, Kishoredas and his wife Roopkumari were giving a performance, singing baul songs and dancing to the tune. Suddenly, Roopkumari screamed out in pain, clutched her stomach and fell to the ground. "O Ma!" she screamed, tossing and turning like a half-slaughtered goat. Her beautiful face turned ashen, struck with a deathly pallor. When I rushed in, she gasped out: "Sir, I won't live long. Starvations have taken a toll; they have led to gastric pain in the stomach! A killing pain!"

I saw Roopkumari again at the Agradweep fair, sitting under the Kadam[17] tree and begging away. Her eyes had sunk horribly, her vision was clouded; she was thin as a skeleton and looked ghastly. A Bairagi known to me whispered in my ears: "Sir, you're right. This is the same Roopkumari. Do you remember how well she used to sing? What sheen and glow her beauty held? Everything is gone."

: "What happened to her? What disease is it?"

The man whispered to me: "It's a vile disease. Do you know how many Bairagis have plundered and literally sucked her out? Indeed, she was a housewife. After becoming a widow, she was seduced out of her home by Kishoredas."

: "Isn't there any remedy against this?"

: "What remedy? They've come and joined this trade out of their own accord. They don't realise the pitfalls initially; when they do, where is the space in society then? Let me tell you, sir, the youth of Bauls and Bairagis don't last out. They end their lives either in hemp or in lust."

The vendor of the tea-stall attached to the cluster also said the same thing: "How many do you think are the truly devotional ones out of the lot that you see here? Most of them are female companions; they just land up here, brought by pimps and middlemen. This is what goes on from cluster to cluster. Those, who have been seduced themselves, would in turn seduce housewives and girls in the name of religion. I have observed so much just sitting here!"

: "Don't the villagers protest?"

: "There are plenty of ignorant and illiterate farmers living here. As if that wasn't enough, most of them are Muslims. If they talk on religion, there would be a riot."

---

17 *Kadam or Kadamba*: *Neolamarckia cadamba*, with English common names burflower-tree, laran, and Leichhardt pine, and called *kadam* locally, is an evergreen, tropical tree, native to South and Southeast Asia. It has scented pale yellow or light orange flowers in dense and spiky globe-shaped clusters

On the way back, a sharp beam of torch-light flashed on my face in the dark. "Who goes there?" This was common practice in the rural aeas. The youth wielding the torch wanted to know my identity. Then he said sarcastically: "Oh, did you come to see the great man?"

Why then did the tea-vendor say that there was no protest? I liked the protesting youth's sarcasm. He kept saying: "You look like an urban-educated city-bred man, but why are you here? Sir, have you been totally trapped? So how much money did the great man ask for—two hundred or two hundred and fifty?"

I was startled and blurted out: "Does he take that much money to initiate?"

By then, moonlight streamed in through the chinks in the little puffs of cirrocumulus clouds, creating an aura of mystery. The unknown youth seemed to be quite well-educated. Taken aback, he said: "Listening to you I first thought you were simply a pretentious Vaishnava. Now I've realised that you know nothing about the great man. You don't know that this is an abortion centre."

It was as though I had been whipped across my face! Now I followed why, on the last occasion, on way to Satgechhiya, the man selling molasses mistook my wife for an unattached female companion. The youth rattled on: "You'll find many such abortion centres if you move from village to village. But it's difficult to identify them from outside. There's a veneer of religion on the surface—with regular keertan in the Lord's name, fairs and carnivals, special days of fasts and feasts. There's always a ring-leader proclaiming that the lost husband will return to the deserted wife, the blind will regain vision, the dumb will find speech and the infertile woman will give birth: these are the public slogans. In reality, these clusters are semi-brothels. In any of these villages, if a girl is found to be pregnant, her parents bring her over to spend a month at such a cluster. They tell the other villagers that the girl has gone to serve the guru. Duly aborted, the girl returns home hale and hearty after a month. Occasionally a couple of them even die in the process. There're people to dig up the sandy river bed, bury the body and make it vanish. The police station is quite far; nevertheless the guru-thakur makes sure to pay his obeisance at regular quarters. Everything continues peacefully and smoothly. This is what our country is like!"

: "Aren't you doing something about it?"

: "We're trying. It's a difficult, very difficult job. In the mean time, we've opened a night school. Many people have come up against us already. The area-chief is also offering resistance. He too is a disciple of the guru-thakur. Any odd day they might organise a mass-beating to finish me off, after laying a pistol in my hand. You might savour a little news story published in the newspaper—about an armed youth being killed by mass beating at Rakhalgachhi village!"

The youth gave a wry smile. He suddenly asked: "Where'll you stay tonight?"

: "I'll put up somewhere. I'm quite used to it."

: "How can that be? I have, of course, a place of my own but of you stay there, you'll have trouble in the morning. Rather, let me take you to Kalo Sayeb's (Black Sahib's) home."

The man was no less strange than his strange name—Kalo Sayeb. The residence of Kalo Sayeb stood across an unstable bamboo bridge, which spanned a dry canal. The generator thundered monotonously, lighting up the entire house of Kalo Sayeb. It was quite a novel sight in the village. The youth slipped away, after introducing me to Kalo Sayeb, bidding a quick goodbye with, "I'll take your leave, brother; we'll meet again tomorrow morning."

Kalo Sayeb was not dark at all, but rather a well-built, light-skinned gentleman, about 60 years old. Extending a very polite and classy welcome to me, he made me sit on a traditional divan. It was a well-appointed room, with a round marble table, the walls displaying framed, nineteenth-century canvases by British painters and a chandelier with lighted bulbs, thanks to the running generator. It all looked wonderful; my eyes seemingly amazed at my apparent 'discovery' of a piece of old traditional Calcutta—scooped out from somewhere beyond the back of a blind lane.

"They call me Kalo Sayeb out of spite," the gentleman tried to explain to me in detail. "I hate this village and those villagers. They are narrow-minded and unclean. That boy Santosh, who brought you here, is the only one with whom I keep company and talk."

: "How does one survive by not mingling with the people of the village? Don't they torture you? Haven't there been robbery attempts?"

: "Attempted, but failed. Sir, I possess three four-bore guns. For myself, my wife and my daughter-in-law are all expert shooters. We're a self-sufficient family. Wait, I'll show you everything. But before that, there should be some tea and snacks."

Kalo Sayeb rose from his seat. He pressed the keys of a home-made intercom which he took from the table and began speaking into it: "Hello, who's it, Bouma?[18] Yes, you might have heard—a guest has come; he will stay the night and have dinner. Yes, the south-facing room on the first floor will be nice. Yes, please send snacks immediately. Is it *luchi*[19], brinjal fries and kheer? That'll be nice. Yes, please send your mother-in-law to this room."

He smiled very pleasantly—a smile of success. Almost simultaneously, a dark, stout, middle-aged woman entered the room. It was a strange contrast. Here was a slim, erect, pale skinned, six-foot tall man paired with a plump, unusually short and dark woman. But they made an extraordinarily happy picture.

18 *Bouma*: Daughter-in-law

19 *Luchi*: A small, round, fluffy, fried bread made of kneaded refined flour, deep-fried till it fluffs up into a ball and served with meat, vegetables or kheer/rice puddings

Kalo Sayeb explained with evident relish: "I was a restless soul. At the age of twenty, I fled home to become a sailor. Later, I trained as a mechanic. After travelling around half the world, I came home to settle down, and marry. I had only one condition in marriage—the bride should be dark and short."

: "Pray why this strange condition?"

: "I had observed from childhood that short, dark girls are looked down upon in our country. But where shall they go? Shouldn't they get married well simply because they are short and dark? I've got my son also married to a dark girl. As I was saying, I earned in plenty in the navy job and I didn't need to slave away at service thereafter. I was the ship's mechanic; I have a penchant for machinery and machine parts. The telephone and the generator at home are my creations. For farming, I drive the tractor myself and so does my son. We don't depend on or owe anything to anybody."

: "Why do they call you Kalo Sayeb?"

: "That's because everything of mine is tip-top. You notice me at home with a dhoti and vest. But when I go out, I wear a full-sleeve shirt, trousers and prope shoes. Casual dressing in lungis, pyjamas, rubber flip-flops and half-sleeved Hawaii shirts is not to my taste. Those have arrived after the Second World War. I don't wear mixed fabrics like the terry-cotton either; my clothes are all pure cotton."

It was nice to hobnob with this funny man. I raise a quick question: "Don't you buy anything from the village?"

: "Why should we? There are plenty of vegetables in my land, there is fish in the tank. Eggs in the poultry. I visit Postabazar once a month and make a monthly purchase of potatoes, onions, ginger-garlic, oil, spices, tea and sugar and load them on the Lalgola Express. I get them downloaded at Murogachha station and subsequently these are transported straight to Rakhalgachhi by bullock-cart. That's all."

Meanwhile, fragrant tea-and-snack time was over. Looking at the man, there was no end to my wonder! This gentleman evidently did not get people to share his thoughts with, so he kept talking without a pause: "This village has gone to the dogs. It's rotten. The air is ridden with the loud monotonous noise from the wheat-crushers, the transistors blare incessantly, cheap and trash varieties of fish are sold in the markets and fairs with horrid-sounding names like tilapia, grass carp and so on. You'll find the local cauliflower, brinjal and raddish tasteless when you try them, since they're poisoned with pesticides. Do you shop yourself? Here's a useful tip from me—always buy spotted brinjals as they are free of pesticides. Those vegetables, which you find to be bright and shining are actually full of phosphates."

I was dying to ask a pertinent question all this while and finally blurted out: "Why can't you tolerate people?"

He laughed raucously to himself and said: "Where do you see the people? Are they anywhere? All are of the IR-8 variety."

: "IR-8? Isn't that the name of a variety of paddy?"

: "Initially it was the name of a paddy-seed. Then came the vegetable IR-8. At the end, it's the human IR-8, which has infested the country. They are highly productive, nice to look at but all empty inside. Devoid of taste! Odd-looking bad characters. There is a surfeit of IR-8 grade of people all over. Haven't you noticed?"

: "I must have, but didn't quite realise. How do you recognise them as IR-8?"

: "Why, by their symptoms. Look at the young man in my neighbouring house, with a pompous name – Sandipan – a graduate. But he can't write a proper application. Did you understand? That's an IR-8 graduate for you! Nanda Gosain's daughter living in the next cluster is a music diploma holder—a 'Sangeet Prabhakar'. But if you asked her to sing, she would either hunt around for her song book, or, try to locate the harmonium to help her hold the scale. She's an IR-8 singer! There's Subal who lives in the house out there; the son of Satish Biswas. He's a teacher but he doesn't attend school half the days. What does he do? He indulges in party politics! The students taunt him in his absence. Look at the local area chief—he's a thief. If you call the police against an injustice, immediately on arrival they'll ask for a bribe and then ask you to go for a mutual settlement. All are IR-8: artificial and false— much like the cheap trash fish. And what lingo do they use? Previously, the mean folks used the expletives; now the literate and educated youth indulge in similar 'bad-mouthing', at every turn. Haven't you heard?"

: "Bad-mouthing?"

: "Means using foul language!"

: "Against so many IR-8s, how will you survive? Besides, if the youth of the present generation don't take control of the society, how will the county run?"

: "I've huge debates on this issue with Santosh. That boy is pure 22-carat gold. He's a great optimist. He believes that the society will change and people will surely undergo a transformation. I only see the reverse; I don't see anything changing for the better. How many boys like Santosh are around? Take a round of the village. They all wear printed terry-cotton, open-breasted Hawaii shirts, lungis and rubber flip-flops. This is now the national dress of this country. The society is a complete trash as are the clothes of the urchins. But then I'm prattling away non-stop; I haven't heard anything about you. You're going round the civil society in dhoti and kurta; you seem to be a rare variety like the sonamug variety of dal."

The simile of 'sona muger dal' – the special golden variety of this dal – was fairly novel. I wanted him to explain. He replied—"In our land, the golden mung seeds were apparently destroyed; it was not grown any more. Have you tasted golden mung lentil ever in your life? How would you do that? The land is filled with horse-mung! You're in the teaching profession; aen't there IR-8 there? Of course, you won't recognise them. There's an English medium school in the next village. It's a wonder; as long as the Englishmen were here there were not too many English-medium schools!"

: "How did so many grow? What's your opinion?"

Kalo Sayeb answered: "That's only natural. Now, the hybrid Jaya-Ratna variety of paddy has taken over the market and has more acceptability than the Aman variety. The silvercarp fish is more popular than the rohu or the *mirgel.* English medium is the cross-breed variety; it would run very well now, like the telapia fish."

Amidst the brilliantly sharp and clear-cut words of the gentleman, there lurked somewhere a note of pessimism. So, in order to escort him gently to another subject, I said: "Everything appears bad to you. But the work for which I move from village to village is, of course, genuine. Do you know the nature of work I'm occupied with?"

: "Yes, I know it very well. I've heard it from Santosh."

There was a sense of indifference and neglect in his attitude, which did not escape my notice. So I brought up the topic afresh. I asked him: "Even my work is not up to your liking. Is that also IR-8?"

: "The work is genuine. You, as a person, are also the 'golden mung' variety. But the songs you're looking for are highly adulterated."

: "How's that? Why?"

: "Then let me elaborate a little. Bauls and Bairagis were earlier mediatator devotees. Now they've become mercantile people. Have you properly scanned those people who sing Baul songs along roads and river-banks, in fairs and trains? They are all fake Bauls."

It was quite a startling statement. Yes, it was true, too. Of course, there were fake Bauls; I had seen them at the Ghoshpara fair. A young Baul, with a huge mop of hair – almost like a halo around his face – wearing saffron robes and butter denim parallels had been singing Baul songs. As soon as the song was over, he took off his robe put on a red nylon vest and began smoking smack. How very true! Curiously, I wanted to know: "How do you discern IR-8 Bauls?"

: "First of all, from thei robes."

: "How come?"

: "Why, haven't you noticed? There are saffron terry-cottons."

: "How's that?"

: "Yes, check them out. The IR-8 Baul always wears saffron terry-cotton robes. What does it mean? It means gorgeous, durable and attractive. Have you heard a saying? It was previously believed: '*Yogi, without colouring the mind, you've coloured your attire.*'

"Changing the saying, do you know how I put it? I say: '*Not a Baul, yet you dress as a Baul, only for earthly pleasure!*' Tell me what you think of it?'"

"You've said it very well," I replied. True, the trendy Bauls that we see on roads, along river-banks and at fairs beg for alms as a profession. They also dess accordingly."

"And how about those strangely odd songs?" Kalo Sayeb enquired, even before I could finish.

"Strange songs?'" I became inquisitive.

"Yes, of course, odd and queer. Haven't you heard? Well wait a while, I had jotted down part of a song. I got it on the train to Lalgola from a 'terry-cotton Baul'. Here it is; listen to the lyrics:

My mind, if you want to ride a bicycle—
First, wear a loin-cloth and clean your heart a trifle!
On foot-pin, put your feet,
Hop forward, don't retreat;
Stand up then on the pin,
Look in front and watch out clean,
And all the while, keep on track the handle.
Sitting on the seat—
Have balance complete,
In core-hymn, turn on paddle!

"So, did you follow?"

: "I understood that this song is a true-blue IR-8 song sung by a terry-cotton Baul. Isn't that so?"

Laughing heartily, Kalo Sayeb said: "You're quite right. However, let me add something. Who has penned the lyric? On checking up, you'll find that it was composed by some Calcutta-based folk-lyricist. It has been set to music by some 'synthetic' man, dubbed 'Khyapa'. That is, all put together, it can be called a genuine collaborative scheme. Now you see that you have a tough task ahead."

: "Why tough?"

: "Isn't it tough? You've to look for cotton in the age of terry-cotton. Is that very simple?"

In bed at night, I continued to wonder where I had started, where and how far I had reached! Just the pull of a word opened up such a large world. The words 'female companion' dragged me to a Sahajiya portal, which seemed to double up as an abortion centre! From there, even though I had landed in Santosh's hands, he brought me over to a strange man whose clear gaze constantly caught the society's double faces and hypocrisy, self-contradiction, artifices and artificialities. IR-8 was such an astonishing metaphor—binding it within a framework was no mean task or no less surprising! Collecting and putting together diverse thoughts I landed in a jumble and subsequently fell asleep at some point.

I woke fairly early, perhaps because of the new surroundings and found myself soaked in sweat. As I brushed my teeth using a twig broken off from the *aash-shyaora* shrub, Santosh turned up. His face lit-up with a bright smile, he said: "Tell me how your shelter was. Our Kalo Sayeb is a straightforward man; there's no complication about him." Pausing a little, he added: "By the way, how are the rural songs that you collect? I'm not interested in religion but the other kind of village songs are within my ambit. Will you take them?"

: "Oh, really?" I was taken aback. "I was looking for the other kind of songs for a long time. I do believe that, outside the body-based doctrine, vocal music and Fakiri songs, there must be a world of other songs. But I haven't got them. Do you have them? Will you give them to me?"

Santosh replied: "I haven't got them with me, but I know where they are. We'll have to go to Kareya village. Can you ride a bicycle? There's a blind singer there, Doyat Ali, by name. If our luck holds, we can get him."

I said: "Why, where will the blind man go?"

: "Most of the days, he leaves in the morning to beg for alms at Barniya, Dhopat and other villages. He returns after the day is done and then he eats."

: "After a day spent in begging, he has to cook, does he?"

: "No, no, he has a wife, Suratannechha. She, too, is blind. It was we who got them married. They seem to be happy. At times, I spend the night with them, listening to songs; they're quite different. Let us start, without any further delay."

Finishing off with tea and breakfast quite quickly and taking leave from all the members of Kalo Sayeb's home, we set off for Kareya. It was a Jaishtha morning, with the air not yet so hot. Breezing through the coolness of the morning – heady with the fresh fragrance of flowers and leaves – we chatted all the way to Doyat Ali's house—a rundown hut. Our luck favoured; the sightless man was sitting on the raised front balcony.

"From the footfall, I can make out its Santosh. Am I right? Who else with him?"

After the introductions were over, Doyat Ali said: "Sir, I'm poor, very poor. But since you've come, you must eat something. I've nothing, save a few palm trees. Have some palm-kernels. My dear, please serve the gentlemen some palm-kernels." Surat, Doyat Ali's wife, stroking my body with the charm of her sightless eyes said: "Please sit down, dears. Take some rest. The man will never change; he'll continue to be like that! Should one offer just palm-kernels? Please have some *batasha* alongside."

The day advanced. Some villagers converged in ones and twos. Doyat Ali said with pride: "They've smelt music!" He picked up his single-stringed drone – the *ektara* – on his shoulder and burst into a song:

Oh, Ta Na, Ta Na Na—
Begging for a fistful of rice, I don't get a belly-full to eat.
Oh mind, in sheer sorrow, to people's doors, I drag my feet!
How often should I knock on others' doors, pray!
How arduous are my chores to this day,
My sunburns get sore along the way,
With whom do I share my sad defeat!

I've a Vaishnavi at my home,
Twenty kilo rice, she eats alone!
She's the Goddess, I'm the God,
I pray and serve, though it is odd!
Yet she calls me the 'Father Divine', her Lord
That makes me angry, listening to her drone!

She is always craving and dreaming food
How can I help her eat healthy and eat good?

Hearing the song, Suratannechha faked rage and retorted: "Santosh, don't you believe a word of this song! When did I hanker for food? Do I polish off twenty kilo rice? Has the blind bugger ever seen twenty kilo of rice?"

Flashing a loving smile, Doyat Ali said: "I'm in the throes of dealing with an ignorant woman! Santosh, you got me hitched to her and look what a sticky pest you put on my free and simple lifestyle! She doesn't have a sense of humour, doesn't follow a song. Dear blind woman, is this song my composition? It's by Kubir Gosain."

Santosh said: "I don't want to listen to this useless brawl between the blind stork and the dry stream. Doya, after the song of humanity, now sing about fruits."

"All are songs about humanity, sir," said Doyat Ali. "Fruit has been created by God for man's consumption; otherwise, what's the value of fruits? But yes, God's highest credit is in creating this fruit in the guise of man. Listen then—

Bar-elahi put fruits on trees, kudrat is his.
First, he places one fruit on two trees
You see his makkar please—
For that fruit's sake, there many a fruit is."

Singing this far, Doyat Ali said: "Sultan, are you there? Explain the meaning of this song to Sir."

Emerging out of the crowd, Sultan said: "Sir, *Bar-elahi* is *Allah. Kudrat* means power. The two trees are Adam and Heba. *Makkar* imples skill. And the fruit is mankind."

Santosh said: "It all means that Allah – with his power and skill – created Adam and Heba first; from those two, man was born. And various fruits were created for the consumption of mankind. Do you agree?"

"Right, right," exclaimed Doyat Ali with joy. "The educated man's knowledge and intellect are very clear...However, listen gradually to the rest. Sultan, you stay near about sir; you'll explain from time to time. Listen—

Paddy, wheat and sesame beans,
We're happy if coconut's in,
On palm, some are keen,
There's brinjal, gourd and other curries green!

Gourds both bitter and pointed, and jujube berry,
Sour juice's tamarind territory,
Sweet'n'sour lemons, the red berry
But nothing like the pulse kheshari's bliss!

Chilli-coriander-fennel-cumin
Are fruits-turned-spices for the cook and the kitchen;
Plantain-pumpkin-gourd you do need,
Cucumber-papaya are to be cooked indeed,
The black and yellow mustards-linseed-hemp – all fruits turned to seed,
They produce the oil when pressed and pasted in!

A vibrant human world gradually took shape before my eyes; a framework of the consumerist food-loving society, linked to life, grew. Doyat Ali had not stopped; his unassailable voice was still resonant:

The wood apple, the cucumber,
The water chestnut in plentiful number,
Acid-fruit, date-palm, musk-melon, et al,
Pomegranate and litchi: thick-skinned and small;
Gourd and other root-fruits, fox-tailed ginger,
Coarse-grained maize: happiness-harbinger;
Black cumin, turmeric, coriander: to make merry:
Seeds of hollyhock, pomegranate and black-berry;
Place myrobalan in a betel-leaf fold—
Sandalwood paste for digestion and cold!

The music continued add infinitum. Both listeners and singer Doyat Ali were lost in the music. But I was wondering what my role here was. Was I not a total misfit in this rural world? Truly speaking, I was not even aware of the many names of fruits, spices and crops named here. How limited was our urban life—how confined and self-contained! Did we have clear knowledge about the various names of crops, their use and nutrition values?

At one point, the song of fruits had ended, making way for the song on iron. Was that any less colourful! A big shock awaited right at the beginning of the song:

For making cane-goods, iron you need,
Had iron not chopped the cane—
It'd have been just a grove of reed.

I had never thought about this aspect! Iron's first task was to chop the cane; only then that cane could be used as the wooden pillar for the thatched roof and could support a window, or the frame of a bullock cart, the seat and the roof. There were sundry other uses. Doyat Ali's cryptic song detailed many uses of iron:

The iron is in the wood chopper's axe and knife,
In the shovel and the pick-up—all common and rife,
From the chichke, to the needle and the shears—
The iron makes even a spade comes to life.

Standing next to me Sultan said: "Sir you may be slightly foxed by the words. I'll explain, please listen. *Chichke* are the thin skewers used for roasting pointed gourds as the rural people can't afford oil to fry them. Shears are used to cut paddy or wheat at harvest. Now listen to some more of the magic of iron...

Iron is plough's tip,
Pasi and the nail,
It is the deadly spear-top and sword's edge,
and of the cane-sheathed cutter;
Shuttle for weaver, kenko for the angler,

The sharpener and pen-knife, lance-knife, angling hook
And chopper: we hail!"

Sultan explained: "*Pasi* is the spot where the tip of the plough is fixed. *Kenko* is an instrument to kill the fish. Listen to this now—

Carpenter's drill and pail,
Anvil and hammer and nail
Baul-hata, kajal-lata,
A thief's foot chain in a jail."

"Oh, how wonderful," exclaimed Santosh. "It counted in the thief's chain, too! Good lord! But I couldn't follow what a *baulhata* was!"

: "Didn't you follow? At village homes, a *baulhata* is a shovel which is used to clear away faeces. But the song continues to flow, do listen:

Forceps, arrows, cannon and gun
Shackles, rake's claws, wok's handle—the whole run,
Duck-trap, husker and huller's hammer-top and pitchfork,
Bhomor badari—the cobbler's implements for leather work."

Sultan enquires, "What, sir, are you confused again? Here is the explanation. Iron is used to make the two top holds of the husker's mace; *bhomor* and *badari* are the iron tools which cobblers use for stitching and nailing shoes as well as for scraping the leather. Now, Doyat Ali, please end your song on iron. The song on birds still emains to be sung. Perhaps I'll sing along.

With iron hammers, all stone is crushed,
Iron for the barber's clippers, blades and scissors—
for the nails, clean shaves, and horse's hair, well brushed.
A boat's body, the ship's deck, nails on the shaft to put,

A range of rustic tools, the umbrella-sticks to push open and pull shut,
A ship's anchor to cling on in deep sea, and to trust!

"Sir, the barber's tools are fine-honed stuff, while a rough iron comb is for brushing clean a horse's body. But this song will go on for a while. You won't like this song."

I pulled Santosh aside and asked: "What pleasure do you derive from such songs? Where's any deep knowledge in this song?"

Santosh replied: "The social cohesiveness, infallible knowledge on the use of various tools and of material life, extensive knowledge of man's needs—can the value of these be totally ruled out? You must have noticed that the villagers have been enjoying the song much more than we have? Could you tell me the reason behind this?"

I replied: "The reason for this is that dimensions of their familiar world are far too little. These become even less under the pressure of life and tensions of livelihood. These three songs have captured the essence of their confined stretch of life. They derive a joy similar to what we experience when we hear about the glory of the splendid life that our fathers and forefathers enjoyed. Isn't that so?"

: "Perhaps it's a lot similar to what you describe. But the canvas of village life is a much larger and a detailed one than our urban life. They are curious to know every detail. The urban man simply knows that rice comes from paddy, that's all. The villager thinks, first, of the selection of paddy followed by the preparation of the soil, adding fertilisers, preparation of the paddy prototype. Then comes sowing, the cultivation and harvest of paddy followed by transportation to the godowns, the process of boiling and husking—all these stages and factors are equally important to them. Along comes the role of the farming machinery. The plough, the sickle, the ladder, the sharp *henso* – the crescent-shaped knife – the husker and the sieving equipment—they have to be careful and vigilant about every detail and every step involved. They have to also take care of the pair of bullocks. Enough fodder has to be stored for feeding them. Perhaps this is why their songs are laden with such minute details."

: "Is this called abundance? Whatever, it was now time to listen to the song of birds."

By then, Doyat Ali had finished his song and lit up his bidi. Sultan tied anklets around his own feet, and began, with a long-drawn cascade of notes:

Arrey arrey arrey, rey rey rey go fly—
Avoid the trap, bird, or else you may die;
Caught on the sly, in a faint you'll lie! Partridge, lapwing, mynah,
The magpie robin, the koel, and the rest—
Hill mynah, cockatoo, the paradise flycatcher,
and the parakeets at their best!
Pigeon, dove and the snipe,
Lapwing, iris, the tree pie and others of their type;
Caught in the trap and captured: they all lie!

Ali told Santosh: "Did you notice the original thoughts of the village songster? While writing about birds, the first thing he remembered was that the bird dies in distress, unless it can avoid the trap. So, the first hindrance against avian survival is the man-made trap. The rest of the song goes like this:

Kites, crows, eagles and other raptors hunt;
Birds prey on birds—
I am witness to such stunt!"

Santosh said: "Now notice another contradiction. Birds prey on birds—this is, truly speaking, the living world's prevailing contradiction. Man himself preys on and kills man in various ways. But let that go. First, let's listen to the song. It's a nice one, isn't it?

Porcupines abound the wind-blown reed-hedge,
'Saltaru' a bird, lives along the sal-wood's edge.
The 'Bou-kotha-kao' hawk cuckoo there—
Their call provides the joy's share.
The honey sucking flowerpeckers flit up and down
Bee-eater, kingfisher, cormorants and waterhens,
Flying cranes and water-birds in marshy land near town."

Santosh said: "You were speaking earlier of abundance, which you'll get only in the villages now. This is nature's own abundance. There is such a wide variety of birds in our land! And what are those? At least a hundred years back, Arjan Shah had composed this song. Do keep in mind—the two World Wars had not taken place then. The air was unpolluted. Land and marshes were not so lacklustre then. There were ripe fruits in the trees. Birds can only survive in such an environment."

All the while Sultan sang, dancing around:

Bulbul, sunbirds and barbets prance to and fro;
The mythical lovebirds of this world, come and go.
Wood-peckers, coucals, peacocks,
sparrows and the 'baya' weaver birds abound;
Minivets, drongos, pipits, tits and many a native bird come around.
Geese, moorhens, teals, plovers, shanks, stilts and herons,
Frogs mate in peace and the hornbills fill the environs.

The music advanced at its own pace. I wondered whether all these birds were still there—in their natural habitats!

Santosh asked: "What are you thinking?"

"I'm not sure why," I mused. "But somehow I remembered Kalo Sayeb...wondered whether any IR-8 bird, by any chance, had mingled with this lot!"

Santosh roared with laughter.

Meanwhile, the musical soiree was over and the place had visibly emptied itself. The day progressed too. Besides, stomachs would not be filled by listening to music. All the working people gradually left on their own errands. Only one remained; he came to me and said in a very low voice: "Sir, I've heard all you said. Therefore I may tell you that even these songs are not the genuine stuff, reflecting the countryman's heart! To listen to those special songs, you'll have to go to another enclave and meet someone. Will you come with me?"

Leaving Santosh behind, I went alone with this man and reached a clay courtyard. A middle-aged man sat there wearing a somewhat annoyed and listless look on his face. Seeing my companion – whose name was Arun – his face lit up with a half smile. Arun said: "Chanduda, this gentleman is looking for genuine village songs. Doyat Ali was singing to him those old and hackneyed songs of fruits, birds and iron. I've brought him along. Would you like to sing him an essentially true village song?"

Chanduda said: "Well sir, I can't vouch for truth or lie. Around my mamarbari – the region of Nalda, Tungi, Shabdanagar, Palashipara, Sayebnagar – the boys sing a kind of song called *bolan,* on the last day of Chaitra. They create their music out of current and contemporary events and call it *Rong Panchali.* Would you like to have a sample? There are no words of wisdom there, but only stark truths. Listen then."

Thereafter, Chanduda looked straight into my eyes and said: "You know, don't you, that government has opened health centres in the villages? Operations are performed at these centres to control the birth of humans. There is a song on it that goes like this:

O brother, the 'man-cutter machine' has come up very well,
For those who wish to be impotent, their ranks swell!
Hekim's – the doctors – producing impotents, in Palashipara, dwell!"

It was as if somebody had whipped me across the face. On that hot day of the month of Jaishtha, I bowed my face in embarrassment.

It is difficult to predict who you might come in contact with, in the course of a human lifetime. I had left no stone unturned in the hope of 'healing' my own mentally challenged daughter. Was there a door I had not knocked upon or a cure I had not tried? My search ranged from the highest-paid topnotch neurologist of Kolkata to the low-grade traditional rustic hakim. On one occasion, a Fakir – reputed to be empowered to utter infallible words of truth and wisdom – came wandering to our town. I did not believe in these miracles at all. But upon the insistence and entreaties of my wife and looking at the pathetic, heart-wrenching face of my disabled child, I could not but visit the Fakir. Visits to such places always had a startling and overwhelming effect, awakening one to an ocean of human helplessness and to the wide prevalence of ailments. At least a hundred men and women thronged the Fakir. Most of them were the parents, with ardent prayers for the cure of their children on their lips. How drenched their words were in tears, how distressful there appeals! "Sir, will my lame son be able to walk?" "Sir, please give my daughter the power of speech!" "Sir, will my boy's mind never be cured and be back to normal?" "Will my daughter's epilepsy never heal, sir?"

The Fakir said stoically: "The world moves at His will. What can I do? Everything is within His power. I dispense medicine in His name. If it can be cured it will. Take His name. Think of Him."

What would I say in that huge crowd? In my arms, my mentally challenged child lay comfortably, swaying mindlessly. There was a touch of mercy; the Fakir threw a glance at me. He asked: "Whose fruit is this? Is it your own?"

I was startled. 'Fruit'? I had never before heard such a unique use of the word 'fruit'. Is the child a fruit, may be the fruit of karma? On seeing me nod my head, he said: "What's the disease of your son?"

: "It's a daughter, not a son."

: "Whoever is the son is the daughter; they're all alike," the Fakir smiled. "Everything is his creation. Only the mould's different. The action is different. God has not given her intelligence, isn't that so? Nothing is likely to change unde my care. But do you know a place called Shyaoratala of Ranabanda? It has the cluster of Aahad Fakir. If you dedicate yourself with ample devotion, there'll be benefits. I know that for sure."

Ranabanda was not too far. There was a direct bus via Chapra from our town. We could perhaps think later about dedicated vows for the correct medicine, but the place could certainly be visited for the moment. On such thoughts, I set out for the place one morning. During the journey, the passengers intimated me about several things. It was perhaps a very responsive portal, they claimed. Who didn't know Aahad Fakir's name in these parts of the country! And was there anybody whose ardent desire had not been fulfilled? Reassuring voices rose from the crowd. A young man – an employee of the Chapra BDO – commented from the side: "The name Aahad seems familiar enough...Yes, I do recall something. He was the same Fakir who was murdered, wasn't he?"

Murder? That too of a Fakir? I shuffled uneasily in my seat.

The bus stopped at Ranabanda. The bus journey was over. One now had to cross a small river to reach Shyaoratala on the other bank. It was around ten in the morning, when I reached. It was a lonely place, surrounded by trees. There were a couple of sheds and one platform. Aahad Fakir used to sit here most of the time.

"Yet, when he sat here, he would always cover his feet with his two hands," said an aged devotee.

: "Oh why? Why did he?"

: "So that no devotee could touch his feet. He had a strong objection against salutation."

: "How did you know?"

: "What nonsense! I've seen him sit on that platform with my own eyes, as clearly as I can see you."

Someone came forward to explain: "Among those who had seen Aahad Fakir with their own eyes are Chhamad (Samad) Ali and Wachhef (Wasef) Ali. This gentleman is Wachhef Sahib."

I greeted him and asked: "Did Aahad Fakir not belong to very old times?"

: "Not too old, I'd say. He died on 10 Magh 1365, which is thirty-three years ago. I was a young man then."

How did he become a myth in such a short time? Probably he was a Fakir of very large proportions. Yet, we knew precious little about Aahad Fakir! How could I get to know more? I was thinking of catching Wasef Ali in this regard, when a handsome youth began singing near the platform. Someone whispered in my ears: "Sir, this singer is a very famous one. His name is Jaharali; he has somewhat monopolised the music scene in our Padmamala-. Ranabanda region." The song began in an open, tuneful voice:

Loving my Kala has been quite a a disaster—
The old lord has become my necklace and my master!
A youthful husband rests at home:
Nothing wrong with his virtues' high dome,
Yet for my old man, I decline an eight jewels' cluster!
Having loved the old one, Day'n'night, my tears run.
Just once, let him come, as my soul's lustre!

Go forward, friend, go around, See if my old lord can be found,
I can't stay hale, hearty and sound,
Gazing ahead through hope's stormy duster!

O Kali, my kind one, See if for the old lord some care be done,
So that I'm not forced to return, O Murshid of mine,
Home to my young man any faster!

I had never before, heard such a strange song belonging to the Vaishnava faith. If Kala was Krishna here, to call him an old, aged lord and master throughout the song was, no doubt a very new and unique concept. To quench my evident curiosity about the song, Wasef said: "This song was a great favourite of our guru, that is, the respected Aahad Shah, who used to sing it often. No sir, I don't' know precisely when he composed it."

I gradually came to know that there was a big annual carnival and feasting on the occasion of Ambubachi. People who took a divine oath had a congregation. Rice, lentils and vegetables donated by all homes were pooled to arrange and sustain an annual rice feast at the festival. Hapu songs, Shabdo songs, Dhuyojari songs continued through the day. And there were night long Fakiri soirees. Why were the events and the place so popular? What exactly were the activities of Aahad Shah—was he a Baul or a Dervish?

Wasef Ali elaborated: "No sir, he was not a Baul. He was a Sufi Fakir. Whatever I know about his life, I can narrate."

: "Please tell me."

: "He was born in the neighbouring village of Ranaband. His faher's name was Madari and mother's name Ametya. They were very poor. After they had given birth to five daughters in a row, the husband and wife prayed to Allah for granting them a male child. They vowed that if it were a son they would consecrate him to Allah. In Allah's mercy, their desire was fulfilled.They named the boy Aahad."

: "What does Aahad mean?"

"In Arabic Wayahedun means One; from this came the name Aahad. Whatever, Aahad was the poor son of an impoverished family. He became a cowherd on hire at other homes. Yet, since his childhood Aahad was pure, religious-minded and of an ascetic temperment. When he was roughly between fifteen and sixteen years of age, he became a *kishani* at the house of Chandrakanta Paramanik."

"What's the difference between a cowherd and a *kishani*?" I enquired.

Wasef Ali said: "Sir, you're an urban gentleman. In the countryside, the young boys tending the cattle and helping in farming are called cowherds; the senior cowherds are called herdsman. Working as a herdsman, he heard by word of mouth that in the village of Baliuro's residence, there was a Peer. Well, Aahad did herdsmanship for the whole day and in the evening he went to the Peer guru. Meanwhile, his parents got him married by force. But within a short time, both parents died; Aahad's wife died, too, of snakebite. All the earthly bondings were snapped. My guru subsequently came to Shyaoratala, established his cluster and built his own hermitage, his ashram. He didn't move anywhere else in his entire life after that."

I asked: "From the time he came to Shyaoratala he never moved out anywhere: is this what you heard?"

: "I have heard this since childhood; besides I've never actually seen him move anywhere as long as he lived. There was another unique element about him, which we as his disciples have closely observed. Nobody had ever seen him take a bath, eat a meal, change clothes or leave his seat to relieve himself. This was after having kept a watch for twenty-four hours. Even...but would you believe this?"

: "Oh, please carry on. It's most fascinating to hear."

: "It's something I've personally observed. The year was 1345 of the Bengali calender, when there was a furious flood drowning all land; yet even then he didn't leave his seat below the tree. When the water rushed in, he tied a rope around his waist, tied the other end to the tree and continued to sit in the open, on flooded grounds. When his disciples came to rescue him on a makeshift banana trunk raft, he told them: "The Merciful wishes me to float. So here I am afloat. You please return home."

With great respect, Wasef folded his hands in honour of the departed divine soul. Then he said in an exulted tone: "He was a man of the greatest dignity. He also had the power of infallible words; his words always rang true. Anyone who devotedly took a vow saw it fulfilled. If you lie prostrate at his portal even now, certain diseases are cured. Just see how many are lying around right now!"

It was indeed true. In front of Aahad's platform, several men and women lay prostrate. How much of it was truth and how much myth: who would say? In the quiet, serene environs of the ashram, even the greatest of atheists would be adequately influenced to question their minds. In my mind's eye flashed the pathetic face of my disabled girl suffering from an incurable disease. I collected myself and clutching on to the last straw, exclaimed: "But have you personally witnessed somebody being healed? Will you please name him?"

"Sir's doubts have not cleared yet," said Wasef with a smile. "Then I've to narrate the story of Dubraj. Dubraj was my guru's very first disciple. I've seen her come to fetch ghee for preparing the customary ghee-kedgeree for Ambubachi."

: "Where was Dubraj's home?"

: "It was at Nutangram-Keshavponta near Andul. She was married off at a very early age and sent to Baliuro village. Unfortunately she fell prey to leprosy Her whole body was afflicted. Asking her husband to marry again, she left home and came over to the Fakir's portal at Shyaoratala. Listening to her wails at midnight, guru ran in and asked: 'Who are you, mother?' After hearing the entire story, he said: 'Pray to him who gave you this fatal disease.'"

:"Was Dubraj's leprosy truly cured?"

: "It was truly and fully cured. I had myself witnessed. In this ashram, everyone called her 'Ma'. Mother died only the other day. That, too, was a wonder. Aahad died on 10 Magh 1356, while Dubraj Ma passed away exactly one year later on 10 Magh, the same day. Wasn't it a wonder?"

Indeed there were many wonders. In this atomic age of electronic marvels, there had been no reduction in the ceremonies of folk goddesses of the land. There had been no dearth either in the pomp of the annual carnivals of Bauls, Fakirs, Dervishes and Gosains. Even after opening a higher secondary school and a health centre in every village, one would observe the same grandeur for the Sheetala worship in the month of Chaitra and Manasa worship during the month of Sravana. The only difference was, instead of the folk *jhaanpan* songs there would be shrill music blaring on the microphone and among all the commodities on sale at the fair would lurk a red-banner-draped book shop for the sale of Leftist literature. Sudeb Sensharma of Brahmanitala had pointed out another novelty in the worship of rural deities; he had remarked: "I've always seen sir, since eternity, the juicy pods of ripe jackfruits being used for the food-offering to the deity Manasa. But these days mother Manasa has had a change of taste. She is consuming the bumper-crop—of pineapples from north Bengal and juicy water-melons from Gangasagar. Is this any less a wonder, sir?"

Finally, I blurted out the question that I had held back for long from Wasef Ali: "Who murdered Aahad Shah? And whatever was it for? Was there a Hindu-Muslim communal angle at all?"

: "Oh, no, no. It was from violence, jealousy, and somewhat from avarice. It was quite true that guru's name, fame and news of activities were spreading to faraway villages. This was also true that a few ailments were getting cured. What happened as a result? All the land and garden around that you see were offerings from his devotees. Didn't that create jealousy and violence among the lower class? But then that was not quite sufficient cause to kill one."

: "Then did his religious faith enrage people?"

: "No, it was not even that. His religious faith was the most catholic one. Hindus, Muslims and Christians continue to sit together for joint meals during the Ambubachi carnival. He used to chant–*'Huq-Allah, bolo Musalman; Huq-Hari bolo Hindu; Huq-Jishu bolo Christian'.* He always used to utter these words. *Huq* means 'truth'; it is indeed, what everbody seeks. Actually what I have gathered is that it has nothing to do with faith, nor with jealousy or violence. He had to sacrifice his life for meeting the illegitimate lust of a group of people."

: "Could you please be a little more explicit?"

Heaving a deep sigh, Wasef said: "It's a very sad episode of ours. Prior to that evening; Fakir Sahib gave some money to his disciples for a special reason. Some disciples present there must have thought Fakir Sahib had stashed away much more money. They returned the same night to demand all the money from the Fakir. The Fakir had given all, still they clamoured for more money. They tied him up. Guru had perhaps recognised them; so they stabbed him to death. The Fakir had pleaded: 'Please don't take my life!' They didn't listen."

With moist eyes Wasef said: "It was my misfortune that I was the first one to find him. It was early dawn and he was still breathing. He was lying in a pool of blood with his hands and legs tied up. It was I who untied him. His soul left him the same night. But till the very end, despite all the exhortations, the Fakir refused to reveal the names of the killers. He had pardoned them; but Allah didn't; there was justice done thereafter."

: "And how?"

: "Will that sound credible enough to you? But we've seen it ourselves. One man in this ashram collapsed vomiting blood. A few came to return the stolen money and banged their heads against the ashram's platform, ardently soliciting pardon. They died a strange death before sunset—agonised, suffering and breathless. The rest of the killers from neighbouring villages died within a month from sudden mishaps. The misfortune was over. From then onwards, this ashram's fame spread far and wide. The Ambubachi fair has seen an increasing rush of male and female devotees. Nowadays, the crowd exceeds fifty thousand."

I felt inquisitive about Aahad Fakir's age when he was killed. Was it an untimely death? Had he been relatively young?

Wasef replied: "His year of birth was 1246 (by the Bengali calendar); death in 1356. It means that he lived for 110 years."

: "Such an eminent personality was killed...were there no police and court-cases?"

: "With whom will those cases be fought? There was no witness. Besides, the Fakir didn't name anyone! But the judgement by Khuda in his own court has been done already. Does anyone take the names of those killers and sinners today? Everyone remembers Aahad's name, shows a lot of devotion and sings his praise. Look at you, having travelled all this distance—simply to find out more about him, haven't you?"

I continued to stare at the divine space with my doubtful and questioning mind hardly responding to what I heard. If I could lie prostrate here for the sake of my spastic daughter, would she get cured? Would her disability disappear? Would her senses return? Would she talk and call me 'father'? It would be that call which I had never heard! Oh Aahad Fakir, give me belief, the belief to rest my faith in your divinity. In folk life, I had not come across anything supernatural. I could not call you with the ardentness of Dubraj. I did not have the unassaible faith of Wasef. Did my eyes moisten at this thought?

In a moment, the rational mind was back on firm ground. I stood at the turning point of the twentieth century, its last years...what were these irrational thoughts of mine? My intellectual mind started re-constructing the wonderful core myth of Aahad. I realised that a mindless killing had transformed the insignificant life of a man into the talking point and folk legend of the region. The stories of the collective deaths of the assassins had lent a memorable touch of supernatural mythology to this entire episode. Would the world continue to move in this manner forever? The atomic age would create an unbelievable world, with the electronic technology regulating an instrumented and robotic social life through remote control. Would Aahad's story still be alive then? Would people still believe them all?

Suddenly the whole ashram exploded in front of me. It seemed that the land was rent with the collective heavy sigh of the eternally deprived mass of humanity. It seemed as though India's five lakh mentally challenged children – as disabled as my own daughter – were seeking freedom to be out of their hapless lives. Finding me quiet, the old Wasef placed his hand on my shoulder and said: "I understand your pain. You lack devotion in your heart. You'll never get peace in life."

I raised my head in frustrated anguish and recollected the confident face of Sufal Sarkar. I also recalled his energetic words alongside: "The greatest enemy of this country is devotion, which does not allow a man to raise his head in dignity. My fight is against this damp and listless notion of devotion."

As soon as I remembered his words, I quickly walked out of Shyaoratala with brisk steps, amidst the surprised stares of Wasef and the group of believing disciples of Aahad. Crossing the river, I boarded the waiting bus. The bus began rolling shortly thereafter. My mind was bent on going over the events surrounding my first meeting with Sufal Sarkar.

It was on an invitation from the district agriculture officer on the annual prize-distrbution ceremony. The successful farmers of the district would be given shields and cups: for a good harvest, for good sizes and for multiple products from the same land. Even though these were routine programmes, I used to attend these to catch a glimpse of the different kinds of village folks. In my quest for Peers, Baul-Bairagi-ascetics, their gurus and their mantras, blind faiths, beliefs, superstitions, and myths, talismans, portals, and their kind of music at fairs and carnivals, I had seen the adversities of village life as well. There was injustice, exploitation and oppression—where humanity stood deprived of all rights. On the one hand there were ample crops of paddy, with tractors running along vast stretches of land, verdant beauty sprawled across the countryside—thanks to the instalment of shallow tubewells. I had seen villagers polish off a full meal during winter harvest of the Rabi crops—the season of plenty. Yet I had also been privy to the sight of matchsticks being sold by the stick, or, a young girl bringing in a small packet of linseed to a grocer's shop in exchange for some kerosene oil.

Villagers in rustic surroundings appeared very different from those at a farmers' gathering in a town, presided by the agricultural officer with a few farmers sitting on a bench on one side. Those that called themselves simple farmers were formally introduced by Akashvani radio as 'farmer-brothers'. I had watched many such programmes in the Indian News Reviews. Normally one saw smiling farmers from Haryana turned out in large, tightly spiralled turbans in such documentary films. On that particular day's awards ceremony, I expected to see our usual stooping, pale, stressed and tired farmers of Bengal. Instead, I was startled to spot in the crowd of farmers – hopelessness writ large on their faces – a man standing ramrod straight! He was Sufal Sarkar, receiver of many awards for multiple harvests in the same plot of land. That was part of the announcement. But, before that, Sufal's one single statement attracted me.

On the table stood the neatly arranged trophies, identity papers and savings certificates stacked in neat piles as well. The district magistrate had arrived to preside over the function, his ready-made smile fixed on his lips. Next to him sat his manicured wife—soft and demure as a rabbit, her sunglasses fashionably in place. In their meticulously planned family, their only child was dressed in a Gazebo outfit. He came in perched on the shoulders of their personal orderly, obliging everybody present with a cute, toothy smile. In front of the DM, the district agriculture officer stood with an ingratiating smile. Other associate officers were busy with the nitty-gritties of the arrangements. There were many posters on the stage. There was a souvenir made available with blessings from the Prime Minister, and Central and State agriculture ministers as well as the lists of strange names of all the shops selling fertilisers and agro-pumpsets of the district. On a bench on one side was seated the invited farmers; apparently this function was theirs. They were wearing over-starched dhotis and shirts. Their dry, scaly and hard workmen's feet were fitted unwillingly with dust-layered boots. But there was no trace of that easy smile on their sunburnt faces. The official stringent photographers exhorted: "Come on, please smile a little for the camera."

Simultaneously came the extension officers, cajoling them likewise: "Smile, smile. It's such a happy day for you. How many prizes will you get! Look this side with a smiling face, please."

At that moment rose Sufal Sarkar. A short, dark man, he wore a dhoti pulled up high above his knees and tucked in with a shirt. He demanded loudly: "Where would the smile come from? BDO Sir has fetched us early in the morning from the village. Our stomachs are on fire, ravaged with hunger! This is a farmer's hunger, sir, like the parched and hungry fields of the month of Jaishtha. A cup of tea and biscuits won't serve the purpose! Give us a good meal and the smiles will appear on their own. What are you doing here? Simply showing off your badges and strutting about with your empty talk!"

I liked Sufal Sarkar and his plain, clear-cut words instantly. He was such a delightfully straightforward man! I simply had to go and meet him. After meeting, he extracted a promise from me: I would have to visit his village Shyampur.

I remember to have visited him within a week or so. It was winter.

The walk began from the bus-stop, along a path flanked on both sides by rolling lush green fields of crops. The two expressions 'unbound' and 'stretched till the horizon' had their true essence revealed only in the countryside. There were a few earthen hutments on the way. Scenes of cane-crushing were interspersed with glimpses of jute twigs laid out in the sun for drying – dabbed in a paste of cow-dung on one end – turning into fuel for household use.

: "Where are you headed to?" was the common point of enquiry from the passers-by.

: "Sufal Sarkar's house."

: "Go straight on and then take the left turn. It won't take more than ten minutes. Sufal-da is at home. I met him a while ago." Due respect for Sufal was hardly concealed in the voice and demeanour.

I reached a while later. The not-quite-middle-aged man was weaving a mat from palm leaves. He rose and offered me an unpolished jackfruit-wood chair. He himself preferred to stand. I noticed the man was of a restless nature. He either scratched the earth with his toes or simply shuffled around restlessly. All the while his restless eyes roved; most careful and yet curious. After an exchange of civilities, I raised the most engaging query about the quiet and peaceful village. "How is your life in this village? It does seem to produce a bountiful harvest. Folks are peaceful and seem to be hard-working in the fields and farms. But is this the real envionment? Is there no party politics? Aren't there robberies?"

The erect man gave a single-word, direct answer: "Why should there be robberies? We all are united."

I was quite startled. I had been going around villages for a very long time. Everywhere robberies were a sensitive issue. Everyone was cowed down by foreboding, always under a menacing threat! So I had to ask: "Does it mean that you're claiming that there is no robbery when people stand united in a village?"

: "How will it happen?" Sufal argued in a very logical way. "In a village society, equality of framework makes for unity. The unequal society fetches dacoits. If you find out the core reasons of a robbery in a village, you'll find some village insider passing on help and information to the robbers. It won't happen here."

: "Why?"

: "Here we are twenty-five farmer families living together. We sow less of paddy, more of vegetables. Now you'll find in their land brinjals, tomatoes and broad beans. One farmer's land measues up to at most five acres. Here robbery won't pay off. An ordinary farmer sells a daily produce of vegetables for a paltry rupees ten or fifteen. Now, do please have the puffed rice and a cup of tea." A thin dusky girl brought tea for us. Sufal said: "This is my eldest daughter, working in the village health centre of the neighbouring Dogachhi village. Today is Sunday: her day-off."

: "It means that you've educated all your children. Is there a school?"

Smiling a little, Sufal said: "There was no school, I have created one: I was firm and obstinate about it."

: "How did that happen"?

: "There was nothing at that time; it was full of rubbles and marshes. Earlier there were apparently tigers. There is a rumour in the neighbouring villages. They also believe that we, the people who migrated from East Bengal, are apparently fiercer than the tigers. Whatever, we are the lower caste people who came from the Erakandi area of Faridpur—all of us belong to the same village. After Partition, one group of ours came to rehabilitate in Bahirgachhi. We were twenty families then. Even after staying for ten years, we could not survive."

: "Why? Was there enmity from the local people?"

: "No, no, it was the flood. Have you been to Bahirgachhi? It's an extremely low-lying place. Every year the harvest would get submerged under water. Finally we discovered this place and settled down after clearing the forest. Even then twenty-five years have passed."

There was a streak of brightness, a firmness of purpose and energetic confidence in the eyes of Sufal, even as a struggling person. Some people had a different flow of the sap of life lying outside the achievements and affluence of some men. It was akin to living and drawing sap from the ground through roots going deep and far. Such men were rare in the village. I wanted to ask with charmed eyes: "You were telling me about opening a school obstinately!"

: "Yes. That created history. You must be knowing that we people from East Bengal have to tolerate much sarcasm and satire, after landing here. We are also of the scheduled caste category—low in rank. Once there was a long queue for tickets at the Sealdah station. I was also standing in the queue. Suddenly a well-dressed clear-skinned man – certainly an uppe caste Brahmin – remarked mockingly: 'What's it, it is such a long queue? Why so? Hasn't the government still not made provision for a separate "reserved queue" for the scheduled caste?' I often have to hear and accept such things as well. In the neighbouring Dogachhi village, it was mostly caste Hindus who predominantly lived there, led by Brahmins. They called us 'Namo' and despised us a lot. Once I had gone to Dogachhi on some errand. It was summer. I was resting on the side of the village tank while a lot of people and children bathed there. I sat enjoying the sight when I suddenly noticed a boy almost drowning, gasping for breath in the middle of the tank."

: "Did you save him and pick him up?"

: "Yes, I belong to the waters of East Bengal. Can someone drown before my eyes? I swam up to the boy and rescued him. He had drunk a lot of water. I swung him around me, got the water out and told him—'Now go! You've been saved boy.' On receiving news of the drowning, in rushed the boy's mother and grandmother in a little while. They enquired as to who had rescued their child, when everyone pointed at me. The old women said: 'You are from Shyampur. Aren't you?' When I agreed, she simply held her grandchild by the neck and ordered: 'Come along, take a cleansing dip in the water. You have been touched by a 'Namo'. Nobody protested, everybody stood in silent agreement."

: "How is that?"

: "Yes, I became obstinate in my mind. 'Dear old hag,' I said to myself. "This is not to merely address you but to all of you in Dogachhi, I shall demonstrate the strength of this 'Namo'. So I have shown them accordingly. Now in that village, there is a lot of respect for me. Everyone flatters me by saying that Sufalbabu is our pride."

: "How did it happen?"

: "I organised and united the village—running back and forth to the town in the process. I created a night school. Now everyone in our cluster of villages is a 'primary school pass', each village with at least four graduates. There are twenty children who have passed the high school exam, higher secondary. We will make everybody educated. We all are united here."

I finally understood the reason behind the man's pride. He was not merely Sufal (fruitful) but successful. But how are the villagers still united? Hasn't party politics entered and tarnished their minds yet? I am yet to see a village in West Bengal where there are no political conflicts or group politics. A Panchayat operated, and so did the votes. I had to ask the question finally.

Sufal answered: "Most of the village politics is empty and rumour-based. Shall I tell you about an incident? Murtipur is the village next to Dogachhi. There two brothers, Sukesh and Janardan Mandal, live next to each other with separate kitchens. They have a relatively small tract of farmland, with which they somehow managed to make two ends meet. Both are CPM, with of course not much political knowledge. In Murtipur, there continues to be a lot of unrest between two left-leaning parties – the RSP (Revolutionary Socialist Party) and the CPI(M) (Communist Party of India – Marxist), with both parties trying to increase the number of their respective cadres. One day when Sukesh and Janardan had both gone to the fields, Sukesh's cow broke through Janardan's fence, entered his courtyard and ate the crops. It immediately created a heated confrontation between the two wives. In the evening when Janardan returned exhausted from work, his wife reported the story with appropriate exaggerations, accompanied by the inevitable weapon of tears. Well, there was virtually a fire raging inside Janardan's head after this episode...

"Was there a murder?" I asked, startled and shaken.

: "No, no, not a murder. But Janardan said: 'Let me go to the RSP office. From now onwards I won't do CPM politics anymore.' Since then Janardan is working for RSP. In that confrontation, the Murtipur votes were divided. In the last Panchayat elections the Left Front was defeated there. So now you see the fundamentals of village politics?"

I lived in a town and got news of village politics by reading the papers. But such news items did not find space even there! So I was most surprised. But more than that, I developed respect for the calm analysis by Sufal Sarkar, by the sequencing of all the events. It was indeed very difficult to know about the man's own self. He did not reveal almost anything personal.

I had to provoke him tactfully and ask him: "You spend the whole day in the fields. What do you do in the evenings? Chant Hari's name?"

The reply came with the utmost defiance: "Hari's name is taken by the sinners and repenters. I have no such hang-ups. I have not sinned. Nor do I believe in the concepts of virtue and vice and nor have I any faith in divinities or devotion for Brahmins. I have believed in humanity. Do you know what I often think? The greatest enemy of this land is devotion, which does not permit man to raise his head. My fight is against this timid devotion."

"But you haven't replied to my question," I said.

: "You didn't tell me what you do in the evening?"

: "I have an ailment. I get attacked by this ailment once it is evening..."

: "Which ailment? How old is it?"

: "This disease has taken hold of my life since my days of youth...that was the time when it intensified. Yes, you can say it's been with me for about thirty to forty years."

: "Is it the asthmatic wheeze?"

: "No sir, it is the disease of studies. Once it's evening, I light the hurricane lamp and start reading. Now while I talk to you I'm waiting for evening to fall soon...wondering when I can begin reading my book. I am keen to know how the book ends."

: "Which book is that?"

: *"Ispaat ('Steel'. How the Steel was Tempered).* It is by Nicolai Ostrovsky. Have you read it?"

I shook my head. But I could not quite express the shock of surprise I received. I was not merely surprised but also awestruck. It was the great wonder! How could the same time, space and environment make men of completely different beliefs? Today, when I tried to recall from far away, I found it difficult to reconcile the two persons: one supertitous like Wasef Ali and the other open-minded like Sufal Sarkar. Both belonged to the same contemporary period. How could it happen? Was it the self-knowledge often cited by Bauls and Fakirs? At least I clearly believed that without invoking God even once, Sufal had reached the zenith of self-knowledge. Yet I had met him not on the straight path of divinity and soul-searching but at the opposite end of that purely divine road leading to the 'man of my mind'—my 'self'.

The end to this gift of a unique striking surprise on the stroke of dusk was no less fascinating. I naturally asked him how – in the remotest of villages – he had procured the world-famous book of Ostrovsky? Was there a library in the village?

A soft smile hanging from his lips, he replied: "In that case you have to get up and walk over to a corner of my home's raised balcony."

I had to get up. There was a simple open bookshelf, made of packing-box plywood, tucked away at one corner. Nearly twenty-five books in Bengali translation, of Soviet and Chinese originals were very neatly stacked there. In passing, he informed me that he had read each volume at least ten times. He had thus collected the hymn of his survival, the weapon of struggle. His formal education till the sixth standard had been honed by an international outlook as well as a socialist and egalitarian approach to life and philosophy, accompanied by progressive thinking. He had bought the book *Ispat* from a recent book fair in the town.

The inner self of the man – hidden for so long – emerged unplugged, all at once, in proud verbosity. How glowing was his face!

: "Have you heard of the Tebhaga movement? I was sucked into its whirlpool at one point of time. I picked up my reading habit since then. Of course, there was an inordinate pressure of work then, too, mosty of the organsational kind. Then came the Partition. We floated like strands of straw: first at Bahirgachhi, and then permanently at Shyampur over the last ten years. Still, to construct a new village in a new land was also a large organisational task—involved explaining the right path to people and getting the job done correctly. Now I'm somewhat relieved of the pressure; I can lead a fairly restful life; give advice and counsel people. l have imbibed a fair amount of knowledge from my own readings and continue to learn something new every day!"

: "Is this village then, under your hold?" I asked.

: "I don't believe in any kind of control. It's a united lifestyle we would like to achieve. We all work hard; we eat hearty meals. We stand next to each other in weal and woe. We are together."

Were Sufal and his group of men still united, I thought to myself, from time to time. Had the upstart middlemen of politics not yet entered their orbit? Did the new young generation of the educated lot still accept Sufal's leadership? Occasionally I did think of visiting Shyampur again. But finally I did not go. Suppose I didn't find the same old picture? Why should I not retain an unsullied picture of good, untarnished memories and cling on to my faith? Who would wish to break the purity of the mind?

When I used to move from village to village in quest of the Sahebdhani community, I had two thoughts in mind. Brittihuda village in the Chapra division had the main portal of the revered guru of the Sahebdhanis. Everyday the principal priest offered meal-services and the evening ceremonial prayer services with lighted lamps to Deendayal. And every Thursday Deendayal received special offerings and ceremonial worships. Taking of from my first thought-stream, I had asked the head 'priest' Sharat Pal: "You're the principal Fakir of the Sahebdhanis. Who initiates the countless disciples and devotees who ae spread all around? Do they all come to you?"

Sharat Pal replied: "No. Out of them – who had adopted Deendayal's true name from this Pal house of ours – those who are good disciples, fairly educated and good orators, are given special permission by us to set up a portal of Deendayal in their own village-homes. They are called 'platformed Fakirs.' They add to our disciples. They worship Deendayal every evening. When the Agradweep fair is held on the eleventh day of the moon in the month of Chaitra, the 'platformed Fakirs' congregate there with their disciples. They contribute rice and lentils for the carnival. They also pay revenue to our portal. In lieu, we gift them a mat and a hubble-bubble."

: "What a strange custom!" I blurted out, as it evoked a good deal of surprise even with my wide experience of folk religions and sects. I asked: "It means that the platformed Fakirs are obligated to you and general disciples are obliged to the platformed Fakirs. Isn't that so? Well, is there a list of names and addreses available with you?"

:"Certainly. Haven't you noticed the accountant of the platformed Fakirs collecting penalty for the platformed Fakirs?"

: "Penalty?"

: "Yes, 'revenue' in our faith is akin to 'penalty'. We're their routine masters!"

: "Well, what a beautiful system! Indeed, a lot of your system is seen; I still have two curiosities. One, to see a platformed Fakir; and, two, to see from close quarters an ordinary disciple of Deendayal. This general disciple will be for me to find out. But, in order to see a platformed Fakir intimately, I'll need your opinion as to whom I should approach, who would show the activities and who would explain best. You'll understand best; a letter from you will be of great value."

Thinking over deeply, Sharat Pal asked: "Which kind of platformed Fakir would you like to meet: Hindu or Muslim?"'

"It won't make any difference to me," I quipped.

With a wry smile, Sharat Pal had asked: "Male or female?"

This time I was taken aback. Could both male and female alike be the intiator-guru in the Sahebdhani faith?

Sharat Pal explained: "Long ago our sect had the most noted women of the times—Jagatimata, Deenuratan Dasi and Lakshmitagar. They had many disciples each. You'll still find some there. However, I'll send to an unusual place. Do visit Akandabere; you know that place, don't you? You should go to Darzee Fakir's residence there. His son's name is Kamal Husain. They are celebrated names, everyone knows them. Darzee Fakir was a very old and renowned platformed Fakir of our sect. His portal continues to be active there. But Kamal Husain didn't adopt Fakiri. Food services, daily worships and ceremonies, sacred vows, hymn-initiation are all performed by Harimati. She is a Hindu though. Kamal calls her 'Didi'[20]. Harimati had addressed Darzee Fakir as 'father'. Since then she stays with them in their home; didn't marry. She is a great devotee of Deendayal."

It was surprise upon surprise. I blurted out: "Do you mean she is a Hindu woman, living in a Muslim household!"

In a slightly offended voice, Sharat Pal had said: "Even after you have understood everything, you seem to get muddled up with the basics sometimes, don't you? Among us, there is no distinction between Musims and Hindus. It's a matter totally of your concern."

I felt terribly embarrassed. Truly we are many types. Sacraments were very strong components of the sect. After my apologies to him, I obtained a letter to Anandabere for Kamal Husain and took leave for the day.

Intimating approximately my date and time of arrival, I had written a letter to Kamal Husain at Akandabere. I was rewarded

20 *Didi*: Elder sister

immediately, when I saw a cosy, thatched-roof ox-cart, standing at the bus-stop. The walk-way to Akandabere would easily be four miles, which I realised while traversing by the cart. In the scorching summer heat, the cart-driver perspired profusely. From time to time, the man threw a respectful glance at me. It was, as though, to size up how great a man I was, for whom a grand man like Kamal Husain had to send his ox-cart. To rid him of his inertia I asked the man a few questions at random. He responded non-commitedly and talked to the oxen, shooting off ample expletives. It was a difficult situation; how long could one continue to be silent? So I expressed a wide area of curiosity: "O dear brother, have you seen the father of Kamal Husain? Well, something has struck me about him."

The driver said: "Speak on."

:"Well, why was the man's name so unusual? What kind of name was Darzee[21] Fakir? Was he doing tailoring as well as Fakiri?"

: "No, sir. He was initially only a tailor, a very poor man. Have you heard of Rukunpur? Once their zaminder called this tailor to repair a very old mattress. Sir, all these we've heard as hearsay. He brought it home at Akabndabere, by loading it on a horse-driven cart. The next day, he was thunderstruck by opening the mattress. All its stitched openings were full of gold coins and only gold coins."

: "Good lord! And then?"

: "He kept striking his forehead and wailing: 'O Allah, what is this trial of mine?' He could neither tell anybody fearing a robbery. By somehow spending that night, he went back to the zaminder. The zaminder was stupefied, after hearing everything. He had no clue about the gold coins; it must have been done by his ancestors."

It seemed I had stumbled upon the purest *Arabian Nights* in a village! I sat up in great anticipation while the driver carried on

21 *Darzee*: Tailor

with his story after taking a breather: "There was an approximate total of three hundred gold coins. In his joy, the zaminder gave away one hundred gold coins to the tailor. The latter's fortune opened up. He built a large grand mansion. There was plenty of associated pomp and grandeur too. With the money came the airs and his head turned too!

"It is not easy to absorb the heat of gold coins, is it? He divorced his faithful wife – who had brought him luck and been wedded for long – and she committed suicide. Kamal was a young child then. Actually the man had his eyes fixed on other material attractions. He soon brought home the pretty and fashionable Saleha bibi home from Beldanga. Suddenly one night, the beautiful Saleha fled home with the remaining gold coins, eloping with her cousin. And as though it had to happen, the huge mansion was suddenly burnt down exactly a week after this incident. Everyone said it was due to the curse of his faithful first wife. Utterly distracted, the man went helter and skelter for a few days. Then, under somebody's counsel, he came over to Sharat Pal's site to seek mercy at Deendayal's feet. Well, his head cooled down; he received Deendayal's mercy and adopted *fakiri.* Deendayal's platform was established at home. He used to sing almost always; since then his name came to be Darzee Fakir."

: "Did you get to see Darzee Fakir?"

: "Yes, I vaguely remember. I was a young boy then. The Fakir sported a long white beard and used to sing all the time, which I still remember."

While talking, we had reached Akandabere at one point of time. Kamal Husain welcomed us with open arms and seemed to be a well-built man of fifty. He wore a long kurta and a lungi. "Welcome to a poor man's cottage," he said, pressing into my palms a costly packet of Filter Kings cigarettes. It was not a cottage at all, but a proper concrete house. There was a wheat mill noisily running in the backyard. He pulled hard at his

Filter Kings and exhaled a self-contented gush of smoke. Our conversation carried on alongside: "On this side of the country, there's only one wheat-smashing macnine, which belongs to yours truly."

I took a hard look at the man this time. The well-built look had added embellishments. The eyes were lined with a fine touch of surma and his hair cascaded down in curls. He was surrounded by a group of useless sycophants. From his attitude it was clear that Kamal sahib was an established and respectable man. Perhaps in this village his word would be the last one. Just that one could not imagine his father to be the all-forsaking Fakir! He appeared quite keen to talk about himself. My natural instinct was to provoke such people a little and watch how they talked without a break. So in keeping with his tone of conversation I asked: "It does seem that not merely the wheat machine but Kamal sahib owns many other items which have no duplicates in this village!"

: "Right you are! No doubt about that. Only the qualified can appreciate class and quality in others. The only Rajdoot bike in the village is parked at yours truly's home. Two double-barrelled guns as well. Only yours truly's daughter attends a college in the city. I'm the one and only quack doctor in the village too. My son Dwini studies Arabic in a Kolkata madrasa.

Perhaps the list of unparalleled possessions was going to be longer. But there was an interruption midway. One of the rural poor came in screaming: "Hakim sahib, my daughter continues to have loose motions; blood-dysentry perhaps. There are contractions in the stomach, with severe pain. My poor suffering girl is groaning in pain!"

The quack doctor made a solemn 'hmm' sound, doubling up now as the Hakim sahib. Looking thoughtful, he turned to me abruptly and said: "Could you catch on to the case? There has been no impact with six tablets of Enterostrep. Should I give an injection?" Then he turned to the man and said: "You better go home now. Let me think it over." Both of us walked ahead. There was a shop next to the house. One section of the shop was used for selling stationery goods like books and papers, notebooks, pencils, pens and ink while the other stacked soil-fertilisers, insecticides, seeds and spray machines. Even after years of village surveys I was yet to come across a more well-stocked shop. Amply surprised, I asked: "Does this shop also belong to you?"

"You've guessed spot-on. This shop is indeed mine. I have placed my unemployed nephew here. How do you find the shop's idea? Learning of life's core values, the sales tactics of the fertilisers Sufala, Urea and learning about soils and fertilisers happen together. Kamal's soil and Khuda's soil are both amenable to farming." He laughed raucously at his own humour and the sycophants joined in the chorus with their stop-gap fake laughs. Deriving quite a bit of fun, I joked: "Kamal sahib, within this short span of time, I've seen so many forms of yours that I'm confused as to how I should address you—the Doctor sahib, Kamal bhai or Mr Husain?"

: "Well, well, wait a while. You haven't yet seen anything much of mine. But you've understood the problem very well. Most of the people of this village know me as Kamal, the son of Darzee Fakir. In the enlightened *alem* society, I'm Saheb. Patients call me Hakim Sahib. Some also call me Master Sir."

:"Do you teach as well?"

: "I'm three types of master. First, I'm the Head Master of the primary school. Second, I am the master of the Alkap music group. Could you tell me what the third one could be?"

: "What else could a third master be after all these?"

: "Well, well, see the letter-box fixed to the wall of my house. I'm also the post master! I sell postcards and envelopes."

Another question of mine – surprised that I was – also hit the target: "Does Haji Sahib also dabble in politics?"

The reply came prompt, in a joyful voice: "Most certainly, I'm the chairman of the panchayat here. So some amount of partying is a matter of course. Without party, land, shop, teaching, a panchayat could not be protected, could it?"

"The town's famous comrades occasionally step in my hutment."

: "You've no trouble in this village then?"

Sensing some fun, and pointing his hand towards the sky, Kamal Husain said: "Everything is under Khudatallah's mercy. To become an enlightened alem of the village, I've constructed a mosque. In order to seek the attention of the pure Muslims, I've sent my son to study Arabic at a madrasa. I've brought under control the common man, the poor and needy population by the practice of Hakimi. Most farmers of the village are in my employment. Bauls and Bairagis respect me as I'm the son of Darzee Fakir. Hindus treat me as progressive since I've sent my daughter for higher education. SDO, BDO all respect me for doing politics."

: "How about the Hindu and Muslim youths and the unemployed sector?"

: "I have built the Alkap group for them. I've arranged employment benefits for many. I fetch the *jatra* troupes in winter."

: "But do you follow Shariat?"

: "I follow everything by norm. I tell everybody—'Go to the mosque', 'read Namaz.' But fundamentally, I don't follow anything. Why is that? Basically I am the product of Darzee Fakir; how can I forget that? My elder sister Harimati-didi is at home, as well as the exalted Deendayal Deenabandhu Goptababaji. In reality, is there any separate creed called Hindu or Muslim? Do you follow me? Would you like to listen to a funny incident?"

: "Tell me. All your incidents are quite interesting."

Exhaling a halo of cigarette smoke, Kamal said: "I have a good-for-nothing nephew. When my cousin sister died at an early age, I brought him over and raised him. He didn't complete his education and is the roving type; he was brought up by Harimati-didi. He can't commit himself to any specific job. But he is honest, my wife likes him a lot. I was at a loss to employ him somewhere. The boy was intelligent though. Once he came and asked, "Uncle, can you lend me some money?" When I asked him the reason he said: "I would like to start a hotel." The spot where you got down from the bus has a stop for Malda, Behrampur and all the North Bengal buses. So the boy set up a hotel right there."

: "How was it possible? Is the common public eating rice meals at a Muslim hotel?"

: "Oh you have to listen to the boy's idea. He has cunning streak in every fold of his mind." Appreceative of the nephew, the uncle gave a warm smile: "There is someone called Ram Chakrabarti in our village; he is handsome and clear-complexioned but empty-headed and completely illiterate. He however is capable of cooking; is a reasonably good cook and is often hired for feasts. My nephew Khudabux approached him and asked him directly whether he wanted to do a job. Ram readily agreed. Well, the boy set up the hotel right on the bus route. The bare bodied Ram Chakrabarti shows off his *paita* – the thick sacred thread of Brahmans – and cooks!"

: "And what about Khudabux?"

: "He is a cunning fox, this boy! He puts on an innocent expression while sitting at the counter and keeps the accounts, shops for fish, meat and vegetables. He is quite an impudent monkey to have given this strange name to his hotel! Would you believe what he calls his hotel? It has been named 'Khudabux's Hindu Hotel'. It's running very well and doing roaring business. As I told you, there is no Hindu -Muslim divide in real life! It's all an eye wash!"

How on earth could such a shrewd and cunning person be so catholic and selfless as well? I developed doubts about his credibility. This man sounded like a pucca realist! He was communal in his practices yet his mind was as clear as water. Did this have anything to do with the basic culture of Deendayal's home? I couldn't resist the temptation to clear my doubts and asked head-on:

: "Master-Sir, sorry, Hakim sahib, how have you named your children?"

: "You've raised a very good and pertinent question. Harimati-didi calls them Gopal and Meera. Their formally registered names are Maqbul Husain and Rokaya Sultana," Kamal replied.

: "Oh but why do they have Muslim names?" I lamented.

: "Well, wait, wait! Cool down please. You sing praises of the Hindu community, that the Hindus are very catholic and open-minded. Would you clarify one doubt of mine, my respected guest? You must have realised now that I don't follow religion. I have Harimati-didi in my home, the icon of Darzee Fakir's Deendayal rests in the inner precincts. Yet I follow Muslim customs and rituals because my children have to be married off. There is something called society, do you follow?"

: "I do care for society. Our urban society has been opening up of late and rigid rules have been relaxed a good deal. But in the cloistered rural community, I understand that there are still many bondages; rules and restrictions do exist."

Kamal protested to say: "Sir, your words and attitude appear too casual and artificial. Now look, let me be brutally plain. In our rural homes and family circles love affairs and love marriages aren't too common you know! Here the parents fix the marriages of their children. Now tell me which Hindu home will accept my Maqbool's hand in marriage? Everyone knows that Deendayal resides in my home and Harimati-didi lives with us. All know full well that I don't observe the 'Puran[22]-Quran' rules from my heart.

22 *Puran*: Colloquial; The Puranas—ancient Hindu religious scriptures, literally meaning 'ancient, old'. A vast genre of Indian literature about a wide range of topics, particularly myths, legends and other traditional lore. They contain narratives about the history of the universe from creation to destruction and the genealogies of kings, heroes, sages, and demigods

But tell me, will you marry off your nephew to my Meera? Even though Meera is very pretty and is an accomplished young lady! She pursues honours in political science. And I can furnish enough money for her dowry as well. Still the Hindus will not accept her. In that case why do you shout from the tree tops about your all-embracing progressive philosophy and catholic outlook?"

Kamal Hosain's words were like a sharp volley of bullets—shooting through the head and hitting right at the core. What reply could I give? Truly, our social frame was a frozen one; sacraments, prejudices and beliefs ran deep. Why just in a village, was it not true even in the urban milieu! If one of our nephews wanted to marry – simply out of catholicity – a Roqeya Khatoon for instance, wouldn't we resist, to start with? Even if we accepted it somehow due to exccesive open-mindedness or due to the groom's personality and social position, would we still be able to print Roqeya's name on the wedding card? Or her father's lineage? Truly, I had never been in such a predicament before. But the trouble still awaited me. In my weakest moment Kamal hit me with another master stroke. He said: "Both you and your wife have been professors. You are also doing a research on the Sahebdhanis. Well, you have a daughter I heard. Will you be ready to give her hand in marriage with a Muslim boy? Well, perhaps you won't have to do it yourself. If the girl herself wants such a marriage, will your professor wife be easily agreeable? Won't she try to dissuade her daughter by saying: 'What a shame! How can you do this, being the daughter of a person of your father's stature? How would I show my face to the larger society and the students in my college?' Tell me, won't you say this? Put a hand on your heart and confess. But the Muslim society will accept my son and daughter. Even if I am an atheist or catholic in my views, they would still accept. That is why I have to be an Aalem. I have to ask everybody to offer Namaz. Do you understand the reason?"

: "What is its reason?"

: "The reason is that, whether good or bad, our country's Shariat-based Muslim society only watches whether the man offers Namaz or not, visits the mosque or not, honours the scriptures or not. If he does and even if there is some amount of hypocrisy involved, the society will accept his conduct and pardon everything else. That is why I am a pure Muslim in conduct. If I had been practising Fakiri like my father, would I be at all respected by my society?"

Almost like a god-sent messenger someone came out to save the hapless me. She was Harimati-didi, wearing a saffron robe and chanting on the rosary beads around her neck. Her skin was very fair and she had a graceful appearance. Walking in with a smiling face from within the house, she reprimanded Kamal: "My dear crazy brother, where is it written in the Shariat that when there is a [23]guest at home, he must not be offered any hospitality but instead abused right and left? You have been shouting senselessly. Won't you bring him inside?"

: "Oh yes, I certainly will. Let's go inside. Please come in, please do. Please be seated inside," Kamal ushered me in, a smile hanging at the corner of his lips.

Making me sit inside, Harimati-didi fanned me with a hand fan: "Is it enough to be a Muslim? Do you know enough about offering hospitality to guests? This was known to our father."

Winking at me, Kamal told his sister: "Now look after your Hindu brother. He has had a lot of trouble. Let your Muslim brother go to hell. But couldn't the kheer, *rabri*[24], *luchi* and the

23 *Kheer*: Dessert prepared with sugar boiled in thickened creamy milk and often flavoured with cardamom and raisins in Bengal. Rice or other similar ingredients added in other parts of India, which is then *payesh* in Bengal

24 *Rabri*: Thickened sweetened milk with layers of *malai* or cream in it. It is flavoured with cardamoms, saffron and dry fruits like almonds and pistachios. Milk is continuously simmered and reduced on a low flame till it reaches a semi thick consistency. Tthe preparation is easy but takes time

other edibles that have been cooked at home since morning also be shared by this rival brother of yours? In matters of food, Hindus and Muslims are brothers."

"Get out from here", Kamal got a beating by the hand-fan.

"Would you spare me by not eating? Aren't you ashamed? Gopal and Meera are not at home; Khudabux hasn't had his lunch! How can you get so greedy?"

"Let me escape, the situation is bad", Kamal left muttering. Just before leaving, he turned around at the door and said: "I shall be back after a short while. Let me go and check on the patients as well. Please have breakfast and speak to Harimati-didi. You particularly intend to talk to her; you have work with her. After lunch, we shall sit and debate again. And yes, it is important; do listen to my sister's song, talk to her with care. My sister is devoid of love and affection, has no illusions, no pain or sorrow. You can see for yourself what a plain-looking frump she is; a complete owl if you ask me! Father could not get her married as a result and left her dangling around my neck like a deadweight. But my sister's singing voice is gorgeous. Earns her meals here because she sings twice a day! Otherwise, we would have thrown her out long back!"

: "Get out, get out of here!" Harimati-didi came forward and hit her brother in jest. "Huh, your money my foot," she strongly objected. "It's all my father's. However, do come back in time for lunch, dear boy."

In such graceful and pleasing environment the mind softens easily in the natural course of things. The thick and creamy kheer, *rabri, luchi,* lovingly preapred by Harimati-didi left a nice aftertaste in me, akin to a wide expanse of a lovely fragrant garden and left me pleasantly overwhelmed and somewhat confused. Realising my confused state of mind, Harimati-didi approached me and spoke lovingly: "Everything is a part of this worldly game of mankind! How much Deendayal has revealed to me! Otherwise, how do I get a place in this home? This house is like heaven. You have seen only my crazy brother. You haven't seen his beautiful wife inside the kitchen yet. She is preparing rice pancakes and chicken curry for your dinner. You haven't seen Meera and Gopal; they are such sweet children. And there is the greatest rascal of them all, Khudabux. Who knows whether he will be back home today or not!"

I thought to myself about the mystique of Deendayal and how he had revealed a good deal for me to see as well. This home – a brilliant picture of charm incarnated – stood on solid grounds of compassion and plain humaneness. I had not seen anything like this anywhere earlier. Being somewhat carried away by emotions, I said: "Didi, I will like to listen to your account. How have you come to this home? Where is your origin?"

Smiling shyly Didi asked: "You have been to the Pal-home of Brittihuda, haven't you? I was raised there. I have certain special ties with them, as I am their 'door- vowed'. Why are you looking like that? Don't you understand the meaning of 'door-vowed'?"

: "No, not quite."

: "Listen, I will explain to you. We are cobblers by caste. My parents used to live in Aarangshorshe next to the Hudo village. For a long time they did not have a child; finally they took a vow and pleaded to Deendayal of the Pal-house for a child. I was born after this. This is termed 'door-vowed'. From early childhood I have been apparently inclined towards religion. So my parents did not get me married, but left me at the Pal-house. Lalchand Pal – the father of Sharat Pal, who sent you here, initiated me into my faith. I am a born ascetic. I lie at Deendayal's feet."

: "How did you come here?"

: "Why, I came with father—the Fakir-baba. Haven't you heard the details and events around Darzee Fakir, father of Kamal?

When his first wife fled and the whole house was burnt down, he turned totally mad. Everything ran smoothly under Deendayal's mercy. But the man became a Fakir at the end. Who would look after the family? Who would perform the daily rituals and offer prayers to Deendayal? Who would look after his son Kamal? I had called Fakir 'Father'. So when Father told me: 'Dear, if you don't take over and come with me, I won't survive', I had to come."

Didi dissolved into a sudden flood of tears. "It has been such a long time since the Fakir has taken to earth", she wept. "He left me bonded with compassion and emotional ties. I have really been trapped, brother, bound with this wonderful family. I am old now. When I leave, who will look after Khudabux? What will happen to Deendayal's service? I worry about all that."

In the afternoon just before lunch, Harimati-didi took me to Deendayal's platform. It was in a cold, dark room with only one lamp burning. There was a small raised platform on one side of the room, with a folded piece of cloth laid on it, and some flowers strewn over it. The trident, the Fakiri stick and the hubble-bubble were arranged neatly at one corner. There was also a pair of wooden sandals of some guru from the Pal-house. It was a very simple and basic arrangement, almost lean. But then Deendayal Sahebdhani did not have a human form.

Didi sat on the mat and started performing many rituals while the attractive fragrance from the burning incense, the spiralling scent of the lamp's burning ghee and the aroma of sandalwood created heady waves in the room. In this quiet, cold solitude of the room Deendayal's day-worship continued. Suddenly didi stood up and began swinging the whisk, all the while singing:

Come and sit on the mat along your path
I receive you with thunderous adulation
I swing the whisk for your satisfaction.
Glory to Deenbandhu, Deenanath.

Then she prostated herself on the floor and said in salutation:

Glory to Deendayal, Atalbihari, Karowadhari
In Deendayal Sahebdhani's name, everyone chant Hari, Hari
Hari bol, Hari bol!

She was then submerged in meditation for a while and then she said:

Kling Kling Deendayal, Sahebdhani as friend—
Sahebdhani, Allahdhani always to attend!
Guru's true, the four ages are true, true are the moon and the sun
True are words, lusts and deeds and all the actions done.
Gosain's the compassionate one,
In this world, without you I have no one.

I kept wondering how unusual this world of folk religion was. It united the sound of 'Hari Bol' with the name of Allah. How dominant was the force of faith which uttered together words like 'Guru was true and lust was true' in the same breath! Were all four ages, the sun and the moon all true? Alongside, the core chant of Sahajiya Vaishnava 'kling, kling' was also a core part of it all? How was it possible? Did the infusion happen as smoothly as it did with the flow of fragrance from the burning incense, the sandalwood and the aroma of ghee from the clay lamps with the lone silence of Deendayal's sanctum sanctorium? This dimly-lit, cool, peaceful and undisturbed room of Deendayal had no link with the scorching heat of summer outside, which was just as much as the lack of a connect between man and man. Once I stepped outside this room, I was a Hindu and Kamal Husain was back to being a Muslim. His son Maqbool would never get married to my daughter.

It was as if to sever my reverie that the worship of Deendayal ended. I came out and sat on the outer balcony, embracing the exhaustion of a scorching summer afternoon. There was unbearable heat on all sides. Harimati-di perhaps by her intuition, empathised with the heat in my mind and my internal pain. She quietly caressed me with her comforting hands and said: "You sit here for a while I sing a song for you. You will get some peace of mind."

Her voice began weaving music at a unique mid octave.

Ram or Rahim, Karim Kalulla Kala
Hari Hari—all in one soul, they give life and might;
With one moon the whole world is bright.
Each to his own and each to her own—
Hindu or Muslim,
The daughter is the 'child' alone.

Lakshmi and Durga Kali Fatema we call her gladly—
Whose son Husain Ali plays at Madina's site;
With Kartik and Ganesh in her lap—
Mother Kamala is sitting tight.

Suddenly I felt an unusual emotion coming over me. Who had penned such a song? Was he thinking much in advance? Like Kartik and Ganesh in the lap of mother Kamala, were I and Kamal Husain sitting in the lap of Harimati-didi? Was the affection and love similarly inaffable? Who was this human genius of a century ago who could graft such a song in the village? The sweet and deep voice of Harimati-didi was gradually drawing to a close:

Some say Krishna-Radha, some say Allah-Khuda,
What's in a name?
There is no thirst or hunger,
All appetites disappear and go asunder;
We are all one: think it over and under!

String a garland of the two names same

In the same tune is running away,
Same water, same earth to stay,
Same air pure, at play,
Under control of a grand name's fame.

I stared at sister Harimati-didi in open-eyed wonder. There were tears in her eyes. Were they of joy or of deep devotion?

Kamal Husain and I sat down for lunch next to each other. Didi sat facing us with a palm leaf hand-fan. Kamal's wife served us. She was a veiled lady of the village, befittingly shy. Wide-eyed wonder in her beautiful eyes spoke out from under the veil. The fairness of her skin threw a rare radiance – like the glowing embers in a hot oven – in the afternoon heat. The cooking was excellent; Kamal visibly appreciated it, singing praises. After lunch we went into one of the bedrooms and settled down on a bed. Lighting a cigarette Kamal called his wife. The veiled lady came in hesitatingly and stood in one corner. Kamal walked up to her and removed his wife's veil. "This is the world's light, Noorjahan," he proclaimed. His wife bounded away, throwing a quick glance with her bright-as-lightening eyes, raising quite a storm in her trail.

Roaring with laughter Kamal said: "I didn't tell you in the morning, I am unparalled in two more aspects. In the ten or twelve neighbouring villages, among all the flourishing Muslims I'm the only one in whose home there is just one mistress – my wife – and not several; the second news ours was a love marriage."

I looked up in appreciation and asked: "You should be around fifty years old, or less?"

: "Take it to be fifty, if you may, but why do you ask?"

: "I wondered how long back this love affair happened! How old were you then?"

: "Oh, how would I remember all that? But to say it in a word, mine was the age to fall in love."

Was there the sound of breaking glass—the sweet tinkle of a chandelier coming crashing down, just beyond the room's threshold? In reality, it was his beloved running away, her anklet bells ringing.

Smiling in a lighter vein, Kamal said: "Life, as you find it, is very nice indeed! Man also wishes to live in joy and peace. But home and the outer world have become two completely separate entities now. Look at this happy, contented and nice man as I stand here now; yet I have to change my demeanour and attitude as soon as I step out. I will have to utter false words, decorative and artificial language, words of flattery. Yet I carry the legacy of Darzee Fakir in my blood. That man did not know nor practice falsehood or pretence. He was a Marfati Fakir."

I said: "I have heard the names Marfat and Shariat on several occasions. Could you please explain to me their difference?"

Harimati-didi entered the room at this point and heard my words. "What would he tell you? He is ignorant!" she exclaimed. "Let me explain. Shariat is like a tree's trunk. If you wish to enjoy the flowers and the fruits will you get it at the trunk? You would have to climb up to the tree's branches. Marfat is that branch and fruit and flower of the tree. From Shariat comes Marfat. To understand Marfat, Shariat is immensely valuable. But once you realise and accept Marfat, what price Shariat?"

I now asked Kamal Husain: "Has there been no social rebuff amongst your fellow Muslims for the fact that a pure Hindu lady like Harimati-didi lives in a Muslim household as respected and important as yours?"

: "It has never really happened and the main reason behind this is because everyone is a devotee of Deendayal and looks up to us. From my father's times the offerings of secred vows in Deendayal's name came in enormous numbers. During carnival time in the month of Chaitra, I don't have to spend a penny from my pocket. All the village people contribute rice, lentils, vegetables and subsidiary products themselves and perform the rice carnival. Call them Hindus or Muslims, the common people here are united in the name of Deendayal. And there is my elder sister, old Harimati-didi. She is the most respected lady in the whole region. Everyone is prepared to follow and serve her! I have actually perceived something unique in my life; would you like to know? A good thing is never struck down. Looking at my mansion, balcony, shop, wheat machine, post office, *hakimi* and partyism, people still fear and respect me. Nobody loves me. If I stand for elections, you know why I might win? Is it because of power? Is it because of money? Not at all; I win at the elections because I am the son of Darzee Fakir. People vote for me, because they know that if I lost my sister will be pained. In that case, is my winning at the elections a real win or defeat?"

Gradually the day advanced, the time to bid farewell came forward. I realised that I hadn't ever seen Deendayal filling a larger space in the hearts of people. I had seen Deendayal's original platform at the Pal house in Brittihuda. I had also witnessed the Fakir's establishment at Akandabere. But I had not actually seen how much space Deendayal occupied in the common man's mind.

Before I crawleded under the thatch of the ox-cart, Noorjahan bade me farewell from a distance, with her glance fixed downwards; charming and perfectly poised. Kamal Husain said: "Please come again to this poor man's home. And along the way do drop in once at the Khudabux Hindu hotel and tell my truant boy that his aunt is waiting with kheer and meat curry-roti for him. That rascal must come home!"

Harimati-didi said: "Let Deendayal bring you to our portal again. But will I be alive then? How long will Deendayal's portal continue at this home? I am getting old. I will die and Deendayal's portal will disappear."

In our land a new word has recently come into vogue. The word is 'field work research'—colloquially referred to as 'area survey'. Those who worked in the fields of sociology, anthropology or folk culture were enchanted by the adventure in 'area survey'. They went to Ayodhya hills or to the Kalighat Poto area (painter's enclave) or to Sati-Ma fair at Ghoshpara. In these cases the groups of students came together under the guidance of one or two very serious and solemn-looking professors. In some cases, the study teams had one or two foreigners as well. Everyone possessed notebook and dot pen. In the group there would be at least one camera and tape-recorder.

There was no harm in confessing one truth here that even before the tape-recorder and cameras came in, great work had been done in the field of research. Kshitimohan Sen or Nirmal Kumar Basu, Mansuruddin, Jogesh Roy Bidyanidhi, Dinesh Chandra Sen had completed a huge volume of research some time back, which have not been equalled by anybody yet. Akshaykumar Dutta, Mr Wilson or Jogendranath Bhattacharjya were even older stalwarts, the mere mention of whose names and achievements bring shame to the current crop of work.

In reality, if one went with a lot of elaborate arrangement, occasionally the good things did not always emerge. Cameras and recorders were items which often made villagers recoil into their shells. Some people took severe objection to these electronic appliances. As a result, they did not reveal much or deliberately said things which were confusing. Sharat Pal of Brittihuda once told me about a folk culturist who wanted to keep evidence of everything by taking photographs. "What was my responsibility to collect so much evidence?" In another case, I was very amused by the words of a village-guru. He said: "Someone like you came on the last occasion. He had brought a woman with him and wanted to put the woman next to me and let her be photographed. Imagine the audacity! I never even allowed my own wife to be photographed with me, let alone some unknown woman from somewhere. What a shame!"

Having seen these area-surveys, I had been very careful. I had one advantage—that I had no group. I had always been severely alone. Occasionally I might have had, for company, a very peaceful type of a student, with whom one could talk on the way back and forth. One could also reconcile his observation with one's own. Taking advantage of young age, he could collect some additional information also from the village youths. Most of all, there were some disadvantages of moving around alone in the village area, unless you knew the village people from beforehand. Thinking of these various matters, I took Monoranjan with me while travelling to Ishwarchandrapur. He was basically a village boy, which meant he would be perseverant and not mind hardships, could walk a lot and would be happy with rice and lentils. Besides, he wouldn't bother me with queries like 'Where is the bathroom?' 'Where shall I take a bath?' Instead, he would go direct to the river or the tank. Ishwarchandrapur was a village of the poor rank. There was no respected landlord like Kamal Husain.

Ganesh Parui was the man in whose house we stayed at Ishwarchandrapur. He sold the *champakala* – a particular variety of plantain – at the Gowari market where I had met him and was his customer. But locating him as a Sahebdhani practitioner was entirely my credit. Once I found him selling good quality ripe fruits and had asked him: "How come, these are not ripenend by carbide, but left to ripen while still on the tree!"

He had replied with great humility: "I used to buy it daily from the wholeseller and sell. Today, I get my own home produce. This is all due to the mercy of Deendayal."

Deendayal's mercy? From this single significant clue, I had caught the man and asked him: "Do you happen to be a disciple of the Pal-bari of Hudo?"

Flashing a gratifying smile, he had said: "Sir, you know about our sect very well. Come to our village once. It is Ishwarchandrapur. Do you know it? My name is Ganesh Parui."

Ganesh Parui seemed to be a very poor man. But being childless he didn't seem to be very impoverished. He had a hut fixed with a cane machan. That was the bed too. And the rudimentary clay oven was in the house's courtyard. Come wet or shine, his wife somehow managed to rustle up two quick, simple meals out in the open. Today his house had a festive air about it with guests. He called out to his wife: "These gentlemen are here. Please make the dal a little thicker and richer than usual."

We went to Ishwarchandrapur for research and intended to stay for two days and two nights. Keeping track of everything, we reached in the morning, carrying with us a few food products, which we unloaded cautiously, keeping in mind to retain Ganesh's honour. There were potatoes, onions, eggs, tea, sugar, milk powder and bread.

: "I hope you didn't mind, did you?"

: "Everything is Deendayal's mercy. Otherwise how did he know that I didn't have a paisa with me? Having been ill for two days, I couldn't go to the market."

The whole day, we went around the village and when evening had advanced a little, I entered Ganesh's house. He was hale and hearty by then. Having refreshed ourselves with puffed rice and tea, we sat in the courtyard after rolling out a straw mat. The fragrance of rice cooking in the courtyard filled the air. It was a full-moon fortnight perhaps, with a large-sized moon in the sky. Bringing a single string drone, Ganesh began strumming it. I wondered what song he would sing other than the typical kind which appealed to an urban audience—'The moon rests on the moon'. I hoped he would move on to sing something else after the first stint. But Ganesh startled me by beginning with a novelty:

I had heard the name of happiness and joy
But had not seen their form,
My home is in the city of sorrow;
My life is born of sorrow; and sorrow is our norm.

The song seemed totally autobiographical. So much surprise was kept in reserve for me by Deendayal in the Ishwarchandrapur evening. Ganesh continued to sing with a deep resentment fuming within:

I thought I would come to a happy land,
Settle down happy in a happy strand,
Sorrow came rushing to disband,
Holding me by hair to conform.
In times of sorrow, in the afternoon,
A sorrowful meal is what we spoon,
Lying in the evening, making the bed of sorrow my cocoon,
I take sorrow's sleep by storm.

Monoranjan thought that the song perhaps ended here. He said effusively: "O, what a song! I would write it down immediately. This is a song for all of us. Who has written it? Was it you?"

Biting his tongue in embarrassment Ganesh stopped the song: "Can I write such a deeply sentimental song ever? I have learnt the song from the Ishup Fakir of Agradweep. I didn't quite get its beginning. But it seems from the meaning that the song is by our Jadubindu. Listen to the rest.

Sorrow is my freedom friend,
Sorrow is my company to attend,

In the heart glows my misery's light till its end
Which is burning my life down
My words for sorrow will remain for the morrow:
Who would prevent its seeds from being sown?

Truly speaking, I had not expected such a song in this village at all. What a gem to discover!

Before going to bed, I had a long chat with Ganesh Parui. Ishwarchandrapur village seemed a monopoly of Deendayal's disciples. "Sir our villages are practically cleaned out of their people during the Agradweep fair; nearly everyone goes. They are all devoted to Deendayal. Our own carnival in the month of Falgun is on the second moon. Sir, please come next time to participate. We will let you hear Ishup Fakir's song. His music brings us great peace."

Next morning we went and sat at one end of Ishwarchandrapur on the banks of river Jalangi, sitting on the top of a cane-thatch, over a banyan tree. Such cane thatches were made below some trees in villages, which were commonly owned. Whoever needed to sit under a shaded area, used these. The previous day a long interview was conducted while sitting on the thatch. Our principal task lay with the common Sahebdhanis, who worshipped Deendayal every Thursday with *panchatattwa*, a kedgeree or hash of boiled rice, lentils and three types of vegetables. They were the ones who slapped the penalties on some of the platformed Fakir and offered worship. These were also the folks who lay prostrate at the portal of Charan Pal in Agradweep. Come to think of it, they formed the main strength of the Sahebdhani sect.

In between the rituals, my eyes continued to follow a lean-looking, middle-aged man. I saw the man at the same place since yesterday, wearing a blue lungi and a dirty, torn vest. For the whole day the man sat on the thatch nonchalantly, swaying his legs. His face was dirty, and hair dry and unkempt. He had no demand, nor a speck of curiosity, and wore a blank expression. Somebody perhaps offered him a bidi which he puffed for a quite a while and appeared very gratified for being able to spend some time. Everybody called him 'Pacha' with great disdain, as though the man Pacha was a rotten left-over. He seemed to be a low-caste man. On Pacha's cheek, there was a fearsome scratch. On calling him up to come and sit, he appeared very confused. I asked him: "Pacha, what is that huge scratch on your cheek?"

: "Sir that was a tiger's scratch mark," came the very indifferent reply.

: "How did it happen?"

: "Well, twenty or twenty-five years ago, a tiger walked into the forest by the neighbouring village. The hunter saheb was sitting on a high machan. We the low-caste people surrounded the forest from four sides and raised an alarm by beating on cannisters. We are called 'beaters'. In the turmoil, the tiger got confused and instead of targeting the bait and the hunter, leapt across to our group. Then the tiger gave a big leap again and while fleeing, left this fatal scratch on my face. It turned into a septic wound. I had to spend two months at the sadar hospital to recover. It was purely Deendayal's mercy that saved my life, but the scar has remained, sir. There are three Pachas in this village. There is one 'tabla Pacha' who plays the tabla[25]. A 'mudi Pacha' who is a grocer. And I am called the 'wounded Pacha'."

He was such an indifferent man that it was difficult to carry on a conversation. Our activity continued, as the afternoon advanced. The sun in the last quarter of Falgun grew brighter and stronger as well. There was a bathing ghat[26] behind us. People gathered there, listened to our conversation for a while, and then scraping out

25 *Tabla*: A pair of small hand drums used in Indian music, one of which is slightly larger than the other and is played using pressure from the heel of the hand to vary the pitch and the fingers to keep the beat and the rhythm

26 *Ghat*: Flight of steps leading down to the river

mustard oil with their fingers from the little cane containers that they carried, tied to their waist-bands for an oil massage, went for a dip. Splashing about in the water for a while, they clambered out after a bath and went home swishing their dripping clothes. After a while, by two or three o'clock, those bathed and fed men returned to our thatch to observe our activity. Their oil-massaged, clean bodies shone and they wore clean dry dhotis. Lighted bidis hung from their lips. But I noticed that Pacha did not come down from his perch, which meant that he neither bathed nor ate. The day advanced, we had with us bread, boiled eggs and bananas. In the morning we had had rice starch with plain rice for breakfast, as we were not supposed to go back in the afternoon to Ganesh's home. He had gone to Gowari market for selling bananas.

During our snack break, we called out to Pacha. "Will you eat bread, bananas and an egg?" we asked.

: "Please give," he said without much ado and wolfed down the food. After a drink of water from the tubewell, he settled down and continued to swing his legs.

Looking at the state of affairs, Monoranjan went up to his thatch and spoke in a low voice. Apparently he did not come across someone like Pacha too often. Thanks to Deendayal's mercy, it did not seem that I would get much information out of Pacha. The man was totally without any character, and very single-tracked. He did not seem even to talk much either. After an hour, Monoranjan came back with suppressed excitement and told me: "Do you know sir, Pacha has no land, no fixed income. He did not receive any formal education. He lives in a hut whose northern-corner roof has broken off. If Deendayal gives me some hay, I could repair the thatch by the end of this Chaitra. Sir, will you give him ten rupees?"

: "Wait, wait", I tried to convince Monoranjan: "Suppose I gave him the money...would that be a permanent solution? What would happen after the ten rupees are spent? There are three

Pachas in this village, but there are many more poor people like Pacha here!" In order to provide some inspiration to Monoranjan, I said: "Please call him. Let me talk to him."

The man came up and stood facing us indifferently, not particularly interested in the world around him, scratching out a figure on the soil with his toes. The afternoon was almost over. I asked him directly: "Pacha, both yesterday as well as today you didn't bathe at noon nor go home. Why?"

: "I am usually very hungry after a bath. I don't go home; what shall I eat there? The kids cry in hunger, my wife abuses me. I can't tolerate all these. So I keep escaping."

: "How many children do you have?"

: "I have two: a boy and a girl."

In my mind a poster and a logo of the health department popped up—with smiling parents and joyous children in a symbolic expression. There is a slogan: 'Small family, happy family.' Getting the better of my emotions, I asked: "Do your children go to school?"

: "They go only for the free bread and escape during tiffin break."

: 'This morning what did you all have?'

: "Sir, today merciful Deendayal has showered upon us half a kg of boiled wheat."

: "But you have been sitting here all day. Don't you feel hungry?"

: "Hunger dies eventually and the stomach stops aching with Deendayal's mercy."

: "Is there no work in the village for you?"

: "The name of this village is Ishwarchandrapur, but there is no special care given by Ishwar—the Almighty. If there is farming work here, one gets a little money or at least wheat. But where is it this year? With Deendayal's mercy, there is no paddy in the fields."

: "Why don't you go outside the village for selling labour?"

: "Even the neighbouring villages have their farming men unemployed. Every season some of us travel to Barasat for cutting paddy. We do get some money and food thrice a day to fill our stomachs. This is about two months' work. The little money that accumulates is spent in buying clothes for the whole year and for buying sweets for the children for one day. We also go to the Agradweep fair to offer the penalty. This year there has been no news from Barasat. Let me stop, sirs, words just add on to words."

Monoranjan asked: "Where will you go now?"

After all this while, at the end of the day 'wounded Pacha' had a smile on his face! He said: "Don't you see sirs, the day is almost over with Deendayal's mercy. After a while, the evening lights will be lit. I will now dive into the river, take a dip with great joy. Then I will run back home."

: "What will you do after going home?"

: "First, the wife will scold me and beat me with kicks and broom-sticks." Pacha smiled shyly: "She wouldn't be at fault! For the whole day she'd have been looking for edible tubular roots, being affronted by people. The two children collect and bring home snails and squids from somewhere. And my wife might have managed to borrow a handful of rice. Mixing and cooking all these in a hash would make the *panchatattwa*. It would be as Deendayal would give. Having eaten that boiled food, I'd have a nice deep sleep. Undisturbed slumber till next morning."

: "What will happen tomorrow morning?"

: "That is known only to Deendayal. If there is nothing else, this thatch is here. It is good enough to spend the whole day up to evening here. Let me go now, glory to Deendayal Deenabandhu."

Like the fading daylight, Pacha melted away to the river bank and the solemn evening descended with a dim glow, as nebulous as Monoranjan's face.

Where was Deendayal, I wondered. Did he reside in the cluster of Sharat Pal in Hudo village, or in the serene countenance of sister Harimati, or in the bottomless depths of sorrow in the lives of folks like Ganesh and Pacha?